RESERVATION POLICY AND JUDICIAL ACTIVISM

RESERVATION POLICY AND JUDICIAL ACTIVISM

P.P. Vijayan

KALPAZ

Published by

Kalpaz Publications
C-30, Satyawati Nagar,
Delhi – 110052
Ph.: 011-47034999, 9811692060
www.kalpazpublications.com
E-mail: kalpaz@hotmail.com

Distribution Network
gyanbooks.com
India, USA, Canada, UK, Australia, France

ISBN: 978-81-7835-419-4 (HB)

Reprint in India, 2024
First Published, 2006

Printed at: Gyan Press, Delhi.

Reservation Policy and Judicial Activism
Author: P.P. Vijayan

Contents

List of Tables

List of Figures

Abbreviation

Art.	Article
AIR	All India Reporter
EPW	Economic and Political Weekly
ILR	Indian Law Reporter
DOPT	Department of Personnel and Training
LSGI	Local Self Government Institutions
OBC	Other Backward Class
OL	Official Letters
OM	Office Memorandum
OUP	Oxford University Press
RTC	Round Table Conference
SC	Scheduled Caste
SEBC	Socially and Economically Backward Class
ST	Scheduled Tribe
SCC	Supreme Court Cases
SOL	Supreme Court Online

K. G. Balakrishnan
Judge
Supreme Court of India

3, Janpath,
New Delhi-110 001
Tel. : 23012393

FOREWORD

For many people in the contemporary world, the most immediate and oppressive form of inequality is that we see as being rooted in race. In most of the countries it is the colour of the skin rather than the income or occupation which is the most visible factor of one's place in society. Men and women belonging to different races have unequal opportunities and when this manifests itself in a more or less fixed pattern of inequality, we say that this society is stratified in terms of race. In a stratified society, the opportunities available to the members of the disfavour races are severely restricted. The resources of the State are not equitably distributed. How one works, earns or lives in the society or brings up one's children, all these are controlled and governed by the race into which one is born and this colour of skin unlike income, or occupation cannot be easily concealed or changed. Those who are placed in disfavour conditions are fated to be in that condition. Apart from the colour of the skin in Hindu religion, the oppressed and downtrodden are believed to be of inferior origin. This birthmark one has to carry with him from cradle to grave. The colonial rule had very little effect on the racial composition of the population in India.

Law is a social phenomenon. But law possesses no magic to change these beliefs. Beliefs are under the operation of moral law controlled by conduct and behaviour of the people. Changes in beliefs may bring changes in the way men live and thus make changes in law also. Therefore, the problem of race relations could not be solved at the legal level. Racial segregation or untouchability will cease only when there is a change in the belief that individual worth does not depend upon the colour of one's skin.

In United States of America, the civil rights movement gathered momentum after a series of decisions of the Supreme Court of the United States of America. It is interesting to note that *Plessy* Vs. *Ferguson* which was decided at the end of the 19th Century was overruled by the Supreme Court of United States of America after a period of 60 years in *Brown* Vs. *Board of Education.* In *Plessy* Vs. *Ferguson,* the Supreme Court of United States of America held that the State can prescribe, as a rule of civil conduct, that whites and blacks shall not travel as passengers in the same railroad coach. The dissenting opinion of Justice Harlan's in *Plessy* Vs. *Ferguson* was an appeal to the posterity. He said:

> "If a State can prescribe, as a rule of civil conduct, that whites and blacks shall not travel as passengers in the same railroad coach, why may it not so regulate the use of the streets of its cities and towns as to compel white citizens to keep on one side of a street and black citizens to keep on the other? Why may it not, upon like grounds, punish whites and blacks who ride together in street cars or in open vehicles on a public road or street? Why may it not require sheriffs to assign whites to one side of a court-room and blacks to the other? And why it not also prohibit the commingling of the two races in the galleries of legislative halls or in public assemblages convened for the consideration of the political questions of the day? Further, if this statute of Louisiana is consistent with the personal liberty of citizens, why may not the State require the separation in railroad coaches of native and naturalized citizens in the United States, or of Protestants and Roman Catholics?"

It took more than half a century to change this opinion expressed in *Plassey* Vs. *Ferguson.* The question of reservation has always been a serious subject matter of litigation. The plethora of the decisions on the question have carefully been compiled and commented upon by the learned author, Dr. P.P. Vijayan who has done extensive research on the subject. The author has delved deep into the subject and has taken meticulous care and considered the series of decisions rendered by various High Courts and the Supreme Court of India. He has given notes briefly of the facts, the question of laws involved in each case and the decision given thereon.

This book is a unique contribution on the subject and I am certain that it would evoke immense interest to the students, law makers, judges, lawyers and social reformers who are interested in the subject of reservation in public employment and admission to educational institution.

[Justice K.G. Balakrishnan]
September 29, 2005

Preface

Discrimination is a significant factor that maneuvers the behavior pattern of human psyche. Overt and covert discriminatory behavior practiced consciously and unconsciously by humans, could be discerned in the socio-political structure. Absence of discrimination may be hailed as a sign of cultured behaviour but the history of human civilization does not present any notable example for this kind of conduct on the part of Homo sapiens. On the contrary how Patricians treated Plebeeians and how Jews were treated in Europe till the end of Second World War and how Varnashrama Dharma disfigured the ancient Indian societies, are some of the glaring illustrations of discriminatory behavior that tends to subvert peace in a polity. As democracy postulates rule of law, Judiciary has to undertake the responsibility of preventing discrimination from taking the centre stage. There is the legal therapy of providing if not, reserving opportunities for those who are discriminated against. But the medicine of reservation has its own side effects. First it consolidates the rival groups of pro-and anti-reservationists, second, merit is given back seat and third it encourages migration of the talented and thereby causing brain drain. There may be other side effects, which are fall out of these. Obviously there is clash of interests. Thus role of judiciary becomes very significant for the fact that being an impartial interpreter of law with a commitment to the spirit of the Constitution.

This book is the modified version of my doctoral thesis. And I am afraid that it might be cliché to state that a research work is the product of intellectual interaction of the researcher with many a scholar in the field.

Many eminent personalities and academics were gracious enough to spend their valuable time in going through my script, if not discussing the topic of the thesis, and offer their enlightening comments. With due respect and gratitude I mention their names: Dr. Mohanan. B (my guide) Professor, Dept. of Political Science and Development Administration, Gandhigram Rural Institute, Tamil Nadu, Prof. M. Bhaskaran Nair, Former Professor and Head of the Dept. of Political Science, University of Kerala;

Prof. M.S. Balakrishnan, Professor of English, M.G. College Trivandrum; Dr. G. Gopakumar, Professor and Head of the Dept. of Political Science, University of Kerala; Prof. Gyanchand, Former Professor and Head Delhi Faculty of Law; Dr. N.R. Madhava Menon, Vice Chancellor, National University of Juridical Sciences, Kolkata; Prof. S. Nagappan Nayar, Law Academy Law College, Thiruvananthapuram; Prof. Naturam, School of Social Sciences, JNU; Prof. M.M. Potty, Principal Government Law College, Thiruvananthapuram, Prof Sukhdeo Thorat, Professor JNU, Prof. T.K. Thampi, Former Professor and Head of Dept. of French, University of Kerala and Sri K.P. Sukumaran, Journalist.

It is only a truism to say that libraries play a vital role in a research of this kind. I am thankful to the staff of the following libraries for their commendable cooperation: Kerala University Library, Public Library, British Library, Govt. Law College Library, Legislative Library and Law Department Library Thiruvananthapuram, Law Department Library, University of Kerala; National Law School Library, Bangalore; Australian Embassy Library, New Delhi; Indian Law Institute Library, New Delhi; Supreme Court Library, New Delhi; Kerala High Court Library, Ernakulam; Library of National Commission for SC/ST, New Delhi; Office of the Backward Class Commission, New Delhi.

I am indeed lucky to have a circle of friends whose candid opinion and timely encouragement made me overcome many a difficulty. May I record their names with a thankful heart, Adv. Dr. K.S. Chauhan, Supreme Court of India, Adv. Sergi Joseph Thomas, High Court of Kerala and Adv. Laila.S, District Court Thiruvananthapuram. Many persons have helped me in collecting data: Sri. S. Babu, Addl. Secretary, Government of Kerala and Dr. K. Surya Prasad, Librarian, Dept of Law, University of Kerala are but a couple of them. My indebtedness to them has no limits. I am indebted to my better half Adv. Jiji Vijayan and children at whose cost it has been possible to complete the work.

In spite of all contributions of my mentors and friends, I may have of course unknowingly, committed mistakes for which I shoulder responsibility with all humility.

P.P. Vijayan

Acknowledgements

Doctoral theses more often get quarantined within the four walls of some University libraries. Some of them may be made into books so that people outside academia could have access to discourses that touch their very lives. The questions of social justice and equality have been and are subject matter for discussions at various levels. At the same time the reality of hierarchical divisions displaying their assertiveness backed by social, political and not the least economic power, is staring at us. These divisions may undergo their own permutations and combinations, yet the divisions in one-way or other perpetuate themselves. In this context reservation or protective discrimination becomes relevant especially when the journey is towards an egalitarian polity. Hence my doctoral thesis too gets a new avatar and I hope discerning readers would welcome it. But there is always the danger that doctrinal detour and dogmatic determinism might mislead you. Hence it becomes imperative to have the guidance of mentors who could help you to avoid mirages of hermeneutical falsity. Obviously the first among these mentors is my teacher and guide, Dr. Mohanan. B, Professor, Department of Political science and development administration, Gandhi Gram Rural Institute, Tamil Nadu. From the very process of selecting the theme and through out my struggle to reach the target, he has been a source of strength, reminding me often of the good old saying that 'time doesn't wait for anyone.'. But for his friendly admonitions, meticulous inspection and timely advice this work would not have attained this shape.

Many eminent personalities and academics were gracious enough to spend their valuable time in going through my script, if not discussing the topic, and offer their enlightening comments. With due respect and gratitude I mention their names: Prof. M. Bhaskaran Nair, Department of Political Science, University of Kerala; Dr. M.S. Balakrishnan, Professor of English, Dr. G. Gopakumar, professor and head of Department of Political Science, University of Kerala; Prof. Gyanchand, Professor and Head Delhi Faculty of Law; Dr. S. Japhet, Professor, Centre for the study of Casteism, Communalism and Law, National Law School of India

University; Prof. (Dr.) N.R. Madhava Menon, Director, National Judicial Academy; Prof. S. Nagappan Nayar, Law Academy Law College, University of Kerala; Prof. Naturam, School of Social Sciences, JNU; Prof. M.M. Potty, Principal Government Law College, Thiruvananthapuram, Prof. Sukhdeo Thorat, Professor JNU and Sri. K.P. Sukumaran, Journalist.

It is only a truism to say that libraries play a vital role in a work of this kind. I am thankful to the staff of the following libraries for their commendable cooperation: Kerala University Library, Public Library, British Library, Govt. Law College Library, Legislative Library and Law Department Library Thiruvananthapuram, Law Department Library, University of Kerala; National Law School Library, Bangalore; Australian Embassy Library, New Delhi; Indian Law Institute Library, New Delhi; Supreme Court Library, New Delhi; Kerala High Court Library,Ernakulam; Library of National Commission for SC/ST, New Delhi; Office Of The Backward Class Commission, New Delhi.

I am indeed lucky to have a circle of friends whose candid opinion and timely encouragement made me overcome many a difficulty. May I record their names with a thankful heart, Adv. Dr. K.S. Chauhan, Supreme Court of India, Adv. Sergi Joseph Thomas, High Court of Kerala and Adv. Laila.S, District Court Thiruvananthapuram, and Adv. Jiji.S. Madhavan, Legal consultant. Many persons have helped me in collecting data: Sri. S. Babu, Addl. Secretary, Government of Kerala and Dr. K. Surya Prasad, Librarian, Department of Law, University of Kerala are but a couple of them. My indebtedness to them has no limits.

P.P. Vijayan

1
Introduction

The policy of reservation as envisaged in the provisions of the Constitution of the Union of India has always been a topic of discussion, wrought sometimes with highly emotive content that involves social, political, economic, administrative and legal ramifications.

Reserving opportunities, resources or offices for individuals or groups for furthering their welfare and thereby ensuring social justice, is the core of the concept of reservation. Socio-economic disability of a person deprives him or her of the chance to compete with others on equal footing. Thus to find out the disability of the person and reserve opportunities for him or her becomes the responsibility of the State when the State is democratic and its objective is welfare of the people. In the Indian political and sometimes even in judicial parlance the term 'reservation' has come to mean reserving opportunities, resources and/or offices for the groups of people who belong to the socially and educationally backward communities or castes.[1]

People got themselves divided into castes, which underwent a metamorphosis and multiplied.

> Hindu society did not attempt to suppress the immense range of racial, social, cultural and economic diversities, which history was creating for it in unending succession. On the contrary it accepted them, gave to each its place and niche, and brought into existence a living association of human groups of all sorts, which was a federation of its parts, without ever trying to be any one thing. Caste system is the name given to this federation. It is, however, less a system than a method.[2]

The federating point of this caste-based society was the Brahmin. And through the Brahministic rituals and beliefs the hierarchy of caste system has been sustained. This has to be eliminated if India has to become democratic in the western sense of the term. Dalits who have been termed outcastes is a bye-product of caste system. Hence Ambedkar believed that the final solution lay in the abolition of caste system itself.[3] But after some time, it seems, he changed his opinion and observed in one of his papers that the caste could not be abolished. He said:

> Caste is religion, and religion is anything but an institution. It may be institutionalised but it is not the same as the institution in which it is embedded. Religion is an influence or force suffused through the life of each individual molding his character, determining his actions and reactions, his likes and dislikes. These likes and dislikes, actions and reactions are not institutions, which can be lopped off. They are forces and influences, which can be dealt with by controlling them or counteracting them. If social forces are to be prevented from contaminating politics and perverting it to the aggrandizement of the few and the degradation of the many then it follows that it will contain mechanisms, which will bottle the prejudices and nullify the injustice, which the social forces are likely to cause if they were let loose. [4]

Such a legal mechanism he was able to incorporate into the Constitution, as he was the Chairman of the Drafting Committee. Yet even today the social mindset has not fully accustomed to the democratic morality of acknowledging the principle of equality in social intercourse. Ambedkar often remarked that 'in the religious sense, if dogmas like caste and untouchability are taken as test, the untouchables are not Hindus'. He was vociferous in his observation that Hinduism was an obstacle to social unity.[5] The capacity of Hinduism to 'federate', of which Nirad Chaudhari speaks, faces a stalemate when it has to absorb the Western concept of 'equality' of treatment of citizens as the basic tenet of democracy. This could be easily discerned if we compare the workings of 'affirmative action' in the USA and 'protective discrimination' in India.

Thus a society based on status has to be restructured into a society based on contract. Though the Constitution of India begins with the phrase 'We, the People of India'- a phrase contractual in nature, at the pragmatic plane performance of the contractual stipulations has been lopsided. In other words 'equality' among the individual members of the society has to be ensured. Thus it is a part of the performance of these stipulations that the policy of 'reservation' for the 'backward' was envisaged. The 'backwardness' may be due to the age-old system of social structure, which in course of time had become so rigid that it would be an insurmountable obstacle in the process of establishing equality among individuals. This social structure also reveals male dominance, which in fact was absent in ancient times.

Process of Social Change in India

The process of Sanskritization and/or Westernization might have helped a few caste groups in attaining a higher social status. But "Sanskritization as model of status improvement for the Scheduled Castes seems to be relatively irrelevant".[6] Westernization, unlike Sanskritization, continues to influence the people of different castes and communities.

This is because of the fact that Westernization implies the benefits of industrialism, which everyone desires to have and Sanskritization cannot deliver those benefits and in such a predicament the latter has been losing its relevance. But the process of Westernization is interlinked with the knowledge of a Western European language. In the Indian context, English education became the trajectory for Westernization.

Thus it would not be wrong to say that the process of 'westernization' sta: .ed when Lord Macaulay introduced English as the official language in Indian Provinces. But the impact was felt mainly on the upper castes and English education being a passport to appointments in Government services, the benefits went to the upper and middle class people while the masses that belonged to lower castes or casteless (the depressed class of people) remained ignorant and backward.[7] This gradually created a cleavage and consequently the civil society got itself divided and the major division being 'Brahmin versus Non-Brahmin' in many regions of India. Among the Non-Brahmin, there were different classes of people based on caste hierarchy. The issue of 'reservation' should be understood in this background. And it is also important to note that 'reservation' to a certain extent prevented the consolidation of the Non-Brahmin communities within the Hindu fold.

To establish a democracy it is essential to ensure equal opportunity for all classes of people so that the dream of egalitarian society could be realized. People should have access to modern facilities, which, in turn, depends on the resources they could command. Here comes the necessity to provide reservation for the classes of people who deserve it. But at the same time 'classes' or 'castes' that had originated in the erstwhile feudalistic era, have been losing their significance and 'individual' is getting more attention in the context of modern, western system of democracy. Yet from the point of view of Social Psychology, the whole process of Westernization has not gone deep into the social psyche of the people in India. This leads to a sort of hypocrisy in public life. People speak about socialist, egalitarian society, but in private life their behaviour reveals the strong faith in the cultural milieu of the past.

The Impact of Social Reform

The attempts in the direction of reforming Hindu society by socio-religious movements in the 19th and early 20th centuries also reflected this contradiction. Instead of creating a casteless and classless society, they strengthened the groups based on caste.[8] Obviously these groups began to demand due representation in government services. Such demands did not assume any dangerous proportions, thanks to the then Governments (both the British ruled Provinces and Princely States) that responded positively to this issue.

The need for such reservations is to be construed as a time-bound 'program' because this action on the part of the State cannot go on forever. The time limit for this program has also been extended, may be, due to political compulsions. Originally when the Constitution adopted 'reservation' regarding representation in legislature it was only for ten years, which was up to 1960; but the time limit has recently been extended to 2010. But the protective discrimination envisaged for education and employment for the Scheduled Castes and Scheduled Tribes and other socially and economically backward classes of people, does not have any time limit. Another argument is that there is a potential danger that the periodical extension of as well as permanent protective discrimination might, instead of effecting equality through gradual regaining of balance between the erstwhile dominant and erstwhile backward classes, create a tendency among the 'backward' to remain formally backward so that the benefits of protective discrimination could continue for ever. In effect this might breed another variety of inequality in the social hermeneutics.[9] Consequently the equality among the citizens might become a mirage and democratic institutions, to that extent, might suffer.

Obviously in such social scenario disputes are bound to arise. Getting education, obtaining positions of power-including positions in lawmaking bodies and administrative posts-and resource sharing are some of the facets of reservation. Rivalry among the communities is bound to occur because once privileged classes are losing their share of power and hitherto depressed classes are given the benefits of 'protective discrimination'. Here comes the role of Judiciary. This study, therefore, focuses this aspect of judicial approach in dealing with this social syndrome. Has Judiciary succeeded in delivering justice-justice as one of the ideals enshrined in the Preamble of Constitution?

References

1. See Articles 15(4) and 16(4) of the Constitution of India.
2. See, Nirad, C. Chaudhari, The Continent of Circe. (New Delhi 1965), p. 56. After having surveyed the literature concerning this issue, Cunningham and Menon say, "The historic caste system in India was truly systemic: everyone had a place within it. As a result caste system not only drastically exploited and disadvantaged certain groups, such as the erstwhile untouchables; it also concentrated advantage in other groups such as the Brahmins. *Both* suffering and success were largely attributable to where one was born into social hierarchy rather than individual effort or virtue. Thus, India's approach to affirmative action has a more complex origin than the comparable civil rights movement in the United States." 'Race, Class, Caste...? Rethinking Affirmative Action' Michigan *Law Review Vol. 97, No. 5 March 1999.*
3. 'Dr. Ambedkar and Caste' *Harijan* February 11, 1933.
4. Dr.Ambedkar Babasaheb, *Emancipation of Untouchables* (Bangalore 1992) p. 30.
5. Dr.Ambedkar Babasaheb, *Writings and Speeches*, Vol. 9, Government of Maharashtra , (Bombay 1990), p. 186.
6. Ravinder Singh Bains, *Reservation Policy and Anti-reservationists.* (New Delhi 1994), p. 17.
7. See: Bhagwan Das, 'Moments in a History of Reservations', *Economic and Political Weekly* October 28, 2000.
8. Susan Bayly, The New Cambridge History of India IV. 3 *Caste, Society and Politics in India* (1999) p. 155. The contradiction that one finds in the preaching of an egalitarian society and defending caste system, is discussed in Chapter IV of the work.
9. O.P. Sharma, *Reservation- A Gimmick* (New Delhi 1994).

3

Conceptual and Analytical Framework

The existing literature on 'reservation policy' will give a kaleidoscopic view on protective discrimination programmes. Legal umpiring is very much required to resolve disputes pertaining to reservation policy. All three wings of the State legislature, executive and judiciary have to act in unison for delivering social, political and economic justice to the citizens. But instead of a healthy co-ordination there is a subtle rivalry among them; especially between the political executive and judiciary.

The *legislature* is influenced if not dominated by partyism in a parliamentary system of democracy. This has led to Scheduled Castes organizing themselves into political parties in various parts of India. The best example is Bahujan Samaj Party (BSP). Scheduled Tribes, to a certain succeeded in having new States for Tribals and Hill people like extent Chattisgarh, Jharkhand and Uttaranchal. Thus parliamentary system has encouraged the power bargaining and power brokering and this has a boost to caste consolidation and not to caste elimination.

This tendency is reflected in the formation of political *executive* namely the formation of Council of Ministers both at the Centre and at the State levels. The permanent executive being dominated by the upper castes is not sincere in implementing the reservation policy in its letter and spirit. This inevitably leads to political as well as legal conflicts and political articulations clearly point out the need for an effective monitoring system to see whether the reservational laws are of help to the backward classes in overcoming their social disabilities. In a sense the backward classes do get political awareness and they often feel that they are being used as 'vote banks'. But this kind of thinking will only encourage divisive tendencies.

The *judiciary*, though in the initial stages approached reservation laws in dry legal way of interpreting laws by letter and grammar, later revealed a more liberal and active approach in interpreting reservation laws with the touchstone of Constitutional provisions.

In legal disputes, often the 'upper castes' approach the court and challenge the reservation laws. But recently this trend has been reversed.

In this study the concern is the contribution of Judiciary in the area of 'reservation', which is one of the policies to achieve social justice. But in relation to the points raised above following specific objectives are pursued in the present study.

Objectives

1. To examine the extent to which Judiciary is successful in balancing the conflicting interests in the area of 'reservation'.
2. how far the judiciary is active in resolving the conflicting interest between reservationalists and anti-reservationalists, or the equality and protective discrimination especially in the scenario of political appeasement of communal vote banks.
3. the contributions of the court in the creamy layer principle and examine whether it is sufficient to deliver justice to the deserving classes.
4. the relevance of reservation in the context of globalization and its offshoot the knowledge society and it.
5. focuses issue of reservation in Kerala.

In addition to the above objectives the study revolves around following.

Hypotheses

1. When judiciary tries to resolve the issues, the political executive sabotages it by Constitutional amendments.
2. Judiciary, though tradition-bound in the initial stages, has become more active and positive in resolving reservation related issues. And at the same time it often voices its concern for efficiency in administration.
3. There are conflicts between executive and judiciary in implementing reservation.

The Concept of Equality

As the study progresses it can be seen that 'equality' emerges as the central theme. On the concept of equality, as it is incorporated in the Constitution of India, Andre Beteille's observation is note worthy.

What was at issue was not simply equality as a right available to all individuals but also equality as a policy aimed at bringing about certain changes in the structure of society.

It is far from my intention to argue that the claims to equality of individuals and collectivities are nicely balanced in the Constitution of India or that they can be nicely balanced. Law and politics in India have, in fact, been bedevilled by these conflicting claims ever since the Constitution came into effect. It cannot be too strongly emphasized that the Constitution treats the provision in favour of Scheduled Castes and Scheduled Tribes.

The main concern of any political society should be the inequality from which some sections suffer. This inequality is to be understood as a historical continuum of an erstwhile ethos of a society. It might have created a social inequality or economic inequality or both and consequently causing political inequality too in the world of realpolitik. Hence constitutional guarantees to social and economic equality along with political equality have become the raison d'etre of the very system of government. This has been duly acknowledged in the Indian Constitution as special provisions. Ambedkar himself argued in the Constituent Assembly that these special provisions should not be allowed to 'eat up' the general provisions of equality of opportunity for all individuals alike. These special provisions continue to be in force, and it cannot be argued that, because they take collective identities into account and perhaps even strengthen them, they are by definition hostile to the spirit of equality.[1]

The crux of the problem in cases relating to reservation can be easily understood if one can discern the conflicting facets of the concept of equality. Whenever the legality and legitimacy of reservation are discussed the concept of equality enshrined in Article 14 of the Indian Constitution becomes the core theme. The policy of reservation is based on the argument that it would be injustice to treat socially and economically backward people on par with the 'upper classes'. The very concept of equality needs to be examined for in Politics as well as in Law the concept has a Western import and obviously the semantic content that West attributes to it may be alien to the Asian mind.

The Origin of the Concept

The Age of Reason contributed to the politics of the day in Europe the forceful slogan of 'Liberty, Equality and Fraternity' made popular by French Revolution[2], which ignited the thinking world to establishing a political system that came to be styled as democracy[3]. As democracy became the system of government accepted as a norm for the polity by the western world, it has become fashionable to assume that democracy is the best form of government and people in other parts of the world too should adopt such a system[4]. In spite of having a long tradition of governance of states, the people of the Indian sub-continent also came under the spell of the colonial system and at least an articulate section of Indian public opinion during the period of freedom struggle was in favour of the political system of the British masters[5]. Even in Britain the democratic system was a product of evolution and only at a later stage the sovereign power began to devolve gradually and the non-rate payers were given the voting right as a beginning to achieve what could be termed 'political equality'.[6]

The concept of equality is an intriguing one. In his Nicomachean Ethics, Aristotle says that 'justice is equality, as all men believe it to be, quite apart from any argument'. It is pertinent to note that in Greek 'equality' and 'justice' are synonyms.[7] An opposite extreme view could be obtained from Nietzsche who said, "Equality of all men is the biggest lie ever told."[8] It is only commonplace to say that individuals differ in many respects. But they have a basic trait that is to be recognized and encouraged. In the beginning of twentieth century L.T. Hobhouse wrote:

> As a matter of the interpretation of experience, there is something peculiar to human beings and common to human beings without distinction of class, race or sex, which lies far deeper than all the differences between them, call it what we may, soul, reason, the abysmal capacity for suffering, or just human nature, it is something generic, of which there may be many scientific as well as quantitative differences, but which underlies and embraces them all. If this common nature is what the doctrine of equal right postulates, it has no reason to fear the test of our ordinary experience of life or of our study of history and anthropology.[9]

Classification of Equality

Equality has its ramifications reflected mainly as natural equality, social equality, political equality, economic equality, legal equality, and ultimately international equality. The list is not complete; yet it is interesting to note that in the social life of humans, a member of the society always faces problems connected with one kind of equality or other. This multi-dimensional aspect of equality generates complex issues. Parliamentary democracies, which demand support of the majority in the legislature for the political executive, makes the problems all the more complicated.[10] Yet within a political society based on a legal framework of constitutionalism these problems should be solved in a peaceful atmosphere observing the legal principles laid down in the basic law of the land.

The concept of equality is intertwined with other social and jurisprudential concepts like 'right', 'liberty', 'fraternity', 'property' and 'justice' thus making the concept a multi-dimensional one. Hence "of all the basic concepts of social, moral and political philosophy, none is more intriguing and none is more baffling than it."[11] Perhaps this intriguing nature of the concept might have made Earnest Barker remark: "Equality is a protean notion: it changes its shape and assumes new forms with a ready facility."[12] However the term equality might evoke a sense of levelling. That is why Laski said; "Undoubtedly it (equality) implies fundamentally a certain levelling process. It means that no man shall be so placed in society that he can overreach his neighbour to the extent, which constitutes a denial of latter's citizenship."[13] He further elaborates this levelling process in the following words:

> It means that my realization of my best self must involve as its logical result the realization by others of their best selves. It means such an ordering of social forces as will balance a share in its gain also. It means that my share in that gain must be adequate for the purpose of citizenship. It implies that even if my voice be weighed as less weighty than that of another, it must yet receive consideration in the decisions that are made. The meaning, ultimately, of equality surely lies in the fact that the very differences in the nature of men require mechanism for the expression of their wills that give to each its due hearing.[14]

The mechanism about which Laski speaks has its legal dimension. Thus the basic law of the land shall contain provisions to ensure equality by a levelling process.

F.A. Hayek, another thinker of renown, says,

> As a statement of fact it is just not true that all men are born equal. We may continue to use this hallowed phrase to express the ideal that legally and morally all men ought to be treated

> alike. But if we want to understand what this ideal of equality can or should mean, the first requirement is that we free ourselves from the belief in factual equality.[15]

He opines that there is a conflict between the concept of equality and the reality of inequality. At the same time he believes that 'equality before law', which is a prerequisite of a free society, would automatically entail equality in material welfare.

The Relevance of the Concept of Equality

Equality becomes an essential ingredient for a better life and better life for their members is the aim of all political societies. A deeper analysis would bring forth the truth that the positive aspect of equality is achieved only when there is "an appropriate opportunity for each; what is to be equalized is not the opportunity to enter a profession or to be successful in business but the opportunity to lead a good life, or to fulfil one's personality."[16] Therefore the sense of justice demands that when the policy of reservation is formulated and executed it must have the nexus with the objectives sought, namely 'to lead a good life' and 'fulfil one's personality'. Whether this ultimate goal is achieved by the political systems, is a pertinent question to be asked both by the decision makers and by the justice deliverers.

Modern democracy postulates 'equality' as the cardinal principle of governance, because of the very fact that democracy presupposes the participation of citizens in the decision making process, and the very decisions the citizens are making or authorize others to make on their behalf affects their future and thereby affects the future of the political society of which they are members. For the better functioning of democratic system political equality becomes the most indispensable ingredient. All democratic states, therefore, ensure equality of citizens by way of giving each one of them one vote. But this 'equality' is inadequate because of the very fact that other inequalities, especially economic and social inequalities, overwhelm the political equality. Thus 'inequalities' in other spheres of life become significant for this will breed inequities, which will, from within, disrupt the very democratic fabric.

Inequality is inherent in humans. The Marxian philosophy would proclaim that the inequalities were caused by the fact of who owns the means of production. And hence the class difference and consequently class-conflict between the 'haves' and 'have-nots' is inevitable. The panacea for resolving this lies in the establishment of socialism. Thus the socialist thinkers make the concept of equality an avowed norm for achieving the utopia of a classless society. Obviously the emphasis of the socialist thinkers is on the economic equality. Criticizing the Marxian approach Bertrand Russell says, "The greatest political evil is not inequality of wealth as the Bolshevik theorists insist, but inequality of power."[17]

More or less in the same fashion Dahrendorf points out authority as the basis for inequality. As Bains remarks:

"[H]is contribution, however, lies in his recognition of authority as the basis of inequality. In conclusion, it may be stated that power plays a major role in the unequal distribution of resources."[18] Thus the concept of equality has an inevitable nexus with that of power. But again power has its own ramifications. A person may try to develop his personality and he may use every avenue of power he has. This could be termed as 'developmental power'. But there are persons who may try to extract advantages from the abilities of others. This could be termed as 'extractive power'. This is the qualitative aspect of power. It all depends on the inherent capacity of persons concerned. It has a value -dimension also, because the society may not approve of any misuse of power. The basic principle that society imposes certain moral as well as legal obligations upon the members should be understood in the light of this basic postulate.[19]

The Nature of Equality

Equality is a normative concept. It implies that all persons should be treated equally by providing equal opportunity so that they could develop their personality and thereby the State may also be benefited. But can all be weighed equally? Thus, in a given socio-politico-economic situation, perfect equality becomes an ideal to be achieved, nevertheless it is a pragmatic program that is to be sincerely adopted and vigorously pursued. How can Law pursue it? In this regard it would be better if the lawmakers take note of what Rawls says. There are two essential aspects of equality. "First each person is to have equal right to extensive basic liberty compatible with similar liberty of others. Second, social and economic inequalities are to be arranged so that they are both

(a) reasonably expected to be everyone's advantage and

(b) attached to positions and offices equally open to all".[20] Rawls goes on to examine the nexus between 'equality' and 'justice'. He considers 'fairness' as an inseparable part of the concept of justice.

The concept of equality, therefore, poses problems both at the philosophical level and on the pragmatic plane. As Ben and Peter's state:

> A positive egalitarianism, demanding similar treatment of all, irrespective of any difference, would clearly lead to absurdities. To sweep away all distinctions would be to commit injustices as inexcusable as any under attack. Moral progress is made as much by making new and justifiable distinctions as by eliminating established but irrelevant 'inequalities'.[21]

What are to be considered 'irrelevant inequalities' is a pertinent question often faced by the lawmakers and judicial pundits? It seems that for the elimination of irrelevant inequalities, what Laski calls, 'the levelling process' is required.[22] However perfect equality is impossible to achieve and hence "equals should be treated equally and the unequal unequally and the respect in which they are considered unequal must be relevant to the differences in treatment that we propose."[23] Yet the question remains who is to assess the inequality and what normative yardstick one has to adopt.

By the middle of twentieth century 'equal treatment' of humans had become a strong political as well as emotional issue. It became a cardinal principle of 'human rights'. The concept of human rights in general acquired an emotional content, especially since the pogrom unleashed by Nazis during World War II. The subsequent Declaration of Human Rights of the United Nations gave a global legitimacy to the concept of 'equality'. The modern democracies invariably incorporated these rights into their Constitutions.[24] It became a significant principle of democratic constitutionalism.

Equality Versus Inequality

Inequality can be viewed from different angles. Inequality in physical stature is an obvious fact and cannot be done away with. Inequality in the realm of mind and brain is also a fact for which reasons abound. In modern times we speak about the 'human resource'; but if that resource were to be utilized properly, it should be made more potent. It means the potentiality of the individual is to be developed to the utmost extent possible. This will also point out to the fact that each person must be given sufficient and relevant opportunity to cultivate his potentialities. Thus it is imperative that a democratic State should make such opportunity available to all citizens. Then only the State could create wealth, which ought to precede the sharing of wealth.

The Concept of Equality and Modern Democracies

But the dilemma faced by the modern liberal democracies, is that to decide the degree of inequality and consequent affirmative action to be taken should 'classes of people' be taken as the basic unit or the 'individual'. This dilemma is reflected in the discussion regarding 'civil rights' questions in the United States. As Nesiah points out: "Thomas Sowell (1981a), among the first Black academics to speak out against preferential policies, argues that affirmative action programmes have made suspect the qualifications and occupational status of every member of the groups benefited. Sowell has been particularly critical of the application of affirmative action within the academic community."[25] Again he continues to reproduce Sowell's arguments:

> Sowell distinguishes between what he sees as two contradictory senses in which the term 'civil rights' is used. In the first, 'civil rights' means that individuals are viewed and treated within a framework, which is 'blind' to their gender or ethnic origins. In the second, 'civil rights' has come to be equated with affirmative action 'biased' towards specific ethnic groups or one particular gender. Sowell's quarrel is with the latter interpretation, and he is particularly critical of the principle of 'proportional equality'.[26]

While not fully sharing the opinion of Sowell, Nesiah observes "In all three countries (The USA, India and Malaysia) there is an inherent elite bias in preferential policies." He says this is evident particularly in India for the benefits usually accrue only to the upper segments of the protected categories.

In this context observations of Professor Ronald Dworkin are indeed relevant. Speaking on affirmative action, he emphasizes the need to distinguish equality as a right from equality as a policy.[27] According to him political theory has virtually ignored this distinction. He further states that there is a distinction between the right to equal treatment and the right to treatment as an equal. The former is 'the right to an equal distribution of some opportunity, resource or burden' but the latter treatment implies the right 'to be treated with the same respect and concern as anyone else'[28] It seems that the latter one has a socio-psychological dimension. In spite of Constitutional commandments and legal provisions that guarantee 'equality', there is hostility and rivalry among the communities. Another observation by Ivan Reid about the British society is indeed thought provoking. "... These issues (relating to social class differences) are based on questions of social equality and justice."[29] Emphasizing the role of education in this regard he says, "For some the provision of equal opportunities is a sufficient end in itself, for others the end is equality of outcome, which is only achieved when educational attainment of the classes, sexes and ethnic groups is identical."[30]

Social Justice

Yet another concept closely connected with equality is 'social justice. Justice is a word with a host of semantic ramifications. It was the fulcrum around which the dialogue on Plato's Republic revolves. And 'ideal state' became the only answer to realize the ideal of justice. Even today the concept is too elusive to be comprehended and too evasive to be implemented. Yet one can safely proceed on the assumption 'that justice is a positive ethical social value.'[31] Stone has described this ethical value content in the following words: "Men can (and often do) judge things to be just or unjust without formulating any norms attendant on the vague notions which base their judgments; but to explain such judgments, they will always be found to resort to propositions which are tacitly, if not expressly, normative."[32] But in realpolitik it has become a slogan to be used and a myth to be perpetuated. Covenants and Constitutions, therefore, invariably incorporate this ideal.

The Preamble of the Indian Constitution too declares Justice, social, political and economic as the noble objective. But unfortunately the Constitutional practice for over half a century presents a sad story of deviation, distortion and dysfunction. Equality of treatment is one of the cardinal principles of a democracy. But in a society that has been practicing inequality as a way of life a sudden shift in the power structure that equality would bring about is something intolerable. But social justice demands this power shift.

Secondly in an unequal society, social justice demands unequals to be treated unequally. In other words those who were at the lower rungs of the social ladder must be given the benefits of 'protective discrimination' for the obvious reason that they cannot compete with those who have already been at the upper strata. But here too social tension is created owing to the process of 'power shift' from the classes of citizens who were enjoying it to some other classes who were deprived of it. This again is to be resolved if social justice is to become reality. The period of transformation inevitably brings in points of conflict. And herein comes the Judiciary that tries to restore justice by umpiring. Hence people often approach the Court in the hope of getting justice. There are many laws including directives in the Constitution for ensuring social justice to the people especially to the underprivileged. Yet even today social justice in its philosophic content has come to become distorted at the pragmatic plane. But this is not something confined to Indian condition. As V.R. Krishna Iyer comments:

> The Statute Book of India contains much legislation designed to lift the Dalits, to abolish their disabilities and to give them special opportunities for advancement in education and in employment. Bonded labour is by law abolished. Untouchability, by Constitution, is forbidden. The Civil Rights Act goes a long way to eliminate injustice inflicted on the Dalits. Especially stern punishments are prescribed for commission of offences against Scheduled castes and Tribes, but these magic remedies sleep as paper tigers. The social evils continue. The economic wrongs go on. The law is dead, vis-à-vis these unfortunates. There are plans and sub-plans, schemes and projects worked out by the administration at the Central and State levels. There are special reservations for employment and education and these facilities look like reverse discrimination. But what are the raw realities? Tolstoy's biting words set the tone for a social audit of the performance. The abolition of slavery has gone on for a long time. Rome abolished slavery. America abolished it, and we did, but only the words were abolished, not the thing.[33]

In the Indian political scenario, social justice became an adjunct to the political discourse when Western political philosophies of 'liberalism' and 'socialism' made inroads into the minds of the educated elite. The elite among the depressed and backward classes came to consider 'social justice' an indispensable agenda and as much important as freeing the country from the colonial shackles. This ideal was symbolized in Ambedkar and his efforts to give social justice its due place in the basic law resulted in the incorporation of provisions for reservation.

Jurisprudence of Equality

The jurisprudential perspective of the problem of resolving the conflicts arising out of inequalities has given rise to certain doctrines like 'reservation', 'protective discrimination' and 'affirmative action'.[34] Among these the policy of reservation is more political in nature for it tries to strike a compromise between the equality principles envisaged by law and the political solution that would appeal to the concerned group of citizens. In doing so the ostensible purpose is to achieve 'social justice.' When this policy is given legal expression by way of constitutional guarantee and statutory protection, the justification is found in the doctrine of 'protective discrimination'. The dynamics of law demands that it must be put into effective action. The role of the executive, therefore, is emphasized in the doctrine of 'affirmative action'. But all these doctrines are only the reflection of various dimensions of the principle of equality in its political ramifications, legislative formulations, executive endeavours and judicial activism.

Judicial Activism

The Court is often called upon to resolve disputes relating to society in general. In settling the questions involved in such disputes, how does the court behave? When the Court plays a positive role the Court is said to be exhibiting 'judicial activism.' To a great extent this depends upon the predilections of the person who tries to assess the merit of the judgment in his/her own way. Hence 'judicial activism' can be described as an ascriptive term.

The positive role can be elucidated to mean that the Court shall interpret law in such a way that the objectives envisaged in the Constitutional scheme could be realized. At times it may approach the question of personal liberty from the broader perspective of 'human rights'. Tracing the evolution of reservational jurisprudence one would wonder whether the Court has displayed judicial activism. The Court has tried, as it wont to uphold law and at the same time it also wants to accommodate the social aspirations of the depressed classes and weaker sections. It has been a balancing act. But before arriving at a conclusion in this regard, one must delineate what judicial activism means.

Obviously in this context the concept of Judicial Activism is to be comprehended in all its ramifications. The perceptions regarding Judicial Activism are varied. Baxi has rightly stated, 'Activism is one word but constitutes many worlds.'[35] According to another author, "Judicial activism has become as much fascinating as the judicial review, of course, with certain amount of hostility, controversy and apprehension."[36] This statement implies that judicial activism and judicial review are two distinct processes. But the same author in a different context says: "Judicial review power of the judiciary aims at activising herself in retaining her domain of judicial activity over the State activity-legislative and executive." Again, "Suffice it to say that judicial policy making stems from the function of interpretation of the fundamental law of the land, and as such judicial activism is the assertion of judicial review which is remarkable feat unparalleled in the history of world constitutional adjudication." Sathe begins his book on Judicial Activism by saying, "This monograph is about judicial review and its role in democracy. Judicial review means overseeing by the judiciary of the exercise of power by other co-ordinate organs of governments with a view to ensuring that they remain confined to the limits drawn upon their powers by the Constitution."[37]

Justice M.N. Rao begins his article on Judicial Activism by saying that "The concept of judicial activism, which is another name for innovative interpretation, was not of the recent past; it was born in 1804 when Chief Justice Marshall, the greatest Judge of the English-speaking world, decided Marbury v. Madison."[38] The cited case is often quoted as a classic example for judicial review. Thus there is some sort of confusion regarding these two processes of judiciary or one may even wonder whether they are in fact two distinct processes at all. Thomas Sowell is of the opinion that that judicial activism has acquired many meanings and hence need for clarification. Judicial activism has its corollary 'judicial restraint' He cites a few logical questions that are usually ignored. "Are judges deemed to be activist or restrained toward (1) the current popular majority, (2) the legislature representing the current popular majority, (3) the statutes passed by present or past legislatures, (4) the acts of current or past executive or administrative agencies, (5) the meaning of the words in the Constitution, (6) the principles or purposes of those who wrote the Constitution, or (7) the legal precedents established by previous judicial interpretations of the Constitution."[39]

While discussing the theoretical paradigms of Judicial Activism, it cannot be ignored that the disputants expect justice from the Judiciary. But again 'justice' in connection with the interpretation of law has variety of meanings. In the words of Tom Campbell,

> Well, we can certainly construe the term 'justice' here in many different ways. 'Justice' may mean anything from (1) the accurate application of authoritative rules of positive law (called formal justice), through (2) treating the parties fairly according to some process model, (that is procedural justice), to (3) dealing with people according to their deserts or their needs, or their moral rights (or however we care to define substantive justice).[40]

One may call Judiciary 'active' when one gets the variety of justice one expects. That is why it has been pointed out that persons according to their own perception of justice use the adjective active to Judiciary.

The traditional role (obviously it is the British legal tradition that Indian Judiciary followed in the initial stages) of the judiciary is that it shall interpret Constitution (if there is a written one) and legislations including delegated legislations. Thus it is entrusted with the responsibility of declaring what exactly law is.[41] One may expect to have formal justice.

Interpretation of law per se for the avowed purpose of settling disputes or balancing interests cannot be said to be either activism or review. But sometimes the Court goes beyond this traditional role and applies its creative mind in interpreting law so that they could find a solution to the problems of the contemporary society, which demands immediate attention such as, interception of telegrams under section 5(2) of the Indian Telegraph Act, 1885. A host of such cases could be cited as illustrations for the liberal interpretation of existing laws. Such interpretations of existing laws are often termed as 'Judicial Review'. Here one may expect to get substantive justice.

However the Court may try to rectify the inadequacy of the existing legal provisions by indulging in innovativeness. For instance in *Vishaka v. State of Rajasthan* the Court held that sexual harassment at workplace is a violation of Article 15 and 21 of the Constitution. The Court went on to enjoin detailed directions on the subject. It observed that all employers, public or private, until suitable legislation is enacted on the subject should, strictly follow the guidelines it offered.[42] Here the Court's observation and order could not be fully termed as 'review' per se. More than reviewing the existing law, the Court went on to legislate in the interest of the public for the issue at hand had to be tackled without delay. It is in a way judicial law making. This could not be termed as mere judicial review and it would not be improper to use the comprehensive term of judicial activism.

Thus it could be safely concluded that one of the techniques of judicial activism is judicial review. If this were comprehended in proper perspective, judicial review would become complementary to judicial activism. The very act of reviewing is prompted by either zeitgeist or volkgeist combined with the Weltanschauung of the Judge. Only an active judge would resort to this kind of reviewing of law. The judicial activism, thus, becomes a comprehensive concept that embraces the judicial technique of 'review' too. There are also limitations set to this sort of 'activism' by the Constitution,[43] if not its Basic Structure.

Judicial Activism—Historical Evolution

The judicial activism, thus construed, has a hoary past. Far back in 1610 natural law doctrine became a weapon in the hands of Justice Coke to invalidate the man made law in Dr. Bonham's case.[44] The Royal College of Physicians tried to impose a fine for the illegal practice of medicine. Lord Coke pointed out the well-established maxim of Common Law that no man can be a judge in his own case. He said,

> ...it appears in our books that in many cases the common law will control acts of parliament and sometimes adjudge them to be utterly void; for when an act of parliament is against common right or reason or repugnant or impossible to be performed, the common law will control it and adjudge such act to be void.[45]

However with the Revolution of 1688 in England the judiciary practically abandoned the doctrine of superiority of Common law as against law enacted by the parliament. Haines discusses the evolution of judicial review both in England and later in the United States. In this context his observations deserve special mention:

> ...The peculiar significance attached to fundamental laws in the United States took definite and concrete form in the period from 1780 to 1803. It was in this period that the American doctrine of judicial review of legislation was formally announced and accepted as a feature of the public law of the states and of the nation. The gradual emergence of the principle that constitutions are fundamental laws with a peculiar sanctity, that legislatures are limited and receive the commission for their authority from the constitution, and that courts are to be considered the special guardians of the superior written laws may be observed in the evolution of political ideas which accompanied the separation from the British Empire and the establishment of an independent government in America.[46]

When an independent government was formed in India, the framers of the Indian Constitution might have thought about the desirability of judicial review. The power of judicial review is not expressly provided in the Constitution; yet Articles 13, 32, 131-136, 143, 226 and 246 give this power to the judiciary. But the parliament has often come with amendments to the Constitution, which try to limit judicial power. Among them the forty-second amendment virtually set at naught the power of the judiciary regarding review of legislation.[47] Then through a series of judgments the Court has restored the power of judicial review.[48] Unlike the United States, India follows the parliamentary system of democracy and this makes amendment to the Constitution easier especially when a single party dominates the parliament. Hence whenever the Court's decision is not acceptable to the legislative-executive wings of the government, the ruling party or coalition comes with a Constitutional amendment. Thus in India within a span of half century of constitutional experience more than eighty amendments has appeared. Many important amendments are aimed at imposing limits on judicial activism. Even in the United States of America, there is a rethinking on judicial activism. Comparing the judicial activism in India with that in Germany K.L. Bhatia says:

> Features of judicial activism or judicial creativity or Judicial craftsmanship are inherent in both the systems but not congruent, because the modules are different Indian modules developed on the basis of Public Interest Law through the strategies of Public Interest Litigation (PIL) or Social Action Litigation (SAL)...German module having basis on Codified Law System is developed by the Federal Constitutional Court through tricky strategy of Abstract Review, Concrete Review and Individual Complaint.
>
> Judicial activism in India is a movement from personal injury to public concern by relaxing, expanding and broadening the concept of locus standi. Judicial activism is correlated...with a progressive movement from "personal injury standing" to "public concern standing" to allowing access to justice to pro bono publico, that is, public spirited individuals, groups and organizations, on behalf of "lowly and lost" or "underprivileged" or "underdogs" or "little men" who on account of constraints of money, ignorance, illiteracy have been bearing the pains of excesses without access to justice...and by 1975 it had struck down over hundred central and state laws as unconstitutional because such laws suffered from the virus of "hostile discrimination."[49]

From the above analysis it can be understood that the 'lowly and lost', 'underprivileged' 'underdog' or 'little men' do not often get justice from the executive wing of the government and they do not know that they could approach the Judiciary. Hence they need help. Most people who come under the umbrella of reservation do come in the above category.

Activism vis-á-vis India Judiciary

Even during the colonial period there were 'activist judges'. More than a century ago, in 1893, Justice Mehamood of Allahabad High Court articulated his 'activist' mind.[50] In a case concerning an under-trial who could not afford to engage a lawyer the judge expressed his dissent by holding that the court could not decide the case by merely looking at the papers. The condition precedent for a case to be 'heard' was not fulfilled. This clearly shows that the judge had treated law as a living organism and not mere letters on the paper. Here the Judge stood for procedural justice.

In the initial stages of post-Constitutional period the Indian Judiciary was rather hesitant to go beyond the letter of the Constitutional provisions. But later gradually Judiciary began to grapple with socio-political realities and started to interpret law beyond the letter and tried to discover the soul and spirit of it. The period of evolution could be classified in accordance with one's perception of political events in the country. It could be as Prof. Baxi points out Nehruvian and the post-Nehruvian or Emergency and post-Emergency or in the case of reservational judgments Mandal and post-Mandal.[51]

In the first decade of the Constitution, Judiciary confined itself to following written law by letter. This was what happened in *A.K. Gopalan*[52] and *Chambakam Dorairajan.*[53] Judiciary in these cases followed a sort of restraintivism. Often it is said that it was a period when the Court gave much importance to Fundamental Rights and non-justiciable Directive Principles of State Policy were considered to be of lesser value. But here too if the Court's decisions were analyzed from a different angle it could be seen that in the case of *A.K. Gopalan* the Court justified State intervention in the fundamental right zone; but when it came to 'reservation' zone, as in the case of Chambakam Dorairajan, the Court resented such State intervention. In *A.K. Gopalan* the issue was the Constitutional validity of the Preventive Detention Act under which the petitioner had been arrested. The fundamental right of 'personal liberty' was at stake. On behalf of the petitioner it was argued that the word 'law' must include not only the lex, i.e., the enacted law but also jus, i.e., the just principle of law. But the Court rejected this argument and went to a narrower construction, if not a literal construction, of the Constitutional provisions. But the Court did not like the intervention of government in matters of admission to the professional college for the Communal G.O. of the Madras government went against Article 14 of the Constitution. Which judicial pronouncement can be ascribed 'active'? The answer depends upon one' own perception. Hence to a certain extent 'activism' is an ascriptive term. But after two decades the Court liberally interpreted Fundamental Rights, especially personal liberty (Article 21) by virtually overruling Gopalan in Maneka.[54] This created a general opinion especially among the persons practising law that Judiciary was active in upholding the basic rights of the citizens. The cautious step adopted by Indian Judiciary could be seen in the context of 'activism.' Often Judiciary in the US is compared with that in India. But a word of caution seems to be necessary.

First, the US Constitutional structure is different from that of India. In the US Constitution the first fourteen amendments that form the 'Bill of Rights' do not contain any restrictive clauses. Thus the Judiciary has got a wider area to act. Whereas in India though the fundamental rights are guaranteed they are subject to Constitutional restrictions, which empower the State to make laws to impose 'reasonable restriction' on those rights. Thus Judiciary is called upon to decide whether restrictions imposed by the State are 'reasonable' or not. To that extent sphere of action of the Judiciary is also limited. Obviously judicial activism does not find a fertile ground under the Indian Constitutional framework.

Secondly regarding legal mechanics too, the terms used in the two Constitutions are different. The US Constitution speaks about 'due process of' law whereas the Indian Constitution mentions 'procedure established by law'.

Thirdly with regard to reservation issues it cannot be said that the Court has been active. This could be seen from the discussions in the chapters that follow. But here too Indian Judiciary faces an indirect challenge from political executive. Many instances could be cited to show where judicial decisions are set at naught by Constitutional amendments engineered by Political Executive. The highlight of this is the forty-second amendment that tried to establish the obsolete doctrine of Parliamentary sovereignty that tried to curtail the jurisdiction of the court. The Court then had to surmount this obstacle by relying solely on judicial review based on Directive Principles of State policy and principles of natural law.[55] In effect the political executive often stifles judicial activism. Respect for the Basic Law, i.e., Constitution by the people in general, and a Legislative and Executive wing in particular, is essential for the Judiciary to function with dignity.

References

1. Andre Beteille, *Society and Politics in India* (OUP 1991) p. 230.
2. The Declaration of Independence by the American states eloquently put forth the ideal of equality. See Declaration of Independence in Congress, July 4, 1776. The second paragraph states: "We hold this truth to be self evident: That all men are created equal, that they are endowed by the Creator with certain unalienable rights; that among these are life, liberty and pursuit of happiness; that to secure these rights, governments are instituted among men...", yet it was French revolution that popularized the idea in the realm of politics. Modern history being Euro-centric, the Asian countries have also been influenced by it.
3. Aristotle terms 'democracy' as the degenerated form of 'polity'. But in modern times the term has acquired some sort of nobility. (It is interesting to note the observation of George Orwell about 'Politics and English Language'.
4. The world history itself is euro-centric in nature. Hence whatever is European is something to be aped.
5. Even Gandhiji, who had been a bitter critic of the British Parliamentary system of democracy, later came to approve of it. See Anthony J. Parel (Ed.) *The Hind Swaraj* (Cambridge 1997) pp. 30-31.
6. Albert Venn Dicey has the following observation regarding Bentham's contribution to the electoral reform in Britain. "Had not Benthamism provided reformers with an ideal and programme, it is more than possible that the effort to amend the law of England might, like many other endeavours to promote the progress of mankind, have missed its mark." *The Lectures on the Relation between Law and Public Opinion in England during the Nineteenth Century. (1981)* p. 176. Parliamentary Reform Act 1832 was in fact a partial realization of Bentham's dream.
7. Vlastos. G, 'Justice and Equality' in *Theories of Rights,* (London 1989) Jeremy Waldron (ed).
8. Quoted in Warwick McKean, *Equality and Discrimination Under International Law.*(London 1983) p.3.
9. L.T. Hobhouse, *Elements of Social Justice.*(London. 1922) p.9.
10. The political parties in their electoral fights encourage socio-economic inequalities and thus cause the inequalities to persist.
11. Frank Thakurdas. 'In Defense of Social Equality', *The Indian Journal of Political Science.* Vol.xxxvii No.1. p.1.
12. Earnest Barker, *Principles of Social and Political Theory.* (London 1967) p.151.
13. Harold.J Laski. *A Grammar Of Politics* (London. 1951) p.153.
14. *Ibid.,* p.153.
15. Hayek. F.A. *The Constitution of Liberty* (London. 1960) p. 87.

16. S. Ben and R.S. Peters, *Social Principles and Democratic State* (London 1975) p.119.
17. Bertrand Russell, *Roads to Freedom* (London 1919) p. 111.
18. Ravindar Singh Bains, *Reservation Policy and Anti-Reservationists* (New Delhi 1994) p. 4.
19. C.B. Macpherson, Democratic *Theory: Essays in Retrieval* (London 1975). p.53 The existence of human capacities "is attributed to divine creation, or to some evolutionary development of more complex organism, it is a basic postulate. It is an empirical postulate verifiable in a broad way by observation. It is at the same time value postulate, in the sense that rights and obligations can be derived from it without any additional value premise, since the very structure of our thought and language puts an evaluative content into our descriptive statements about man."
20. John Rawls, *A Theory of Justice.* (London 1972) p. 61. If Articles 15(4) and 16(4) are examined one could find that they reflect the second aspect of Rawls analysis.
21. S. Ben R.S. Peters *op.cit* p.133.
22. Harold Laski *op.cit* at 21.
23. Harold Laski *op.cit* at.114.
24. Article 1.4 of the International Convention on Elimination of All Forms Of Racial Discrimination states:

    Special measures for the sole purpose of securing adequate advancement of certain racial and ethnic groups or individuals requiring such protection as may be necessary in order to ensure such groups or individuals equal enjoyment or exercise of human rights or fundamental freedoms shall not be deemed racial discrimination, provided, however, that such measures do not as a consequence, lead to maintenance of separate rights for different racial groups and they shall not be continued after the objective for which they were taken, had been achieved. (United Nations. 1969).
25. Devanesan Nesiah, *Discrimination- with reason?* (OUP 1997) p.30.
26. *ibid* at p.31.
27. Ronald Dworkin, *Taking Rights Seriously,* (London 1977) pp. 223-39.
28. *Ibid.* p. 227.
29. Ivan Reid *Social Class differences in Britain* (London 1989) p.13.
30. *Ibid.*
31. Julius Stone, *Human Law and Human Justice* (Bombay 1965) p.31.
32. *Ibid.*
33. V.R. Krishna Iyer, *Social Justice and Undone Vast* (New Delhi 1991) p.71.
34. See Clark D Cunningham and N R Madhava Menon, 'Race, Class, Caste...? Rethinking Affirmative Action.' *Michigan Law Review* Vol. 97, No 5 March 1999.
35. Upendra Baxi in his Preface to S.P.Sathe's *Judicial Activism in India* (OUP 2002) p.x.

36. K.L. Bhatia, *Judicial Review and Judicial Activism* (1997) p.115.
37. S.P. Sathe, *Judicial Activism in India* (OUP 2002) p.1.
38. M.N.Rao, *Judicial Activism*, appeared in *Ebc India* from web. Even back in 1825 a contrary view was expressed by Justice Gibson of the Pennsylvania Supreme Court. In *Eakin v. Raub* he observed:

    The constitution of Pennsylvania contains no express grant of political powers to the judiciary. But, to establish a grant by implication, the constitution is said to be a law of superior obligation; and, consequently, that if it were to come into collision with an act of the legislature, the latter will have to give way. This is conceded. But it is a fallacy, to suppose that they can come into collision *before the judiciary*.

    The constitution and the right of the legislature to pass the act may be in collision. But is that a legitimate subject for judicial determination?

    Quoted in C.Herman Pritchett, *The Federal system in Constitutional Law.* (1978) p. 37.

    But the above argument is not applicable in the Indian context. Article 13 (2) clearly states that "The State shall not make any law which takes away or abridges the rights conferred by this Part and any law made in contravention of this clause shall to the extent of the contravention be void." But the Constitutional Amendment do not come under the purview of this Article; because the legislature asserted the its power through twenty fourth amendment that added clause 4 to Article 13. It says, "Nothing in this Article shall apply to any amendment of this Constitution made under Article 368." This again has set an unpredictable limitation to the review power of the judiciary.
39. Thomas Sowell, 'Judicial Activism Reconsidered' *http://www.amatecon.com/etext/jar/jar.html* accessed on 08-07-2003
40. Tom Campbell, *Judicial Activism- Justice or Treason?* Working paper Number 2002/17

    http://law.anu.edu.au/news/webdocuments/ tom Campbell notes.pdf. accessed on 08-07-2003
41. See Art. 141 of the Constitution of India.
42. AIR 1997 SC 3011
43. Analyzing the Constitution as a political document in the American context Martin. H Redish writes:

    In sum, in a society committed to the value of popular sovereignty, the inertia must lie in favour of the policy choices made by those representative of and accountable to the electorate. It is only when the text of the countermajoritarian governing document provides a rule of behaviour or structure that is contravened by majoritarian action that unaccountable judiciary has license to invalidate that action. Hence in a democracy the only justification for judicial review by a non-representative governmental organ is the desire to insure that the majoritarian branches adhere to the countermajoritarian limitations imposed by the constitution. Judicial invalidation of the majoritarian will on any other grounds would erode the basic democratic principle that non-constitutional value and policy choices are to be made by those responsive to public will.

Martin H. Redish. *The Constitution As Political Structure.*(New York 1995) p. 8.

44. See Charles Grove Haines, *The American Doctrine of Judicial Supremacy* (New York 1959) p.33.
45. *Ibid.*
46. *Ibid.* p.66.
47. Twenty- fourth amendment introduced clause (3) to Article 368. This clause stated, "Nothing in article 13 shall apply to any amendment made under this article. But the forty-second amendment was portentous in the sense that it cut off the jurisdiction of the Court in a significant way, perhaps with an object of incorporating the doctrine of 'parliamentary sovereignty'. It introduced clause (4) and (5) and the latter clause read' "For the removal of doubts, it is hereby declared that there shall be no limitation whatever on the constituent power of Parliament to amend by way of addition, variation or repeal the provisions of the Constitution under this article."
48. Clauses (4) and (5) of the article 368 were held *ultra vires* because they exclude judicial review, which is a basic feature of the Constitution. See *Minerva Mills Ltd.* v. *Union of India.*, AIR 1980 SC 1789, *Subhash* v. *Union of India.* AIR 1991 SC 631.
49. K.L.Bhatia, *op.cit.*, p.115-116.
50. Interview with J.S. Verma (Justice) by Manoj Mitta, *India Today* 15th March 1996.
51. S.P. Sathe, *Judicial Activism in India* p.x.
52. *A.K.Gopalan v. State of Madras.* AIR 1950 SC 27.
53. *State of Madras v. Champakam Dorairajan* AIR 1951 SC 226.
54. *Maneka Gandhi v, Union of India* AIR 1978 SC597.
55. *Minerva Mills v. Union of India.* AIR 1980 SC 1789.

3

Reservation Policy in India: Origin, Growth and Recent Trends

Historical Bakground

Legislations regarding 'reservation' could be traced back to the colonial period. By the middle of 19th century there emerged reformers in many parts of India. One such reform was the byproduct of proselytizing the natives especially the depressed classes by the Christian missionaries. This might have inspired the Hindus to effect social reforms or they might have felt ashamed to have such practices as caste discrimination. Consequently there were such moderate reform movements in many parts of the subcontinent. For instance a movement was started in the Madras Province in 1852.[1] In 1858 the Government of Bombay Presidency declared that 'all schools maintained at the sole cost of Government shall be open to all classes of its subjects without discrimination. But this policy was hardly enforced. For instance a Mahar boy was refused admission and the Bombay Education Department justified the action of the school by saying that 'it would not be right for the sake of a single individual, the only Mahar who had ever yet come forward to beg for admission into a school attended only by pupils of caste, to force him into association with them, at the probable risk of making the institution practically useless to great mass of natives.'[2] By 1923 the same Government decided to cut off aid to educational institutions that refused admission to members of the Depressed Classes.[3] But often the reform movements addressed issues, which were considered anachronistic and superstitious. The reform movements were concerned not with the evils of caste system as such, but of broader social issues like widow remarriage and education of women and opposition to child marriage. As Galanter says they are issues, ' which reflected higher caste practices, and options' Caste system as such was not challenged[4]. Some authors tried to discover 'Brahminism' as the root reason for the discriminatory behavior.

Jyotiba Phule, a social activist felt the necessity of reforms within the Hindu fold. In 1860 he called attention to the deplorable conditions in which the depressed classes lived and also the discriminatory treatment meted out to them. In 1858 the Government of Bombay Presidency (present Maharashtra and Gujarat were parts of it) declared that 'all schools maintained at the sole cost of Government shall be open to all classes of subjects without discrimination.' During that time the British Government took a serious view of the question of depressed classes. In 1880s, the British administration set up scholarships, special schools and other beneficial programmes for the Depressed Classes. The progressive minded princes in the native states like Baroda, Kolhapur, and Travancore took similar initiatives.[5] Tracing the historical evolution of the policy of reservation, the Committee on the Welfare of Scheduled Castes and Scheduled Tribes stated:

> Realising the inequatious distribution of posts in the administration between different castes and communities, the rulers of some of the then princely states, who were genuinely interested in the upliftment of disadvantaged sections of the society, took initiatives and introduced reservations in the administrative posts in favour of backward castes and communities in their States as early as in the first quarter of 20th century. Mysore and Kohlapur were amongst the first to do so. Because of the movement for social justice and equity started by the Justice Party, the then Presidency of Madras initiated the reservation in Government employment in 1921. It was followed by the Bombay Presidency comprised of the major portion of present states of Maharashtra, Karnataka and Gujarat. Thus the first quarter of the 20th century saw reservation in Government employment in almost whole of South India.[6]

The census of 1910, classified the population into (a) Hindus, (b) Animists and Tribals and (c) The Depressed classes. Thus the plight of the depressed classes was addressed for the first time.

Eight years later in 1918, the Maharaja of Mysore, having received a petition from the depressed class people, appointed Miller Committee to go into the question of adequate representation of non-Brahmin communities in the services of the State. When the First World War started in 1914, Britain began to pay more attention to the war. And, perhaps to elicit the support of the people in India Britain thought about some Constitutional reform. In the political history of India an association in Madras Province initiated representation to the depressed classes. There was also a strong public opinion in favour of this demand. A minute of dissent by Sir C. Sankaran Nair clearly reflected this trend in the political atmosphere of that time. According to him, "the non-Brahmin and depressed classes have awakened to a sense of their political helplessness and to their wretched condition, and no longer contend to rely upon the Government which has left them in this condition for the past hundred years, claim a powerful voice, in the determination of their future."[7] Thus increasing political awareness among the non-Brahmin Classes and Britain's need to have Indian people's cooperation in war efforts prompted the British rulers to adopt a policy of encouraging the 'gradual development of self-governing institutions with a view to the progressive realization of responsible government in India as an integral part of the British empire'.[8]

After studying the views expressed by various organizations in India, it was decided to provide representation in the Provincial Assemblies and the Central Legislative Assembly. In the provinces ruled by the British a systematic attempt for the betterment of the Depressed Classes was started with the introduction of Montague-Chelmsford Reform incorporated in The Government of India Act, 1919. A demand for the adequate representation in the legislatures was justified on the ground that the depressed classes were subjected to the intellectual and cultural domination of Brahmin priest class.[9]

A Significant Poltical Movemnet in Madras Province

In fact the non-Brahman movement had organized into the South India Liberal Federation in 1916. Later it came to be known as *Justice Party* after the name of its English newspaper, edited by T.M. Nair, a physician by profession. "As a first step, the party agitated for reserved seats for non-Brahmins in the legislative councils, ushered in by the Montague-Chelmsford Reforms."[10] The main objective of the *Justice Party* was getting communal representation in the Government offices.

> In reply to a question raised in the Madras legislative Council in the year 1914 it was answered that that the total of registered graduates of the Madras University was 650 of whom 452 were Brahmins, 12 non-Brahmin Hindus and 74 belonged to other communities. The Madras legislative Council, the Senate of the Madras University and other local and public bodies

> composed of a large number of Brahmins and the non-Brahmins had hardly a chance of entering these bodies. Out of the 128 permanent District Munsifs in 1919, 93 were Brahmins, 25 non-Brahmin Hindus and the rest consisted of Muslims, Indian Christians and Anglo-Indians. Out of 1007 Gazetted posts 609 were filled with Brahmin as against 398 posts held by non-Brahmins, Muslims and Christians. Out of 17,225 clerical posts 9813 were held by Brahmins...[11]

Moreover not a single non- Brahmin was elected to the Legislative Council during the first three decades since it started functioning in 1882 when it was started to 1917. Thus it was no wonder that when under the Government of India Act 1919 elections were held the *Justice Party* came out successful and formed ministry. The Indian national Congress had not participated in the elections. It was this Government of Madras that introduced what was later termed as 'Communal G.O., which, in the post-Constitutional period, was challenged in *Chembakam Dorairajan v. State of Madras.*[12] It will not be wrong to state that there was a widespread awakening among the 'depressed classes' and this led to their claiming for adequate representation in the legislatures. Jaswal writes:

> The result of the First Dispatch on Indian Constitutional Reforms was that the existence of depressed classes was recognized for the first time in Indian History under the Government Of India Act 1919 with the result that among the fourteen non-official members nominated by the Governor general to the Central Legislative Assembly, one was the representative of the 'depressed classes'. In the provincial legislatures the depressed classes were represented by four nominations in the Central Provinces, two in Bombay, two in Bihar and one each in Bengal and United Provinces. In Madras ten members were nominated to represent nine specified depressed classes.
>
> It was after the Act of 1919 that the Scheduled Castes, popularly known as depressed classes became a 'political entity' for consideration in future set up of constitutional reforms. A thorough examination of the Report of the Thirty second Indian National Congress shows that the Congress has mustered enough strength to pass a resolution to urging the people of India to remove all disabilities that were imposed by custom upon the depressed classes.[13]

In Madras Province Periyar E.V. Ramasamy spearheaded the non-Brahmin Movement. He declared that 'communal justice' was only a means to an end and the end would be casteless society. Periyar E.V. Ramasamy broke with the Congress in 1925 on the issue of dominance of Brahmins within the Indian National Congress in the Madras Province and started the Self Respect Movement with a view to bringing about all round change in Tamil society."[14] So with the positive urge to protect the rights of depressed classes, there emerged the negative force of anti-Brahminism. Often casteism was identified with Brahminism and due mainly to the impact of Western ideals of equality and socialism the non-Brahmin, if not anti-Brahmin, movements emerged in different parts of India.

The Government of India Act 1919 had a provision that a statutory Commission would be appointed after ten years to report on the matter of establishing a responsible government in India. In keeping with this provision, the British Government appointed Simon Commission. The Commission did not have any Indian member in it and was 'all-white' one, in spite of protests from the Indian National Congress and Gandhi the Commission toured every Indian province. The Commission went through memoranda from Government of India, from Committees appointed by the provincial legislative councils and from non-official sources. Obviously the final report contained recommendations for reform. One of the recommendations was the need to safeguard the minorities and other depressed classes of people. The report of the Commission focused the issue of the depressed classes not only as a social issue of caste, but also as an issue with serious political ramifications. The Commission was of the opinion that the uplift of the depressed classes depended on their gaining political influence, if not participation in the governmental processes. Obviously the representatives of the depressed classes were to be present in the legislature. Many provinces like Bihar and Orissa suggested they would opt for 'nomination' because the depressed classes were too backward to choose their own representatives. But the Commission did not favour this idea for it felt that depressed classes needed opportunities for getting used to ideas and practices of self government.

The Role of Colonial Constitutional Reforms in Establishing Equality

The depressed classes demanded a separate electorate. But the Commission did not favour this. However the Commission was not against reserving seats for them. The Commission recommended to reserve seats for the depressed classes in general constituencies and these seats would be filled by election in which both depressed classes and others would participate.

In 1923 government decided not to give grants to those aided schools that refused admission to the children of the depressed classes. In 1928 Government of Bombay set up a Committee under the chairmanship of O.A.B.Starte to identify the Backward Classes and recommend special provisions for their welfare. In the meanwhile under the leadership of Ambedkar the Depressed Class people had begun to articulate forcefully their demands. The Simon Commission, which came to study and make recommendations for Constitutional reforms held negotiations and consultations with different groups of people. The representatives of the 'untouchables' participated in them. In the words of Galanter, "Dr.Ambedkar, by this time recognized as an important spokesman, appeared before the Commission to demand reserved seats for the untouchables in legislative bodies, special educational concessions, and recruitment to Government posts recommendations substantially accepted in the Commission's report." [15]

He argued:

> The depressed classes in India present definite problem in political and social evolution. They are the resultants of historical forces, religious, economic and social. They are the embodiment of exploded (sic) social ideas and the disabilities imposed on them by the original framers of Hindu polity have been aggravated by long centuries of segregation and neglect. The origin of these classes and the beginning of their woes rightly belong to the domain of historical research but their betterment, economic and educational, is an imperative problem. Their class-consciousness is growing, stimulated partly by the sympathy of the Government and partly by the belated awakening of the Hindu social conscience.[16]

In the Report submitted in 1930 backward people were categorized: (a) Depressed Classes, (b) Aboriginals and Hill Tribes and (c) Other Backward Classes. But there was stiff opposition to the recommendations of the Simon Commission Report. Therefore the British Government convened a Round Table Conference in November 1930, to which delegates from different parties and interest groups were invited. Unfortunately the Indian National Congress, which claimed that it was the only organization that truly represented the people of India, did not participate for it was engaged in The Civil Disobedience Campaign against the Government. Though Gandhi, the unquestioned leader of the National Movement, was opposed to any kind of reservation, later changed his position and conceded to setting up separate electorates to religious minorities like Muslims, Sikhs and Christians. But he opposed vehemently separate electorate for the 'depressed classes'.[17] The Round Table Conference ended in failure. Subsequently the British Government appointed Lothian Committee in December 1931, to formulate a system of franchise whereby all sections of the people would be represented in the legislatures. The Committee was specifically required 'to investigate the need, justification and methods to ensure adequate representation for the Depressed Classes.' As one writer observes:

> The Hindu members of the Lothian Committee, the members of the provincial Franchise Committees, and the Hindu witnesses in several provinces conspired to minimize the number of untouchables. Perjuring themselves, the witnesses denied the existence of untouchables in their province. In the United Province, for example, the Franchise Committee reported the number of untouchables as just 0.6 million as against the 1931 (census) figure of 12.6. In Bengal the Franchise Committee figure was 0.07 million whereas the census figure was 10.3 million. Before the RTC the census figures of the untouchables had not been challenged. When the upper castes found that the untouchables would get representation and facilities based on their population, they resorted to lies to deny the existence of untouchables. Is not such a calculated conspiracy to deny the right of the untouchables going on in different forms even today? [18]

Simon Commision Report and After

In 1931 six months after the publication of Simon Commission Report, a Round Table Conference was convened in London to review the Commission's Report and how a new Constitution for India could be worked out on the basis of the recommendations of the Commission. Ambedkar and Rao Bahadur Srinivasan represented the Depressed Classes in this Conference.

The focus of the Conference was the position of minorities in the future structure of Government in India. Ambedkar and Srinivasan demanded separate electorate and adult franchise. But the separate electorates were not to be a permanent feature. But the discussion went on without reaching an agreement. Subsequently there was convened the Second Round Table Conference. This time Gandhi also participated; but he vehemently opposed to the system of separate electorate for the Depressed Classes. He criticized the separate electorate as a devise of the British strategy of 'divide and rule'

The Franchise Committee of the Conference was unable to reach an agreement on the representation of minorities. Thus the then Prime Minister of Britain Ramsay Mac Donald was authorized to make an award, which would be binding on all parties. Called as Communal Award, announced in August 1932, it 'granted their demand for separate electorates in areas where they were concentrated in addition to regular votes they would cast as members of general electorate.'[19] The award proclaimed:

> Members of the depressed classes qualify to vote, will vote in general constituency. In view of the fact that for a considerable period those classes would be unlikely by the means alone, to secure adequate representation in the legislature, a number of special seats will be assigned to them...These seats will be filled by election from special constituencies in which only member of the 'depressed classes', electorally qualified, will be entitled to vote. Any person voting in such special constituency will, as stated above, be also entitled to vote in a general constituency. It is intended that these constituencies should be formed in selected areas where the depressed classes are most numerous and that except in Madras, they should not cover the whole area of the province.[20]

The Poona Pact

Gandhi was opposed to this award.[21] After a month he started a fast unto death to resolve the issue of representation of depressed classes of people in the Assembly. A modern historian writes:

> ...his (Gandhi's) friends as well as his opponents wondered why he chose this particular issue for so terrifying a tactic, since it seemed directed more against the untouchables than the British Government. Gandhi considered this issue central to the very survival of Hinduism. However for that reason he was willing to concede more reserved seats to Ambedkar for his party than the British had done. All he asked was that the

depressed classes should not think of themselves as members of any religious community but Hinduism."[22] Gandhi openly declared, "I believe that if untouchability is really rooted out it will not only purge Hinduism of a terrible blot but its repercussion will be world wide. My fight against untouchability is a fight against the impure in humanity."[23]

The mediators between Gandhi and Ambedkar put in all their effort and both of them met at Yervada jail where Gandhi had been a prisoner of the British Government. It was here that he started his 'fast unto death' against the separate electorate for Depressed Classes. Now the responsibility of saving the life of Gandhi fell on all sections of Indians. But Ambedkar had a different opinion. It did not seem that Ambedkar at first took the fast of Gandhi seriously. On 19 September 1932, he issued a statement focusing on the following points:

1. Why should Gandhi stake his life on a relatively small issue as the communal question?
2. Why were the Depressed Classes singled out whereas at the RTC Gandhi had opposed special rights to all except Muslims and Sikhs?
3. His conscience was not aroused if the nation was split by the arrangement of special electorates for classes and communities other than the depressed classes- Why?
4. If there was any class, which deserved special political rights, it was the depressed classes.
5. The only path for the depressed classes to succeed in the struggle against organized tyranny was a share in political power.
6. The Mahatma staked his life to deprive the untouchables of the little they got.
7. The Communal Award itself was a compromise between the two principles of separate electorates and joint electorates.
8. At the time of RTC the Mahatma was opposed to any system of special representation to the Depressed Classes even in a system of joint electorates.
9. Gandhi had suggested a convention-based scheme under which the losing untouchable candidate would obtain a court verdict that he was defeated because of untouchability and continue to contest and keep on getting court verdicts *ad infinitum.*
10. All Mahatmas had failed in the mission of removing untouchability and absorbing the depressed class.

11. Reformers who preferred to sacrifice principles at moments of crisis rather than hurt the feelings of their kindred could not be trusted by the depressed classes.
12. The Mahatma's fast would result in acts of terrorism by his followers against the depressed classes.
13. Gandhi's fast was releasing reactionary forces and fostering hatred.
14. If the Mahatma did not want hatred reaction and terror to spread on a large scale, he should reconsider the decision to fast unto death.

But Gandhi viewed the Award 'an attack on Indian unity and nationalism and harmful to both.' By that time Gandhi had become hero of millions in India and even the depressed class leaders like M.C.Raja thought it their duty to save the life of Gandhi. Hence the mediators between Ambedkar and Gandhi actively intervened and at last Ambedkar agreed to meet Gandhi at Yervada prison. After much haggling they reached an agreement.

According to this historic agreement depressed classes would get 147 seats in the provincial councils instead of 71 promised in the Ramsay MacDonald's award. The Depressed classes could get 18% of the seats in the Central Assembly also. The British Government accepted this agreement between Ambedkar and Gandhi and incorporated it as an amendment to the Communal Award of the Prime Minister of Britain. Subsequently Gandhi ended the fast and the following week was celebrated as Untouchability Abolition Week.[24] It seems that Gandhi knew the rising political awareness among the backward classes and depressed classes. These developments reflected in the next Constitutional document namely Government of India Act 1935.

The Government of India Act 1935 replaced the term 'depressed classes' with 'Scheduled castes'.[25] Accordingly separate lists of scheduled castes were notified for various provinces in 1936. The Act also defined 'scheduled castes' as 'such castes, races or tribes or groups within castes, races or tribes which appear to His Majesty -in- Council to correspond to the classes of persons formerly known as the depressed classes as His Majesty-in-Council may specify'. Even though seats in the legislature were reserved both for the 'minority' communities and for the 'depressed classes', reservation in the public service was denied to the 'depressed classes', whereas the minority communities enjoyed 'reservation' in the public services. The reason stated for this was: "In the present state of general education in these classes the Government of India considers that no useful purpose will be served by reserving for them a definite percentage of vacancies out of the number available for Hindus as a whole, but they hope to ensure that duly qualified candidates from the depressed classes are not deprived of their opportunities of appointment merely because they cannot succeed in open competition."[26]

Political Strategies of Gandhi and Ambedkar

While Gandhi started Harijan Sevak Samaj to uplift the Depressed Classes, Ambedkar formed the Independent Labour Party (1936) to put pressure on Government for obtaining more resources for the Depressed Classes. Later in 1942 it became All India Depressed Classes Federation. When in 1942 Gandhi and the Congress opposed war efforts and started the famous 'quit India' movement, Ambedkar, by contrast supported the British policy and its war efforts. He became a member of Viceroy's Executive Council. He used his position in the Government to further the interests of the Depressed Classes. During this time in a 'Memorandum' he submitted to the Government, he demanded reservations not only in legislative seats but also in education and Government employment. This was perhaps a crucial moment for the Colonial Government and thus his demand was accepted and this became the basis for the policy of India when it was framing the Constitution. Ambedkar played his card well by cooperating with the Colonial Government and made available some concrete gains for the Depressed Classes. The Independent India could not go back on this commitment of the previous government. It had to recognize these gains and the framers of the Constitution had to evolve a policy of protective discrimination based on this already accepted principle. The pertinent question here is, would the framers of the Constitution have incorporated protective discrimination clauses in the basic law if Ambedkar had not made the British Government recognize the plight of the depressed classes and won for them the valuable concessions from the then Government.

Thus in 1942 the scheduled castes obtained 8.5 per cent reservation in Central services. The framers of the Constitution adopted the policy of reservation as the continuation of the policy that had been followed by the British Government in India. In many Provinces and native States legislations were enacted for uplifting the Depressed Classes.

Thus the socio-political scenario of the thirties of the twentieth century was one in which the so-called Depressed Classes had begun to articulate their aspirations and in principle at least the upper class Hindus had to recognize the rights of the Depressed Classes. In many regions in India the Hindu Temples were opened to depressed Classes people. This was a significant step on the path of the social uplift of the Depressed

Classes. And rightly Ambedkar was able to articulate effectively the aspirations of depressed classes and adopt befitting political strategies to make gains for them.

The Maharaja of Travancore issued Temple Entry Proclamation in 1936.[27] In 1938 Madras Presidency enacted Madras Removal of Civil Disabilities Act followed by Bombay Government's Bombay Harijan Temple Entry Act, 1943 and the United Provinces Removal Social Disabilities Act, 1947. Perhaps these initiatives in the form of even legislations paved the way for a silent socio-political revolution and this changing scenario became the backdrop for the discussions of the framers of the Constitution.

Kerala

Kerala till the last quarter of 19th century presented a picture of feudalism reinforced by casteism. Between the 12th century when Chera kingdom disintegrated and the late 19th century that witnessed a new awakening among the non-Brahmins and especially among the depressed classes.

Kerala comprises the erstwhile princely states of Travancore and Cochin, and Malabar, which was a part of Madras Presidency. In the Madras Presidency the Non-Brahmin movement was demanding reservation for the depressed classes of people and consequently some kind of reservation was introduced through a Government Order in 1920.[28] Cochin was a very small state where reservation was not at all an important issue.

Evolution of Constitutional Government in Travancore

Travancore had begun its journey towards participatory government in 1888 when the Travancore legislative Council[29] came into existence. It could not be said that it was a truly representative body and moreover it had only the power to make tentative suggestions and requests to the Maharaja of Travancore. Yet the body enabled the Sovereign –King-to come into contact with different shades of public opinion. In 1898 and 1904 Regulations were made for increasing the number of members in the Council. In 1904 The Sri Mulam Popular Assembly was formed.[30] But politics in the princely State of Travancore embarked on its innings on the slippery pitch of demand for reservation in government posts. Nairs and Brahmins dominated the administration and consequently the other communities like Ezhavas, Pulayas who belonged to the Hindu fold, and also Christians and Muslims organized themselves. They had their own separate organizations,[31] which later came under the common platform of 'Aggrieved Communities' that formed Joint Political Congress (JPC).[32] Because of the Communal dimension of the politics of the day, the Indian National Congress did not have any strength in this part of the country.

Agitation Through Memorials

Travancore was one, if not the best-administered state in the Indian subcontinent.[33] Yet with regard to political conditions it could not be said that Travancore displayed any social harmony. Until the middle of 19th century slavery was practiced.[34] The feudal social system enabled the upper castes to exploit the depressed ones in many ways. First the opposition emerged from the dominant community namely Nairs. *Malayali Sabha* an organization of educated young men that was formed in 1884 reflected the discontent of the Nair youth against the administration dominated by foreign Brahmins.[35] Their indignation found expression in *The Malayali Memorial* submitted to the Maharaja of Travancore in 1891. There started a series of Memorials because the monarch's government placated Nairs by offering posts in the government services. This caused divisive thinking among the Travancoreans. Ezhavas, a backward Community in the Hindu fold submitted their *Memorial* in 1895 but to no great advantage. The *Memorial* described the condition of the Ezhava community and the need for action on the part of the Government. It said:

> Government schools in the State were all closed to them in Travancore till a few years ago; and although some have been since opened, yet owing to the absence of State patronage, even these slight educational facilities have not been as largely availed of as might be desired. Even as it is the number of Tiyas (Ezhavas) returned in 1891 as educated are 25,000 or 12.10% of the male population, while the percentage in 1875 was only 3.15. This increase considering the absence of any kind of inducement from Government and the fact that most of the schools in the state were closed to them goes to show that the community is certainly not indifferent to education.[36]

Thus the *Ezhava Memorial* pointed out the need for affirmative action at least in the case of one depressed community. But the Government of Travancore was not prepared to embark upon any radical changes in the existing system. Thus having been frustrated the Ezhavas submitted a similar *Memorial* to Lord Curzon in 1900, but this also did not bear fruit.

Reforms by the Monarch

Lord Curzon on his visit to Travancore in 1900 said, obviously having a reference to the memorial detailing the grievances of the Ezhavas that "in the history of States no rulers are more esteemed by posterity than those who have risen superior to the trammels of bigotry and exclusiveness and have dealt equal mercy and equal justice to all classes... including the humblest of their people." T.K. Ravindran adds, 'The Maharaja of Travancore was quick to act on the advice and a wave of reforms followed. But his officers were not ready to do away with the customary rules and that is why the schools declared open to lower castes still remained virtually inaccessible to them.'[37]

It would not be right to say that the Travancore Government was not responsive to the demands of the backward classes. There are many occasions as when a representative of Ezhava community Kumaran Asan, the famous Malayalam poet, thanked the Government of Travancore for admitting the students belonging to depressed classes in Government institutions. For instance Asan 'thanked the Dewan for showing special attention in redressing the educational grievances of the Ezhavas...'[38]

Gradually Communities other than Nairs, Kshatrias and Brahmins began to organize themselves.[39] These *Memorials* demanded representation in the administration and in the Popular Assembly. From the given statistics below[40] one could easily understand the reason for their demands.

Table–3.1

Total Number of Members to be Returned by Open Election to the Popular Assembly

	1922	*1925*	*1928*	*1931*
Total seats.	23	23	23	23
Christians	7	7	6	4
Ezhavas	0	0	0	0
Muslims	0	0	1	0
Nairs	12	13	14	15
Other Caste Hindus	4	3	2	3
Backward Communities	0	0	0	1

Source: Confidential file No. 1126/1933. Kerala Secretariat

Table–3.2

Total number of persons in the Government service and the community wise distribution

Community	*Population*	*Appointments Held*
Nairs	868411	13384
Non-Malayali Brahmins	54141	2833
Ezhavas	869863	912
Muslims	353274	609
Catholics	809390	923
Marthomite	142486	960
Protestants	208725	658
Jacobites	337872	1353

Source: Confidential file No. 1126/1933. Kerala Secretariat.

Yet it could not be said that the Dalits were not represented in the legislature, a forum for discussion created by the King. As one scholar observes,

> ...the primary purpose, for which SJPS (Sadhu Jana Paripalana Sangham) was established, was to place the *Dalits* in the political realm of Travancore. The effort bore fruit soon. In 1911 P.K. Govinda Pillai was nominated as the representative of the Scheduled castes to the Sri Mulam Praja Sabha – legislature-(sic) and on December 5, Ayyankali himself became a member, a position in which he continued until 1933. Soon many other members of the community found their way to the Sabha. Charakan Soloman (Dalit Christian, 1913), Vallikkara Chothi (Pulaya, 1914), Kandan Kumaran (Paraya, 1915), Pandit Abraham Isaac (Dalit Christian 1916), Karumban Daivathan (Pulaya 1917), M.M. Ratna Swamy (Sambava, 1921) Poikayil Yohannan (Dalit Christian, 1921) and Pampadi John Joseph (Dalit Christian, 1922) were a few other notables who adorned the House and in some areas – for instance in education and land question- attained moderate success as well.[41]

Communal Representaion in Administration

'Communal Representation' was an issue discussed in the Sree Moolam Popular Assembly as far back as 1925. The then Chief Secretary of the Government of Travancore explained the inability of the

Government to give representation to each and every small community. At the same time the Chief Secretary placed before the Government certain broad principles regarding recruitment to public service. Weaker sections of the Travancore population were given representation even in the not so democratic Sri Moolam Popular Assembly (Sree Moolam Praja Sabha).[42]

Again this issue came up before the Assembly in the form of a cut motion on the budget in August 1929. The Government then appointed a Committee consisting of both official and non-official members. In September 1933 this Committee submitted its report that came up for discussion in the legislature in May 1934. Subsequently the Government realized the importance of the matter and hence decided to study all aspects of the issue. The Government thus appointed, Dr. G.D. Knox, a former Judge of the High Court of Travancore, to examine all available material and make a report on the principles to be observed, in laying down Government's policy. Based on the report, Government subsequently issued an Order on 25th June 1935 [43].

The Communities other than Nairs and Brahmins considered themselves isolated from the administration. This feeling made them unite against the Government, which was alleged to be dominated by dictates of the Dewan. The aggrieved communities came together to form a common political platform that came to be known, as Joint Political Conference later became Joint Political Congress.[44] One of the demands of the Joint Political Congress was to have due representation of aggrieved Communities in the posts in Government services. With statistics the aggrieved communities argued for their cause. Thus reservation of posts in the Government service was a significant platform for the political movement in the erstwhile Travancore to come together.

Constitutional Experiments and Communal Representation

Travancore had a debating body called The Travancore Legislative Council established far back in 1888 and the Sree Moolam Popular Assembly in 1904. Even after the demise of Sree Moolam Thirunal, the Constitutional experiments continued and in 1933 a bi-cameral legislature came into existence namely Sri Mulam Assembly, the Lower House and Sri Chitra State Council, the Upper House. There emerged the question of due representation to different communities in this body, which became a vociferous demand. It is interesting to note that the Indian National Congress had only a negligible influence in the State. Since 1935 alleged autocratic rule of the Travancore Dewan (incidentally the Dewan Sir.

C.P. Ramaswamy Iyer, was a Tamil Brahmin lawyer and former member of Indian National Congress) became the core issue that united all Communities. For the time being forgetting the communal differences, politically conscious people came forward to form the Travancore State Congress. Popular figures from among the Nairs also joined the movement which gave it an all-community color. However, it was dominated by the former organization namely JPC. The political scene of the pan Indian politics was charged with the sentiments of anti-colonialism and in Travancore it was anti-Dewan. Since 1937 when Travancore State Congress was formed this struggle against the Government had been going on.

In 1947 the British left Indian subcontinent. But as soon as the colonial rule ended and subsequently democratic institutions too replaced the princely rule, the question of caste and community emerged as the most significant factor in deciding policy matters including the formation of ministries. Each community being organised and capable of acting as effective pressure groups, reservation in principle was something of a political reality to be reckoned with. Even the first ministry in the erstwhile Travancore represented three dominant groups. In the opinion of a contemporary political activist as the first ministry did not represent other minority or backward communities it did not last its full term. Had it been more representative of different Communities in the State, the first ministry would have had a longer life.[45]

Reservation in Administration

Malabar part of Kerala already had reservation in the form of Communal G.O.[46] Reservation in the administration was introduced in Travancore in 1936 and in Cochin in 1937. Dr. G.D. Knox, who was appointed by the Government of Travancore, framed the rules for Public Service Commission. These rules reserved 40 per cent jobs in the intermediate category for the backward and depressed classes. At the lower level the posts were to be filled in proportion to the population of each community. This was the arrangement until the Travancore-Cochin State came into existence in 1952.

Post–Independence Period in Travancore–Cochin

Since the accession of the princely States to the Indian Union the reservation policy of the States has been guided by the policy of the Central Government. In 1951 the Government of the newly formed Travancore-

Cochin State constituted a committee to go into the question of reservation of posts for the Backward Classes and Scheduled Castes and Scheduled Tribes. Having considered the report of the Committee Government passed an Order on 17th September 1952 declaring the classes of citizens who are to be regarded backward for the purpose of Article 16(4) of the Constitution.

They were: 1. Ezhavas 2. Muslims 3. Kammalas 4. Hindu Nadars 5. SIUC 6. Latin Catholics. 7. Other Hindus 8. Other Christians. (that is Scheduled castes and backward community members converted to Christianity). Scheduled Castes and Scheduled Tribes specified as such by the President of India under Articles 341 and 342 of the Constitution. For the purpose of reservation, the government posts were divided into three classes based on the salary they were entitled to. There was no reservation of posts at the first category or what was called Higher Division. The appointments would be solely based on merits. But at the intermediate and lower levels 45 per cent of the seats would be reserved for backward classes of people including Scheduled Castes and Scheduled Tribes who together enjoyed 10 per cent reservation and the rest 35 per cent went to other backward communities. In this distribution of reserved seats Scheduled Tribes had only ½ percent. Among other backward classes of people Ezhavas enjoyed 13 per cent reservation and Muslims came next with 5 per cent whereas SIUC had only 1 per cent. There was also an inbuilt safeguard for the reservation. On 14 June1956 the Travancore-Cochin Government issued orders allowing a lesser standard of qualification to the candidates belonging to Scheduled castes and Scheduled Tribes compared to the required qualification for the general category of candidates.

On 1st of November 1956 the State of Kerala came into existence as a result of the formation of linguistic states and necessary order regarding reservation was issued in 1957.[47] Along with this the exemption given in the qualifying test to the Scheduled castes and Scheduled Tribes was extended by an order dated 27 June 1958.

Constituent Assembly of India

At the same time at the pan-Indian stage Constituent Assembly came into existence in December 1946. But the birth of the Constituent Assembly was not without the birth pangs.[48] Though not a sovereign body in the beginning, the Constituent Assembly assumed sovereignty later.[49] Comparing the Constituent Assembly of India with Philadelphia Convention (1787) and to the States-General of France (1789) a scholar points out that the American and French bodies constituted towards the end of eighteenth century were "articulate only in the general way, while in India a strong political factor had emerged by the time the Constituent Assembly was convened. That was the party system. It is in and through the political parties that the socio economic forces in India had crystallized."[50]

The Constituent Assembly worked for about three years in framing the largest constitution of the world. The ideals, about which the Freedom Movement had spoken, were to be translated into Constitutional provisions. One of them was the protection of the socially backward communities. The rhetoric of establishing an egalitarian society found its vociferous expression in the words of Nehru.[51] According to Anirudh Prasad, "At that time the issue of reservation was pleaded, explained, accommodated and accepted with the national spirit to assimilate sections of society including the intended beneficiaries of the reservation policy into the main stream of national life."

In the present context of affairs in regard to these unfortunate countrymen of ours who have not had these opportunities in the past, special attempts should be made, of course, in the educational and economic field and even in the political field to see that they have a proper place till they find their own legs to stand upon without the external aid. [52]

Constitutional Objective

The debate on the resolution moved by Nehru in the Constituent Assembly regarding 'aims and objects' that later formed the Preamble of the Constitution, clearly reveal the sentiments of different sections of the people. Even though majority of the members wholeheartedly supported the resolution Ambedkar had his own apprehensions. He said:

> ...I must confess that, coming as the Resolution does for Pandit Jawaharlal Nehru who is reported to be a socialist, this Resolution, although non-controversial is to my mind very disappointing. I should have expected him to go much farther than he has done in that part of the Resolution. As a student of History I should have preferred this part of the Resolution not being embodied at all. When one reads that part of the Resolution, it reminds one of the Declarations of the Rights of Man which was pronounced by the French Constituent Assembly. I think I am right in suggesting that after the lapse of practically 450 years, the Declaration of Rights of Man and

> the principles which are embodied in it has become part and parcel of our mental make up. I say they become not only the part and parcel of the mental make-up of modern man in every civilized part of the world, but also in our country which is so orthodox, so archaic in its thought and its social structure hardly any one can be found to deny its validity. To repeat it now as a Resolution does, is to say the least, pure pedantry. ..The Resolution suffers from certain other lacuna. I find that this part of the Resolution, although it enunciates certain rights, does not speak of remedies...[53]

Leaders of the Congress party were very articulate in upholding the rights of the Depressed Classes and offer them adequate safeguards for exercising those rights. But doubts were also expressed regarding the effectiveness of these measures.[54] On the one hand a member from Madras criticized separate electorate as an effective safeguard for Scheduled Caste reservation:

> ...Even if the Harijans are given this percentage of votes and this kind of electorate system, the Harijans are in a position to withstand the attractions that they will have to face at the time of elections. So many parties can set up candidates and they can purchase the Harijans and put up any candidate they desire, and any candidate can come up in the Assembly, and certainly he may not represent the community though he may get percentage of votes that is desired by this system. As long as the Scheduled castes, or the Harijans, or by whatever name they may be called, are economic slaves of other people, there is no meaning demanding either separate electorate or joint electorates or any other kind of electorates with this kind of percentage (cheers) (sic). Personally speaking I am not in favour of any kind of reservation in any place whatsoever.[55]

On the other hand a Harijan Member, Nagappa vociferously argued for reservation for the ancient people who had been exploited by those who came later and dominated them. Quoting the number of Scheduled caste members and their population in various parts of the country, he tried to focus on the point that 'reservation' was essential with regard to Scheduled Castes and Scheduled Tribes.

Unlike Scheduled Caste representatives, the Scheduled Tribes representatives expressed their voice of dissent by asserting that they being the original inhabitants need to be treated with dignity. Jaipal Singh from Bihar said:

> ...If there is any group of Indian people that has been shabbily treated, it is my people. They have been disgracefully treated, neglected for the last 6000years. The history of the Indus valley civilization, a child of which I am, shows quite clearly that it is the new comers- most of you here are intruders as far as I am concerned-it is the new comers who have driven away my people from Indus Valley to the jungle fastness. This Resolution (Resolution Regarding Aims and Objects, moved by Nehru) is not going to teach Adivasis democracy. You cannot teach democracy to the Tribal people; you have to learn democratic ways from them. They are the most democratic people from earth. What my people require is not adequate safeguards as Pundit Jawaharlal Nehru has put it. They require protection from Ministers, that is the position today. We do not ask for any special protection. We want to be treated like every other Indian...the whole history of my people is one of continued exploitaiion and dispossession by the non-aboriginals of India punctuated by rebellions and disorder, and yet I take Pundit Jawaharlal Nehru at his word. I take you all at your word that now we are going to start a new chapter, a new chapter of Independent India where there is equality of opportunity, where no one will be neglected. There is no question of caste in my society. We are all equal. Have we not been casually treated by the Cabinet Mission, more than 30 million people completely ignored? It is a matter of political window dressing that today we find six tribal members in the Constituent Assembly. How is it? What has the Indian National Congress done for our fair representation? Is there going to be any provision in the rules whereby it may be possible to bring in more Adivasis and by Adivasis I mean not only men but women too.

Again he remarked:

> ...I think there has been juggling of words going on to deceive us. I have heard of resolutions and speeches galore assuring Adivasis of a fair deal. If history has to teach me anything at all, I should distrust this Resolution, but I do not.[56]

The discussion went on to the question of representation in the legislature and many expressed hope that the proposed Constitution would guarantee equality and at the same time protect the rights of the Depressed Classes.

But there are also voices of frustration. For instance H.J. Kandekar came with his own experience. He said: "I remind you of the Poona Pact. I place before you the example of my own province. In Central Provinces where we constitute 25 per cent of the population and we are entitled to 28 seats, we are given only 20 seats in pursuance of Poona Pact. Where have our eight seats gone?... Harijans cannot tolerate such injustice. They should be given representation according to their numerical strength."[57]

Provision regarding 'untouchability' in the draft Constitution was generally welcomed. Eventually the fundamental right of 'not being subjected to any discrimination' came to be qualified by the provisions to procure 'protective discrimination'. According to Nesiah, unlike Martin Luther King. Jr, Ambedkar was in a position of authority for as the Chairman of the Drafting Committee of the Constitution and Minister of Law, 'he was vested with both real and symbolic authority at the highest level'. Hence he was able to intervene effectively for the emancipation of Dalits. According to one member the inclusion of Ambedkar in the cabinet showed that there was a change of heart on the part of the caste Hindus.[58] But later events revealed the fact that it was not really a change of heart, but only a political expediency that made the Congress leadership offer Ambedkar such a position. But the relevant question is whether Ambedkar could or did exercise any real power.[59] It would be safer to say that his skill as a lawyer was utilized by the then Congress Government.

Discussion on the Report on Minority Rights

Report on the Minority Rights, based on which the discussion on political safeguard of the depressed classes was carried on. Sardar Vallabhbhai Patel, who presented the Report said in conclusion:

On the whole this report is the result of careful sifting of facts on both sides. One thing I wish to point out. Apart from representation in the Legislature and the reservation of seats according to population, a provision has been made allowing the minorities to contest any general seat also. There was much controversy about it, both in the Advisory Committee and in the Minorities Committee; but it has been passed by a majority. There was also another point which was a matter of controversy and that was on behalf of the Muslim League and a section of the Scheduled Castes. The point was raised that a certain percentage of votes should be considered necessary for a successful candidate. This was a matter of controversy and amongst the Scheduled Castes themselves a very large majority sent me a representation yesterday saying they were against this.

But in the Advisory Committee it was discussed and it was thrown out by a large majority. [60]

Speaking on the Report. P.S. Deshmukh said that the report was highly satisfactory; but at the same time he voiced the fear that the so-called majority might be marginalized. He said:

> I am content that no minority is going to try any more to deprive others of what legitimately belongs to them. For many years past it was the majority that has been tyrannized. Unfortunately, the so-called majority is dumb and deaf and although many of us try always to speak in their name, I have no hesitation in stating that we have completely failed in translating our words into action…I, therefore, urge that at least when the minorities are content to have only their fair share of power in the Cabinets and a reasonable proportion in Government Services, our rulers will pay some more attention to the oppressed and neglected rural population which has even under the sacred name of the Congress has been more undone than assisted …Let this be borne in mind in distributing power and posts among the various Hindu Communities and let the policy of the 'Devil – take - the hindmost' cease, at least from now. [61]

On the other hand members from depressed classes, like S. Nagappa and Jaipal Singh, demanded representation in proportion to their population and representation in cabinets too. With regard to reservation of seats in parliament and state legislatures, originally the Constitution proposed a time limit of ten years. Though this was not agreeable to the Scheduled Castes, they accepted the advice of the political masters. For instance in the words of a member:

> We almost all Harijan members of this House sat together and Honourable Pandit Nehru was kind enough to explain to us that in our own interests this will be the best thing. According to his advice we have come to a decision on this point. After all this is a question that has to be reopened by Parliament. If after ten years our position happens to be the same as it is today, then, it is open to the Parliament either to renew it or abolish it.

But even in the same Constituent Assembly speaking on the minority report, Mahavir Tyagi was highly critical. He observed that giving reservation would not benefit even the so-called Scheduled Castes.

In fact Parliament considered this question from time to time and extended the period of reservation in legislature.[62]

Constitutional Provision for Protective Discrimination

As the Preamble of the Constitution envisions achieving equality is *sine qua non* of a democratic polity, the Constitution of India has incorporated provisions, both *general* and *specific*, for this purpose.' Equality as a right' is envisaged in the Constitution under Article 14, 15 and 16, whereas 'equality as a policy' is implied in those provisions that ensure reservation for the socially and economically backward class of people, which inevitably includes scheduled castes and scheduled tribes. The right to be treated with respect and concern as anyone else is implied in Article 17 and also in The Protection of Civil Rights Act. To a certain extent Abolition of Titles in Article 18 also emphasizes equality among citizens. Articles 25 to 28 confer certain rights relating to freedom of religion on all persons in India. Again Article 46 directs the State to take steps to protect educational and economic interests of the weaker sections and in particular, of Scheduled Castes and Scheduled Tribes.

The Universal Adult Franchise adopted by the Constitution also goes to show that the Indian Union is committed to political equality.

The specific provisions are made for safeguarding the rights and interests of Scheduled Castes and Scheduled Tribes as well as other backward classes. Articles 15 (2), (3) and (4)[63] and Clause (3), (4), (4A) and (4B) of Article 16 that come under Part III titled Fundamental Rights and Articles 330 to 342.

Every fundamental right guaranteed by the Constitution is qualified by certain restrictions. The 'right' is for the individual citizen; but the unbridled right might bring more harm than good. Hence to protect the social interests, restrictions on the rights of the individual do become essential. Whether there is too much of a right or too much of a restriction, is to be decided by the Court. What in legal parlance has come to be called 'balancing of interests' is of course, the responsibility of the Judiciary.[64]

Obviously when this balancing is done the court must look into the question of what is 'societal interests'. It does not mean equal status of the citizens alone, because the 'equal status' to a significant extent, especially in an industrialized society, depends on the 'economic equality'. A meaningful economic equality could be achieved only with the development of economy. The latter is possible only when people are given opportunity to develop their inherent talents. But unfortunately this fact is forgotten and 'protection' has come to mean only providing government jobs, which are comparatively less productive. Hence it is expedient that a new thinking is needed in this area.

During the debates in the Constituent Assembly it was generally agreed that sufficient protection for the backward communities was to be given. The attitude of the Christian leaders was not in favor of reservation *per se.* Anirudh Prasad comments:

> Rajkumari Amrit Kaur, a Christian opposed both reservations of seats and weightage for any community. She had reasons to argue so *first*, in her opinion there was no reason to believe why the interests of any individual or community would not be safe in the hands good persons irrespective of their religion. *Second,* privileges and safeguards really weaken those who demand them. *Third,* reservation or weightage was wrong in principle and when it was given on the ground of religion, it was doubly wrong, for all religions stood for brotherhood of man and none for separatism. In her opinion reservation and special privileges would lead to the fragmentation of the Indian Union. [65]

However the framers of the Constitution did not heed to such warnings. Even leaders like Nehru had apprehension regarding reservation. He observed:

> There is a great danger, whether you deal with an individual or group or community, of giving certain props to that community which give it a false sense of strength which does not belong to it, and when they are removed, suddenly make the community weak. A nation ultimately ought to stand on its own feet. So long as it relies on some external prop, it is not strong. It is weak. So these external props, as I might call them, that is reservation of seats and the rest-may possibly be helpful occasionally in the case of backward groups, but they produce a false sense of strength, and ultimately, therefore, they are not so nearly as important as real educational, cultural and economic advance which gives them inner strength to face any difficulty or any opponent. [66]

Another danger that lurks behind reservation is that it consolidates the scheduled castes and the members of the caste do not want any removal of caste identity. The ramifications of reservation goes further that most of the educated young persons, who cannot find government employment because of the fact that they belong to the 'upper caste', try to emigrate and thereby they cause 'brain drain' in the country. Having no vision to foresee such consequences the Constituent Assembly eventually made a compromise mainly because of political compulsions.[67]

Represention in Legislatures

Regarding representation in Legislature, a joint electorate was accepted. Thus separate electorate and weightage were rejected. Reservation of seats for minorities based on religion was also not accepted by the Constituent Assembly. But reservation of seats for SCs and STs in Lok Sabha and State legislatures for ten years was agreed upon. But the period has been extended from time to time. Presidents and Governors were to nominate members to represent unrepresented Anglo-Indian community in Lok Sabha and State legislatures. In State or Central cabinets no statutory reservation for minorities was provided, but the President at the Center and the Governors at the states could appoint practicable numbers of ministers from minority communities. This was aimed at the smooth functioning of democracy. But the political realities point out to the fact that the Chief Minister exercises the power to choose his or her ministers. He or she might choose ministers as political expediency warrants.[68]

Representaion in Services

The Constituent Assembly did not envisage any reservation for minorities as such. Backward classes were to be given adequate representation in the services under the state. The claims of people belonging to Scheduled Castes and Scheduled Tribes were to be taken into consideration. Thus there arose mainly three categories of people who deserved the benefits of Protective Discrimination: the backward class, the Scheduled castes and the Scheduled Tribes. Speaking in the Constituent Assembly, Ambedkar elaborated on this aspect. He was not in favor of giving undue reservation for it would have an unfavourable impact on the whole concept of reservation itself.[69] Again the reservation policy should be carried out *in keeping with efficiency of administration* (emphasis added) Special provision for Anglo-Indian Community to posts in Railway, custom, postal and telegraph services of the Union for the continuance of reservation was under the stipulation for periodical reduction and the reservation was only for a maximum period of ten years from the commencement of the Constitution.

The rights of the depressed classes of people were to be protected and for this purpose an administrative mechanism was designed. Provisions were made for appointing special officers for Scheduled Castes and Scheduled Tribes and a Statutory Commission for socially and educationally backward classes. Scheduled Castes and Scheduled Tribes could be comparatively easily identified. But the issue of identifying 'socially and economically backward' classes is more complicated. Considering the 'upper castes' as a whole, as economically forward cannot be justified. Many influential caste groups demand that they should be included in the 'backward' list so that they could continue to enjoy the benefits of 'protective discrimination'.

According to Sivaramaya[70] Indian policy is based on four principles: compensation (for past injuries), protection (of the weak under article 46 of the Constitution), proportional equality and social justice (incorporation distributive justice and social welfare). Regarding the first principle, whether it is reasonable that the present generation should shoulder the burden of the sins of the past generation when they had their own notions of social morality and custom-based laws. The second principle of 'protection' for the weaker section can be justified, but there must be valid, reasonable and legal parameters for assessing 'weaknesses' of individual or class. The third principle of proportional equality too can only be transitory. Social justice, the fourth principle, is couched in such a vague phrase that it could be interpreted according to the predilections of the person who interprets.

Reservation in Kerala State

The history before the formation of Kerala would reveal the fact the fight for 'rights' was a combined effort of the communities other than the dominant ones. And the political movement that was to translate this aspiration too reflected it in the form of Joint Political Congress. Hence to treat the question of evolution of reservation in the case of Scheduled Castes and Tribes on the one hand and Other backward Classes on the other in separate streams would be repetitive. Moreover the issue of reservation with regard to Scheduled Castes and Scheduled Tribes had not become controversial. There were only a few questions as to which communities were to be included in the Scheduled Castes Lists and whether a particular Community was to be included in the list of Scheduled Tribes. For instance as one scholar puts:

Looking at the progress achieved in implementing reservation, it could be safely concluded that the Constitutional mandate in this regard is scrupulously respected in political representation both at the national and state level. But with regard to representation of Scheduled Castes in administration and admission in educational institutions, trends are often contradictory between the all India pattern and that of Kerala. While at the central level SCs are grossly under represented in both fields, Kerala pattern shows satisfactory results in many respects though some gray areas are still noticed. [71]

On 1st of November 1956 the State of Kerala came into existence as a result of the formation of linguistic states and necessary order regarding reservation was issued in1957.[72] Along with this the exemption given in the qualifying test to the Scheduled castes and Scheduled Tribes was extended by an order dated 27 June 1958

Kumara Pillai Commission

In 1965 the Kerala Government had been reserving seats in Medical, Engineering (including Polytechnics) Agricultural, Veterinary colleges and in Arts and Science Colleges for students of Backward Class, Scheduled Castes and Scheduled Tribes. Against the reservation Orders of the Government writ petitions were filed in the High Court and the Court allowed the petitions. Though an appeal was filed, the Division Bench too allowed the petitions with a few exceptions. However the Court directed the Government to set in motion a fact -finding enquiry so that appropriate Orders could be issued on an objective basis. The Court also suggested a probable time limit, 'before the beginning of the academic year 1965-1966'. In pursuance of this direction of the Court, the Government appointed a Commission under the Chairmanship of Kumara Pillai and with three members other than the Chairman and a member-Secretary. The Commission came into existence on 8th July 1964.

The terms of reference were: 1. to enquire into the social and educational conditions of the people and report on what sections of people- other than Scheduled castes and Scheduled Tribes- should be treated as backward for reserving seats in the higher educational institutions and 2. to recommend the quantum of such reservation and the period during which it may remain in force.

The Commission submitted its report on the last day of 965. Based on its recommendations the Government issued Orders in May 1966. A salient feature of the report was that the very first recommendation suggested economic criterion along with caste or community for determining backwardness. The report said, "Only citizens who are members of families, which have an aggregate income (i.e. income of all members of the family from all sources taken together) of less than Rs. 4200 per annum and which belong to the caste and communities mentioned in Appendix VIII constitute socially and educationally backward classes for the purpose of Art. 15 (4) ..." In issuing Order based on the recommendation, the Government changed the amount of annual income of the family to Rs. 6000. Reservation based on regions is also recommended. The fourth recommendation said, "In the Medical, Engineering (including Polytechnics) Agriculture and Veterinary Colleges 20% of the general seats may be allocated between the Malabar area and the T.C. area in the ratio of 5:8 on the basis of merit."

Recommendation 6 is significant for it proposed to reserve 25% of the seats in the Medical, Engineering (including Polytechnics) Agriculture and Veterinary Colleges (seats remaining after the allotment for the managements of Private institutions and for special cases such as for nominees of the Government of India etc.) for the socially and educationally backward classes and the seats so reserved may be as follows:

Ezhavas	9%
Muslims	8%
Latin Catholics other than Anglo-Indians	2%
Other backward Christians including SIUC and convert to Christianity from Scheduled castes	1%
Other backward Hindus	5%
Total	25%

The Government accepted the above recommendation. It also accepted the recommendation that unfilled reserve seats must go to open merit pool. The reservation was recommended for ten years beginning from the academic year 1966-67. The report also proposed financial help to the students of backward classes.

Nettur Commission

For deciding the question of backwardness and also the quantum of reservation to be made for the backward classes the Government of Kerala constituted a Commission in 1967 subsequent to the decision of the Kerala High Court in *V.Hariharan Pillai v. State of Kerala.* In the beginning it was a committee of which Nettur P. Damodaran was the chairman. In February 1968 the committee was redesigned as a Commission. The terms of reference to the Commission are:

(a) What are the main factors, which lead to backwardness of citizens?

(b) What should be the basis for classifying sections of people into backward and non-backward?

(c) In the light of answers to (a) and (b) above, what classes of citizens in the State should be treated as backward for the purpose of Article

16(4) of the constitution and which of such classes are not adequately represented in the services under the State and,

(d) What should be the quantum of reservation and the period for which it is to remain in force so far as the reservation of 40% to "other backward classes" is concerned?

At that time 50% of the appointments in the public services were set apart for open competition on the basis of merit. In the rest 50%, 10% was set apart for Scheduled Castes and Scheduled Tribes and 40% for other 'backward classes'. The Government of Kerala asked the Commission not to include the matter of SCs and STs and the terms of reference was to be confined to "40% to other backward Classes". This may be because of the fact that there was, as it has already been pointed out, not much dispute regarding reservation to the Scheduled Castes and Scheduled Tribes. More controversy one may find with regard to the determination of the groups that constitute Other Backward Classes (OBCs).[73]

The factors leading to backwardness, the basis of classifying people into 'backward' and 'non-backward' and the Classes of people who are not adequately represented are one of the items included in the terms of reference. Thus the Commission went into the question of 'backwardness' and made certain concrete and reasonable recommendations.

In the course of determining the factors responsible for backwardness, the Commission observes that conditions vary from State to State. After analyzing various case laws and the speech made by Dr.Ambedkar in the constituent assembly, the report enumerates the factors that must be present to determine 'backwardness'. According to the findings of the Commission, test of residence or habitation, test of occupation, test of caste, test of education, economic test, test of appropriation of appointments and test of social backwardness due to historical reasons. In conclusion the Commission states:

> [Thus], the Supreme Court and High Court of Kerala have both used the term 'social backwardness' as meaning 'economic backwardness' and 'social backwardness due to historical reasons of caste, occupational stigma etc'. Therefore it is clear that the expression 'socially and educationally backward' used by the Supreme Court and the use of the term 'socially, educationally and economically' used by (sic) by the High Court of Kerala is one and the same. This construction recognizes the factual existence of classes of citizens who are backward 'educationally', 'economically' and 'socially due

to historical reasons'. We have already adopted *the economic test, as one of the tests for backwardness*. It is therefore not necessary to include 'poverty' again as a constituent social backwardness due to historical reasons. Thus, the all round retardation due to the practice of caste till the recent past, backwardness due to the vestiges of caste in the present, backwardness due to the occupational stigma, purdah, aversion of Muslims till recently, to education through the medium of English, other social taboos resulting in social backwardness will be the constituents of 'social backwardness due to historical reasons'. We would therefore suggest *that social backwardness due to historical reasons may (sic) be one of the four tests*. (Emphasis supplied) [74]

Thus the Commission followed an economic criterion in determining backwardness of different classes of people. The above analysis of the various factors that go to cause backwardness might be sound when the contemporary socio-economic and political conditions were considered. But almost all these conditions are transient. Hence it is obvious that the validity of the observations of the Commission needs to be reexamined from time to time. However the Commission's report did not evoke any sharp reaction. Based on the report the government also issued necessary orders. Another significant aspect is the Commission's adoption of economic criterion for assessing backwardness. Later the Supreme Court in *Indra Sawhney* has recognized this to a certain extent.

Commission is quite sound when it says:

> ... I have to emphasize one aspect, it may be true to say that the Ezhavas, Muslims and Latin Catholics belong to communities that are socially and educationally backward. However the possibility of there being a section large or small in these communities who are advanced and who are not backward, socially, economically or educationally cannot be ruled out. If there is such a section no reservation can be made in favour of the members of that section.

Echo of *Indra Sawhney* Decision in Kerala

In the post- *Indra Sawhney* period the Central Government appointed Justice R N Prasad Committee in accordance with the direction given by the Supreme Court to fix the criteria for exclusion of creamy layer from the Backward Classes. In the Judgment the Supreme Court had made it clear that the State Governments were also to take steps for exclusion of creamy layer among the backward classes from the benefits of reservation under Article 16(4) for the appointments in the state government services. Some States acted promptly and fixed the criteria for exclusion.

The State of Kerala did not do anything in the matter for a few years. This led to the initiation of contempt of court proceedings against the Chief Secretary to the Government of Kerala and the then Chief Secretary was directed to appear before the Supreme Court. There after the State Government passed the *Kerala State Backward Classes (Reservation of Appointments of posts in the services under the state) Act* 16 of 1995 declaring that having regard to known facts in existence in the State of Kerala there are no socially advanced sections in any Backward Classes who have acquired the capacity to compete with forward classes, that the Backward Classes in the state were not adequately represented in the services under the state and they would continue to be entitled for reservation under clause (4) of Article 16 of the Constitution.

Challenge to Kerala Act 16 of 1995

The Nair Service Society and others challenged the validity of the Kerala Act 16 of 1995 before the Supreme Court. The Court requested the Chief Justice, High Court of Kerala to appoint a retired Judge of the High Court to be Chairman of a High level Committee to collect necessary information regarding the creamy layer and forward its report to the Supreme Court within three months. Subsequently Justice K.J. Joseph Committee came into existence. It submitted its report on 27-5-1997 to the Supreme Court. The Court jointly heard the contempt matter and writ petitions challenging the validity of the Kerala Act. The Supreme Court declared that the provisions of sections 3, 4 and 6 of the Kerala Act are unconstitutional. The SC also held that the guidelines and criteria fixed by Justice Joseph Committee are reasonable so far as the state of Kerala is concerned. Consequently the SC accepted Justice Joseph Committee report in toto subject to the addition of the communities and sub castes as pointed out in the affidavit of the State.

The Supreme Court further directed the State of Kerala to find out the 'creamy layer' and exclude it from the purview of 'backward class'. For that purpose suitable provision should be made. Until that time the recommendations of Justice K.J. Joseph Committee should apply. Finally the Court said:

> Any fresh alternative provision that may be made by the State of Kerala, it is needless to say will be subject to such further decision of this Court in case the validity thereof is questioned.
>
> In the event of alternative provisions being made by the State of Kerala is either by executive order or by legislative measures or by way of Rules, no Court shall entertain any challenge thereto, and all proceedings in relation thereto shall have to be taken out only in this Court.

Regarding the stand taken by the State of Kerala, Supreme Court was highly critical. The callous indifference shown by the State Government in implementing the decision of the apex Court, in fact, amounts to contempt of Court. Yet the honourable Supreme Court was gracious enough to adopt a lenient view. In this context it would only be appropriate to quote the words of the Court:

> On account of the inaction of the State of Kerala in spite of inaction of extensions of time in implementing Indra Sawhney ...in appointing commission to identify the creamy layer, this Court felt "vexed" and issued contempt notice on 20-3-1995. Pursuant to that notice on 10-07-1995 the State of Kerala filed an affidavit that it had already passed the Kerala Act 11 of 1993 on 17-4-1993 appointing a Commission, which could go into this issue but that the said Commission stated that it had no jurisdiction to go into the question of 'creamy layer' as per the provisions in that Act of 1993. The affidavit then stated that the matter was referred again to the Commission on 13-10-1993; a meeting took place on 10-5-1994 that the Commission again refused to identify the creamy layer, that a Bill was then contemplated to amend Kerala Act 11 of 1993 to confer powers on the said Commission to go into this issue as well, that in the meantime, the State constituted the Justice Khalid Committee on 8-7-1995.
>
> In our opinion, these events were set out in the above affidavit filed by the Chief Secretary only to ward off any penal action for contempt of this Court. The above explanation was naturally found to be wholly unsatisfactory and this Court held, in its order dated 10-7-1995 that the State of Kerala represented by its Chief Secretary had acted in "willful disobedience" of the orders of this Court and that it had committed contempt of Court. This Court granted time till

> 11-9-1995 to the State of Kerala to purge itself of the contempt. It appears that there was then a cabinet meeting on 13-7-1995 and thereafter it was decided on 14-7-1995 that a Standing Committee should go into the question but that instead, it was suddenly decided on 27-7-1995 that the "existing system be continued". Then Act 16 of 1995 was passed on 31-8-1995 to give effect to that decision. The Act received the assent of the Governor on 2-9-1995 and became effective retrospectively from 2-10-1992, thus allowing the existing reservation to continue in full force. In effect no creamy layer was identified. As per sub-clause (a) of S.3 of the Act it was declared that in view of 'known facts' the legislature was of the view that "no section of any backward Class in the State of Kerala who had acquired capacity 'to compete with' the forward classes." As per Cl. (b) it was stated that Backward Classes were not still adequately represented in the public services of the State. Section 4, therefore, continued the 1958 scenario of Backward Classes without excluding the creamy layer and S. 6 spoke of retrospective validation.[75]

The observations of the Court truly reflected the lack of political will on the part of the Kerala Government to identify the creamy layer among the backward Classes for these Classes command a considerable chunk of ballots. Thus the fear of losing 'vote bank' made the ruling conglomerate find excuses if not adopt stoic silence. The delaying tactics adopted by the Legislature as well as Executive pushed the Executive to the dangerous brink of contempt of Court.[76] Subsequently a Commission was appointed to into the question of 'creamy layer' first and then that of 'adequacy of representation of backward Classes in the services of the government.

Narendran Commission (S)

This Commission that was appointed on 13th January 2000 might be called the First Narendran Commission, because there was another Narendran Commission that was appointed for studying and reporting on the adequacy or otherwise of representation of the Backward classes in the services of the State Government, Public Sector Undertakings, Autonomous Bodies and Institutions under the State Government including Universities, on 11th February 2000.

The terms of reference of the First Narendran Commission were:

(a) What should be the criteria to be adopted to exclude those who belong to the creamy layer among other Backward Classes from the benefits of reservation in accordance with the observations in the judgment of the Supreme Court or what criteria should be adopted to provide maximum protection to those belonging to such communities in accordance with above mentioned judgment.

(b) Whether there is any class, which may be excluded from the creamy layer on the basis of hereditary occupation or otherwise.

(c) (i) Whether there should be different criteria regarding income/ property for different categories coming within the creamy layer.

(ii) If so, what should be the ceiling for such income/property?

(iii) While calculating the income whether it is necessary to exclude income from any particular source or sources. While making the recommendations, the Commission will take into account the existing socio-economic conditions and the special features of the Other Backward Classes in the State

(iv) The Commission should submit its report to Government within one month.

(v) The Office of the Commission will be at Thiruvananthapuram and its headquarters Ernakulam.

It seems that the Commission was satisfied with the response it received from the public. In the words the response was 'tremendous'. The Commission also said, "A perusal of the various representations makes it clear that not only the Backward Classes but some of the members of the forward classes also have made their valuable suggestions". In the opinion of the Commission, therefore, the question of reservation is of 'considerable importance to all sections of the people in the State'.[77]

But at the same time the bureaucrats did not view this question of considerable importance to the public with the much seriousness that it deserved. The Commission wrote to the Chief Secretary to the Government of Kerala to make available a community-wise list of officers in the Government Secretariat. A request was also made to furnish similar lists of officers in the offices of the Heads of Departments from the rank of section officers to the Heads of Departments. In the words of the Commission, "For reasons not known the Chief Secretary to Government is also keeping quiet."[78]

In paragraph 10.2 the Commission refers to caste system as a prelude to assessing social backwardness. According to the Commission 'nobility' attached to an occupation decided the caste in the past and it continues to a certain extent. But in the past it was the 'Brahminical' doctrines that decided the 'nobility' of a vocation and made it more or less 'hereditary'. The impact of Westernization unfortunately did not permeate the lower rungs of different societies in India. Since the adoption of Indian Constitution, 'caste' stands abolished legally and officially. Yet in one way or other it has to be reckoned with when the policy of reservation is discussed. There is tendency to get oneself into a lower caste group so that the benefit of reservation could be obtained. Thus even the Court is invited to discuss caste.

In *Kerala Pattikajathi Samrakshana Samithy v. State of Kerala*[79], this conflict of interests could be clearly seen.

The anomaly in emphasizing the phrase 'socially and educationally backward' and the importance of the 'economic' factor are being revealed when the Commission observes,

> It goes without saying that in any recommendation the Commission is to make the Commission cannot ignore their existing social and economic conditions and the special features of the Other Backward Classes in the State. The 20th Century is over and we are already on the threshold of the 21st century. In the 20th century especially in the last half of that century revolutionary changes were witnessed by the whole society in the State. The social advancement made was tremendous and it cannot be said that the Backward Classes in the State were not also benefited by this. The economic conditions also improved and more and more people who were under the poverty line could be brought above the line. All these developments in a way very much improved the living conditions of the Backward Classes who form the majority of the population in the State. Though the vast majority of the Backward Classes are yet to attain the capacity to compete with the forward Classes in all walks of life, the number among them who are in a position to compete the forward classes has increased to some extent. [80]

In paragraph 11.2 the Report says "that restrictions imposed on the Backward Classes should not be such that they are denied the legitimate rights that they have to get into the Government service and partake in the power sharing that is essential to make democracy really meaningful" It seems that the Commission is under the impression that the mere acquiring of government office is the means to achieve meaningful democracy. In which case all, if not, the majority of the citizens will have to occupy a position in the governmental establishment. Democracy and its effective functioning depend on the legislature elected by the enlightened electorate and an executive (of which the civil service is a part) dedicated to 'public service' and an independent Judiciary. The Commission itself has had the bitter experience of lack of cooperation from the part of the bureaucracy when it did not care to respond to Commission's requests.

Moreover the Second Narendran Commission has discovered that the Backward Classes have acquired such a share in the Governmental service, which has gone beyond the quota if not reached the quota level.

With regard to determining the lower limit to the income of the parents whose wards are to be excluded from the protective umbrella, the Commission says, "Considering all aspects of the matter the Commission is of the view that the gross annual income has to be fixed at Rs.300, 000/- ..."[81] It would have been better if the Commission had linked the determining of the income limit to money value, so that there could be automatic alterations in accordance with the changing value of rupee.

Having argued to the effect that the traditional occupation of the member of the scheduled caste is a factor determining backwardness and hence those who follow traditional occupations have to be excluded from the creamy layer test. Here also it is submitted that the Commission has not appreciated the trends available in the present day society in the state. There are persons belonging to the Brahmin community who work in companies manufacturing and selling shoes and chappals. According to the ancient customs in India anything connected with making footwear's was considered very low in social ranking. The poor Brahmin who works in this area does not get any benefit of protective discrimination. On the other hand a carpenter who is engaged in the traditional occupation in, say, an Arab country earns a lot of money and in fact does neither need nor deserve any benefit of protective discrimination. Therefore it is felt that the sweeping statement made by the Commission that 'these persons (who are engaged in the hereditary occupations) of all backward classes from the Creamy layer' is not justifiable, if not unrealistic.

Again, the Commission's helplessness is revealed in Para 14. In some States like Karnataka, there is a division within the backward classes as Backward, more Backward and the most Backward. As there is no such division in Kerala, the most backward classes do not benefit when the vacancies are fewer in number. Conceding this argument, the Commission goes on to say.

But the division of these communities on the basis can be made only on the basis of their present representation in the services. This can be ascertained only on the basis of reliable data. A division not on the basis of data may prove to be harmful to some of these communities. The abolition of quota system and make all Backward Classes to compete for the 40 per cent seats put in a pool may also prove to be equally counter productive. It goes without saying that the more advanced sections among the Backward Classes will have a monopoly as the more backward among the Backward Classes will not be in a position to compete with them. *But the Commission is not making any recommendation on this point for want of reliable data.* (Emphasis added).

In Para 15.1 the Commission comes to the conclusion that "A considerable number of posts and that too in the higher grade are still kept out of the purview of reservation. Not only that a good number of Corporations and Public Undertakings are yet to be brought under reservation." Again the Commission is unable to offer any specific number or percentage of posts to be reserved. Moreover the Commission has not taken into consideration the change in the policy of the Union Government since it signed the World Trade Organization Agreement. Hence international norms both on efficiency of the personnel and appointments on the basis of 'equal opportunity' have to be considered. It is a sad fact that the Commission is silent on this aspect.

The Commission has dealt with the inordinate delay caused by bureaucratic indifference it recommends: "At any rate the certificate should be issued within ten days of the receipt of the application and if in case the certificate is to be refused the refusal also should be communicated to the applicant within the same time limit." Thus the present position with regard to reservation for the Other Backward Communities (OBC) is that those parents whose income exceeds Rs. 300, 000/- per annum cannot claim the reservation rights for their wards.[82]

However, the vote-bank politics has been to the fore in the move of the Government to include religious minorities among the 'backward'. Susan Bayly comments: "In October 1994 the Kerala State Government decided to include the state's entire Muslim population in the OBC category, thus making them eligible for employment reservations and other benefits. To do this the Government adopted the simple device of classifying all Kerala Muslims as *Mappilas,* that is, as members of the one named non-Hindu 'community' that had originally been placed on OBC register.'[83]

The *Report* of the second Narendran Commission came to light on 9th November 2001. This *Report* presents a thorough study of the communal representation in the administrative hierarchy. The Commission held fifty-one sittings and three sittings were held in the cities of Kozhicode, Kochi and Thiruvananthapuram. The inordinate delay in collecting data is indeed unjustifiable these days when technology in communication has made long strides. This indeed is a reflection on the efficiency of the administration. The *Report* says:

> On the expiry of the last date specified by the Commission (31-12-2000) for receipt of data from Government and Public Service Commission, the matter was reviewed by the Commission. The data received from Secretaries till then covered only about twenty percent of the employees. Some of the Secretaries to Government had written to the Commission seeking extension of time for collecting the data. Data from Public Service Commission also got delayed. It was therefore obvious that, in spite of the best efforts of the Commission and cooperation from the Secretaries to Government, work would not be completed by 10-2-2001 when the first six months extension would run out. Hence ...the Commission sought extension for six more months...[84]

On the other hand there was tremendous response from the public. Many organizations and individuals of upper classes too approached the Commission to articulate their studied opinion. There was an anonymous representation that described the claim of the Backward Classes as farce.[85] Statistical inaccuracies, ignorance 'consolidated fund' and 'budget' and demanding representation for hitherto unknown backward communities are some of the interesting aspects of the public response elicited by the Commission. After conducting an exhaustive survey by way of collecting data and processing them, the Commission states:

> The total number of the employees in all the Government Departments and the Judiciary together is 3,25,554. Out of this 1,57,008 belonged to all the Backward Classes together. The reservation quota for all the Backward Classes together is 40 per cent. The actual position is that all the backward Classes taken together have got 48.23 percent of the total number of posts. The forward Classes have got 38.73 percent.[86]

Yet the Commission arrived at the conclusion that

> There should be different types of governmental and social action to help backward classes to get rid of their social and

educational backwardness. One such-perhaps the most important - action is practicing a system of reservation to ensure a minimum level of representation for backward classes in public services. The level should certainly not be too low compared to their population ratio. Simultaneously, backward classes should be encouraged to increase their share in open merit competition also. This is exactly the system we are following. [87]

But the Commission is of the opinion that in the case of certain communities the position of their representation in the service is satisfactory. Therefore the Commission recommends 'intelligent and imaginative corrective action'. But unfortunately the Commission does not suggest any corrective action. And a government managed by groups of political parties engaged in their unscrupulous race for power the nature of corrective action would be an endeavour to appease the predominant caste-group, if not the vote-bank.

In the final analysis as it has been pointed out at the outset of the discussion Kerala cannot be said to be a problem State with regard to the implementation of the reservation policy. Reservation for the socially and educationally backward communities has been accepted principle since the thirties of twentieth century in the Travancore area and the Malabar area, which was part of the erstwhile Madras Province, also had rules regarding Communal representation.[88] Thus it can be safely remarked that the public in Kerala has internalized the policy of reservation based to a certain extent on the principle of equity. That was why there was little political reaction subsequent to 'declaration of reservation policy' based on *Mandal Commission Report* by the Central Government. It is left to the future political decision makers to formulate policies when the impact of liberalized economy in the form of privatization, is felt.[89]

Regarding the reservation of seats in the state legislature for Scheduled Castes and Scheduled Tribes, there is no controversy at all. Subsequent to the Constitution (Seventy-third and seventy fourth Amendment) Act 1993 the Kerala Government enacted *The Kerala Panchayat Raj Act.1994.*[90]

Recent Trends–Reservation of Seats in Local Self Government Institutions (LSGIs)

Two recent trends are available in this regard: one is, new states, which predominantly Tribal have been formed. This could offer sufficient political power for the Tribals to govern themselves and come up in life. But how far could they play an effective role in the pan-Indian politics is a pertinent question that might be answered only in future. Moreover could it help bringing them to the mainstream of Indian life?

Secondly the LSGIs regime envisaged in the Constitution (Seventy-Third and Seventy – Fourth Amendment) Act 1992 has given rise to legislation regarding Panchayat Raj at the village level and Nagar Palika at the urban level. This is significant in the sense that one, the object of participatory democracy demands that people at the village level should understand the intricacies of democratic mechanism. Here too the Scheduled Castes and Scheduled Tribes are given the benefit of reservation. For instance Constitution (seventy-third Amendment) Act 1992 adds to the Constitution anew Part (Part IX) titled "Panchayats'. In this Part, Article 243D provides that there shall be reservation of seats for the Scheduled Castes and Scheduled Tribes in every Panchayat and 'number of seats so reserved shall bear as nearly as may be, the same population of Scheduled Castes in that Panchayat area or of the Scheduled Tribes in that Panchayat area to the total population of that area and such seats may be allotted by rotation to different constituencies in a Panchayat. The same Article in clause 2,3 and 4 provides for the reservation of seats for Scheduled castes and Scheduled Tribes women as well as for other women. Again the State legislature is empowered to make provisions for women Chairpersons in Panchayat. But these reservations are interlinked with Article 334 that specifies the time limit for the reservation of seats in the legislative bodies.[91]

References

1. Dr. P. Jagadeesan, *Marriage and Social Legislations in Tamil Nadu.*(Madras 1990) p. 31 Srinivasa Pillay and his like- minded colleagues founded the Hindu Progressive Improvement Society in November 1852. The major aims of the Society were the promotion of widow remarriage, the encouragement of female education and the uplifting of the depressed classes"
2. Quoted in Marc Galanter, *Competing Equalities* (Oxford 1984) p.21
3. Department of Social Welfare, Government of India, *Report of the Committee on Untouchability, Economic and Educational Development of the Scheduled Castes and Connected Documents* (1969). p. 3.
4. *Ibid* at p. 22..
5. V.A.Pai Panandiker, ed., *The Politics of backwardness: Reservation Policy in India* (New Delhi1997) p. 94.

6. See. *Sixteenth Report*, Committee on the Welfare of Scheduled castes and Scheduled Tribes (2001-2002) submitted to Lok Sabha on 27th August 2001.
7. Quoted in S.S. Jaswal, *Reservation Policy and the Law*. (New Delhi 2000) p. 34.
8. Sir Harcourt Butler, *India Insistent* (1931) p.73 the policy announcement was made by the then Secretary of State for India Edwin Montagu.
9. B. R. Ambedkhar *Writings and Speeches* Vol. pp 252-3.
10. A.N.Sattanathan, 'Reaction to Brahminism: DMK's Heritage' *The Indian Express (Madurai Edition)* 24 August 1967.
11. P.Venugopal, 'Implementation of Social Justice through Reservation' website accessed on 29th March 2003.
12. See Chapter IV.
13. S.S.Jaswal, *op.cit* pp 34-35.
14. P.Jagadeesan, *op.cit* pp. 97-98.
15. Marc Galanter, *Competing Equalities.*(1984) p. 30.
16. Quoted in J.R. Kamble, *Rise and Awakening of Depressed Class in India* (New Delhi 1979) p.86.
17. Lord Irwin, Viceroy of India, hoped that by releasing Gandhi, he would be able to reach an agreement with him. In March 5, 1931 Gandhi-Irwin Pact was announced and 'civil disobedience' was discontinued. Again as per the agreement Gandhi took part in the Second Round Table Conference held from September to December 1931. But the conference failed to solve the problem of 'communal representation' in the legislative bodies.
18. Thomas Mathew, *Caste And Class Dynamics - Radical Ambedkarite Praxis.*(New Delhi 1992) p 12.
19. Galentar *op.cit.* p. 31.
20. Gwyer and Appadorai, *Speeches and Documents on Indian Constitution* (London 1921) Vol. I p.4.
21. A modern Indian historian alleges that the Communal Award of Prime Minister Mac Donald was aimed at 'divide and rule' Bipin Chandra, *India's Struggle For Independence.* (New Delhi 1999) p. 290.
22. Stanley Wolpert, *A New History of India* (OUP 1982) pp. 319-320.
23. *Ibid.*
24. Six days after the pact between Ambedkar and Gandhi, the latter started *Harijan Sevak Samaj.* (Servants of the Untouchables' Society) and its weekly journal *Harijan.*
25. See. The Government of India Act 1935. It is to be noted that Gandhi gave the name *Harijan* (people of God) to the depressed classes. But this name they resented for they consider the term patronizing and condescending. In 1990 the Government of India prohibited the use of this word to denote the depressed classes. In fact the term *Harijan* acquired a pejorative meaning among the upper caste people and thus caused a psychological untouchability

26. *Gazette of India* Part I July 7, 1934.
27. In fact it was the socio-political undercurrents, which were responsible for this progressive step. The native kings of Travancore always encouraged education and this led to political awareness of the backward classes. They joined with the religious minorities of the State formed Joint Political Congress. Some powerful backward Classes even threatened that they would embrace some other religion like Christianity or Buddhism. The then Dewan of the Travancore in a tactical move to throw open all Hindu Temples under the Government management to Hindus of all castes. See Robin Jeffrey, *The Decline of Nayar Dominance* (London 1976) pp. 259-260.
28. This Communal G.O. as it was referred to, was the impugned law in *State of Madras* v. *Champakam Dorairajan.*
29. The regulation II of 1603 of Malayalam Era establishing The Travancore legislative Council was framed on the lines of the Indian Councils Act as it stood then. Ramakrishnan Nair, *Constitutional Experiments in Kerala.*(1964) p.3.
30. According to the Government the object was 'solely to give people an opportunity of bringing to the notice of Government, their requirements, wishes or grievances on the one hand, and on the other to make the policy and measures of Government better known to the people so that all possible grounds of misconception in regard to the action of Government may be removed.' *Ibid* at p.7.
31. SNDP, Pulaya Mahajana Subha, etc.
32. See for instance *T.M.Varghese and the Struggle For responsible Government* Ph.D. Thesis.
33. V.P.Menon, *The Story of The Integration Of the Indian States(1961)* P.262.
34. T.K.Ravindran, *Asan and Social Revolution in Kerala* (1972) pp 6-7.
35. Robin Jeffery *op.cit.*, p. 13.
36. Ezhava Memorial, Bangalore 13th May 1895. as quoted in T.K.Ravindran, *Asan and Social Revolution in Kerala* (1972) p 4. An upper caste man like G.P. Pillai also expressed similar sentiments supporting Tiya cause.
37. T.K.Ravindran, *Asan and Social revolution in Kerala* (Trivandrum. 1972) pp., 18-19.
38. *Ibid.* p. 29.
39. Sree Naryana Dharma Paripalana Yogam, Ezhava Mahajana Conference, Ezhava Political League, Latin Christian Mahajana Subha and Christian Political Conference were some such organizations.
40. K. Chandra Mohan, *T.M.Varghese and the Struggle For responsible Government* Ph.D. Thesis.
41. J. Prabhash, *Affirmative Action and Social Change* (2001) p. 51.
42. *Ibid.*, p. 84.
43. *Report of The Backward Classes Commission, Kerala* 1970 Vol. II p. 15.

44. K. Chandra Mohan, *T.M.Varghese and the Struggle For responsible Government* Ph.D. Thesis. (Kerala University) Chapter IV 'United Front of Aggrieved Communities'.
45. M.M.Varkey *Ormakaliloode* (Kottayam 1974) p. 242.
46. See Chapter IV.
47. See *Justice K.K.Narendran Commission Report* 2000. In the erstwhile State of Travancore and Cochin Backward Classes were entitled for reservation of posts in Government services from 1936 onwards. In the erstwhile Malabar District, which now forms part of Kerala also, Backward Classes were having reservation for appointments in Government Services from 1921 onwards. In some other south Indian states also backward classes were given the benefit of reservation for appointments to Government services. But the position was different as far as Central Government Services were concerned. In the states of North India also Backward Classes were not having the benefit of reservation for appointments in Government services.
48. S.K. Chaube, *Constituent Assembly of India.* (Calcutta 1986) Chapter III. Birth of the Constituent Assembly. pp 30-55.
49. Ibid. pp 86-96 Ivor Jennings went to the extent of saying that "The greatest difficulty, was, however, in finding out where the 'sovereignty' of the Constituent Assembly came from." Ivor Jennings, *The Constitutional Problems in Pakistan* (London 1951) p. 24.
50. *Ibid.*, p. 101.
51. The sixth item in the Objective Resolution moved by Nehru in the Constituent Assembly read: "Wherein adequate safeguards shall be provided for minorities, backward and tribal areas, and depressed and other backward classes..."
52. Anirudh Prasad, *Reservation, Policy and Practice in India* (New Delhi 1991) p.17.
53. H.S. Saksena (ed) *op.cit.*, pp. 3-4.
54. Marc Galanter went to the extent of saying, "The Constitution sets forth a general programme for the reconstruction of Indian society. In spite of its length, it is surprisingly undetailed in its treatment of the institution of caste and existing group structure in Indian society." *Competing Equalities.* (1984) p. In the Constituent Assembly, S. Nagappa expressed doubts about the implementation of these provisions.
55. H.S. Saksena (ed) *op. cit* pp. 173-174.
56. H.S. Saksena *op. cit* pp. 7-8.
57. *Ibid* p.13.
58. Ibid at p.150. "The very inclusion of Dr. Ambedkar in the present Dominion Cabinet is a change of heart of the caste Hindus that the Harijans are not anymore to be neglected." Shri.V.I. Muniswamy Pillai (Madras general).

59. K.V. Rao, *Parliamentary Democracy of India: A Critical Commentary*, (New Delhi *2nd* Ed.) p.12 "My reading of the Constitution makes me feel that it is inappropriate to call Dr. Ambedkar 'the father of the Constitution'. If any people are entitled to be called so, they are Nehru and Patel, but I would like to call them the presiding Deities, the sources of ideas of the Constitution-the real makers of the Constitution. I would like to attribute fatherhood to them as well as the members of the Drafting Committee in common, but would not like to single out Dr. Ambedkar for this honour. We may call him, more appropriately, the 'mother' of the Constitution-and I am not using it in any deprecating or jocular sense. Dr.Ambedkar had to bear, in fact, others' ideas and nurture them and bring them out as his own, and this he did remarkably well.
60. H.S. Saksena, *op.cit* at p. 148.
61. *Ibid* pp. 149-150.
62. The period has been extended from time to time by means of Constitutional Amendments. The Constitution (Seventy-ninth Amendment) Act 1999 section 2, that provided for the special reresentation to cease after sixty years (from the commencement of the Constitution). It means that the reservation of seats for the SCs and STs would continue up to 2010.
63. This Clause 4 was added by the Constitution (First Amendment) Act 1951.
64. For further discussion see Chapter IV
65. See Anirudh Prasad, *op.cit.*, p. 112.
66. See *Nehru: The First Sixty Years* (ed.) Dorothy Norman. Asia Publishing House, (Bombay 1965) p.400.
67. The post independent socio-political scene would vouch for it. See the Conclusion (chapter IV).
68. Constitutional provisions regarding the powers of the CMs.
69. CAD Vol. II pp. 1-36 Dr. Ambedkar said "Let me give an illustration. Supposing for instance reservations were made for a community or a collection of communities, the total of which came to something like 70 per cent of the total posts under the state and only 30 per cent are retained as the unreserved. Could anybody say that the reservation of 30 percent as open to general competition would be satisfactory from the point of view of giving effect to the first principle namely that there shall be equality of opportunity. It cannot be in my judgment."
70. Sivaramaya.B. 'Affirmative Action: Scheduled Castes and Scheduled Tribes. In *International Perspective on Affirmative Action.* USA; Rockefeller Foundation. (1984)
71. J. Prabhash. *op cit.* p.87. The difference in the development of Backward Classes-including SCs and STs- is mainly due to the historical factors for often a researcher in India forgets the sub-continental dimension of India where there were innumerable polities. Even in recent history one may find that the Travancore Kings were comparatively benevolent and the Princely State was the best administered one.

72. See *Justice K.K.Narendran Commission Report* 2000. In the erstwhile State of Travancore and Cochin Backward Classes were entitled for reservation of posts in Government services from 1936 onwards. In the erstwhile Malabar District, which now forms part of Kerala also, Backward Classes were having reservation for appointments in Government Services from 1921 onwards. In some other south Indian states also backward classes were given the benefit of reservation for appointments to Government services. But the position was different as far as Central Government Services were concerned. In the states of North India also Backward Classes were not having the benefit of reservation for appointments in Government services.
73. Since the publication *of the Mandal Commission Report* and subsequent judgment in the *Indra Sawhney case* 'backwardness' has come under judicial srcutiny.
74. *Nettur Commission Report* pp. 80-81.
75. *Indra Sawhney v. Union of India* AIR 2000 SC 498 (512).
76. Another dangerous tendency this might encourage is that people might lose their respect for the judiciary. People may think that if the government itself could defy the Court's verdict, why they could not do that.
77. *R eport of the Justice K.K.Narendran Commission* 11 April 2000. para 6.2
78. This is not an isolated case. The civil service in India has a general tendency of lethargy, indifference, sometimes even arrogance and it never realizes the meaning of the word 'public service'.
79. ILR (Kerala Series) 1995 (3) pp. 3-41.
80. *Report of the Justice K.K.Narendran Commission.* 11 April 2000. para 11.2.
81. *Ibid* Para 11.6.
82. The list of the OBC is given in the appendix to the *Report.*
83. Susan Bayly, *Caste. Society And Politics In India, (*OUP 2000) p. 305.
84. *Justice Narendran Commission Report* dated 9th November 2001 p. 4.
85. *Ibid* p. 13.
86. *Ibid* pp. 41-42.
87. *Justice Narendran Commission Report* dated 9th November 2001.
88. The GO, which was held void by the Court in *Chembakam Dorairajan*
89. See 'Conclusion'.
90. *The Kerala Panchayat Raj Act, 1994*. The Act has been amended seven times the last amendment was in 2001.
91. See Article 243 D Clause (5).

4

Judicial Creativity Towards Rationalisation of Reservation

One of the important objectives stated in the Preamble of the Constitution is 'social justice'. The Court is expected to interpret law in such a way that this avowed objectives could be made a reality. Justice V.R. Krishna Iyer emphasizes this aspect of Judicial Activism when he says:

> A pragmatic approach to social justice compels us to interpret constitutional provisions liberally with a view to see that effective policing of the corridors of power is carried out by the court until other Ombudsman arrangements are made. Court's function, of course, is limited to testing whether administrative action has been fair and free from the taint unreasonableness and has substantially complied with the procedural norms set for it by the rules of public administration and that the action of the administration is not *mala fide*[1]

Reservation is mainly in the area of admissions in educational institutions,[2] employment in government services[3] and seats in the legislature[4]. Regarding reservation of seats in the legislatures including union parliament, there is practically no dispute. Moreover this reservation is only for Scheduled Castes and Scheduled Tribes and originally this reservation was only for 15 years but it has been extended till 2010 through amendments to the Constitution. Other Backward Classes (OBC) do not enjoy any reservation of seats in the legislature. But in the sphere of education and government services OBCs do enjoy reservation. In some States like Kerala, OBCs have become a dominant force in the bureaucracy. Thus the transience of backwardness has given rise to clash of interests both at the political and legal levels.

In this chapter cases that came before the supreme court of India have been discussed and analysed to get a clear picture of the nature of judicial activism vis-à-vis social justice. For the convenience of analysis cases have been grouped into four categories viz., education, employment, promotion and miscellaneous.

Education

In *State of Madras* v. *Champakam Dorairajan,*[5] the Court was unwilling to uphold the validity of the Communal Government Order of Madras Government, for the impugned Order went against the principle of 'equality before law' enshrined in the Constitution. There were two similar cases of admission to the Medical College and to the Engineering College.[6] According to Justice S.R. Das,

> The Chapter of Fundamental Rights is sacrosanct and not liable to be abridged by a legislative or executive act or order except to the extent provided in the appropriate article in Part III. The directive principles of State policy have to conform to and run as subsidiary to the chapter of fundamental rights. In our opinion that is the correct way in which the provisions found in Part III and IV, have to be understood... However so long as there is no infringement of any fundamental right to the extent conferred by provision in Part III there can be no objection to the state acting in accordance with the directive principles set out in part IV, but subject again to the legislative and executive powers and limitations conferred on the state under different provisions of the Constitution.[7]

The Court's verdict was nullified by the legislative action, for the Parliament came with an amendment to the Constitution and introduced Clause 4 to Article 15. This amendment is described as 'a crushing response to that challenge (the decision of the Court).[8] This indeed marked a portentous trend of the beginning of a subtle conflict between Legislature and Judiciary.[9] In *CR Srinivasan* v. *state of Madras;*[10] the Court rejected the caste as the only criterion for reservation. This judgment also reflected the spirit of 'equality' as envisaged in Article 14. In a similar vein Andhra High Court held[11] that any provision that prohibits backward classes to compete with others was held to be violative of Article 15 and 29(2) (b). It was also directed that a minimum percentage for reservation be fixed.

In *Kesava v. State of Mysore*[12] the issue involved was whether the decision of the State to identify backward classes was valid, as State Government had declared every community except Brahmin as Backward Community. The High Court held that State was doubtless the sole authority to classify the communities as 'backward classes'.[13]

In *M.R. Balaji and others v. State of Mysore and others*[14] the Court was trying to keep a just balance between the conflicting interests of those who would like to have as much reservation as possible and those might lose their chance even if they are the deserving ones. The issue in this case is about the admission to the Medical course. "According to the petitioners, but for the reservations made by the impugned order, they would have been entitled to the admission in the respective colleges for which they had applied." The impugned Order was issued on 31-07-1962 and it reserved seats for candidates belonging to the backward classes whose average of student population was the same or just below State average. This resulted in 68 per cent of seats available for admissions to the Engineering and Medical Colleges and to the other technical institutions is reserved for backward classes, more backward classes, Scheduled Castes and Scheduled Tribes. The classification of the socially backward classes of citizens made by the State, proceeds on the consideration only of their castes without regard to other factors, which are undoubtedly relevant. It was argued that this might lead to a virtual reservation for nearly 90 per cent of the population, which might come under different categories of backwardness. This would be at the expense of those classes of people whose members may perform well but may not get an opportunity.

After analyzing facts and probing the legal nuances, the Court came to the conclusion that caste alone could not be the criterion for backwardness. The Court also observed that reservation should not go beyond 50 per cent. The Court said:

> When it is said about an executive action that it is a fraud on the Constitution it does not necessarily mean that the action is actuated by mala fides. An executive action which is patently and plainly outside the limits of Constitutional authority conferred on the State in that behalf is struck down as being ultra vires the State's authority. If, on the other hand, the executive action does not patently or overtly transgress the authority conferred on it by the Constitution, but the transgression is covert and latent, the said action is struck down as being fraud on the relevant constitutional power... We have already noticed that the impugned order in the present case has categorized the Backward classes on the sole basis of caste which, in our opinion, is not permitted by Article 15 (4) and we have also held that the reservation of 68 per cent made by the impugned order is plainly inconsistent with the concept of

> special provision authorized by article 15 (4). Therefore it follows that the impugned order is a fraud on the Constitutional power conferred on the State by Article 15 (4).

On the whole the apex court succeeded in giving a well balanced judgment.

Caste could not be the sole criterion for identifying social backwardness. But castes, poverty, occupation, place of habitation are some of the relevant factors for determining social backwardness. It is unconstitutional to classify backward classes into backward and the most backward. Above all the Court observed that the upper limit for reservation could only be 50 per cent. It is open to question whether by fixing the upper limit, Court was not interfering in matters of policy, encroaching thereby the domain of legislature. Moreover fixing a limit in such a question would become inappropriate when the socio-economic changes become more manifestly rapid. The Court changed its observations in accordance with the provisions in the first amendment to the Constitution namely, Article 15(4) is held to be valid and not contradictory to Article 15(1). A reasonable extent of discrimination was to be permitted by law. But the honorable Court did not go into the essential social data regarding the proportional strength of the communities in the whole of the population, the educational progress made by each community and the standard of life enjoyed by them. The Court simply went on to pronounce the judgment based on the recent amendment to the Constitution and the philosophy behind the amendment. Perhaps the honorable Court took the stand that was politically correct at that time.

In *Chitralekha v. State of Mysore*[15] the Supreme Court gave some leeway to caste by saying that caste could be considered as one of the relevant factors in determining social and educational backwardness. But at the same time it was made clear that the terms 'caste' and 'class' are not synonymous. The Court observed:

> We do not intend to lay down any inflexible rule for the Government to follow. The laying down of criteria for ascertainment of social and educational backwardness of a class is complex problem depending upon many circumstances, which may vary from State to State and even from place to place in a State. But what we intend to emphasize is that under no circumstance a 'class' can be equated to a 'caste' though the caste of an individual or a group of individuals may be considered along with other relevant factors in putting him in particular class. We would also like to make

it clear that if in a given situation caste is excluded in ascertaining a class within the meaning of Art. 15 (4) of the Constitution, it does not vitiate the classification if it satisfied other tests.

In *P. Rajendran v. State of Madras*[16] the Supreme Court upheld the ratio in *Hariharan Pillai's* case. The question was whether caste could be considered the sole criterion for determining socially and educationally backward classes. The Court observed that if the caste as a whole was socially and educationally backward reservation could be made in favor of such caste within the meaning of Article 15(4) The Court also struck down district-wise distribution of seats in the Medical Colleges on the basis of population in each district to the total population of the State. This could not be permitted under Article 14. But at the same time in *Nishi Maghu v. Sate of J & K*[17] the classification of 'social castes' made with reference to the nature of occupations and the classification based on areas adjoining actual line of control and 'bad pockets in Jammu and Kashmir being really backward areas' and residents of these areas being socially and educationally backward were valid.

In *P. Sagar v. State of A.P.*[18] the High Court reiterated the stand that caste should not be the sole criterion for measuring backwardness. The question was whether the list of backward classes based solely on caste was legal. The Court answered this question in the negative. It observed that the impugned order infringed Article 15(1). In *B.Sayeed Ahamad v. State of Mysore*[19], the High Court felt that the occupation and income of the parent fell very much within the category of backwardness. The same Court ruled that family income could be the basis for deciding backwardness in *Shetty v. State of Mysore*[20].

A. Periya Karuppan v. State of Tamil Nadu[21] was indeed a landmark case in respect of the issue of reservation. The candidates challenged the unit-wise selection of Medical Colleges including the reservation for backward classes. Another significant question was the determination of backwardness on the sole basis of caste. Hegde J. observed that 'a caste has always been recognized as a class'. The learned Judge perhaps was not aware of the consequences of such observations. The pertinent question, here is, will it help abolish caste. The question whether 41% reservation for Scheduled Castes, Scheduled Tribes and Other Backward classes could be valid. The apex Court declared that the unit-wise reservation for SCs, STs and OBCs was violative of Articles 14 and 15. But the classification of backward classes on the basis of caste was held to be within Article 15 (4). The Court also observed that 41% reservation was not excessive. Commenting on this aspect of the judgment Anirudh Prasad (1991) writes: "Rajendran, *Balaram* and *Periyakaruppan* appear to present a 'retreat' from judicial efforts to search secular and rational criterion."[22]

The Bombay High Court held that the proportion of population of backward classes, SCs and STs to the total population of the state being the basis for determining the quantum of reservation, valid and reasonable. The provision for the carry forward of vacant reserved seats of the one of the sub-groups of backward class to that of the other sub-group was held to be valid.[23] The adoption of criteria of income and occupation for identifying backward classes was not against Article 15(4) and 16(4). Notification to this effect was held valid by the High Court in *G.N.Guidigar v. State of Mysore*[24].

In *Paravatnalini v. State of Orissa and Others*[25] it was held that reservation under Article 16(4) be read along with Article 355. Reservation under Article 16(4) was not binding on the state. It may be left to the discretion of subject to the satisfaction of a minimum standard of suitability. How this discretion is exercised by the state depends on the political situation that warrants that the party in power uses the power of discretion in such a way as to satisfy the 'vote bank'. This is one of the fallouts of the 'majoritarian principle' that governs the working of parliamentary democracy.

The Supreme Court favored the decision of the state to use caste as the basis for determining backwardness. It observed that if the entire caste was socially and educationally backward, caste could be taken as the basis for identification of Backward Class and this is not violative of Article 15(4)

In *Subash Chandra v. State of U.P.*,[26] the Allahabad High Court held that people of rural areas, hill area and Uttarakand division belong to socially and educationally backward classes under Article 15(4) but the same court in *Dilip Kumar v. State of U.P.*[27] held that the number of candidates from reserved areas appearing in the Pre-medical test and also the shortage of Higher secondary schools in that area were not adequate reasons for classifying all the residents of that area as belonging to educationally backward.

In *State of A.P. v. U.S.V. Balaram*[28] the Supreme Court heard three appeals together. The State of A.P. was the first appellant. The appeals were directed against the judgment of the High Court of Andhra Pradesh that struck down Rule 9 in the Rules relating to the selection of candidates for admission to the Government Medical Colleges. One aspect of the impugned Rules was about reservation of seats in the professional colleges, for Backward Classes. Incidentally the conclusions arrived at by the Backward Classes Commission of Andhra Pradesh was also challenged. Observation of the Supreme Court in this regard is significant. "In fact the Commission has categorically stated that the information received from various schools showed that the percentage of education was slightly higher than the State average in respect of some small groups, but in view of the fact that their living conditions were deplorably poor, the slightly higher percentage of literacy should not operate to their disadvantage." Indirectly at least the Court has acknowledged the economic factor in backwardness. The Court in this regard has said:

> No doubt our attention was drawn to a decision of the Kerala High Court, which has held that reservation is irrespective of some of the candidates belonging to the backward classes getting admission on their own merit. The Andhra Pradesh High Court has taken a slightly different view. If a situation arises wherein the candidates belonging to the groups included in the list of Backward Classes, are able to obtain more seats on the basis of their own merit, we can only state that it is the duty of the Government to review the question of further reservation of seats for such groups. *This has to be emphasised because the Government should not act on the basis that once a class is considered as a Backward Class it should not continue to be backward for all time.* (emphasis added) If once a class appears to have reached a stage of progress, from which it could be safely inferred that no further protection is necessary, the State will do well to review such instances and suitably revise the list of Backward Classes. In fact it was noticed by this Court in AIR 1971 SC 2303 that candidates of Backward Classes had secured nearly 50 per cent of seats in general pool. On this ground this Court did not hold that further reservation made for Backward Classes is invalid. On the other hand it was held:
>
> "The fact that the candidates of Backward Classes have secured about 50 per cent of the seats in general pool does show that time has come for a de novo comprehensive examination of the question. It must be remembered that the Government's decision in this regard is open to judicial review."

In *Pradip Tandon v. State of U.P.*[29] the Supreme Court held that reservations in favor of rural areas were not justified under the reservations for socially and educationally backward class of citizens. In the present case the relevant Government Order that reserved seats for candidates from rural, hill and Uttarakhand areas. This was held unconstitutional.[30] The Court by way of interpretation to Article 15 (4) said:

> The backwardness contemplated under Article 15 (4) is both social and educational. Article 15 (4) speaks of backwardness of classes of citizens. The accent is on classes of citizens. Article 15 (4) also speaks of Scheduled Castes and Scheduled Tribes. Therefore socially and educationally backward classes of citizens in Article 15 (4) could not be equated with castes. In *M.R.Balaji v. State of Mysore* and *State of A.P. v. Sagar* this Court held that classification of backwardness on the basis of castes, would violate both Article 15 (1) and15 (4).

In *Kumari K.S. Jayasree v. State of Kerala*[31] the Supreme Court went into the merit of the State Government's Order dated 2 May 1966, that those OBC candidates seeking admission to Medical Colleges and whose parents' income is above Rs. 10,000 per annum would not come under reservation benefits. The Court said:

> The problem of determining who are socially and educationally backward classes is undoubtedly not simple. Sociological and economic considerations come into play in evolving proper criteria for its determination. This is the function of the State. The Court's jurisdiction is to decide whether the tests applied are valid. It appears that the tests applied are proper and valid the classification of socially and educationally backward classes based on the tests will have to be consistent with the requirements of Article 15 (4).

The Court in its judgment upheld the validity of the Kerala Government Order and thereby indirectly recognized the economic factor in deciding backwardness.

The question in *Aarti Gupta v. State of Punjab*[32] whether the Government could make relaxation in mark for the Scheduled Caste and Scheduled Tribe candidates. According to the first notification of the Punjab Government SC/ST candidates had to secure only 35 per cent of marks in the competitive exam to qualify for medical admission. Yet for 100 reserved seats only 32 qualified. The general candidates claimed those reserved seats. However the Government issued a notification reducing the minimum percentage to 25. This was challenged by the general candidates before the High Court, which dismissed the petition. Hence they approached the Supreme Court.

The Supreme Court rejected the argument that the Medical Council of India prescribed 40% as the minimum and Universities could not reduce it further. But the Court did not accept the argument. Citing earlier decisions, the Court observed that how the selection has to be made out of the eligible candidates is a matter, which depends upon circumstances prevailing in a particular state. In an earlier case *M.P. V. Nivedita Jain*[33] the State Government fully deleted the prescription of the percentage of marks in the selection examination. Though the case was worse than the present one the Court upheld the Government decision. Here too therefore the Court upheld the Order of the Government, which was in favour of reservation that could not be encroached upon by general candidates.

In *State of Punjab v. Dayanand Medical College and Hospital*[34] it was held that though in a sense the Medical Council of India could also be a 'State' for certain purposes, such a body would not be suited to make the necessary reservation in respect of socially and educationally backward classes in terms of Art. 15 (4) of the Constitution because of the need or the necessity for prescription, taking into account several considerations such as different levels of social, economic and educational development of the State or different regions in the State. Such considerations arise in the context of Article 16 as well. It is well known that the States often do appoint Backward Classes Commission to identify the socially and educationally backward classes of India, though in the context of fixing the standards and the extent of backward classes and the manner in which their backwardness have to be ameliorated. These vital aspects of policy necessitated equally by great public and general importance can *be properly appreciated by the Government, Central or State, rather than the Medical Coun*t to which the difference in standards have to be maintained between the general category and the reserved category must be left to Medical Council of India. Thus, proper balance will have to be struck both by the Medical Council of India and by the Government, Central and State exercise of their respective powers. The Medical Council of India, a creature of a statute, cannot be ascribed with such powers to reduce the State Governments to nothing on and in respect of areas over which the States have constitutional mandate and goal assigned to them to be performed.

In *Rajesh Kumar Verma v. State of M.P.*[35] a Government Order relaxing the minimum mark requirement was the issue. Admission to Medical Courses was governed by Rules made by the State Government (in this case Madhya Pradesh). The State Government provided reservation for Scheduled castes and Scheduled Tribe candidates. The Rule also provided that in case eligible candidates to the extent of reservation in any category are not available, the vacancies of the reserved category will be filled from the waiting list of candidates in general category. There was also relaxation of marks. For English minimum mark prescribed is 25%, but that will not be included in the aggregate. In the present case it so happened that out of 87 seats available to Scheduled Caste candidates only 40 students qualified for ad mission and regarding Scheduled Tribes only 30 students qualified and the number of seats was 87. This resulted in the fact that out of 174 seats reserved 94 fell vacant. In the ordinary course these should have gone for general candidates. But the State Government in the meanwhile by an Order reduced the minimum qualifying marks in English to 15% for Scheduled Caste candidates and 10% for Scheduled Tribe Candidates. This Order was challenged through a Writ petition before the Division Bench of the High Court. The contention was that those unfilled seats should go to the general candidates and Order was not justifiable. The High Court accepted the argument and ordered so. But in appeal the Supreme Court pointed out that in the absence of any law to the contrary it was open to the State Government to relax the rule prescribing the minimum qualifying marks to ensure the interests of these category of students was protected and they receive protection to the extent it was necessary for their upliftment.

In *Ritesh R. Sah v. Dr. Y.L.Yamul*[36] the Court observed that if a candidate belonging to the backward class got admission to a course on merit- in the instant case admission in the Medical College-it could not be considered to be admitted against reserved category. The apex Court instructed the Maharashtra Government that the 'above said directions should be borne in mind and the rules should be made accordingly.'

In *Dr. Sadhana Devi v. State of U.P.*[37] the Government of U.P. issued a circular dispensing with the requirement of minimum mark for the admission to Postgraduate course in Medicine for the Scheduled Castes and Scheduled Tribes candidates. The Supreme Court held:

> The importance of merit being the only criterion for admission to post-graduate medical courses viz. MD, MS and the like was also emphasized in *Dr. Pradeep Jain v. Union of India.* (1984) 3 SCC 654: (AIR 1980 SC 1420).
>
> But this line of inquiry need not detain us here in this case because the case of the petitioners is not that there should be no reservation for the candidates belonging to the three special

categories mentioned hereinabove at the post-graduate level. Their contention is that candidates belonging to the three special categories must be able to secure the minimum qualifying marks in the admission tests in order to gain admission to post-graduate medical courses. If they fail to secure even the minimum qualifying marks, then the seats reserved for them should not be allowed to go waste but should be made available to the candidates belonging to general category. This contention must he upheld. Otherwise, to borrow the language used in *Dr. Jagdish Saran* case, (AIR 1980 SC 820), this will be a "national loss."

Before we part with this case, we may refer to another judgment of this Court in, *Mohan Bir Singh Chawla* v. *Punjab University*. Chandigarh, 1996 (9) SCALE 351, in which it was observed after a review of the case law "the higher you go, in any discipline, lesser should be the reservations - of whatever kind."

In that view of the matter, this writ petition succeeds. The decision contained in the letter dated 31-8-1995 addressed by the Principal Secretary. Uttar Pradesh Government to the Director General, Medical Education and Training, Uttar Pradesh directing that there shall be no minimum qualifying marks for Scheduled Castes/Scheduled Tribes/Other Backward Classes candidates in the written examination for admission to postgraduate and diploma courses is quashed. It is directed that if the seats reserved for SC/SC/OBC candidates cannot be filled up on account of failure of the candidates belonging to these categories to obtain the minimum qualifying marks, then such seats should be made available to the candidates belonging to the general category.

Admission to Medical Colleges again became an issue in *Rajiv Mittal v. Maharshi Dayanand University.*[38] There were 49 seats in the open category and 11 seats for reserved category for M.B.B.S. at Rohtak Medical College. In the first counseling there were a few vacant seats in the general category and hence second and third counseling were held and candidate with serial number 60 was admitted. Sunil Yadav who belonged to the backward community came with the rank of 62 in the merit list. There was again one seat vacant in the general category. As candidates with 61, 62, 63, 64, and 65 did not join the general candidate with 66th rank was offered the seat.

Respondent No. 3 who belonged to the reserved category could not get admission in the Rohtak Medical College inasmuch as his merit position in the reserved category was at serial No. 12 while the number of seats in this category in that college was only 11 and all those seats had been filled. He thereupon filed a writ petition in the Punjab and Haryana High Court contending that Sunil Yadav should have been adjusted against the general category seat which had been allotted to the appellant herein in the second counseling held on 26-9-1996, and if this is done, one seat in the reserved category would @page-SC681 fall vacant which would naturally fall to respondent No. 3.

On behalf of the respondent No. 1, it was argued that Sunil Yadav could not be considered in the first counseling in the open category because he did not fall among those open category candidates who had been given admission against 49 open category seats. Candidates up to merit position 53 had been offered admission against these seats at the time of first counseling. Thereupon, Sunil Yadav was called for first counseling for reserved seats and was granted admission against the backward category quota. He, having thus secured the seat, lost his claim for open category and, therefore, did not attend the second counseling held on 26-9-1996.

The High Court, allowed the writ petition filed by respondent No. 3 as it held that it was "settled principle of law that a candidate from the reserved class, if is entitled to get admission to a course of his own merit in the general list, he must be treated on his merit and not accommodated against the reserved vacancy". It thereupon came to the conclusion that Sunil Yadav should have been adjusted against the one seat in the general category which had been offered to the appellant at the time of second counseling and that the reserved seat, which would be so vacating by Sunil Yadav, should be offered and admission granted to respondent No.3.

But the Supreme Court did not agree with the findings of the High Court. The apex Court observed:

> On behalf of the appellant, it has been contended that the High Court could not direct that Sunil Yadav should be considered as having been given the general category seat in the second counseling when he had already secured admission in the first counseling in the reserved category. On the other hand, the respondents have relied on the judgment of the High Court and in particular Note 2 of the Information Brochure and contended that Sunil Yadav could only be adjusted against the open category seat and he could not be considered for the reserved category. In our opinion, the High Court erred in

allowing the writ petition and directing that the admission, which had been granted to the appellant, should be cancelled. The system of counseling for the purpose of granting admission to the various medical colleges in the State is now regarded as most equitable one where options are given of various seats to the students in accordance with their overall merit position in the combined entrance examination, which examination is competitive in nature...

An appropriate analogy of this system is that of a booking chart for a dramatic performance, which has to take place in the future. The people standing in the queue reserve or book their seats out of those, which are available according to their preference. Once the chart fills up the booking closes. Only sometimes, if tickets are returned they may be reissued. But once the dramatic performance starts no one is allowed to enter. Just as counseling for seats to medical colleges must stop once the courses of study commence.

The Court, thus, set aside the judgment of the High Court, the result of which would be that the writ petition filed before the High Court would stand dismissed.

In *Dr. Preethi Srivastava v/ State of M. P.*[39] the Supreme Court considered six petitions together. The issue was whether there could be provisions for reservation of seats in specialty and super specialty courses in Medicine. The State of U.P. fixed the cut off percentage of 20 per cent marks for reserved candidates as against 45 per cent for the general candidates. The State of M.P. fixed 20% for Scheduled Castes and 15 per cent for Scheduled Tribes and 40% for other backward Classes. According to the Court "The disparity of qualifying marks being 20 per cent for the reserved category and 45 per cent for general category is too great a disparity to sustain public interest at the level of post graduate medical training and education."

In *K. Duraisamy and another, v. State of T.N. and others*[40] the Government Order that provided 50 per cent quota for in-service and 50 per cent for non-service candidates for admission in the specialty and super specialty courses in Medicine was challenged. The Court held the Order valid. According to the Court 'quota' and 'reservation' are different concepts. Therefore the matter does not come under Article 15 (4).

A case came before the Supreme Court where a similar notification of the Punjab Government was challenged. In *State of Punjab v. Dayanand Medical College and Hospital*[41] the impugned notification fixed the quota of 60 per cent for in-service candidates and 40 per cent for non-service.

The Court held the notification valid. But the Court observed that with regard to marks in the tests the State could not make any relaxation.

But the apex Court would quash any unreasonable fixing of quota. This happened in the case of *A.I.I.M.S. Students Union v. A.I.I.M.S.*[42] the rule regarding admission to Post-Graduate Course in AIMS was based on the quota of Institutional reservation of 33 per cent coupled with 50 per cent reservation discipline-wise. This was held super reservation and hence it infringed the equality principle of Article 14.

In "*Dr. Narayan Sharma v. Dr. Pankaj Kr. Lehkar*[43] the questions before the Court were, 1. Whether reserving seats in the Assam Medical College for the postgraduate course to candidates from North Eastern Council area. 2. Whether there could be reservation for the teachers in medicine for the postgraduate course. The Court held both these reservations were constitutionally valid. The impugned law in this case was Assam Medical Colleges (Regulation of Admission to Post- Graduate Courses) Rules (1997).

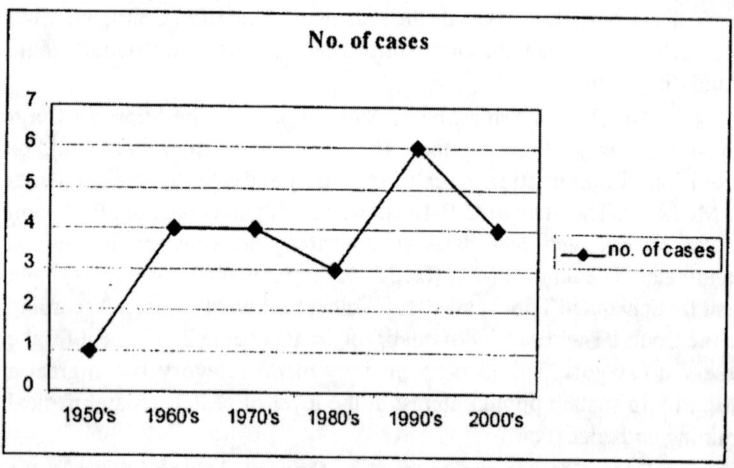

Figures 4.1

The Trend of Supreme Court Cases on Education from 1950 to 2003

Table 4.1

Supreme Court Cases on Reservation Policy in Education (1951–2002)

Sl. No.	Name of the Case	Year and citation	Facts	Questions of law/Articles	Decision/Activism
1	Champakam Dorairajan v. State of Madras	AIR 1951 SC 226	Admission to Medical College was denied because the selection was based on Communal Government Order of the Madras Government.	1. Whether reservation made under Article 16(4) be made on the basis of caste alone? 2. Whether reservation for backward classes are applicable for admission or in service or both.	The Court struck down the Communal GO as violative of Fundamental rights under Articles 14 and 15
2	M.R.Balaji v. State of Mysore.	AIR 1963 SC 649	Large number of professional College Candidates filed writ petitions it the SC alleging that but for the reservation made by the State govt. they would have been admitted students with less marks admitted. The extent of reservation was unreasonable 68% reservation	(I) What was the role of 'caste' in determining social backwardness. (ii) What were the criteria for identifying the social and educational backwardness? (iii) Whether the sub-classification of backward classes into categories valid? (iv) Whether quantum of reservation (68%) excessive?	Caste alone could not be the criterion for deciding the backwardness. Poverty, occupation and place of habitation and such other things have to be considered. Sub-classification into 'backward ' and 'most backward' is unconstitutional. Total reservation could not exceed 50%

Sl.No.	*Name of the Case*	*Year and citation*	*Facts*	*Questions of law/Articles*	*Decision/Activism*
3	R. Chitralekha v. State of Mysore	AIR 1964 SC 1823.	Validity of the order issued and signed by an under-secretary was challenged. Secondly the system of selection based on viva voce examination was challenged on the ground that it is arbitrary.	(i)Relevance of 'Caste in determining social and educational backwardness. (ii) Whether 'Caste' and "Class' synonymous?	(i) Caste could be considered as one o the relevant factors in determinin social and educational backwardness (ii) The term 'Caste and 'Class' wer not synonymous.
4	Minor P. Rajendran v. State of Madras"	AIR 1968 SUPREME COURT 1012	Seat in the medical college could not be obtained because of the reservation of seats district-wise. This Government Order was challenged.	Article 14 and 16 (4) and the impugned Order of the Government.	The provision of district-wise reservation was struck down as violative of Article 14. The impugned Order does not offer proper reservation.

Sl.No.	Name of the Case	Year and citation	Facts	Questions of law/Articles	Decision/Activism
5	P.Sagar v. State of AP	AIR 1968 SC 1379	Andhra Pradesh Govt. reserved Medical seats in the various colleges on several criteria like SC/ST, Children of Ex-servicemen displace goldsmith & women. 20% of seats were reserved for BC is Andhra & Telungu area. HC ruled Reservation for BCs in valid	(I) Whether the list of backward classes based solely on caste was legal.	(I) Reservation was made in favour of caste and not classes. Therefore it infringed Art 15(1). The criterion for determining backwardness must not be based solely on religion, race, caste, Sex or place of birth. The backwardness being social and educational must be similar to the backwardness from which SC/ST suffer. List prepared solely on basis of caste criterion was invalid.
6	A.Periakaruppan v. State of T.N	AIR 1971 SC 2303	The admission to Medical college was denied because of the unit-wise reservation followed by the Government.	(i)Unit-wise selection whether violation of Art 14 & 15. (ii) The determination of backward classes on the sole basis of caste, whether constitutionally permissible. (iii) Whether 41% of reservation for SC's, ST's and BC's excessive?	(I) Unit-wise selection held to be violative of Art's 14 & 15. (ii) Classification of backward class on the basis of caste held to be within the Art 15(4). (iii) 41% of reservation was not excessive.

Sl.No.	Name of the Case	Year and citation	Facts	Questions of law/Articles	Decision/Activism
7	State of A.P. v. USV. Balarama	AIR 1972 SC 1375	Denial of admission to the MBBS course because of discrimination between Higher secondary and Pre-University students and also reservation based caste-backwardness.	1. Whether 'Caste could be taken as the basis for enumeration of backward classes? 2. 43% of reservation, is it excessive?	(I) If the entire caste was socially and educationally backward, caste could be taken, as basis for identification of BC's and including it in the list of BC not violative of Art 15(4). (ii) The 43% of reservation is well within 50 percent limit laid down by the SC, so it is not excessive.
8	Pradip Tandon v. State of U.P.	AIR 1975 SC 563	College admission denied because of the reservation made for people from rural and hilly areas.	Whether a reservation for rural, hill and Uttarkhand areas as socially and educationally backward classes under Article 15(4) was constitutional?	Reservations for the candidates belonging to hill areas and Uttarkhand area were justified whereas reservation in favour of rural area was not justified under socially and educationally backward class of citizens.

Sl.No.	Name of the Case	Year and citation	Facts	Questions of law/Articles	Decision/Activism
9	K.S.Jayasree v. State of Kerala	AIR 1976 SC 2381	Denied admission to Medical College because of the Government Order regarding income ceiling to determine backwardness.	(I) Whether ceiling on family income could determine one from enjoying the benefits of reservation under Art 15(4). (ii) Whether Caste could be made sole criterion for determination of social and educational backwardness under 15(4).	(I) Ceiling the family income could be imposed on the reservation benefits under Art 15(4) to the backward classes. (ii) In ascertaining social backwardness, caste cannot be the sole test. Backwardness could be the result of poverty. Therefore, both caste and poverty should be considered, not just are of them. (Fixing of family income limit valid.)
10	Dr. Jagdish Saran v. Union of India	AIR 1980 SUPREME COURT 820	Rule regarding 70% of seats at the Post Graduate (Medicine) seats reserved for Delhi University students Challenged because of this rule inspite of good marks and performance at the test, he was denied admission	Article 15. The Rule regarding the reservation of 70% seats for the students of Delhi University.	The Rule was unconstitutional and hence void. The rule went against Art. 14 and 15
11	Nishi Maghu v. State of J&K	AIR 1980,SC 1975	The selection of candidates to the Government college in Jammu was challenged 18 per cent seats were reserved for rectifying regional imbalances and some seats for 'social castes'	Whether 18 per cent seats reserved for rectifying regional imbalances and some seats for 'social castes' valid.	The Supreme Court ruled that selection of candidates to the State medical college to "correct regional imbalances" without identifying the areas was illegal. But it upheld selection on the basis of 'social castes' with reference to occupation.

Sl.No.	Name of the Case	Year and citation	Facts	Questions of law/Articles	Decision/Activism
12	Aarti Gupta v. State of Punjab	AIR 1988 SC 481	Candidate of general category challenged president's notification reducing the minimum percentage of marks for reserved category of SC/ST from 35 to 25 per cent.	whether the government can reduce the qualifying marks if sufficient number of candidates from the reserved category are not available	Held reduction of marks not arbitrary.
13	Ritesh R. Sah v. Dr. Y.L. Yamul	AIR 1996 SUPREME COURT 1378	A candidate of reserved category by his own merit got the selection but he was admitted to the MBBS course against the reserved category. This was challenged	Article 15. The Rules of admission to the MBBS course issued by the Government of Maharashtra.	The rules of admission of the Government are not valid for the seats for SC/ST are reserved and a candidate who is selected on merit cannot be admitted against the reserved seats.
14	State of Karnataka v. Kumari Gowri narayana ambiga	AIR 1995 SC 1691	Special Rule providing for appointment only local candidates of SC/ST.	Article 16 (4) and 309 and Karnataka State Civil Services (Direct recruitment of SC/ST) to Class III posts.	High Court had held the rules void and the Supreme Court upheld the judgment of High Court.
15	Dr.Sadhana Devi v. State of U.P	AIR 1997 SC 1120	The candidate belonging to the general category challenged the notification of the U.P. Government providing reservation in the Post graduate speciality and super speciality courses in medicine.	Article 32, 14, 15 Reservation in admissions; Minimum qualifying marks	If the reserved category candidates fail to obtain minimum qualifying marks, the seats reserved for them should be thrown to general category so that no loss is caused to the nation.

Sl.No.	Name of the Case	Year and citation	Facts	Questions of law/Articles	Decision/Activism
16	Jagdish Negi v. State of U.P	AIR 1997 SC 3505	This was originally a Public Interest litigation for benefit of reservation to the residents of Hill and Uttrakhand area	Articles 15 (4) and 16 (4) U.P. Public Service (Reservation for SC/ST and Other backward Classes) Act 1994	The petition was partly allowed.
17.	Rajiv Mittal v. Maharshi Dayanand University	AIR 1998 SC 680	Case against HC decision "settled principle of law that a candidate from the reserved class, if is entitled to get admission to a course of his own merit in the general list, he must be treated on merit and not against reserved vacancy"	Articles 15 (4)	Supreme Court reversed the order of H.C. High Court erred in allowing the writ petition and directing that the admission, which had been granted to the appellant, should be cancelled
18.	Dr. Preeti Srivastava v. State of M.P	AIR 1999 SC 791	U.P Government by an Ordinance gave concession in marks to the P.G. Medical Entrance candidates belonging to SC/ST. There is a wide disparity. This law is challenged.	Article 14 and 15 (4) and the relevant Rules and Ordinance.	Too much disparity in marks obtained, especially at the post-graduate level of Medical education could not be permitted. No relaxation in marks is permissible at the highest level in Medical institutions.
19.	Dr. Narayana Sharma v. Dr. Pankaj Kr. Lehkar	AIR 2000 SC 72	In fact three appeals were heard together. Reservation of seats in Medical colleges in Assam for candidates recommended by the North Eastern Council	Articles 15 (4) and 29 (2)	Such reservation is not constitutionally invalid.

Sl.No.	Name of the Case	Year and citation	Facts	Questions of law/Articles	Decision/Activism
20.	K.Duraisamy v. State of T.N	AIR 2001 SC 717	The Govt. Order that was challenged , provided 50% quota for in-service and 50% for non-service candidates for the admission in the speciality and super speciality courses in Medicine	Article 15 (4) and 16 (4) and Tamil Nadu Govt. Order 55 D of 9-2-1999	held valid for quota and reservation are different concepts
21.	State of Punjab v. Dayanand Medical college and Hospital	AIR 2001 SC 3006	The appellant State of Punjab issued notification regarding admission to Post Graduate Course in Medicine 60% for in-service candidates and 40% for non-service	Article 15 (4) and Relevant Regulations of State of Punjab and Medical Council Act.	State action held valid. But with regard to marks in the tests the State cannot make relaxations.
22.	A.I.I.M.S Students Union v. A.I.I.M.S	AIR 2001 SC 3262	Admissions to Post Graduate Course in AIIMS- Institutional reservation of 33% coupled with 50% reservation discipline-wise	Article 14	Amounts to super reservation. Hence could not be held valid.

Employment

Probably, the first case where Constitutional provision for 'protective discrimination' for weaker sections, was tested on the touchstone of Fundamental Right of equality of treatment, is the one concerning 'equality of opportunity in employment'. This was *B.Venkitaramana v. State of Madras*[41] where the aggrieved party namely a Brahmin candidate for the post of Munsif approached the Court for he was alleged to have been discriminated against by the Public Service Commission. The Supreme Court held that this discrimination was illegal and unconstitutional. He suffered from this discriminatory treatment because of the rules of reservation envisaged in the Communal G.O. of the government of Madras. The Court observed:

> For instance the petitioner may be far better qualified than a Muslim or a Christian or a non-Brahmin candidate and if all the posts reserved for those communities were open to him, he would be eligible for appointment, as is conceded by the learned Advocate-General of Madras, but, nevertheless he cannot expect to get any of these posts reserved for those different categories only because he happens to be a Brahmin. His ineligibility for any of the post reserved for the other communities, although he may have far better qualifications than those possessed by members falling within those categories, is brought about only because he is a Brahmin and does not belong to any of those categories. This ineligibility created by the Communal G.O. does not appear us to be sanctioned by cl. (4) of Article 16 and is an infringement of the fundamental right guaranteed to the petitioner as an individual citizen under Article 16 (1) and (2). The Communal G.O., in our opinion, is repugnant to the provisions of Article 16 and is as such void and illegal.

Again the Court in this case directed the government to "consider and dispose of the petitioner's application for the post after taking it on file on its merits and without applying the rule of communal rotation."

The Supreme Court gave a favourable verdict in the case of reservation of selection posts in the railway service in *Rangachari v. G.M. Southern Railways.*[42] The Supreme Court held that the very term 'Backward Classes' included Scheduled castes and Scheduled Tribes. The Court interpreted Article 16(4) thus:

> Article 16(4) clearly shows that the power conferred by it can be exercised in cases where the State is of the opinion that any backward class of citizens is not adequately represented in the service under it. In other words opinion formed by the

> State that the representation available to the backward class of citizens in any of the services is inadequate is a condition precedent for the exercise of the power conferred by Article 16(4) and so the power to make reservation as contemplated by Article 16 (4) can be exercised only to make the inadequate representation in the services adequate. If that be so both "appointments" and "posts" to which the operative part of Article 16 (4) refers and in respect of which the power to make reservation has been conferred on the State must necessarily be appointments and posts in the services. It would be illogical and unreasonable to assume that for making the representation adequate in the services under the State a power should be given to the State to reserve posts outside the cadre of services.

Again the Court went on to elaborate:

> The condition precedent may refer either to the numerical inadequacy of representation in the services or even to the qualitative inadequacy of representation. The advancement of socially and educationally backward classes requires not only that they should have adequate representation in the lowest rung of services but that they should aspire to secure adequate representation in selection posts in the services as well. In the context of the expression 'adequately represented 'imports considerations of "size" as well as "values", numbers as well as the nature of appointments held and so it involves not merely the numerical test but also the qualitative one.

Thus the Court arrived at the conclusion that;

> ...and if that be so, it would not be reasonable to hold that the inadequacy of representation can and must be cured only by reserving proportionately higher percentage of appointments at the initial stage.

In *T. Devadasan v. Union of India*, where the Court invalidated the unreasonable 'carry forward rule' is another landmark

The central issue in *Prem Prakash and others v. Union of India*[43] is the refusal of appointment to certain Scheduled Caste candidates because of lack of reserved vacancies. They had to be accommodated. In January 1980 the Delhi High Court held an examination for recruiting officers to the Delhi Judicial Service. It was stated that out of 16 vacancies 2 were reserved for Scheduled castes and 1 for Scheduled Tribes. In addition there were two carry forward vacancies for members of Scheduled Tribe. If Scheduled caste candidates were not available they might be transferred as reserved vacancies for Scheduled Caste candidates. After the written examination and viva voce test only 11 candidates passed. Seven out of these 11 had competed for open seats while four had competed for seats reserved for the Scheduled Castes. In normal course vacancies, which are intended to be filled by holding an examination in any particular year are filled from amongst candidates who had appeared for that examination. But the matter was made complicated by the fact that two Scheduled caste candidates who had passed the tests in 1979 and had not been appointed due mainly to the official error, were accommodated in 1980 vacancies as a result of the writ petition they had filed. But in doing justice to them (and delayed justice for that matter) justice was denied to the Scheduled caste candidates who passed the tests in 1980. The apex Court observed:

> The error from which the calculation of the High Court suffers is that the number of vacancies available for the Scheduled caste candidates was fixed according to the number of candidates who qualified for the general seats. The counter-affidavit states expressly that the availability of vacancies for reserved category was determined on the basis that only seven candidates had qualified for the general seats. This according to us is neither justified by the Rules and administrative instructions nor indeed does such a method of fixation of reserved vacancies disclose any acceptable basis. 16 vacancies were advertised in the first instance out of which 11 were for general candidates and 5 for reserved candidates. Administration is not found to fill all the vacancies, which are advertised. But the availability of vacancies for the reserved categories cannot be made to depend upon the accidental circumstances of how many candidates have qualified for general seats. In the first place that would be contrary to the instructions...Secondly such a method will lead to the absurd and undesirable consequence that no candidate of the reserved category will be appointed at all if only one or two candidates from general category qualify in the examination.

And the Court allowed the writs.

Again the one-post issue came up in *Chakradhar Paswan v. State of Bihar*[44] and the Supreme Court has held that if there is only one post, it could not be reserved because reservation under Article 16(4) does not permit the creation of monopoly of certain class on certain category of posts.

In this case, the State Govt. of Bihar directed that separate Directorate should be created each for Indigenous Medicines, the Director being from one of the systems of medicines namely Ayurvedic, Unani and Homeopathic. When separate Directorate was created the Government sanctioned the posts of two Deputy Directors for each of the two remaining systems. The State Government had in accordance with the decision of the Supreme Court prescribed a 50-point roster to implement the policy of reservation to posts and appointments for members of the backward classes under Art. 16(4). It was laid down that "if in any grade, there is only one vacancy for the first time, then it will be deemed to be unreserved and for the second time also, if there be only one vacancy, then it will be deemed to be reserved". Acting upon the roster the Joint Secretary to the Government, General Administration Department (Personnel) made a proposal for reservation of the post of Deputy Director (Homeopathic) for members of the scheduled castes. He said that in the Directorate of Indigenous Medicines, three posts had been sanctioned - (1) Director of Indigenous Medicines' (2) Deputy Director (Homeopathic) and (3) Deputy Director (Unani). All these posts were Class I posts. He suggested that according to the roster of appointments, out of these three posts the first, namely, that of Director be treated as unreserved, the second should be treated as reserved for scheduled caste candidate and the third should be unreserved. According to him, all the posts could be grouped together from the point of view of reservation.

The Supreme Court did not accept the arguments of the Bihar Government. The Court observed that though the Directorate of Indigenous Medicines comprises of four posts, namely, that of the Director and three Deputy Directors, which were Class I posts, the posts of Director and Deputy Directors would not constitute one "cadre". They are members of the same Service but do not belong to the same cadre. According to the 50 point roster, if in a particular grade a single post falls vacant, it should, in the case of first vacancy, be considered as unreserved i. e. general and on the second occasion when a single post again falls vacant, the same must be treated as reserved. Admittedly, the post of the Director is the highest post in the Directorate of Indigenous Medicine with a higher pay scale while the posts of the Deputy Directors carried a lower pay scale. The posts of the Director and those of the Deputy Directors constitute different cadres of the Service. It is manifest that the post of the Director of Indigenous Medicines, which is the highest post in the Directorate carried a higher grade or scale, could not possibly be equated with those of the Deputy Directors on a lower grade or scale. In view of this, according to the 50-point roster, if in a particular cadre, a single post falls vacant, it should, in the case of first vacancy, be considered as general. That being so, the State Government could not have directed reservation of the Post of Deputy Director (Homeopathic) which was the first vacancy in a particular cadre i. e. that of the Deputy Directors, for candidates belonging to the Scheduled Castes. Such reservation was not in conformity with the principles laid down in the 50-point roster and was impermissible under Art. 16(4) of the Constitution and clearly violative of the guarantee enshrined in Art.16 (1). Clause. (4) of Art. 16 is by way of an exception of the proviso to Art.16 (1). The reservation of the post of Deputy Director (Homeopathic) would amount to 100% reservation, which was impermissible under Art. 16(4) as otherwise it would render the guarantee of equal opportunity in the matter of public employment under Art. 16(1) wholly elusive and meaningless. If there is only one post in the cadre, there can be no reservation under Art.16 (4) of the Constitution. *The whole concept of reservation for application of the 50-point roster is that there are more than one post, and the reservation as laid down by the Supreme Court can be up to 50 per cent. The three posts of Deputy Directors of Homeopathic, Unani and Ayurvedic, are distinct and separate as they pertain to different disciplines and each one is an isolated post by itself carried in the same cadre. There can be no grouping of isolated posts even if they are carried on the same scale.*

In *P.Rajendran v. State of Madras*[45] the Supreme Court upheld the ratio in *Hariharan Pillai.* The question was whether caste could be considered the sole criterion for determining socially and educationally backward classes. The Court observed that if the caste as a whole was socially and educationally backward reservation could be made in favor of such caste within the meaning of Article 15(4). The Court also struck down district-wise distribution of seats in the Medical Colleges on the basis of population in each district to the total population of the State. This could not be permitted under Article 14. But at the same time in *Nishi Maghu v. State of J & K*[46] the classification of 'social castes' made with reference to the nature of occupations and the classification based on areas adjoining actual line of control and 'bad pockets in Jammu and Kashmir being really backward areas and residents of these areas being socially and educationally backward were valid.

Posts and Telegraphs Department undermined the policy of reservation by introducing a common norm for reservation of its personnel. In 1983 an agreement was arrived at between the Ministry of Communications and certain associations of employees working in the

Posts and Telegraphs Department. Consequently a fresh order relating to the policy of promotion to be adopted in the Posts and Telegraphs Department was issued in suppression of the scheme of reservation followed till then. Under the said new policy irrespective of the fact whether an employee belonged to the general category or to the category of the Scheduled Caste and the Scheduled Tribes he would be able to get promotion to the higher cadre on the completion of 16 years. Thereby the comparative advantages which the members belonging to the Scheduled Castes and the Scheduled Tribes were enjoying were taken away and all the employees, namely, the employees belonging to the Scheduled Castes, the Scheduled Tribes and to the other categories were placed at par.

In *P and T Scheduled caste/Tribe Employees Welfare Association (Regd:) v. Union of India*[47] the Court held that this order deprived the right of the Scheduled Caste/ Scheduled Tribes for they had been enjoying the advantages of 'protective discrimination'. This also violated the equality clause of the Constitution. Persons belonging to the Scheduled Castes and the Scheduled Tribes in other Departments were enjoying similar advantage and only the employees of P. and T. Department had been deprived of it. The Court observed that it could not issue a writ on this matter for Article 16 (4) was only an enabling provision. Justice Venkataramaiah pointed out the significance of Article 46 of the Constitution. It provides that the State shall promote with special care the educational and economic interests of the weaker sections of the people, and, in particular, of the Scheduled Castes and the Scheduled Tribes, and shall protect them from social injustice and all forms of exploitation.

In *State of Karnataka v. K.B. Urushabendra Kumar*[48] the question is whether a person could claim appointment on the basis of the income of his adoptive family. In August 1987, applications were invited by the State of Karnataka for appointment of Sericulture Extension Officers. Two posts were shown reserved for members of the backward classes-Group 'D'. Regarding one post there is no dispute. Regarding the other there arose dispute between respondents 1 and 2. It appears that these respondents on the basis that they were members of the backward classes of the kind applied for the post and rubbed shoulders before the Karnataka Public Service Commission. The Commission rejected the candidature of respondent No. 1 on the basis that he did not fulfill the income criteria inasmuch as his natural family had income above Rs. 10,000/- per annum making him ineligible even though his adoptive family had income less than Rs. 10,000,/- per annum. The adoption of respondent No. 1 as such was never disputed. The Commission on rejecting the candidature of respondent No. 1 in the backward class category treated him as a candidate in general category and did not show him in the order of merit for appointment in the later category. Consequently No. 2 was selected and recommended for appointment on that basis. The Government accordingly appointed him somewhere in the year 1989 and he has continued in the post thereafter. In the meanwhile Respondent No. 1 challenged the view of the Commission in rejecting his candidature before the Administrative Tribunal, Bangalore. The Tribunal took the view that since adoption was valid evidence as it was by a registered deed of the year 1979, there had been severance of relationship of respondent No. 1 with his natural family and consequently he stood uprooted from that family and transplanted in his adoptive family whose income alone could be taken into account. The Court observed:

> When the factum of adoption and its legality remains unquestionable the law of the Hindus on the subject must necessarily have its consequences. Having gone to his new family, respondent No. 1 rightfully acquired their economic status. It is just a matter of fate that in his adopted family he has comparatively been worse off but it could be the other way had his adoptive family been affluent. The view of the Tribunal in these circumstances appears to us reasonable requiring no interference at our end.

Thus the Court agreed with the Tribunal and thereby restored the claim of respondent No.1 in *P.S. Ghalaut v. State of Haryana and others.*[49] The Court was concerned with the Constitution of India, Art.16 (4) vis-à-vis the Haryana Medical Education Service Rules (1965) regarding inter se seniority. Public Service Commission showed general candidate as more meritorious than reserved candidate. He shall be senior to reserved candidate but applying roster points made the appointment. Thus the reserved candidate steals seniority over general class candidate. The Supreme Court observed that this was not arbitrary.

In *State of U.P. v. Dr. Dina Nath Shukla*[50] the question whether Faculty wise and/or Discipline wise reservation is ultra vires. The confusion was mainly in the advertisement. The Court observed that if the subject wise is adopted in each service or post in each cadre in each faculty, discipline, speciality or super-speciality, it not only be clear to the candidates who seek recruitment but also there would be no overlapping in application of the rule of reservation to the service or posts as specified and made applicable by the relevant Act...If there is any single post of professor or Reader or Lecturer in each faculty, discipline, speciality or super-speciality, which can not be reserved for reserved candidates, it should be clubbed and roster applied and be made available to the reserved candidates in terms of the Section 3 (5) of U.P. Public Services (Reservation for Scheduled Castes, Scheduled Tribes and Other Backward Classes) Act (4 of 1994) The Court said such an interpretation would sub serve and elongate Constitutional objective and public policy of socio-economic justice...mandated and envisaged in Articles 335 and 16 (4) read with Articles 14 and 16 (1), Preamble, Article 38 and 46 of the Constitution and all other cognate provisions.

In. *S.R. Murthy v. State of Karnataka*"[51] the question is promotion in single promotional post. In the Government Polytechnic in Karnataka though the appellant was the senior most person eligible for promotion, he was not promoted because in accordance with the roster point a Scheduled caste candidate was to be appointed and thus a junior person got promoted. Citing previous decisions the Supreme Court held that the application for the purpose of promotion was not permissible.

In *Ajit Singh v. State of Punjab*[52] the Court went into the question of seniority of reserved candidates and general candidates. The Court was not concerned with the reservation policy of the State or with the validity of any procedure fixing roster points for purpose of promotion of reserved candidates. The Court was dealing only with a limited question relating mainly to seniority of the reserved candidates promoted at roster points. According to the Court Articles 16 (4) and 16 (4A) open with a non-obstante clause for it begins, "Nothing in this Article shall prevent the State from making any provision for reservation..." and hence these Articles do not confer any fundamental right. Hence they do not impose any Constitutional duty and writ of mandamus could not be issued to provide for reservation or for relaxation

In *State of Punjab v. G.S.Gill*[53] the respondent was appointed as Junior Technical assistant in the Department of Industries of the state of Punjab. The next promotional cadre was Assistant Superintendent Quality Marking Center (Textile). But this post was reserved for Scheduled Caste candidate. The respondent's contention was that the in the case of solitary post reservation would amount to 100 per cent reservation and hence it would be a violation of Articles 14 and 16 (1). But the Court did not agree with this argument. When the respondent approached the High Court it had agreed with the contention and said that in a single post cadre there could not be any reservation at all. Thus the government appealed before the Supreme Court. The Court pointed out that the reservation was made according to the rule that is in accordance with the roster. Focusing on similar cases the Court arrived at the conclusion that the decision of the High Court was wrong because 'reservation provided to single post on the basis of rule of rotation is not unconstitutional'.

The above decision was reiterated in *Union of India v. Brij Lal Thakur* [54]. The post of E.C.G. Technician in the Grade became vacant on November 30, 1993 in the Central Hospital, Northern Railway due to retirement of the incumbent. For promotion of Theater Assistants to the said post, trade test was conducted in which Smt. Prakash Kaur belonging to Scheduled Castes and two others were called. The vacancy to be filled up was reserved for Scheduled Castes in a carry forward post as per the rotation of the roster. In the trade test Smt. Prakash Kaur was found suitable and she was accordingly promoted as E.C.G. Technician w.e.f. December 9, 1994. The respondent an unsuccessful candidate filed O.A. in the Tribunal contending that since the post of E.C.G. Technician is the solitary post, reservation as per roster is unconstitutional, as it would lead to 100% reservation. The contention found favour with the Tribunal. Accordingly, it set aside the appointment by promotion of Smt. Prakash Kaur and gave direction to treat it as unreserved post and to consider the case of the respondent for appointment to the post according to Rules. The controversy is no longer res integra. The Court in *Union of India v. Madhav s/o Gajanan Chaubal,* [55] by a Bench of three-Judges considered the entire case law following the Constitution Bench judgment in *A. R. Choudhury v. Union of India,* [56] *Commr. of Commercial Taxes v. D. Sethu Madhava Rao,* [57] *: 2248), Venkateswarlu v. Govt. of A. P.* [58] *and State of Bihar v. Bageshwarki Prasad* [59] It was held that "even though there is a single post, if the Government have applied the rule of rotation and roster point to the vacancies that had arisen in the single point post and were sought to be filled up by the candidate belonging to the reserved categories at the point on which they were eligible to be considered, such a rule is not violative of Articles 14 and 16(1) of the Constitution". In that case the post of Secretary in the National Savings Scheme Service was a single point post to which 40 point roster was maintained to the vacancy in the said post. When the Scheduled Tribes candidate was selected for promotion on the basis of the rule of rotation, it was held by the Tribunal that the promotion was violative of Articles 14 and 16(1) of the Constitution. Reversing that order it was held that:

> Thus, the Government has adhered to the rule of rotation to a single post and the 40 point roster to the single post was applied and the vacancy reserved for the Scheduled castes and Scheduled Tribes as and when had arisen, was sought to be

> filled up, when the candidates were available. Thus, we hold that the roster point No. 4 in the vacancy of the Secretary reserved for the Scheduled Tribes was valid and constitutional. When the officer available and was eligible to be considered, he was entitled to be considered in accordance with the rules and be promoted as Secretary. The Tribunal, therefore, was not right in directing that the rule of rotation to the single post could not be applied. It is brought to our notice that the original promotee died pending the proceedings and, therefore, as and when vacancy arises as per rule of rotation as per roster the same would be filled up in accordance with law.

In *Jatinder Pal Singh v. State of Punjab* [60] the single post reservation was again challenged. Reversing the decision of the High Court, the Supreme Court reiterated its earlier stand that a single post could be reserved.

The Supreme Court has categorically held in 'Mandal case' that a person, who belongs to a backward class and who becomes member of IAS, IPS or any other All India Service, his children cannot avail the benefit of reservation. The States of Bihar and Uttar Pradesh have added further conditions such as salary of rupees ten thousand or more per men sum, the wife or husband to be graduate and one of them owning a house in an urban area. So far as the professionals are concerned, an income of Rs. 10 lakhs per annum has been fixed as the criterion. It is further provided that the wife or husband is at least a graduate and the family owns immovable property of the value of at least rupees twenty lakhs. Similarly, the criteria regarding traders, industrialists, agriculturists and others is wholly arbitrary apart from being contrary to the guidelines laid down by Supreme Court in 'Mandal case'.

Multiple conditions have been provided in all the categories. With almost every category the conditions like the 'spouse' being a graduate and holding property in urban area, are attached. These conditions have no nexus with the object sought to be achieved. Since the conditions are not severable the two criteria as a whole have to be struck-down. Thus the criteria laid down by Bihar Reservation of Vacancies in Posts and Services (for Scheduled Castes, Scheduled Tribes and Other Backward Classes) (Amendment) Ordinance, 1995 and S. 3(b) of the U.P. Public Services Reservation of Scheduled Castes and Scheduled Tribes and Other Backward Classes Act, 1994, for identification of "creamy-layer", would be violative of Article 16(4), wholly arbitrary - violative of Article 14 - and against the law laid down by Supreme Court in 'Mandal case'.

Thus the Division bench declared that the creamy layer formula of both the states as invalid for being against the norms indicated by the Court in *Mandal* case.

Though the Government appointed a Commission to determine 'creamy layer', it went on to amend the Constitution so that reservation could be made available to the concerned communities in promotion also.[61]

Sometimes the executive makes rules in such a way that this sabotage the spirit of reservation. A case in point is *Scheduled Castes and Scheduled Tribes Officers Welfare Council v. State of U.P.*[62] The issue was the validity of the memo prescribing norms for promotion in State Medical Health Department. It was alleged that Department relaxed the criteria only when general candidates were to be promoted. Separate list of candidates as per roster was not prepared. Moreover it increased the minimum length of services for promotion and the selection would be subject to efficiency test. The Court held that the impugned Memo was issued *mala fide* to deprive SC/ST candidates of their chance of promotion. Hence the Memo was quashed.

The Supreme Court reiterated that the application of roster for single post cadre an appointment to carry forward rule is valid and constitutional with a view to give adequate representation in public service to the reserved category candidates, the opportunity given to them is not violative of Articles 14 and 16(1).

The questions involved in *Chatter Singh v. State of Rajasthan*[63] whether it was legal that the Rajasthan State and Subordinate Services (Direct Recruitment by Combined Competitive Examinations) Rules (1962C), R.13 does not prescribe any minimum of lowest range of marks for admission to main exam. It was argued that the object of R. 13 is only to eliminate unduly long list of candidates. Rule 13 provides that the Public Service Commission shall conduct competitive examination in two stages, namely, Preliminary Examination and Main Examination. As per the Scheme specified in Rule 7 and Schedule III, Preliminary Examinations are conducted on the subjects as per the syllabus and aggregate marks are taken into consideration to call the candidates for Main Examination. Marks obtained in the Preliminary Examination by a candidate would not be counted for the purpose of Main Examination to determine the final order of merit. The Rule provides that if the candidates belonging to the Scheduled caste/Scheduled Tribe could not reach the prescribed range of marks, there could be 5% cut off from the last range worked out for the general candidates and make the Scheduled caste/Scheduled Tribe candidates qualified for the Main examination. The writ petition was to get this concession for the Other Backward Classes (OBCs). The argument was that the reservation applicable to the Scheduled caste/Scheduled Tribe candidates should be made available to OBCs and the latter be treated on par with the former. The Court did not accept the argument. It held:

> Though OBCs are socially and educationally not forward, they do not suffer the same social handicaps inflicted upon Scheduled Castes and Scheduled Tribes. Articles 15(2) and 17 furnish historical and social dissatisfaction inflicted on them. The object of reservation for the Scheduled Castes and Scheduled Tribes is to bring them into the mainstream of national life, while the objective in respect of the Backward Classes is to remove their social and educational handicaps. Therefore, they are always treated dissimilar and they do not form an integrated class with Dalits and Tribes for the purpose of Article 16(4) or 15(4). Obviously, therefore, proviso to Rule 13 confines the 5% further cut-off marks in the Preliminary Examination from the lowest range fixed for general candidates. So, it is confined only to the Scheduled Castes and Scheduled Tribes who could not secure total aggregate marks on par with the general candidates. The Rule expressly confines the benefit of the proviso to Scheduled Castes and Scheduled Tribes. By process of interpretation, OBCs, cannot be declared alike the Scheduled Castes and Scheduled Tribes. *Therefore, the contention that the doctrine of fusing "any Backward Class of citizen" in Article 16(4), further classification of Scheduled Castes and Scheduled Tribunes and OBCs, as distinct classes for the purpose of reservation and omission to extent the same benefits to OBCs violates Articles 14 is devoid of substance.*

In *Superintending Engineer, Public health, U.T. Chandigarh v. Kuldeep Singh,*[64] the Court held that the reserved posts between Scheduled caste and Scheduled Tribes are interchangeable. It means that in a vacancy, which has been reserved for Scheduled Tribe, in accordance with the roster and the Scheduled Tribe candidate is not available, the claim of Scheduled caste candidate could be considered.

In *Suresh Chandra v. J. B. Agarwal* it was held that in case of a solitary isolated post on the basis of rule of rotation, the benefits and facilities should be extended to the reserved candidates, namely, Scheduled Castes and Scheduled Tribes.

In *P.G.Institute of Medical Education and Research etc., v. K.L.Narasimhan*[65] the Supreme Court held that reservation to single post, applying the rule of roster, was constitutionally valid. To another question whether Court could give direction to throw open the reserved vacancies to the general candidates by a writ of *mandamus*, the Court expressed its inability to do so. The Court has observed that it cannot give *mandamus* to disobey the Constitution and the principle of reservation enshrined in Article 15(4) and 16(4). The Court is not competent to direct authorities to disobey the constitutional mandate. It would be manifestly illegal to seek a *mandamus* or a direction and the Court would not be justified to issue such *mandamus* or direction to the appropriate Government to de-reserve the vacancy.

The Supreme Court has observed that the fusion of posts are constitutional and permissible and also that the rules of rotation and roster are to be applied. The advertisements are required to be issued so that the reserved and the general category candidates would apply for the consideration of their claims for recruitment in accordance therewith and sub serve the socio-economic justice as envisaged in and mandated by Article 14 and 16(1) 16(4), 38, 46, 335, Preamble and other cognate provisions.

In *P.G.Institute of Medical Education and Research Chandigarh, v. Faculty Association*[66] Reversing many previous decisions the Supreme Court declared that a single post could not be reserved. The Court observed:

> We...approve the view taken in Chakradhar's case that there cannot be any reservation in a single post cadre and we do not approve the reasoning in Madhav's case (1997 AIR SCW 3113), Brij Lal Thakur's case and Bageswari Prasad's case (1995 Supp (1) SCC 432) upholding reservation in a single post cadre either directly or by device of rotation of roster point. Accordingly, the impugned decision in the case of Post-Graduate Institute of Medical Education and Research cannot also be sustained. The Review Petition made in Civil Appeal No. 3175 of 1997 in the case of Post-Graduate Institute of Medical Education and Research, Chandigarh, is therefore, allowed and the judgment dated May 2, 1997 passed in Civil Appeal No. 3175 of 1997 is set aside.

In *State of Bihar v. Bal Mukund Sah*[67] the Supreme Court held that, appropriate Legislature or Governor can regulate the recruitment and conditions of service of persons appointed to public services and posts in connection with the affairs of the State concerned. Proviso to that Article permits the Governor of the State to fill up the gap, if there is no such statutory provision governing the aforesaid topics. For that purpose, the Governor may make rules regulating the recruitment and the conditions of service of persons appointed to such services and posts until provision in that behalf is made by or under an Act of the competent legislature, which may intervene and enact appropriate statutory provisions for the same. Independently of general provisions of Article 309, the Constitution has made special provisions for certain Services. Even if they may be part of public services, still separate Constitutional schemes are envisaged for regulating recruitment and conditions of services of officers governed by such Services. Chapter VI of Part VI deals with the subordinate Courts. It is in Chapter VI dealing with the Subordinate Courts provision is made for appointment of District Judges under Article 233, recruitment of persons other than the District Judges to the Judicial Services under Article 234 and also Control of the High Court over the Subordinate Courts as laid down by Article 235. Article 236 deals with the topic of 'Interpretation' and amongst others, defines by sub-article (b) the expression "judicial service" to mean a service consisting exclusively of persons intended to fill the post of District Judge and other civil judicial posts inferior to the post of District Judge. It becomes, therefore, obvious that the framers of the Constitution separately dealt with 'Judicial Service' of the State and made exclusive provisions regarding recruitment to the posts of District Judges and other civil judicial posts inferior to the posts of the District Judge. Thus these provisions found entirely in a different part of the Constitution stand on their own and quite independent of Part XIV dealing with Services in general under the 'State'. Therefore, Article 309, which, on its express terms, is made subject to other provisions of the Constitution, does get circumscribed to the extent to which from its general field of operation is carved out a separate and exclusive field for operation by the relevant provisions of Articles dealing with Subordinate Judiciary as found in Chapter VI of Part VI of the Constitution. The Court further observed that a particular category of post forming the judicial wings has been carved out in Chapter VI in Articles 233 to 235 so far as the question of recruitment is concerned. When Article 309 itself uses the expression "subject to the provisions of this Constitution" it necessarily means that if in the Constitution there is any other provision specifically dealing with the topics mentioned in said Article 309, then Article 309 will be subject to those provisions of the Constitution. Thus the judicial services of the State is concerned Articles 233 to 237, would override any law made by the appropriate legislature in exercise of power under Article 309 of the Constitution. Appointment to the judicial service is carved out in the Constitution itself.

The Court further stated that Article 16 sub-article (4) of the Constitution enables the State to make provision for reservation of appointments or posts in favour of any backward class of citizens, which, in its opinion, is not adequately represented in the services under the State. This provision has to be read with Article 335 which deals with claims of Scheduled Castes and Scheduled Tribes to services and posts and lays down that "the claims of the members of the Scheduled Castes and Scheduled Tribes shall be taken into consideration, consistently with the maintenance of efficiency of administration, in the making of appointments to services and posts in connection with the affairs of the Union or of a State

The Governor (that is State Government) can make no recruitment to the post of a District Judge without recommendation from the High Court. Similarly, appointments to Subordinate Judiciary also cannot be made by the Governor save and except according to the rules framed by him in consultation with the High Court and the Public Service Commission. Any statutory provision bypassing consultation with the High Court and laying down a statutory fiat as is tried to be done by enactment of Section 4 by the Bihar Legislature has got to be held to be in direct conflict with the complete Code regarding recruitment and appointment to the posts of District Judiciary and Subordinate Judiciary as permitted and envisaged by Articles 233 and 234 of the Constitution. Section 4 of the impugned Act shall not apply for regulating the recruitment and appointments to the cadre of District Judges as well as to the cadre of Judiciary subordinate to the District Judges and such appointments will be strictly governed by the Bihar Superior Judicial Service Rules, 1951 as well as by the Bihar Judicial Service (Recruitment) Rules. The plain and grammatical meaning of the words used in Section 4 reveals that the State Legislature in the garb of making law in consonance with Article 16(4) encroaches upon Article 234. The argument that reservation is intended to fulfill the Right of Equality under Article 16(1) read with 16(4) and the question whether there has been adequate representation of a particular backward class of citizens has been left to the satisfaction of the State Government in Article 16(4) and, therefore, the State Legislature cannot be denuded of its right to make such law to fulfill the aforesaid Constitutional mandate proceeds on a premises that the Governor, when frames rules in consultation with the High Court and the Public Service

Commission under Article 234 will not take into consideration the constitutional mandate under Article 16(1) or Article 16(4). The premises on which the argument is based, is wrong. It is indeed painful to notice, some times law makers unnecessarily feel that the High Court or the Judges constituting the High Court are totally oblivious to the Constitutional mandate underlying Article 16 and more particularly, Article 16(4). This indeed is a significant verdict for the policy of reservation at least in Judicial Service is subject to the 'consultation' with the Judiciary.

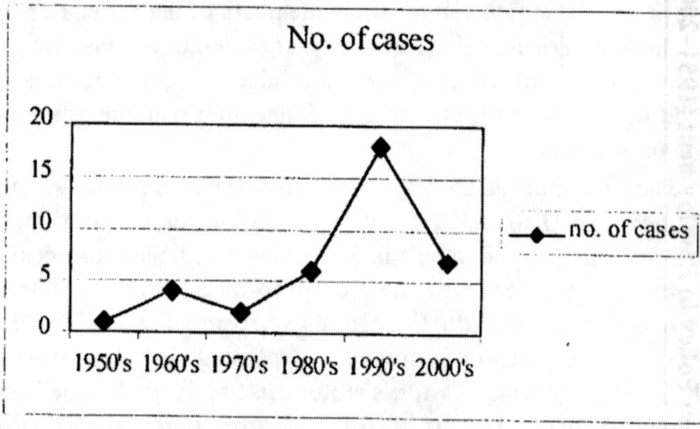

Figures 4.2.
The Trend of Supreme Court Cases on Reservation in Employment From 1950 to 2003

Table 4.2

Supreme Court Cases on Reservation Policy in Employment (1951–2002)

Sl. No.	*Name of the Case*	*Year and citation*	*Facts*	*Questions of law/Articles*	*Decision/Activism*
1	B.Venkataramana v. State of Madras and others	AIR 1951 SC 229	The petitioner was denied the appointment as munsiff inspite of having requisite qualification. Post was denied to an upper caste person because of selection based on the Communal GO of the Government of (then) Madras.	Whether the Communal GO of the Government of Madras infringed fundamental rights guaranteed under Articles 14 and 16.	The Communal GO infringed fundamental rights under Articles 14 and 16. The said Order is repugnant to the provisions of Article 16 and is as such illegal and void.
2	General manager Southern Railway v. Rangachari	AIR 1962 SC 36	Selection post was denied to the petitioner based on the departmental circular reserving the seat for SC/ST	(A) Whether reservation could be made for 'selection' posts, which are 'promotions'. And (B) whether the term 'backward classes' includes SCs and STs and (C) whether retrospective operation could be given to an order of reservation?	By a majority decision the Court held that reservation could be made both for initial appointment and promotion. The term backward class includes both SC and ST. Retrospective operation of an Order is possible.

Sl. No.	*Name of the Case*	*Year and citation*	*Facts*	*Questions of law/Articles*	*Decision/Activism*
3	T.Devadasan v. Union of India.	AIR 1964 SC 179	Selection post was denied based on the departmental circular reserving the seat for SC/Steven though the upper caste candidate had secured a very high percentage of marks. Moreover the actual reservation exceeded the legal limit.	(I) Whether the carry forward rule was unconstitutional rule was unconstitutional as violation of Art 16(1) or Art 14? (ii) Whether the impugned provision of reservation of posts for SCs & STs offends Art.16 (4)?	Majority struck down carry forward rule (4:1) 1. Reservation in a year through carry forward formula, if exceeds the limit of 50% then these are unconstitutional. 2. Art 16(4) was a provision or an exception to Art 16(1). Therefore a provision cannot be interpreted to nullify or destroy the main provision. Reservation provided under Art 16(4) not violative of either Art 16(1) or 14. Dissenting: - Art 16(4) independent of Art 16(1). It grants unlimited power to govt, in reservation. Two conditions are that there must be backward citizens and they are not adequately represented in service.

Sl. No.	*Name of the Case*	*Year and citation*	*Facts*	*Questions of law/Articles*	*Decision/Activism*
4	C.A.Rajendran v. Union of India & Others	AIR 1968 SC 507	Government Office memo of Railway Board secretariat Service, was challenged on the ground that it violated Article 16 (4)	Whether a constitutional duty was imposed on government by Article 16(4) to make reservation in favour of backward classes?	Article 16(4) did not confer any fundamental right on backward classes as regarding reservation of posts. Rather, it was a discretionary power on the state to make a reservation of appointments in favour of backward class of citizens which in its opinion was not adequately represented in the service of the States. The govt. was even empowered to give up the policy of reservation, if adopted earlier, by a subsequent order.
5	Minor P. Rajendran v. State of Madras"	AIR 1968 SC 1012	Seat in the medical college could not be obtained because of the reservation of seats district-wise. This Government Order was challenged.	Article 14 and 16 (4) and the impugned Order of the Government.	The provision of district-wise reservation was struck down as violative of Article 14. The impugned Order does not offer proper reservation.

Sl. No.	Name of the Case	Year and citation	Facts	Questions of law/Articles	Decision/Activism
6	Makhan Lal v. State of J & K	AIR 1971 SC 2206	Petitioner challenged the J&K Government Rules regarding reservation. (Refer Trilokinath case)	Whether reservation on communal ground was valid under Article 16(4) for the backward classes?	Court rejected the plea to make reservation on the communal lines as done by the State of Jammy & Kashmir because these reservations were contrary to the provisions of Article 16(4) of the Constitution.
7	Arati Roy Chaudhary v. Union of India	AIR 1974 SC 532	Petitions a teacher to be promoted to the post of headmistress in Kharagpur School of SE Railway. RB prepared a roster in which 17.5% vacancies reserved for SC/ST. If only one seat should be treated as unreserved. A reserved vacancy was treated as unreserved the reservation carried forward to 2 subsequent years. SC teacher got the post 4 petitioner lost her chance under this rule.	1. What should be the maximum limit for the reservation of the SCs, STs and backward classes?	SC set aside selection made by promotion committee. 1. Expression 'backward class of citizen" under article 16(4) was synonymous to the term 'socially and educationally backward classes under Art 15(4). Backwardness must be decided on the basis of both social and educational backwardness and net either of them.

Sl. No.	*Name of the Case*	*Year and citation*	*Facts*	*Questions of law/Articles*	*Decision/Activism*
8	Nishi Maghu v. State of J&K	AIR 1980,SC 1975	the selection of candidates to the Government college in Jammu was challenged 18 per cent seats were reserved for rectifying regional imbalances and some seats for 'social castes'	Whether 18 per cent seats reserved for rectifying regional imbalances and some seats for 'social castes' valid.	The Supreme Court ruled that selection of candidates to the State medical college to correct regional imbalances without identifying the areas was illegal. but it upheld selection on the basis of 'social castes' with reference to their occupation.
9	Akhil Bhartiya Soshit Karamchari Sangh v. Union of India.	AIR 1981 SUPREME COURT SC 298	The validity of the ten circulars issued by the Railway Board favouring SC/ST candidates is to be declared	Whether reservation for backward classes could be made against a single post? Art. 14,16,46,335	If there was only one post, the vacancy could not be filled on the basis of reservation. However, the reservation for backward classes could be carried forward to the next year. The circulars were held valid
10	Prem Prakash v. Union of India	AIR 1984 SC 1831	The petitioners were denied appointment even after being selected because the SC/ST candidates who had not been appointed had to be accommodated.	Article 16, 310 and Delhi Higher Judicial Service Rules (1970) R.28	Sub-rule 12 (2A) does not contravene Article 14, 15 and 16. Different avenues for promotion to SC and ST candidates are justifiable.

Sl. No.	Name of the Case	Year and citation	Facts	Questions of law/Articles	Decision/Activism
11	Soosai v. Union of India	AIR 1986 SC 733	A person of Adhi-Dravida community, when converted to Christianity, was denied the privileges accorded to Scheduled Caste/Scheduled Tribe people.	Article 14 and 341 of the Constitution and Constitution (Scheduled Caste) Order 1950, para 3	The impugned Rule had to be amended so as to incorporate the object of Article 16 (4)
12	Dr.Chakradhar Paswan v. State of Bihar	AIR 1988 SC 959	The appellant was appointed the Deputy Director of Indigenous medicine. The appointment was successfully challenged in the High Court of Bihar. This appeal before the Supreme Court is caused thus.	Whether only post in a cadre could be reserved under the provisions of Article 16(4) ?	The decision of the High Court reversed. SC/ST candidates should be given promotion.
13	P&T Scheduled Caste /Tribe Employees Welfare Association (Regd.) v. Union of India	AIR 1989 SC 139	The concession that was given to the SC/ST candidates in regard to promotions was indirectly withdrawn by executive decisions. Hence this writ petition.	Articles 14, 15, 16, 29, 330, 332 and 335. The new policy of promotion in P&T does not provide the advantage that SC/ST candidates enjoyed	Caste-cum-means approach could be adopted to identify the backward classes. Caste alone could not be the criterion for such delineation. Poverty should be given due weight age while deciding about the backward classes.

Sl. No.	*Name of the Case*	*Year and citation*	*Facts*	*Questions of law/Articles*	*Decision/Activism*
14	Indra Swahney v. Union of India	AIR 1992 SC 477	When, based on the Mandal Commission Report Central Government decided to reserve 27% seats to Backward classes in the Central Service, it caused a serious social and political backlash. Consequently many Public Interest petitions were filed in the Supreme Court questioning the legality of the decision. These writ petitions were heard together.	(a) Whether reservation for backward classes under Article 15(4) based on caste was valid? (b) Whether economically weaker sections could be given reservation under the provisions of socially and educationally backward classes under Article 15(4)? (c) Whether for the reservations, backward classes could be classified into 'backward' and 'most backward'? (d) What should be the extent of reservations to backward classes under Article 15(4)? (e) Whether reservations to the backward classes be given only in the initial appointment or promotions as well?	The extra advantage to SC/ST must be restored to them. They must be given those advantages as other departments provide to such candidates.

Sl. No.	Name of the Case	Year and citation	Facts	Questions of law/Articles	Decision/Activism
15	State of Karnataka v. U.B.Urushabendra Kumar	AIR 1994 SC 1528	The case is connected with the appointment as Sericulture Extension Officer. The concerned person's adoptive family has an income below Rs.10,000 whereas his natural family has an income above that amount. He was considered ineligible on that count.	Article 16 and 335. Whether a person belonging to backward class and has been adopted to another family, could get reservation benefits.	The discrimination was held illegal
16	Union of India v. Rajiv Yadav IAS	AIR 1995 SC 14	Reservation for SC/ST Indian Adm. Service men in the process of being allocated to various States is challenged; because the Govt. made a reservation for them as far as possible in their home states.	Article 16 (4) 307. Indian Administrative Service (Cadre) Rules 1954.R.5. Govt. Letter dated 31-5-1985	Appeal by the Government allowed.

Sl. No.	Name of the Case	Year and citation	Facts	Questions of law/Articles	Decision/Activism
17	Ashoka Kumar Thakur v. State of Bihar	AIR 1996 SC 75	Criteria for determining creamy layer as laid down by State were challenged.	Article 16 (4) Bihar Ordinance 1995 and U.P. Act 1994.	In the event of non-availability of a reserve candidate at the roster point it would be open to the State government to carry forward the point in a just and fair manner.
18	P.S. Ghalaut v. State of Haryana	AIR 1996 SC 351	In Haryana Medical Education Services, appellant whose seniority was ignored and a junior was promoted. This was challenged.	Article 16 (4). Haryana Medical Education Services Rules 1965.	When appointments are made to fill up the vacancies in the order of roster, the order of merit prepared by the Selection Committee gets changed. Hence appeal dismissed.
19	Valasamma Paul v. Cochin University	AIR 1996 SC 1011	These apeals by special leave arise from judgment of Kerala High Court, regarding appointment of Law lecturers in the Law Department of Cochin University.	Whether a candidate born in forward class, but subsequently transplanted into backward class by marriage, adoption or any other voluntary act can claim reservation under Art 15(4)or 16(4) ?	With regard to promotions within Class I there cannot be any reservation. Only concession could be allowed.

Sl. No.	Name of the Case	Year and citation	Facts	Questions of law/Articles	Decision/Activism
20	Commissioner of Commercial Taxes, A.P Hyderabad v. G.Sethumadhave Rao	AIR 1996 SC 1915	The appeal arises from the Order of the Administrative Tribunal Andhra Pradesh. AP State and Subordinate Service Rules -not applicable in the case of Assist. Comm. Tax . Officer.	Article 16 (4) (4A), 309 and Relevant GOs of Andhra Pradesh Subordinate Service Rules	The stand taken by the Tribunal would apply only for direct recruitment and not for promotion, is illegal. Appeal allowed.
21	Chatter Singh v. State of Rajasthan	AIR 1997 SC 303	Candidate belonging to OBC, challenges the Government Rules regarding recruitments	Article 15 (4), 16(4) and Rajasthan State and Subordinate Services (direct Recruitment by Competitive Examination) Rules 1962	High Court had held the rules void and the Supreme Court upheld the judgment of High Court.
22	State of Punjab v. G.S. Gill	AD 1997 (4) SC 0605	Appeal from the judgment of the High Court in regard to a single post reserved for SC/St candidates. The single seat became reserved due to roster point.	Article 16 (4) (4A) Whether the carry forward rule is constitutionally permissible ?	Criteria laid down by the State were arbitrary and violative of Article 16 (4).

Sl. No.	Name of the Case	Year and citation	Facts	Questions of law/Articles	Decision/Activism
23	Scheduled Castes and Scheduled Tribes Officers Welfare Council v. State of U.P."	AIR 1997 SC 1451	Challenging the Memo issued by the U.P.Government that introduced merit and ability as criteria for posts and promotions in the Health Department. Memo was alleged to be mala fide.	Article 16, 162 and The Memo issued by the U P Government.	The Court quashed the memo. And other incidental instructions.
24	Union of India v. Brij lal Thakur	AIR 1997 SC 2101	Single post reservation was alleged to be 100% reservation and hence challenged successfully before the Central Adm. Tribunal. Hence the appeal by the Union Government.	Article 16, 14 and the relevant Rules.	When appointments are made to fill up the vacancies in the order of roster, the order of merit prepared by the Selection Committee gets changed. Hence appeal dismissed.
25	Superintending Engineer, Public Health, U.T.Chandigarh v. Kuldeep singh	AIR 1997 SC 2133	Post reserved for ST, but suitable candidate was not available. Hence Sc claims the post.	Articles 16 (1) (4) (4A)	The claim of the Sc candidate was to be considered. But promotion could not be given to a general candidate and eligible SC candidate was to be preferred.

Sl. No.	*Name of the Case*	*Year and citation*	*Facts*	*Questions of law/Articles*	*Decision/Activism*
26	Union of India v. Madhav Gajanan Chaubal	AIR 1997 SC 3074	Appeal from the judgment of the central Adm. Tribunal, Bombay. A single post promotion- hence no promotion. This decision of the Tribunal was challenged by the Union Government.	Article 16 (4)	Appeal allowed
27	Jagdish Negi v. State of U.P	AIR 1997 SC 3505	This was originally a Public Interest litigation for benefit of reservation to the residents of Hill and Uttrakhand area	Articles 15 (4) and 16 (4) U.P. Public Service (Reservation for SC/ST and Other backward Classes) Act 1994	The petition was partly allowed.

Sl. No.	Name of the Case	Year and citation	Facts	Questions of law/Articles	Decision/Activism
28	Post Graduate Institute of Medical Education and Research etc. v. K.L.Narsimhan & and others	AIR 1997 SC 3687	Single post cadre reservation was challenged.	Reservation in appointment to the posts of Assistant Professors in various disciplines in the institute clubbing of single point post of Assistant Professor in various disciplines of the institute - Whether violative of Articles 14 and 16(1) of the Constitution ? Whether reservations in post graduation specialities or super specialities are detrimental to the high degree of efficiency and violative of Article 14?	Too much disparity in marks obtained, especially at the post-graduate level of Medical education could not be permitted. No relaxation in marks is permissible at the highest level in Medical institutions.
29	P.G.Institute of Medical Education and Research Chandigarh, v. Faculty Association	AIR 1998 SC 1767	Single post cadre reservation was challenged.	Whether in a single cadre post reservation for backward classes namely scheduled caste, scheduled tribe and other backward classes can be made either directly or by applying rotation of post	There cannot be any reservation in a single post cadre either directly or by device of rotation of roster points.

Sl. No.	*Name of the Case*	*Year and citation*	*Facts*	*Questions of law/Articles*	*Decision/Activism*
30	State of Maharashtra v. Kumari Tanuja	AIR 1999 SC 791	Whether nomadic tribe from Sindh could be considered as Scheduled Tribe in Maharashtra	Article 16 (4) and the Resolution issued by the State of Maharashtra.	Appeal by the State of Maharashtra was dismissed. Judgment went in favour of Bawa community.
31	Ajith singh v. State of Punjab (Ajith singh II)	AIR 1999 SC 3471	Seniority vis-à-vis promotion of the reserved candidate challenged	Article 16 (1) 16 (4) 16 (4A) and 335	The Court upheld the policy.
32	Haridas Parsedia v. Urmila Shakya	AIR 2000 SC 278	Relaxation of marks by 10% for reserved candidates for recruitment in the Transport Department. Of M.P.	Articles 16, 16 (4) and 309 Transport Department service Rules(1971) R. 11 A, 20	Article 16(4) and Article 16(4A) do not confer any fundamental right nor do they impose any constitutional duty on the State to promote the SCs and STs. It is only an enabling provision vesting direction in the State to consider providing reservation if the circumstances mentioned in those Articles so warranted and the court also linked up 'efficiency' factor as found in Article 335.

Sl. No.	Name of the Case	Year and citation	Facts	Questions of law/Articles	Decision/Activism
33	S.R.Murthy v. State of Karnataka	AIR 2000 SC 450	Single post cadre reservation- Head of section of Ceramics- was challenged.	Article 16 (4)	The roster promotion even if in a single post is not unconstitutional. Tribunal's decision was incorrect. Hence the appeal allowed.
34	Indra Sawhney v. Union of India	AIR 2000 SC 498	State of Kerala did not comply with the guidelines given by the Supreme Court. Hence the case The guidelines were declared in Indra Sawhney I	Law declared by the Supreme Court regarding 'creamy layer'	The person to be treated as scheduled caste. The decision of the Tribunal upheld.
35	Union of India v. Dudh Nath Prasad	AIR 2000 SC 525	A person belonging to a scheduled caste in West Bengal stayed in Bihar for studies. He claims the status of reserved category for his parents still lived in West Bengal	All India Services Act 1951 and Article 16 (4) of the Constitution.	The High Court decision was held wrong. Appeal allowed
36	Jatinder Pal singh v. State of Punjab	AIR 2000 SC 609	The argument of the petitioner was that the single post of principle could not be reserved. This was not accepted by the High Court. Hence this appeal.	Article 16 (4) and 309 and Punjab Educational Service (School Inspectors cadre) Class II Rules 1976 R.10 (3) post of Principal	The relevant Bihar Act was declared ultra vires.

Sl. No.	Name of the Case	Year and citation	Facts	Questions of law/Articles	Decision/Activism
37	State of Bihar v. Bal Mukund Sah	AIR 2000 SC 1296	The case arises from the Patna high Court judgment	Articles 309, 233 and 234 Bihar sate service Rules	Seniority of the general candidates to be restored.
38	M.G.Badappanavar v. State of Karnataka	AIR 2001 SC 260	The general candidates challenging the promotion of reserved candidates beyond certain level- to the level of Executive engineers.	Article 16 and Karnataka Government Servants (Seniority) Rules 1957 R.4	Seniority of the general candidates to be restored.

Promotion

In *M.G. Padappanavar v. State of Karnataka*[68] the issue was conferring seniority after promotions between the general candidates and the reserved candidates. In the instant case the initial recruitment of general candidates and the reserved candidates was as junior engineers (later designated as Assistant Engineers) and the next promotion was to the post of Assistant Executive Engineer and then to that of Executive Engineer. Beyond Executive Engineer's post there is no roster operating. That is up to level three, that is, up to the post of Executive Engineer there is roster according to which the candidates are promoted. The appellants were along with the respondents recruited as junior engineers. The reserved candidates thereafter got promotion as per roster points up to the third level (Executive Engineer). In the meanwhile general candidates got promotion as per seniority or selection and reached level 3. By the time the reserved candidates were at level 3. But the reserved candidates were promoted to level 4 as if they were senior to general candidates. This was done considering the fact the reserve candidates reached the category of Executive Engineers earlier than the general candidates. In accordance with earlier decisions of the Court[69] if by the date when the reserved candidates were promoted as Superintending Engineers, the general candidates had already reached the said by normal promotion system, then the general candidates must be treated as seniors as Executive Engineers to the reserved candidates. The general candidates had a right under Article 14 and 16 to be considered for promotion as Superintending Engineers as seniors. This was not done. This has to be corrected. Seniority of the general candidates has to be restored.

Another landmark case is *T. Devadasan v. Union of India.*,[70] where a modified rule of the Union government was challenged on the ground that it was unconstitutional. The rule as modified in 1955 provided that 17½ per cent of the total vacancies in a year would be reserved for being filled from amongst candidates belonging to Scheduled castes and tribes. It further provided that if in any year suitable candidates were not available from amongst such classes the reserved posts would be de-reserved, filled by candidates from other classes and a corresponding number of posts could be carried forward to the next year. If in the subsequent year the same thing happened, the posts unfilled by the candidates from the Scheduled castes and Tribes could be carried forward to the third year. In the third year the number of posts to be filled from amongst the candidates of Scheduled Castes and Tribes would thus be 17 ½ per cent of the total vacancies to be filled in that year plus the total unfilled vacancies which had been carried forward from the two previous years. The rule thus permitted a perpetual 'carry forward' of unfilled vacancies in the two years preceding the year of recruitment. This resulted in more than 50 per cent reservation. In 1961 out of 45 vacancies actually filled 29 went to the Scheduled caste and Tribe candidates thus raising reservation to 64 per cent .

The Court did not say that the carry forward rule *per se* was bad, but it held that the carry forward rule as modified in 1955 was bad and must be struck down as invalid and unconstitutional.

The Court observed: *If the reservation is so excessive that it practically denies a reasonable opportunity for the employment to members of other communities the position may well be different and it would be open then for a member of a more advanced class to complain that he has been denied equality by the State.* (emphasis added). It seems that the honorable Court was trying to placate the wounded feelings of the other communities.

The important aspect of the case is whether 'equality before law' and prohibition of discriminatory treatment laid down by the basic law (Constitution) of the land are more fundamental or less fundamental than the exception to prohibition of discrimination or validating 'protective discrimination' envisaged in Article 16 (4)? Between these two a balance is to be struck. The balancing of interests in such issues does have different ramifications. The first question is concerned with the political aspect of it. Policy -making is a political task. Policy is made into law by the legislature if the law goes against the constitutional provisions when it is implemented, what should the Court do?

The Supreme Court gave a favourable in the case of reservation of selection posts in the railway service in *Rangachari v. G.M. Southern Railways.*[71] The Supreme Court held that the very term 'Backward Classes' included Scheduled castes and Scheduled Tribes. The Court interpreted Article 16(4) thus:

> Article 16(4) clearly shows that the power conferred by it can be exercised incases where the State is of the opinion that any backward class of citizens is not adequately represented in the service under it. In other words opinion formed by the State that the representation available to the backward class of citizens in any of the services is inadequate is a condition precedent for the exercise of the power conferred by Article 16(4) and so the power to make reservation as contemplated

by Article 16 (4) can be exercised only to make the inadequate representation in the services adequate. If that be so both "appointments" and "posts" to which the operative part of Article 16 (4) refers and in respect of which the power to make reservation has been conferred on the State must necessarily be appointments and posts in the services. It would be illogical and unreasonable to assume that for making the representation adequate in the services under the State a power should be given to the State to reserve posts outside the cadre of services

Again the Court went on to elaborate:

The condition precedent may refer either to the numerical inadequacy of representation in the services or even to the qualitative inadequacy of representation. The advancement of socially and educationally backward classes requires not only that they should have adequate representation in the lowest rung of services but that they should aspire to secure adequate representation in selection posts in the services as well. In the context of expression 'adequately represented ' imports considerations of "size" as well as "values", numbers as well as the nature appointments held and so it involves not merely the numerical test but also the qualitative one.

Thus the Court arrived at the conclusion that;

...and if that be so, it would not be reasonable to hold that the inadequacy of representation can and must be cured only by reserving proportionately higher percentage of appointments at the initial stage.

B.N.Tewari v. Union of India [72] was about the 'carry forward' rule. The carry forward rule, which has been discussed in *Devadasan* is again challenged in this case. The petitioner was Assistant in Grade IV of the Central Secretariat Service. The next post, which he could expect was that of Section Officer (Assistant Superintendent). Recruitment is made in the following manner:

(i) 50 percent by direct recruitment from those who obtain lower ranks in the Indian administrative Service, etc., examinations.

(ii) 25 percent by promotion from Grade IV on the basis of a Departmental examination held at intervals by the Union Public Service Commission. And

(iii) 25 percent by promotion from Grade IV on the basis of seniority-cum-fitness.

In the meanwhile there were many cases on reservation that came before various High Courts. The judgments in general, were against such subdivisions within backward classes. *Ramakrishna Singh v. State of Mysore* (1960), on the ground that the subdivision restricts on the number of places each of the protected groups can compete for. If carried to its logical conclusion, this principle prevents separate reservations for Scheduled castes, Scheduled Tribes and 'other backward classes'.[73]

Some subsequent judgments have, however, permitted finer subdivision of reservations, e.g., *Balaram v. State of Andhra Pradesh.* (1972). In *Regumula v. State of Andhra Pradesh,* the High court observed that instead of fixing a maximum percentage of reservation for the backward classes, a minimum percentage should be fixed. A very significant observation of the Court is that the reservation for protected groups can serve as minima but not as maxima. It means that the provision for reservations for backward classes does not prevent them from securing unreserved places in open competition.[74]

Regarding the communities to be included in the list of backward classes, the Karnataka High Court held in *Kesava v. State of Mysore* that the State is the sole authority to decide in the matter. To a certain extent this is an acknowledgement of the diversity in what that is found in various regions in India.

The scope of Article 16 was examined in *Sukhanandana* v. *State of Bihar.* The High Court held that the Article was wide enough to incorporate both the initial appointments and promotions as well. In *P.Sudershan v. State of Andhra Pradesh* it was held by the High Court that the principle of reservation for backward classes should be preserved even if candidates belonging to the backward classes secure more than the prescribed seats in the general competition.

For the first time promotion vis-à-vis reservation became the central issue in *P.K.More v. Union of India.* The Andhra High Court held that as the scope of Art. 16(1) was wide enough to incorporate both the appointments and promotions so was the Article 16(4). Thus the Article 16(4) could b applied in cases of promotion also.

But with regard to sub-groups within the backward classes, the court held that the prohibition of each sub-group of backward classes from competing with other groups was unconstitutional. It was because this would abridge the right of the backward classes under Article 29(2). The provisions of Article 15(1) cannot support it. Article 16(4) could be applied both to the appointment and to promotions was reiterated in *Mohindar v. State of U.P.*

The judicial decision in *S.A.Partha v. State of Mysore* introduced certain flexibility in the judicial approach to reservation. It was held that that those who are getting a certain percentage of reservation, as Scheduled castes and Other Backward Classes (OBCs) could not ask for more seats than those included in the reservation policy. However the reservations for this section should not be in the nature of compartmentalization, but on the basis of guaranteed minimum. Another issue in this case was whether it was constitutional to transfer the unfilled seats meant for Scheduled Castes and Scheduled Tribes to OBCs under Article 15 (1) and 29 (2). The Court held that such transfers are unconstitutional.

The apex court categorically stated that the reservations under Article16 (4) could cover both initial appointments and promotions. Moreover it also held that the reservation could be provided both prospectively and retrospectively. Retrospective operation of law, which is only rarely resorted to, has been adopted in the case of reservation. In spite of this decision of the apex court, the Railway Trade Unions continued their actions against reservations in promotions. Again the Court was of the opinion that inadequacy of representation posited by Article 16 (4) may refer to the numerical inadequacy of representation in the services or even to the qualitative inadequacy of representation. The Court said, "In the context the expression 'adequately represented' imports the consideration of 'size' as well as 'values' numbers as well as the nature of appointments held and so it involves not merely the numerical test but also the qualitative one." But there is no data available to show that any qualitative has been made in the light of the principle set forth in *Rangachari.*

In *Abdul Latif v. State of Bihar* (1964) the Patna High Court held that it was unconstitutional to reserve exclusively for SC and ST candidates. Article 15(4) should not be interpreted in such a way as to destroy or nullify the meaning of Article 15(1), which guarantees equal treatment.

A Pro-reservation attitude could be seen in the decision of Kerala High Court in *Jacob Mathew v. State of Kerala* (1964). According to the Court if the whole or substantial portion of a caste was educationally backward then the caste can be considered socially and educationally backward class. In *Subhashini v. State of Mysore* it was held that 50 per cent reservation limit did not include reservation otherwise made. In deciding backwardness, Kerala High Court held, that annual income of the family alone could not be criterion.[75] The social backwardness should be evaluated from the point of social psychology. It is rooted in the attitude of the members of the society and again the attitude develops from the traditional belief of the society as a whole. The belief of the people in the caste hierarchy that has been built on a sort of theistic sanction cannot be obliterated with the political slogans or judicial commandments. The decision that caste alone could not be the criteria for backwardness was reiterated in Dasu *Rayadu v. A.P.Public Service Commission*[76]. The Court also observed that Article 15(4) and 16(4) are to be treated in equal manner in this regard.

In *Trilokinath Tiku v. State of J&K* the Supreme Court observed that mere inadequate representation of a class in the services of the State was not a criterion for backwardness. Whether the class of citizens was backward in social and educational terms should also be taken into consideration. In this case the petitioners challenged the validity of the order of the Director of education, Jammu and Kashmir State that promoted eighty teachers by applying the norms of reservation, which denied promotion to the petitioner who in fact deserves to be promoted. The alleged norms were:

1. 50 per cent of the Gazetted posts to be filled by promotion are given to Muslims.
2. about 60 per cent of the remaining 50 per cent of the posts are filled by Jamvi Hindus (Hindus from the province of Jammu in the State and majority of them are Dogras) and
3. the remaining 40 per cent of the 50 per cent of the posts are given to Kashmiri Pandits; sometimes one or two posts are given to Sikhs out of turn.

It means out of every 100 gazetted posts, 50 went to went to Muslims of the entire state of Jammu and Kashmir, 30 went to the Hindus of Jammu and the remaining 20 went to Kashmiri Pandits out of which one or two went to the Sikhs. The said norm was not disclosed in any order of the State. It was also alleged that that promotions were made not on the basis of merit and seniority, but purely on the ground of religion, caste and on place of birth.

The Supreme Court could not come to a definite conclusion in the above case. In the words of the Court, "We find it very difficult to come to one conclusion or other on the material placed before us. It is, therefore, necessary to call for a report before we can finally dispose of the writ petition."

Trilokinath Tiku v. State of J&K[77] again came before the Supreme Court after a year. Though the Government tried to produce voluminous evidence 'a formal order making a provision for reservation of appointments or posts in favour of any backward classes of citizens does not find a place.' The Court went on to point out, "The only evidence to which our attention has been invited is the statement of Malik Ghulam Nabi who deposed, 'that the policy laid down by the Government in matters of employment to the State services is that 50 per cent of vacancies are reserved for Muslims of Kashmir (for the entire State). Out of the remaining 50 percent, 40 per cent are reserved for the Jammu Hindus and 10 percent for Kashmir Hindus. There are a number of Government orders by which this policy has been laid down, but due to the short time at my disposal, I have been able to get only one copy of such order, which is signed by the Chief Secretary whose handwriting I know and identify.' The Court was very candid in saying that "The witness was unable to speak to the criteria on the basis of which the order was issued" Thus the Court ordered that the promotions granted to respondents 3 to 83 were declared contrary to the provisions of article 16 (1) and (4) of the Constitution and therefore void. "This will not however prevent the state from devising a scheme, consistent with Constitutional guarantees for reservation of appointments posts or promotions in favour of any backward classes of citizens..."

According to the Court an attempt has been made to circumvent the law declared by the Supreme Court in *Trilokinath Tiku v. State of J&K.* The Court observed thus in *Makhan Lal Waza v. State of J. and K.*[78] In this case the petitioner has given instances to show that 'in spite of the judgment of this Court certain teachers who had been promoted to the post of headmasters are still headmasters though they are very much below Kashmiri Pundit teachers in the list of seniority.' The Court after examining the issues involved came to the conclusion that the promotions made were based on 'communal' standards and not on the criterion of 'backwardness'. The Court could not accept considering all Muslims in Kashmir as backward. The Court said, "All the promotions made to the higher posts or the higher grade pursuant to the communal policy would have to be revised and reconsidered and appropriate orders must be passed..."

The question of 'promotion' cropped up in *R.N.Paramanik v. Union of India.* The issue was whether merit alone should be considered in the matter of promotion to a higher grade when the original appointment had been made against reservation for Scheduled Castes. According to Calcutta High Court the provision under Article 16(4) should be read with Article 335, so no reservation in favor of SCs is carried to the length of impairing 'efficiency of administration'. Hence merit should be the only consideration for promotion to a higher grade even though reservations for SCs were there in 16(4).[79]

In another landmark case, *C.A.Rajendran v. Union of India and others*[80], the apex court declared that Article 16(4) did not confer any fundamental right on backward classes as regarding reservation of posts. It was more of a discretionary power of the state to make reservation of appointments in favor of backward classes. The government is empowered to give up the policy it adopted earlier by a subsequent order.

In this case the petitioner, C. A. Rajendran has obtained a ruling from this Court calling upon the respondents to show cause why a writ in the nature of mandamus under Art. 32 of the Constitution should not be issued for quashing the Office Memorandum dated November 8,1963 which is annexure 'C' to the Writ Petition, and for directing respondent No. 1 to restore the orders passed by it in Office Memorandum No. 2/11/55-RPS dated May 7, 1955 and No. 5/4/55-SCT (1) dated January 4, 1957. Cause has been shown-by the Attorney General on behalf of the respondents to whom notice of the rule was ordered to be given.

In supersession of all previous orders in this regard the Government decided that for

1. Class I and Class II appointments there will be no reservation for Scheduled Castes and Scheduled Tribes in appointments made by promotion to a Class II or a higher service of post, whether on the basis of seniority-cum-fitness, selection, or competitive examination limited to departmental candidates and in the case of promotions made in or to Class I or Class II on the basis of seniority subject to fitness, cases involving suppression of Scheduled Castes and Scheduled Tribes Officers, will, however, continue to be submitted for prior approval of the Minister or Dy. Minister concerned.
2. Regarding Class III and Class IV appointments: in grades or services to which there is no direct recruitment whatever, there will be reservation at 12 1/2 and 5 per cent vacancies for Scheduled Castes and Scheduled Tribes respectively in promotions made by (i) selection or (ii) on the results of competitive examinations limited to departmental candidates. Lists of Scheduled Castes and Scheduled Tribes Officers should be drawn up separately to fill the reserved vacancies officers belonging to these classes will be adjudged separately and not along with other officers and if they should be included in the list irrespective of their merit as compared to that of

the other officers. Promotions against reserved vacancies will continue to be subject to the candidates satisfying the prescribed minimum standards. There will be no reservation in appointments made by promotion on the basis of seniority subject to fitness; but cases involving super session of Scheduled Caste and Scheduled Tribe Officers, if any, will as at present be reported within a mouth to the Minister or Deputy Minister concerned for information.

"The above decisions take effec^t from the date of issue of these orders except where selections by the Departmental Promotion Committee under the old orders have already been made, or rules for a competitive examination published."

The petitioner argued that this Office Memorandum violates the guarantee given to backward classes under Art. 16 (4) of the Constitution and is illegal and ultra vires. It was alleged that the impugned Office Memorandum made discrimination by making provision for reservations in certain types of Class III and IV Services only and not in Class II and I Services, and the classification was discriminatory and there was no rational nexus sought to be achieved by the impugned Office Memorandum. It was also argued that Art. 16 (4) was not an exception engrafted on Art. 16, but was in itself a fundamental right granted to Scheduled Castes and Scheduled Tribes and backward classes and as such it was untrammeled by any other provision of the Constitution. The petitioner accordingly prays for the grant of a writ in the nature of mandamus quashing the Office Memorandum (Annexure 'C') and directing respondent No. 1 to restore retrospectively the orders made in its Office Memoranda No. 2/11/55-RPS dated May 7, 1955 and No. 5/4/55-SCT-I dated January 4, 1957 and to consider the claim of the petitioner as member of the Scheduled Castes for promotion as Section Officer in the Railway Board Secretariat Service.

The apex Court did not accept the argument that 16 (4) confer fundamental right on backward classes of people. It is only a discretionary power of the State and on the issue of Government's policy of placing Class I and Class II posts beyond reservation net, the Court justified the policy. (emphasis added) It observed:

> "The respondent stated in the counter-affidavit that in Class I and II posts a higher degree of efficiency and responsibility was required and therefore reservation was considered harmful so far as Classes I and II were concerned..." The Court therefore considered the policy, reasonable.

In *Hariharan Pillai v. State of Kerala*[81], the Kerala High Court justified the reservation of seats in Kerala Judicial Service where classification was made on the basis of caste because of backwardness by and large of the members of that caste; the dominant criterion was not caste but the backwardness. Subsequent to this the Government of Kerala appointed a Commission to go into the questions regarding the method of determining backwardness and the basis of classification into backward and non-backward classes and also the quantum of reservation.[82]

Rules regarding reservation could be amended by the executive and it could not be considered violative of Article 16(4).

In Triloknath v. State of J&K[83], the Supreme Court categorically said that a test solely based on caste, community, race, religion, sex, descent, place of birth or residence could not be the criteria for backwardness. A community of people is backward not because they belong to that community, but because the members of the community are, at the given point of time, backward in social, economic and educational scale of values. The Court has also clarified that backward caste or community is not synonymous with the term backward class.

When the state disposed of almost 100 per cent of the river- bed land to some backward groups, it was held unconstitutional by the High Court of Gujarat, because the quantum of reservation was in excess of 50% limit prescribed by the Court.[84]

In *Sudhakar v. State of Orissa,*[85] the High Court examined the scope of Article 16(4). The Court said that the 'post' given in the said article was related only up to the initial appointments. However it should be observed in the light of efficiency in administration.

Clubbing together two services was declared unconstitutional in *N.Natarajan v. D.G.P.T. New Delhi.* It provided excessive reservation under Article 16(4) and violated 50 per cent limit.

In *Santhakumar v. State of Mysore*[86] the Court went into the question whether by virtue of adoption into a socially and educationally backward class, the adopted person could claim the benefit of reservation. The Court observed that this was not possible because the adopted person had not suffered from such conditions. The logic of this could be questioned. Again the Court went on to say that the income and occupation of the natural father and not the adoptive father would be considered. This again is not compatible with logical thinking, because the adopted person is going to live with the adoptive father.

In *State of Punjab v. Hiralal* the Supreme Court stated that reservation under Article 16(4) was not violative of Article 16(1). In

Mohan lal v. State of J&K the Supreme Court rejected the plea to make reservation on communal lines for they were contrary to the provisions under Article 16(4).

In *Janaki Prasad v. State of J&K*[87] the Supreme Court went on to examine the scope of the expression 'backward class of citizens' under Article 16(4). The Court held that the expression is synonymous with the 'socially and educationally' backward classes under Article 15(4). Backwardness must be decided on the basis both of social and educational backwardness and not either of them. In *Gurindarpal Singh v. State of Punjab* the Court also observed that reservations for residents in the backward areas were not permissible under Article 15(4).

The term '*Harijan*' was given the judicial interpretation in *B.C.Swain v. Secy. W.T.Department.* According to the Court *Harijan* is not a caste but groups of people of different castes who were considered untouchable. They are, therefore, socially and educationally backward.

In *K.S.Nair v. ONGC and others* the Gujarat High Court upheld the reservation made through an executive order. It is one of the basic principles of Rule of Law that it should be open. Hence the said order should have been published.

In *Shameem v. Medical College, Trivandrum*[88] the Kerala High Court held exclusion of persons belonging to socially and educationally backward classes on the basis of higher income was not warranted under Article 15(4). But this has become irrelevant since Indra Sawhney.

An interesting question came before the Delhi High Court whether by marriage to a Scheduled caste husband; a high caste woman could claim that she should be treated as backward. The court answered this question in the negative. It observed that such a claim, if allowed, would defeat the very purpose for which such reservations were introduced.[89] The honourable Court did not go into the social impact of such marriages. In fact a lady who marries a lower caste person invites social alienation and reprobation. Moreover by not providing protective discrimination such marriages are discouraged. Social consequences of such judicial approach will not be conducive in realizing the goal of casteless society.

The court in *Haripada Ray v. Union of India* upheld that the Article 16(4) related both to the initial appointment and further promotions. It was stated that the phrase 'in all appointments or posts' includes reservation for both the initial appointment and promotion.

A very significant case before the Supreme Court was *State of Kerala v N.M.Thomas*[90] where validity of Rule 13AA of the Kerala State and

Subordinate Services Rules 1958, and other relevant Rules were challenged. The respondent was a lower Division clerk in the Registration Department. Promotions are made on the basis of passing tests namely, Account Test (Lower), Kerala Registration Test and Test in the manual of office procedure. The respondent's plea is that in view of certain concessions given to members of Scheduled Castes and Scheduled Tribes, they were able to obtain promotions earlier than the respondent though the members of the Scheduled Castes and Scheduled Tribes who were promoted had not passed the tests. The Rule gives exemption in this regard to Scheduled Castes and Scheduled Tribes for a period of two years. The respondent's contention was that the said Rules and promotions made there under were violative of Article 16 (1) and (2). On the other hand the State argued that the Rules were legal and valid and the classification rational under Article 16.

A.N.Ray CJ expressed the majority view thus:

> All legitimate methods are available for equality of opportunity in services under Article 16 (1)... Article 16 (4) indicates one of the methods of achieving equality embodied in16 (1). 16 (1) using the expression "equality" makes it relatable to all matters of employment from appointment through promotion and termination to payment of pension and gratuity. 16 (1) permits classification on the basis of object and purpose of law or State action except classification involving discrimination prohibited by 16 (2). Equal protection of laws necessarily involves classification. The validity of the classification must be adjudged with reference to the purpose of law. The classification in the present case is justified because the purpose of classification is to enable members of Scheduled Castes and Tribes to find representation by promotion to a limited extent. From the point of view of time a different treatment is given to members of Scheduled Castes and Tribes for the purpose of giving them equality consistent with efficiency.

Supreme Court held that reasonable classification of employees could be made for the purpose of appointments and promotions for the reservation made under article, 16(4) and the said article is not an exception to Article 16(1), but an emphatic statement.[91] Caste could be one of the criterion but not the sole factor in determining the backward classes. But backwardness must be both social, and educational but not either. Hence the impugned government order was held violative. The result of the carry forward rule was that in a particular year out of 51 vacancies 34 were filled by the Schedule Caste candidates. The majority decision in fact did not give any clear picture regarding the legal doctrine that might support the decision. Having justified the carry forward rule the Honorable Justice went on to say: " In fact the carry forward rule is not allowed to be adopted it may result in inequality to the backward classes of citizens who will not be able to be absorbed in public employment in accordance with the full quota reserved for them by the Government." Hence in some years it may result in going beyond 50% limit.

In *S.S. Sharma and others v. Union of India,*[92] a central government regulation providing for limited departmental examination for determining eligibility of members of Scheduled castes and Scheduled Tribes was challenged. As vacancies reserved for Scheduled castes and Scheduled Tribes had not been filled due to the non -availability of suitable candidates for promotion to Grade I in the Central Secretariat, the Government decided to hold a limited departmental competitive examination confined to members of Scheduled castes and Scheduled Tribes. Accordingly, Regulation 1979 was promulgated to that effect. The petitioners argued that the Government of India was not empowered to fill up the reserved vacancies by recourse to a departmental competitive examination for candidates from the Scheduled castes and Scheduled Tribes. Instead the Government should have de-reserved the vacancies and made them available to candidates from general category. The Court did not accept the argument, for, it observed:

> Whether or not reserved vacancies should be de-reserved is a matter falling primarily within the administrative discretion of the Government. There is no right in the candidates seeking to fill the vacancies belonging to the general category to insist on de-reservation of reserved vacancies so long as it is possible in law to fill the reserved vacancies. If at all, a claim in that behalf can arise only if no valid arrangement can be made for filling the reserved vacancies and de-reservation is called for by reason of the prohibition, in clause (v) of paragraph 2 of the Office Memorandum dated 20th July, 1974 against the carry forward of reservations from year to year in the event of an adequate number of Scheduled castes and Scheduled Tribe candidates not being available in any particular year. Before reaching this extremity, the Government acts wholly within its power in adopting an alternative arrangement for filling the reserved vacancies. De-reservation as a process should be

resorted to only when it is not reasonably possible, within the contemplation of law, to fill the reserved vacancies. The process of de-reservation would otherwise be antagonistic to the principle embodied in Article 16 (4) and Article 46 of the Constitution.

A grievance that the qualifying standard for the Scheduled caste and Scheduled Tribe candidates appearing for the limited competitive examination is low was also made. The Court answered this by observing that " It is now well accepted and has been affirmed by successive decisions of this Court, that relaxed eligibility criteria would be justified in the case of candidates of backward classes."

The Supreme Court in another landmark decision[93] held that if there was only one post, that vacancy could not be filled on the basis of reservation. However reservation for backward classes could be carried forward to the next year.

The Punjab and Haryana High Court declared that Article 16(4) did not confer any fundamental right on backward classes regarding reservation of posts. It was the discretion of the State to make such reservation and hence this could not claim as a matter of right. A similar view was expressed in a few other cases.[94] It was even opined that reservation in such a way as to obliterate the equality of opportunity guaranteed under article 16(1) could not be held valid.

The core issue in *Bihar State Harijan Kalyan Parishad v. Union of India*[95] is the denial of the justice with regard to benefits enjoyed by Scheduled caste and Scheduled Tribe. The Court observed, "The appellant is rightly aggrieved with letter...from the Ministry of Steel and Mines addressed to the Chairman of the Steel Authority of India and a letter...from Steel Authority of India Limited to Chief Personnel Manager, Bokaro Steel Plant, Bokaro. The effect of these letters...is to deny to the Scheduled Castes and Scheduled Tribes the benefit of reservation in the matter of promotion

P & T Scheduled caste/Tribe Employees Employees' Welfare Association (Regd.) v. Union of India[96] presented a problem that emerged from an executive Order.In1983 an agreement was arrived at between the Ministry of Communications and certain associations of employees working in the Posts and Telegraphs Department. Consequently a fresh order relating to the policy of promotion was adopted in the Posts and Telegraphs Department. The order was alleged to have suppressed the scheme of reservation, which had been followed till then. Under the new policy, contained in the letter bearing No. 31-26/83-PE-1 dated 17-12-

1983 addressed to all heads of circles, irrespective of the fact whether an employee belonged to the general category or to the category of the Scheduled Caste and the Scheduled Tribes he would be able to get promotion to the higher cadre on the completion of 16 years. Thus the comparative advantages which the members belonging to the Scheduled Castes and the Scheduled Tribes had been enjoying were taken away and all the employees, namely, the employees belonging to the Scheduled Castes, the Scheduled Tribes and to the other categories were placed at par.

The Court held that the deprivation violated the equality clause of the Constitution. Persons belonging to the Scheduled Castes and the Scheduled Tribes in other Departments were enjoying similar advantage and only the employees of P. and T. Department had been deprived of it. While it may be true that no writ can be issued ordinarily compelling the Government to make reservation under Article 16(4) which is only an enabling clause, the circumstances in which the members belonging to the Scheduled Castes and Scheduled Tribes in the Posts and Telegraphs Department are deprived of indirectly the advantage of such reservation which they were enjoying earlier while others who are similarly situated in the other departments are allowed to enjoy it. Hence the appeal was allowed.

The Supreme Court held that reservation by way of promotion is not permissible. Again principle of reservation does not apply to an isolated post. This was in *Smt. Chetana Motghare v. Bhide Girls Education Society, Nagpur.*[97]

In *R.K. Sabharwal v. State of Punjab*[98] it was decided that when a percentage of reservation is fixed in respect of a particular cadre and the roster indicates the reserve points, it has to be taken that the posts shown at the reserve points are to be filled from among the members of reserve categories and the candidates belonging to the general category are not entitled to be considered for the reserve posts.

The petitioners and respondents 4, 5 and 6 are members of the Punjab Service of Engineers (Class I) (the Service) in the Irrigation Department of the State of Punjab. The respondents are members of the Scheduled Castes whereas the petitioners belong to the general category. The conditions of service of the members of the Service are governed by the Punjab Service of Engineers Class I P. W. D. (I. B.) Rules, 1964. The Punjab Government by the instructions dated May 4, 1974 provided reservations for the Scheduled Castes and Backward Classes in promotions to and within Class I and II services under the State Government. It was laid down under the said instructions that 16 percent of the posts to be filled by promotion were to be reserved for members of the Scheduled Castes and Backward Classes (14 percent for the Scheduled Caste and 2 per cent for the Backward Classes) subject to the conditions that the persons to be considered must possess the minimum necessary qualifications and they should have satisfactory record of service. It was further provided in the Instructions that in a lot of 100 vacancies occurring from time to time, those falling at serial numbers mentioned below should be treated as reserved for the members of Scheduled Castes: 1. 7, 15, 22, 30, 37, 44, 51, 58, 65, 72, 80, 87, 91 and so on. Vacancies falling at serial numbers 26 and 76 should be treated as reserved for the members of Backward Classes. It is stated in writ petition that the petitioners are at serial Nos. 19, 23, 26, 29, 30, 31, 34 and 38 of the seniority list of the service whereas the respondents are at serial Nos. 46, 140, and 152 . Respondent-Rattan Singh was promoted to the rank of Chief Engineer against the post reserved for the Scheduled Castes by superseding 36 senior colleagues including the petitioners. Similarly, respondents Surjit Singh and Om Prakash were promoted as Superintending Engineers against the reserve vacancies by superseding 82 and 87 senior colleagues respectively. According to the petitioners at the time of promotion of these respondents the petitioners were already working as Superintending Engineers for several years. It is further averred in the petition that respondents 4, 5 and 6 were in fact working as Executive Engineers when the petitioners were holding the posts of Superintending Engineers.

The Court observed:

> We may examine the likely result if the roster is permitted to operate in respect of the vacancies arising after the total posts in a cadre are filled. In a 100-point roster, 14 posts at various roster-points are filled from amongst the Scheduled Castes/ Scheduled Tribes candidates, 2 posts are filled from amongst the Backward Classes and the remaining 84 posts are filled from amongst the general category. Suppose all the posts in a cadre consisting of 100 posts are filled in accordance with the roster by December 31, 1994. Thereafter in the year 1995, 25 general category persons (out of the 84) retire. Again in the year 1996, 25 more persons belonging to the general category retire. The position which would emerge would be that the Scheduled Castes and Back ward Classes would claim 16 per cent share out of the 50 vacancies. If 8 vacancies are given to them then in the cadre of 100 posts the reserve categories would

be holding 24 posts there by increasing the reservation from 16% to 24% . On the contrary if the roster is permitted to operate till the total posts in a cadre are to be filled by the same category of persons whose retirement etc. caused the vacancies then the balance between the reserve category and the general category shall always be maintained. We make it clear that in the event of non-availability of a reserve candidate at the roster-point it would be open to the State Government to carry forward the point in a just and fair manner.

We, therefore, find considerable force in the second point raised by the learned counsel for the petitioners. We, however, direct that the interpretation given by us to the working of the roster and our findings on this point shall be operative prospectively.

In *National Federation of S.B.I. v. Union of India*[99] Office Memorandum dated March 26, 1970 which set out that in promotions by selection to posts within Class I, which carry an ultimate salary of Rs. 2250/- in the revised scale of pay per month, or less, the Schedule Castes / Scheduled Tribes Officers, who are senior enough in the zone of consideration for promotion so as to be within the number of vacancies for which the select list has to be drawn up, would be included in the list provided they are not considered unfit for promotion. This does not provide for reservation as contemplated by Art. 16(4) of the Constitution of India; it only provides for concession which the State can always provide under Art. 16. The letters of the Ministry of Finance dated May 30, 1981 and the subsequent ones do not amend or modify the Office Memorandum dated March 26, 1970 but merely explain it. They make explicit what is implicit in it.

The concession is that those Schedule castes / Scheduled Tribes Officers who are senior enough in the zone of consideration for promotion so as to be within the number of vacancies for which the select list has to be drawn up will be included in the select list provided they are considered unfit for promotion. The position of such candidates included in the select list would, however, be the same as is assigned to them by the Departmental Promotion Committee on the basis of their record of service. The said candidates would not be entitled, for the purpose of the said selection, one grading higher than the grinding otherwise assignable to them on the basis of their record of service. This is also the purport of Para 9 of the Brochure insofar as it deals with promotions within Class I.

In the absence of such reservation, the forty-point roster prepared by the Government of India cannot be applied or followed because the roster is prepared merely to carry out the rule of reservation. Further, since none of the relevant Memorandum and orders referred to above provide for carry-forward rule, each year has to be treated as the unit for applying the rule of reservation of concession, as the case may be. Thus it can be applied and followed only when a selection takes place. As there is no rule to that effect, the said concession cannot be given effect to retrospectively.

In *S. Vinod Kumar and Another v. Union of India and others*[100] the Court reiterated that no concession can be allowed to the reserved categories in matters of promotion. The Court said, "We are, therefore, of the opinion that so far as provision for lower qualifying marks or lesser level of evaluation in the matter of promotion is concerned, it is not permissible under Article 16 (4) in view of the command contained in Article 335 of the Constitution."

In *State of Karnataka v. Kumari Gowri Narayana Ambiga*[101] Karnataka State Civil Services (Direct Recruitment of Scheduled castes, Scheduled tribes and Backward Tribes to Class III Posts) (Special) Rules (1997) R.3 regarding 'Local candidate' is the issue to be resolved - Procedure laid down by special Rules is inconsistent with maintenance of standards of efficiency in State services. Hence Special Rules are violative of Arts. 16(1) and 335 of Constitution.

The direct recruitment to various cadres in Class III service in the Karnataka State is on the basis of merit list prepared on the basis of competitive examination or selection made on the basis of objective criteria provided in the various Rules. The Special Rules on the other hand provided entry to Scheduled Caste, Scheduled Tribe and Backward Tribe candidates into various cadres of Class III service without undergoing the process of selection. They are appointed as local candidates in the first instance and thereafter under the Special Rules they are inducted into various cadres of Class III service without going through the process of selection. Thus procedure provided under the Special Rules becomes inconsistent with the maintenance of standards of efficiency in the State Services. *The Special Rules neither provide for any reservation nor any other affirmative action permissible under Art. 16(4). The Rules, therefore, cannot be protected under Art. 16(4) of the Constitution of India. They infract Article 16(1) of the Constitution of India.* (emphasis added).

In *Ajit Singh Januja v. State of Punjab,* the Supreme Court decided two appeals. These appeals have been filed against the judgment of a Full Bench of the Punjab & Haryana High Court filed on behalf of the appellants. The petitioners in were working on the posts of Superintendent Grade I, Superintendent Grade II and Assistant, in Punjab Civil Secretariat, Chandigarh. They were members of the cadre of Punjab Civil Secretariat. Some other petitioners were working on the posts of Under Secretaries/ Superintendent Grade I, in the Punjab Civil Secretariat, Chandigarh, and were members of the cadre of Punjab Civil Secretariat. The petitioners were working against the posts of Deputy Secretaries/Under Secretaries in the Punjab Civil Secretariat and were members of State Service Class-I.

The Primary grievance made on behalf of the different petitioners, was that the policy for reservation in respect of candidates belonging to Scheduled Castes and Backward Classes, was being implemented by the State Government in a manner, because of which the members belonging to the Scheduled Castes and Backward Classes were holding posts in excess to their reservation quota. This was not only prejudicial but also detrimental to the right of the petitioners for being considered for promotion to higher grade. Several other similar writ petitions had also been filed on behalf of others, which were heard together and were dismissed by the common impugned judgment.

The State has been issuing from time to time Government Orders in respect of reservations for members of Scheduled Castes and Backward Classes.

One such order was issued on 19-10-1949, making 15 per cent reservation of posts in favour of Scheduled Castes to be filled up from amongst candidates who held minimum qualification for the posts. By another order dated 19-8-1952, the percentage of 15 per cent was increased to 19 per cent . By yet another order, dated 29-1-1959-roster system was introduced for implementing the policy of reservation. By an order dated 14-1-1964 reservation was fixed in all classes of posts i. e. I, II, III and IV. However, by an order dated 23-8-1966, the State withdrew reservation for Class I and II posts but the reservation in respect of Class III and IV posts were increased to 20 per cent . On 19-7-1968 the State Government saying that in direct recruitment the roster points shall be taken as seniority points for Scheduled Castes issued a clarification. By an order dated 4-5-1974, reservation was re-imposed even in respect of Class I and II posts and it was fixed at 16 per cent (14 per cent for Scheduled Castes and 2 per cent for Backward Classes). This reservation was to be provided by applying the roster system. The reservation of 14 per cent posts for

Scheduled Castes was the substantive provision. IN June the Government issued an Order increasing the reservation quota for the Scheduled Castes to 25 per cent and for the Backward Classes 5 per cent . On 7th January 1980 the Government issued another Order making it clear that "those Scheduled Castes / Backward Classes employees who get appointed/ promoted against reserve points on the basis of their merit/seniority should not be counted for the purpose of reservation but that reserve point should be carried over to the next point at the roster and filled by a candidate/ employee belonging to Scheduled Castes / Backward Classes so that deficiency of representation in service is made up.

The controversy which has been raised in the present appeals is: whether, after the members of Scheduled Castes/Tribes or Backward Classes for whom specific percentage of posts have been reserved and roster has been provided having been promoted against those posts on the basis of 'accelerated promotion' because of reservation of posts and applicability of the roster system, can claim promotion against general category posts in still higher grade on the basis of their seniority which itself is the result of accelerated promotion on basis of reservation and roster? The learned counsel, appearing for the appellants, took a clear and definite stand that they have no grievance or objection if members of the Scheduled Castes or Backward Classes, for whom reservation has been made and roster has been prescribed even in the promotional posts, get accelerated promotions against those posts. But the question is: whether, on this basis such 'accelerated promotees' from lower grade to higher grade in service can claim promotion against the general category posts in still higher grade of service merely because they had been promoted before the general category candidates, who were senior to them in the lower grade and have been promoted later in their turn? In other words, is the benefit of extra seniority obtained by a reserved category candidate by earlier promotion under the reservation policy to the reserved post, also available to him for competing with his otherwise senior general category candidate, who got promoted to the same cadre later only because of the reservation policy, for promotion to a general category post also in the next higher grade.

The High Court has relied on circulars dated 19-7-1969 and 8-9-1969 for purpose of holding that even after the percentage reserved in a cadre is filled and the roster is complete, the members of the Scheduled Castes and Backward Classes can be promoted against general category posts on basis of seniority. It may be mentioned that the aforesaid circulars do not refer anything about reservation in promotional posts or in respect of roster to be maintained in the form of a "running account". It appears that it was by oversight that for purpose of coming to the conclusion aforesaid reference has been made to those circulars. However, the circular which is relevant in this connection is No. 1494-SWI-74/8105 dated 4-5-1974, which had been challenged by the appellants before the High Court.

After analyzing various aspects of reservational laws, the Supreme Court said:

> Whenever a question arises for filling up a post reserved for scheduled caste/tribe candidate in still higher grade then such candidate belonging to scheduled caste/tribe shall be promoted first but when the consideration is in respect of promotion against the general category post in still higher grade then the general category candidate who has been promoted later shall be considered senior and his case shall be considered first for promotion applying either principle of seniority cum merit or merit cum seniority. If this rule and procedure is not applied then the result will be that majority of the posts in the higher grade shall be held at one stage by a person who has not only entered in service on basis of reservation and roster but have excluded the general category candidates from being promoted to the posts reserved for general category candidates merely on the ground to their initial accelerated promotions. This will not be consistent with the requirement or the spirit of Article 16 (4) or Article 335 of the Constitution.
>
> 17. According to us, the Full Bench was not justified in saying in the case of Jaswant Singh v. Secretary to Govt. of Punjab (1989) 4 SLR 257 (FB) (supra) that non consideration of Scheduled Castes candidates against general category posts on basis of their prior promotion will be hit by Articles 14, 15 and 16 of the Constitution. That view shall be deemed to be against the pronouncement of this Court by the nine Judges Bench in the case of Indra Sawhney 1992 (Supp) 3 SCC 217 (supra) as well as the view expressed by the Constitution Bench in the case of R.K. Sabharwal (1995) 2 SCC 745 (supra). Accordingly, the appeals are allowed and that part of the judgment of the Full Bench in the case of Jaswant Singh v. Secretary to Govt. of Punjab (supra) is reversed. Now the case of the appellants and others similarly situated should be considered in the light of this judgment. We are not inclined to examine individual grievances and to work out the effect

of the views expressed by us. That shall be done by the State Government.

In *State bank of India Scheduled caste/Tribe Employees Welfare Association v. State Bank of India* the reservation policy framed by the State bank of India was challenged. The same policy had already been challenged before the Andhra Pradesh High Court

In January 1978, the Government of India advised each of the Nationalized Banks to formulate its own policy of reservation on the basis of a scheme already formulated by the Reserve Bank of India for its own employees and on the basis of various guidelines issued by the Government in this regard in the past from time to time, with such modifications as each bank may consider necessary. Accordingly, the State Bank of India issued a Circular dated 3-4-1978 setting out its scheme of reservation in favour of its Scheduled Caste and Scheduled Tribe employees in the matter of promotion. The scheme was to be operated with effect from 1st of March 1978. Under the scheme so framed, a reservation to the extent of 15 per cent is made in favour of Scheduled Caste employees and 7 1/2 in favour of Scheduled Tribe employees (Paragraph 1.3). Paragraph 1.6 states that the number of reserved vacancies, which cannot be filled, should be carried forward from one year to the next year up to a period of three years. If at the end of the third year, such vacancies reserved for Scheduled Caste and Scheduled Tribe employees cannot be filled by suitable employees belonging to these categories, such reservations will be treated as having lapsed. Under Paragraph 2.3, if an adequate number of SC/ST employees with normal length of service are not available, service norms will be relaxed in the case of SC/ST employees by two years where such service norms for general candidates is eight years' or above. Where the norm is less than eight years' service of general candidates, the norm shall be relaxed by one year in the case of SC/ST employees. Under Paragraph 3.3 a common written test will be held for all the candidates including Scheduled Caste and Scheduled Tribe candidates. The SC/ST employees will be granted relaxation to the extent of 5 per cent of the required qualifying marks. Under Paragraph 3.4, interviews of SC/ST employees who qualify at the written test will be held in separate sittings in order to avoid comparison of their standards with the standards of general candidates. The SC/ST employees will be granted relaxation to the extent of 10 per cent of the required qualifying marks in the interviews. For the purpose of these promotions, the number of candidates who are required to be considered is in the ratio of 3:1 bearing in mind the number of vacancies. In order to decide the norm of number of years of service for being eligible for consideration, the number of candidates in the zone of consideration is first decided on the basis of anticipated vacancies multiplied by three. In the order of seniority, the requisite number of candidates in the zone of consideration is decided upon. The service put in by the last eligible candidates is the minimum service norm. On the basis of this service norm, relaxation is given to SC/ST employees as per paragraph 2.3 of the scheme. The State Bank of India from 1-3-1978 applied the reservation policy. In the year 1978, in the Hyderabad Circle, the posts to be filled in the promotional cadre were 371, out of which 83 posts were reserved for SC/ST candidates. The minimum service requirement for eligibility in that year for general candidates was 7 years. The norm for SC/ST candidates was, therefore, 6 years. In that year no candidate belonging to the Scheduled Caste and Schedule Tribes was found available. In the year 1979, 547 posts became available out of which 123 posts were reserved for Scheduled Caste and Scheduled Tribe candidates. The minimum service fixed for general candidates in that year was 7 years and 8 months. The service norm for Scheduled Caste and Scheduled Tribe candidates was accordingly 6 years and 8 months. Yet only 20 employees belonging to Scheduled Castes and Scheduled Tribes could be promoted. Similar problems continued up to the year 1982. The main reason for the difficulty in implementing the circular of 3-4-1978 appears to be non-availability of a sufficient number of Scheduled Caste and Scheduled Tribe candidates with the required years of service for promotion. This may be because reservation for Scheduled Castes and Scheduled Tribes candidates in recruitment were made in the State Bank of India only in the year 1974. Whatever may be the reason, by 1982-83, the State Bank of India took remedial measures to correct this non-selection of Scheduled Caste and Scheduled Tribe employees in the promotional posts.

State Bank of India, Central Office, issued a circular dated 28th of July, 1983 to its Chief General Managers in all parts of the country pointing out that there were backlogs in promotions with regard to Scheduled Caste and Scheduled Tribe employees. The Government of India had urged that efforts should be made to ensure that reservations of 15 per cent and 7 1/2 per cent for SC/ST employees were adhered to. However, the maximum reservation in any year should not exceed 50 per cent of the vacancies/promotions. The circular urged that the backlog should be cleared expeditiously. It stated, "One possible reason for this shortfall in promotion is the high cut-off point (for service norm) arrived at by the circles even taking into account the relaxation involved at present." It had, therefore, been decided (a) (sic) to relax the service limit in the case of SC/ST candidates to the extent that enough candidates were available to satisfy the ratio of 1:3. However, if it became absolutely essential to reduce the service criterion below 5 years, the matter should be referred to the Central Officer with full particulars. The circular also stated that where considered necessary, exclusive tests for SC/ST candidates should be conducted to clear the backlog of promotions in this category.

In February 1984, it was decided to hold a special test exclusively for Scheduled Caste and Scheduled Tribe employees for promotion to the Junior Management Grade Cadre by relaxing the service norms. In view of the special test being proposed for Scheduled Caste and Scheduled Tribe employees, it was also announced that in the general test which was proposed to be held immediately afterwards, only the candidates belonging to the general category would be eligible to participate. This led to the boycott of the special test by most of the Scheduled Caste and Scheduled Tribe employees.

The employees of the Hyderabad Circle, challenging the service norms fixed for Scheduled Caste and Scheduled Tribe employees as too high, resulting in frustration of the reservation policy and also the circular of 28th of filed three writ petitions in the Andhra Pradesh High Court in July, 1983 in so far as it provided that only 50 per cent of the vacancies could be made available in any given year for being filled by Scheduled Caste and Scheduled Tribe employees. The petitions also prayed for retrospective relaxation of service norms from 1978 onwards in order that all lapsed vacancies could be retrospectively filled. The same contentions have been raised in the writ petitions, filed by the Chandigarh Circle SC/ST Employees' Welfare Association. The Andhra Pradesh High Court upheld the provision in the Circular of 28-7-1983 which provided3 that a maximum of 50 per cent of vacancies in any year should be made available for being filled by Scheduled Caste/Scheduled Tribe employees, to reduce the backlog of reserved vacancies. The High Court further held that the service norms for Scheduled Caste and Scheduled Tribe employees should be reduced to five years so that sufficient number of candidates would be available in the zone of consideration for filling up the reserved vacancies. The High Court correspondingly fixed the service norms for general candidates at six years. The State Bank of India has come in appeal before us under a certificate of fitness granted by the High Court.

During the pendency of these matters, under an interim order of Supreme Court dated 22-11-1985, it was directed that no posts meant for Scheduled Caste and Scheduled Tribe categories should be allowed to lapse. As a result, all vacancies, which are reserved for Scheduled Caste and Scheduled Tribe candidates, are now being duly filled in. In fact, at one stage it seems to have been the grievances of the Scheduled Caste and Scheduled Tribe employees that by reduction of service norms (as per the High Court's order) now far too many Scheduled Caste and Scheduled Tribe employees are within the zone of consideration for promotions. Directions were sought from the Andhra Pradesh High Court to keep the ratio of eligible Scheduled Caste and Scheduled Tribe candidates at 3:1 depending upon the number of vacancies and fix service norms accordingly. This seems to indicate that the anomalies in working out the reduced norms for selection of Scheduled Caste and Scheduled Tribe employees in the matter of promotion to JMC cadre have been ironed out.

The petitioners contended that from 1978 onwards and until a further relaxation of service norms was provided for under the circular of 28-7-1983, various unfilled vacancies reserved for Scheduled Caste/Scheduled Tribe employees lapsed after the expiry of three years. Further these vacancies should not be allowed to lapse. These lapsed vacancies should be filled in. It seems to have been the grievances of the Scheduled Caste and Scheduled Tribe employees that by reduction of service norms (as per the High Court's order) now far too many Scheduled Caste and Scheduled Tribe employees are within the zone of consideration for promotions. Directions were sought from the Andhra Pradesh High Court to keep the ratio of eligible Scheduled Caste and Scheduled Tribe candidates at 3:1 depending upon the number of vacancies and fix service norms accordingly. This seems to indicate that the anomalies in working out the reduced norms for selection of Scheduled Caste and Scheduled Tribe employees in the matter of promotion to JMC cadre have been ironed out.

The petitioners contended that under the circular of 28th July 1983 unfilled vacancies reserved for Scheduled Caste and Scheduled Tribe employees lapsed after the expiry of three years. The contention was that these vacancies should not be allowed to lapse. Again from 1978 onwards and until a further relaxation of service norms was provided for under the circular of 28-7-1983, various unfilled vacancies reserved for Scheduled Caste/Scheduled Tribe employees lapsed after the expiry of three years and it should not be allowed to lapse. These lapsed vacancies should be filled in retrospectively on the basis of subsequent relaxation granted by the circular of 28-7-1983. Another argument was that the direction in the circular that in any given year, not more than 50 per cent of the vacancies should be available for being filled in by Scheduled Caste/Scheduled Tribe candidates is violative of Article 16. Both these contentions, namely, about the carrying forward of reserved vacancies for a period of three years at the end of which they lapse, and the provision that in any given year not more than 50 per cent of the available vacancies should be reserved, have been negatived by this Court in *Akhil Bharatiya Soshit Karmachari Sangh (Railway) Represented by its Assistant General Secretary on behalf of the Association v. Union of India.*[102] In that case a similar provision for carrying forward of reserved vacancies for Scheduled Caste and Scheduled Tribes for a period of three years was upheld by this Court. This Court also upheld the instructions issued by the Railway Board in that case to the effect that in any given year not more than 50 per cent of the promotional posts should be made available to the reserved category of Scheduled Caste and Scheduled Tribe candidates; holding that the carry-forward rule should not result in any given year in the selection or appointment of Scheduled Caste and Scheduled Tribe candidates in excess of 50 per cent (p. 242). In the light of this judgment, the scheme formulated by the State Bank of India under the two circulars of 3rd of April 1978 and 28th of July, 1983, cannot thus be faulted.

It is contended on behalf of the employees that in the light of the subsequent relaxation in service norms granted by the circular of 28-7-1983, which was in excess of the relaxation originally granted under the circular of 3-4-1978, the lapsed vacancies should be retrospectively filled. We find it difficult to accept this contention. In the first place any relaxation granted in favour of Scheduled Caste and Scheduled Tribe employees in respect of service norms is a matter of policy. Undoubtedly, Article 16 (4) enables the Government to make reservations for Scheduled Castes and Scheduled Tribes either at the initial stage of recruitment or at the stage of promotion. This Court in the case of *C. A. Rajendran v. Union of India*, (1968) 1 SCR 721 (AIR 1968 SC 507), has stated that Article 16 (4) does not confer any right on the petitioner and there is no constitutional duty imposed on the Government to make such a reservation. Article 16 (4) is an enabling provision and confers a discretionary power on the State to make reservation either at the stage of the initial recruitment or at the stage of promotion in favour of a backward class of citizens, which in its opinion, is not adequately represented in the service of the State.

The same view has been reiterated by this Court in *P & T Scheduled Caste/Tribe Employees' Welfare Association (Regd.) v. Union of India.*[103]

After analyzing the facts of the case the Court observed:

> From the applications which have been made to the Andhra Pradesh High Court that adequate number of SC/ST candidates

are now available for filling promotional vacancies under the further relaxed service norms set out in the circular of 28-7-1983. In view thereof, the directions given by the Andhra Pradesh High Court to the effect that for filling up of reserved vacancies the service norms for Scheduled Caste and Scheduled Tribe candidates should be five years' service and for general category candidates, six years' service appears to have become unnecessary. The circular of 28-7-1983 clearly provides that service norms set out in the circular of 3-4-1978 can be further relaxed to the extent required up to five years so as to obtain three candidates for every reserved vacancy. Even a further relaxation is permissible with the approval of the Central Officer. The provision for relaxation under circular of 28-7-1983 thus adequately safeguards the interests of Scheduled Caste and Scheduled Tribe employees and provides a fair opportunity to them for filling up reserved vacancies as they arise. The further direction, therefore, given by the Andhra Pradesh High Court can now be ignored.

In the premises, the writ petitions are dismissed. The appeals from the judgment of the Andhra Pradesh High Court are also dismissed with the above observations.

In *Commissioner of Commercial Taxes, A.P. Hyderabad v. G. Sethumadhava Rao*[104] the question was concerned with the Constitution of India, Art.16 (4), and Art.16 (4A). When Scheduled Castes and Scheduled Tribes are not adequately represented in promotional posts in certain class or classes or service under State, posts could be reserved for them. In *General Manager Southern Railway v. Rangachari* [105] and in *State of Kerala v. N. M. Thomas*, and in *Akhil Bharatiya Soshit Karmachari Sangh (Railway) v. Union of India* the Court reiterated the principle that that appointment would include promotion. The Court also pointed out the fact that "The Parliament by amending the Constitution and introducing Art. 16(4A) has removed the base as interpreted by this Court in Indra Sawhney's case, (1992 AIR SCW 3682), that appointment does not include promotion by making express provisions that when the State forms an opinion that members of the Scheduled Castes or Scheduled Tribes are not adequately represented in any service or to any class or classes of base in the service under the State, the State is empowered to make provisions for reservation by promotion. Article 16(1) does not prevent the State from making such a provision..."

In *Union of India v. Virpal Singh Chauhan*[106] the important points raised were concerned with Art.16 (4) of) Constitution of India, which deals with reservation of posts in favour of scheduled castes and scheduled Tribes and also operation of roster. The roster is to be given effect till number of posts reserved for scheduled castes and scheduled tribes are filled by operation of it. In determining the number in the roster candidates of reserved category selected on their own merit are not to be counted as reserved category candidates.

> The Constitution Bench has, however, made it clear that the rule enunciated by them shall operate only prospectively. It has further been held that the "percentage of reservation has to be worked out in relation to the number of posts which form the cadre strength (and that) the concept of vacancy has no relevance in operating the percentage of reservation." (As a matter of fact, it is stated that this batch of cases was also posted for hearing before the Constitution Bench along with R. K. Sabharwal (1995 AIR SCW 1371) batch of cases but these cases were de-linked on the ground that they raise certain other issues which did not arise in R. K. Sabharwal). Be that as it may, as a result of the decision in R. K. Sabharwal and the views/findings recorded by us hereinabove, the following position emerges:
>
> (i) Once the number of posts reserved for being filled by reserved category candidates in a cadre, category or grade (unit for application of rule of reservation) are filled by the operation of roster, the object of rule of reservation should be deemed to have been achieved and thereafter the roster cannot be followed except to the extent indicated in Para-5 of R. K. Sabharwal. While determining the said number, the candidates belonging to the reserved category but selected/promoted on their own merit (and not by virtue of rule of reservation) shall not be counted as reserved category candidates.
>
> (ii) The percentage of reservation has to be worked out in relation to number of posts in a particular cadre, class, category or grade (unit for the purpose of applying the rule of reservation) and not with respect of vacancies.
>
> (iii) So far as Railway Guards in Railway services are concerned that is the only category we are concerned herewith - the seniority position in the promoted category

as between reserved candidates and general candidates shall be the same as their inter se seniority position in Grade 'C' at any given point of time provided that at that given point of time, both the general candidates and the reserved category candidates are in the same grade. This rule operates whether the general candidate is included in the same batch of promotees or in a subsequent batch. (This is for the reason that the circulars/ letters aforesaid do not make or recognize any such distinction). In other words, even if a Scheduled Caste/ Scheduled Tribe candidate is promoted earlier by virtue of rule of reservation/roster than his senior general candidate and the senior general candidate is promoted later to the said higher grade, the general candidate regains his seniority over such earlier promoted Scheduled Caste/Scheduled Tribe candidate. The earlier promotion of the Scheduled Caste/Scheduled Tribe candidate in such a situation does not confer upon his seniority over the general candidates even though the general candidate is promoted later to that category.

If the above three rules are observed and followed, there may not remain much room for grievance on the part of the general candidates. While in the very scheme of things, it is not possible to give retrospective effect to these rules- a fact recognised in R. K. Sabharwal (1995 AIR SCW 1371) the above rules, operated conjointly, should go a long way in maintaining a balance between the demands of merit and social justice.

Thus Supreme Court declared that rule of reservation could be applied in cases of promotion if and when the State is of the opinion that Scheduled Castes and Scheduled Tribes are not adequately represented in the promotional posts in certain class or classes of services.[107]

Regarding roster Supreme Court gave an important decision in *R.K.Sabharwal v. State of Punjab*[108]. The Court observed that the roster implemented in the form of 'running account' from year to year can operate only till the quota provided is reached and not thereafter Once prescribed percentage of post is filled and the numerical test of adequacy is satisfied, then the roster does not survive.

In *Jagdishlal v. State of Haryana*[109] the Supreme Court observed that Article 16(4A) is a fundamental right. The Court was examining the question whether denial of seniority to general candidates would negate the right of equality to them violating Articles 14 and 16(1) The Court said that after the 77th Amendment Act Article 16(4A) gives fundamental right to Dalits and tribes to promotion to post or service in a state. It is a facet of Articles 14, 15 and 16. When competing rights between general and reserved candidates require adjudication and adjustment with the right of general candidates, the doctrine of violation of Article 14 has no role to play since the protective discrimination itself is a facet of that Article and it does not deny equality to reserved candidates.

Another question that was considered by the Court was whether prior promotions are open to judicial review. In this regard the Court observed that if the candidate has already been further promoted to higher echelons of service, his seniority is not opened to judicial review. The Court observed:

> It is true that Indra Sawhney's ratio on reservation in promotion became a torch bearer to the general candidates but before it could become pathfinder, the Parliament enacted 77th Constitution (Amendment) Act and brought on the Constitution Article 16(4A) as a part of the Constitutional Scheme of reservation in promotion to a post. The legislative judgment put off the steam generated by Indra Sawhney's case, (1992 AIR SCW 3682). It is constitutionally a valid principle which was declared to be so in several judgments referred to and followed and ultimately held as valid in A.K. Gupta's case, (1997 (3) SCALE 289

The Supreme Court reiterated its earlier decision that 16(4A) gives fundamental right to Dalits and Tribes in *Asok kumar Gupta v. State of U.P.*[110] The Court observed that Article 16(4A) read with Articles 16(1) and 14 guarantees a right to promotion to Dalits and Tribes as fundamental right where they do not have adequate representation consistently with the efficiency in service. Whether 'reservation' could be treated as a fundamental right or Article 16(4A) is only an exception or restriction on article 16(1)

Another interesting question was whether the direction in the *Mandal* case postponing the operation of the judgment of reservations in promotions for a period of five years is violative of article 14 read with Article 16(1). In Supreme Court's opinion it is part of the scheme of Judicial Review being an innovative device to mete out justice to Dalits and Tribes giving breathing time to the executive to bring about suitable legislative measures, if they desired and if no action is taken by amending the law after the expiry of five years

In *Hari Shamrao Nimje v. Union of India*[111] the appellants who were promoted from Data processing Assistant to Data Processing Supervisors, but they were put into Data Processing Assistant Grade 'A', which is entry grade. It was held to be not proper. They should have been put into Grade 'B' which was a promotional grade. The promotion should have been to 'B' grade and not to 'A' grade, which is an entry point.

In *Chief General Manager, Telecom, Kerala Circle, Trivandrum v. G. Renuka*[112] the respondent had challenged the manner in which the reserved vacancies had been filled. Out of the 54 posts of Junior Telecom Officers 43 were general 9 reserved for Scheduled castes and 4 for Scheduled Tribes. In the competitive examination conducted for promotion certain Scheduled Caste candidates and Scheduled Tribe candidates had not reached the requisite standard in securing the marks for promotion. As the candidates had not qualified for promotion a Review Committee was constituted and the Committee went into merits of the case and their selection and consequent appointments were made. The respondent challenged the appointments on the ground that the Government had no such power. The Tribunal accepted the argument and observed that the Government could carry forward the vacant posts for future recruitment. But the Supreme Court differed and declared:

> A reading of it would indicate that in examinations where the required number of Scheduled Castes/Scheduled Tribes candidates has not acquired the general qualifying standards, their cases should be reviewed on the basis of confidential report, the overall performance in the examination etc. by a Committee of senior officers so as to assess their suitability/unsuitability. In this case, the Committee of three senior officers of the Department came to be appointed. It had considered their suitability by considering previous records and performance in the examination and given them relaxation of marks and awarded grace marks. On that basis, they became qualified. This was done on consideration of their overall confidential reports and their performance in the examination. Under these circumstances, the Government was within their power to review the selection and declare the candidates belonging to Scheduled Castes/Scheduled Tribes as eligible for promotion. Consequently, they came to be appointed. The necessity to carry forward the vacancies would arise only in

> cases where the Review Committee considers and finds them not qualified for three recruitment years. There is no doubt that the respondents, as general candidates secured higher percentage of marks over candidates belonging to Scheduled Castes and Scheduled Tribes. But that is not the correct way to consider the cases of reserved categories. Under these circumstances, it was not necessary for the Government to carry forward the unfilled vacancies and fill up the vacant posts with the general candidates.

In *Ajit Singh v. State of Punjab*[113] the Court went into the question of seniority of reserved candidates and general candidates. The Court was not concerned with the reservation policy of the State or with the validity of any procedure fixing roster points for purpose of promotion of reserved candidates. The Court was dealing only with a limited question relating mainly to seniority of the reserved candidates promoted at roster points. According to the Court Articles 16 (4) and 16 (4A) open with a non-obstante clause for it begins, "Nothing in this Article shall prevent the State from making any provision for reservation..." and hence these Articles do not confer any fundamental right. Hence they do not impose any Constitutional duty and writ of mandamus could not be issued to provide for reservation or for relaxation.

Overruling *Jagdish lal v. State of Haryana* the Supreme Court held:

> The seniority rule relating to "continuous officiation" in promotion is part of the general scheme of recruitment by direct recruitment, promotion, etc. on basis of seniority cum merit and is based upon a principle of equal opportunity for promotion. It is only to such promotions that the seniority rule of "continuous officiation" is attracted. The promotion rule of seniority cum merit is interlinked with seniority rule of continuous officiation. In other words, only in case the officers have reached the promotional level by competition and on consideration of their cases on the basis of seniority-cum-merit, can the seniority Rule relating to continuous officiation be applied. In the case of roster point promotees, the said candidate, who gets promoted as per the roster, having not been promoted upon consideration of their cases on the basis of seniority-cum-merit they cannot rely upon Rule dealing with seniority from the date of "continuous officiation". It is not permissible to delink the seniority Rule from the recruitment Rule based on equal opportunity and apply it to promotions made on the basis of the roster which promotions

are made outside the equal opportunity principle. The general candidates who are senior at feeder level and who have reached promotional post before the reserved candidate moved to still higher level, will have to be treated as senior to the roster promotees in the promotional post and it is on that basis that promotion to still higher level must be made, upon first considering the cases of the senior general candidates.

The roster point promotees (reserved category) cannot count their seniority in the promoted category from the date of their continuous officiation in the promoted post, vis-à-vis the general candidates who were senior to them in the lower category and who were later promoted. On the other hand, the senior general candidate at the lower level, if he reaches the promotional level later but before the further promotion of the reserved candidate, he will have to be treated as senior, at the promotional level, to the reserved candidate even if the reserved candidate was earlier promoted to that level.

In *Ram Prasad v. D. K. Vijay*[114] the Court decided on the question of promotion at the roster point vis-à-vis the promotion of non-reserved or general candidates. The Court held:

> So far as the seniority of the roster point promotions is concerned, the reserved candidates have contended that upon promotion at the roster points, the promotees can reckon seniority and that senior general candidates who later got promoted cannot be treated as seniors at the promotional stage. But in view of what has been decided in our separate judgment in Ajit Singh No. 2... today, the above contention cannot be accepted. Thus, there are no merits in the appeals filed by the reserved candidates

In *Haridas Parsedia v. Urmila Shakya*[115] the question of law involved was concerned with Constitution of India, Art.16, Art.16(4), Art.309 and M.P. Transport Department Subordinate (Class III Executive) Service Recruitment Rules (1971), R.11(A), R.20 - Recruitment exam. The Rule provided relaxation of passing marks to SC/ST candidates. It was the result of policy decision of State Govt. taken in 1964 and reiterated in 1985 and 1990 to grant relaxation in passing marks to SC/ST candidates in direct recruitment and departmental exams.

The Court was of the opinion that it would be erroneous to hold that the decision of the Government for relaxation of passing marks for SC/ST departmental candidates at the departmental examination can be applicable only when in such examination, the departmental candidates belonging to general category also compete with the SC/ST candidates and not otherwise.

> The general sweep of the policy decision already taken by the State Govt. under Art. 16(4) cannot get diluted on the basis of such an irrelevant and fortuitous circumstance. R. 11(A) provides for direct recruitment on post of Transport Sub-Inspector from service by limited competitive exam. R. 11(A)(2) clearly provide that, out of the vacancies reserved for Ministerial Service Officers for being appointed to the post of Transport Sub-Inspectors, 16 per cent vacancies would be reserved for Scheduled Caste and 20 per cent for Scheduled Tribe candidates. It, therefore, becomes obvious that for direct recruitment by limited competitive examination to be undertaken by Ministerial Service candidates, total 36 per cent posts would be reserved for SC/ST candidates. Meaning thereby, 64 per cent of the posts would be available to the general category candidates. All these candidates belonging to Ministerial Service, whether being general category or SC/ST category, will have to appear at the departmental examination based on the same subjects and confined to the same syllabus. It is easy to visualize that if such posts are to be filled up by limited direct recruitment from Ministerial Staff and the examination is held for filling up all 100 per cent promotion posts comprised of the reserved as well as general category posts at a time, then SC/ST candidates would be entitled to 10 per cent reduction of passing marks. To say that relaxation of marks will not be available to SC/ST candidates if at the departmental examination based on same subjects and same syllabus, they have no competition from general category candidates and the examination is confined only to the reserved category candidates. It is difficult to countenance this contention. Such a denial of relaxation will be ex-facie discriminatory and arbitrary. It would also fly in the face of established government policy of relaxation of 10 per cent passing marks under Art. 16 (4) for such reserved category candidates.... Holding general examination for all types of candidates at a time or separate examinations for only SC/ST candidates for bring appointed to the reserved posts on the one hand and for general category candidates on the other

> wherein SC/ST candidates can also compete for unreserved posts, is totally irrelevant for judging the efficacy of the relaxation policy.

In. *S.R. Murthy v. State of Karnataka*[116] the question is promotion in single promotional post. In the Government Polytechnic in Karnataka though the appellant was the senior most person eligible for promotion, he was not promoted because in accordance with the roster point a Scheduled caste candidate was to be appointed and thus a junior person got promoted. Citing previous decisions the Supreme Court held that the application for the purpose of promotion was not permissible.

In *Ram Prasad v. D. K. Vijay*[117] the Court decided on the question of promotion at the roster point vis-à-vis the promotion of non-reserved or general candidates. The Court held:

> So far as the seniority of the roster point promotions is concerned, the reserved candidates have contended that upon promotion at the roster points, the promotees can reckon seniority and that senior general candidates who later got promoted cannot be treated as seniors at the promotional stage. But in view of what has been decided in our separate judgment in Ajit Singh No. 2... today, the above contention cannot be accepted. Thus, there are no merits in the appeals filed by the reserved candidates

In *Dr. (Mrs.) Sandhya Jain v. Dr. Subhash Garg*[118] the appeals were directed against the judgment of the Tribunal. The law involved was M.P. Medical Education (gazetted) Service Recruitment Rules (1987). The Dental College sanctioned five posts of readers. The Recruitment Rules provide procedure for filling only four posts of readers in four disciplines. In such circumstances the past practice was to fill up the fifth post by appointing a lecturer from any one of the branches. It is left to the administrative decision of the government. This was challenged and the Court did not see any merit in the challenge. It upheld the appointment of Dr. Garg.

In *State of Punjab v. Surjit Singh*[119] the issue was that the Circular letter to all head of Departments. The respondent joined service as a clerk in the Civil Supplies Department of the erstwhile State of PEPSU on 3rd of August 1951. Due to the abolition of Civil Supplies Department the plaintiff was absorbed as an untrained teacher on 13th of October 1953. On 1st January 1956 the plaintiff, who belongs to Scheduled Caste, was given regular appointment as a language teacher and his name was shown at Serial No. 72 in the seniority list. In November 1967, 55 teachers were given Selection Grade. In 1969 a further 60 teachers were given Revised Selection Grade. According to the respondent there is a reservation for Scheduled Castes candidates in granting of Selection Grade. Had this reservation been enforced, he could have obtained Selection Grade in 1967 or 1969. Therefore he filed a suit for the grant of Selection Grade to him. Suit was dismissed since the trial Court found that as per the order of 31st of May 1971 there were no reservations in granting of the Selection Grade. The 1st Appellate Court also dismissed the appeal. The High Court in Second Appeal decreed the suit of the respondent. Hence, the present appeal.

The original circular, which is relevant for the purpose of grant of Selection Grade, is the circular dated 17th of September 1956 from the Chief Secretary, Government of Punjab to all Heads of Department. It lays down procedure to be followed in selection of Officers/Officials for promotion to higher posts and lays greater emphasis on merit rather than seniority for such selection. There is no mention in the entire circular anywhere about any reservation. These instructions also state that they supersede all previous instructions. Thereafter the position is again clarified by a Circular Letter dated 31st of May 1971 from the Chief Secretary, Government of Punjab to all Heads of Departments. The subject of the circular is Reservation for Scheduled Castes while filling up Selection Grade Posts. The circular makes a clear difference between selection posts and granting of selection grade. It states that selection grade is provided to avoid stagnation at the highest slab in the grade. It implies that when an employee has reached the maximum of his scale or he continues to work in the same scale for a number of years, he may lose interest on account of stagnation. Therefore, the Government has evolved the system of giving incentives for such an employee by providing for selection grade. This is quite different from promotion to a higher post and there is no question of any reservation in granting a selection grade since that will run counter to the very purpose of providing selection grade.

In the light of these two clear circulars, both the trial Court as well as the 1st Appellate Court, rightly came to the conclusion that there was no reservation provided as far as granting of selection grade was concerned. The High Court was clearly wrong in holding that there was such reservation. High Court seems to have relied upon some interpretation given by Secretary, Scheduled Castes to the Circular of 17th of September 1956. Unfortunately, this interpretation is not on record anywhere. We, however, fail to see how the Circular of 17th September 1956 can ever lead to a conclusion that there would be reservation in the grant of selection grade. The appeal is, therefore, allowed. The impugned judgment and order of the High Court is set aside and the suit of the respondent is dismissed.

In K. *Ameerkhan v. A. Gangadharan* [120] the issue was an order of the Central Administrative Tribunal, Madras Bench in which the selection against 30 per cent quota for the post of Assistant Controller of Stores in the 'Stores Department of the Southern Railway through limited Departmental Competitive Examination held in June, 1994 was challenged on the ground that no reservation for Scheduled Caste/Scheduled Tribe had been made as required. The Railway Board had instructed that while computing the reserved quota such of employees belonging to the said class already- in the grade had to be taken if it was more than the prescribed percentage no reservation shall be provided and if such quota was less, reservation must be provided. A clarification was subsequently issued to the effect that Scheduled Caste/Scheduled Tribe candidates who have been promoted on their own merit and seniority should not be counted as reserved candidates and this has been the declaration of law made by this Court in *R. K. Sabharwal v. State of Punjab, (1995) 2 SCC 745: and Union of India v. Virpal Singh Chauhan, (1995) 6 SCC 684.(AIR 1967 SC 96 at pp. 97-98)*

However, in the selections made by the second respondent the requisite number of posts had not been reserved for Scheduled Caste and Scheduled Tribe candidates. Out of 7 posts at least 2 posts should have been reserved for them, which was available against 30 per cent quota. Therefore, the Administrative Tribunal gave certain directions to offset the imbalance caused by the wrong application of the instructions issued by the Railway Board. Thus the view stated by the Administrative Tribunal appeared to be correct and it called for no interference. However, in the application of the decision certain factors will have to be taken note of in present case. The appellants have been selected quite sometime back and the first appellant has been promoted to a higher grade. The appellants were not responsible for the wrong computation of vacancies done by the second respondent. After the empanelment and appointment of the appellants, it is brought to our notice that there have been fresh promotions to the post of assistant controller of stores at least on two occasions in June, 1995 and May ,1997. In a new section 5 Scheduled Caste candidates and 4-Scheduled Tribe candidates have been selected. The appellants could not participate in the same as they had already been promoted to the higher grade.

Now, when the appellants have been working in the higher grade from 1994 onwards, it would not be equitable to disturb their promotions. However, the second respondent will have to enlarge the panel in order to accommodate two more candidates belonging to Scheduled Caste/ Scheduled Tribe in the next recruitment that may take place and appropriate seniority be given to suitable candidates whether already promoted or now to be promoted with effect from 17-8-1994 when the first appellant was promoted as Assistant Controller of Stores. In such an event equity would stand balanced.

Thus the Court upheld the Order of the Administrative Tribunal which was consistent with the view taken by the Court in several decisions, including *R. K. Sabharval v. State of Punjab and Union of India v. Virpal Singh Chauhan*[121] .

Evolution of reservation jurisprudence has been described as 'Judicial Gerrymandering' The principle of equality, caste-class confusion, reconceptualization of Article 16, increasing the quota of the reserved seats, reservation in promotions and the principle of 'carry forward' are some of the major issues where the Court is called upon to decide.

Reservation for Scheduled Castes, Scheduled Tribes is not at all questioned. Summarizing the evolution of judicial observations, Nesiah says: "The courts have largely followed the lead of the legislature and the executive and when they did intervene occasionally it was mainly to regulate and modify, rather than to innovate or redirect policies. Except during a brief period...the role of the Supreme Court in advancing preferential policies had, up to the nineties been modest. But some recent judgments, notably *Indira Sawhney* (1993), may be heralds of enhanced judicial action in the years to come."[122] What enhanced judicial action is in store for the future cannot be predicted. But the issue of reservation has been highly politicized and consequently a judicial settlement of emerging issues will also be wrought with political paradigms.

Only a few cases regarding reservation have come before the Supreme Court in the twenty-first century. This does not mean that the question of reservation has been settled forever. The lot of the Dalits and Scheduled tribes has not improved a great deal. The number of cases that came before the Court clearly reveals that it is at the implementation level that the conflicts arise; the delegated authority of the administration is challenged and these cases confine themselves mostly to appointments in government services.

A very pertinent question here remains to be answered. If caste in fact means a class of people can a class instead of individual in a democracy be taken as a unit for purpose of reservation based on backwardness? In other words could caste be a criterion for backwardness? Could caste be considered one of the criteria or the only criterion? In the case of Scheduled Castes, Scheduled Tribes it has become almost the sole criterion and thereby a degree of rigidity has been injected in to the segregating tendency of the caste system. The backward classes too would like to have their caste identity remain intact so that they could argue for the benefits of 'protective discrimination'. This would prevent the considerable sections of people from merging themselves into the mainstream of the society.

In a serious work on 'Reservation Policy', it is observed that there is 'lack of proper datas, pros and cons the protective measure.' Again the author of the work says that both the petitioners and the government have not provided any valid data regarding backward classes. Commenting on *P. Rajendran. v. State of Mysore*[123], the author goes on to say that 'no research work was done by the petitioner to show that any of castes enumerated in the order was not backward. Had the petitioner placed material facts to prove so, the Court could not have conceded caste as a determining factor of backwardness.'[124] Government also failed to provide any reliable statistics regarding this matter.

It is only commonplace to say that continuing the caste-based reservation would only perpetuate the caste system and individual's merit would be disregarded to the disadvantage of the society as a whole. Justice VR Krishna Iyer rightly pointed out when he said that a lasting solution to the issue of backwardness would come 'only from improvement of social environment, added educational facilities and cross-fertilization of castes by marriages sponsored as a massive State programme.'[125]

From the principle of substantial equality to license to increase quota of reservation and to the reservation at the promotional stage and 'carry forward' principle what the judicial decisions have revealed is described as Judicial gerrymandering.[126] But what was the reason for the Judiciary to indulge in such a Gerrymandering? Has Judiciary been able to offer an appropriate proposition to the executive in this regard? Can Judiciary be portrayed 'active' or whether Judiciary has been following what is 'politically correct'.

The reasons why Judiciary has indulged in gerrymandering can be summarised in the following way: the philosophy of Judges might influence their thinking, the Parliaments response to judicial pronouncements has often been by way of amendments to the Constitution and this reduced the leeway that judges look forward to when they interpret law and finally the Court often finds itself entrapped by caste based backwardness vis-à-vis backwardness-especially economic backwardness - of the individuals concerned.

Hegde.J invoked a doctrine of substantial equality. The voice of an activist judge is heard when he says:

> Advantages secured due to historical reasons cannot be considered as fundamental rights guaranteed by the Constitution. The nation's interests will be best served - taking a long-range view-if the backward classes are helped to march forward and take their places in a line with the advanced sections of the people.[127]

An effective monitoring mechanism to study the impact of protective discrimination and the judgments based on it is very essential. A periodical review of the progress in the implementation of the policy of reservation is necessary in the interests of the society in general. Without such a mechanism the laws and regulations and judgments would not be of any use and the realization of an egalitarian society would continue to be a Utopia.

Protective discrimination is justified to a greater extent in the area of education; but the same cannot be justified in the services for efficiency should not suffer. The Constitutional provision regarding this is very clear. But unfortunately the very talk of efficiency is resented. This will justify the need for assessing the impact of reservation upon administration.

Another important question is why the Scheduled Castes, Scheduled Tribes and other backward classes have not made economic progress as expected. A recent study of the conditions in three states clearly reveals that "the assistance has not narrowed the differentials in the economic conditions between the caste groups in the state."[128]

Moreover the Scheduled Castes, Scheduled Tribes and other backward communities have been engaged in vocations in which they have acquired much expertise.

Thus it would be better if they were given opportunities to develop their own specialized skills. This does not mean all members of a community should engage themselves in a particular vocation. They may be provided with opportunity either to follow their traditional vocation and make innovations in it or to follow a vocation in accordance with their aptitude. The focus should gradually be shifted from community to individual. Only then could a casteless society be achieved.

Miscellaneous

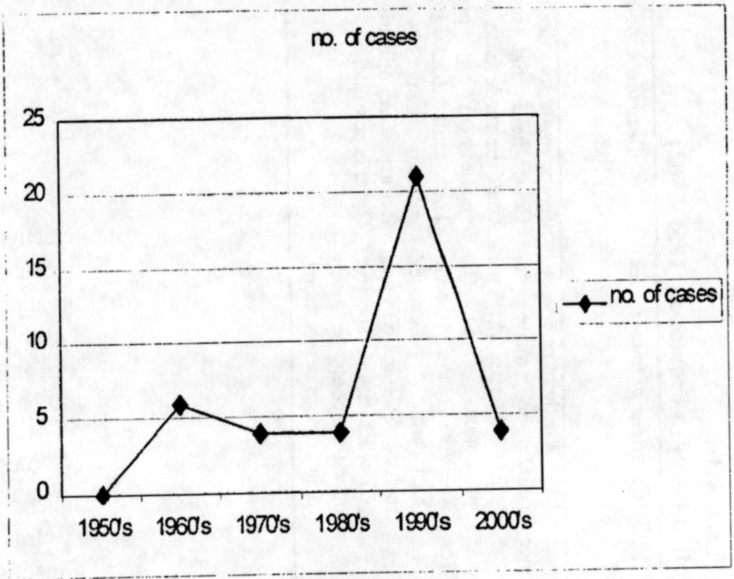

Figure 4.3.

The Trend of Supreme Court cases on Reservation in Promotions from 1950 to 2003

Table 4.3

Supreme Court Cases on Reservation Policy in Promotion (1951–2002)

Sl. No.	*Name of the Case*	*Year and citation*	*Facts*	*Questions of law/Articles*	*Decision/Activism*
1.	General manager Southern Railway v. Rangachari	AIR 1962 SC 36	Selection post was denied to the petitioner based on the departmental circular reserving the seat for SC/ST	(A) Whether reservation could be made for 'selection' posts, which are 'promotions'. And (B) whether the term 'backward classes' includes SCs and STs and (C) whether retrospective operation could be given to an order of reservation?	By a majority decision the Court held that reservation could be made both for initial appointment and promotion. The term backward class includes both SC and ST. Retrospective operation of an Order is possible.

Sl. No.	*Name of the Case*	*Year and citation*	*Facts*	*Questions of law/Articles*	*Decision/Activism*
2.	T.Devadasan v. Union of India.	AIR 1964 SC 179	Selection post was denied based on the departmental circular reserving the seat for SC/Steven though the upper caste candidate had secured a very high percentage of marks. Moreover the actual reservation exceeded the legal limit.	(I) Whether the carry forward rule was unconstitutional rule was unconstitutional as violation of Art 16(1) or Art 14? (ii) Whether the impugned provision of reservation of posts for SCs & STs offends Art.16 (4)?	Majority struck down carry forward rule (4:1) 1) Reservation in a year through carry forward formula, if it \exceeds the limit of 50% then it is unconstitutional. 2. Art 16(4) was a provision or an exception to Art 16(1). Therefore a provision cannot be interpreted to nullify or destroy the main provision. Reservation provided under Art 16(4) not violative of either Art 16(1) or 14. Dissenting: - Art 16(4) independent of Art 16(1). It grants unlimited power to govt, in reservation. Two conditions are that there must be backward citizens and they are not adequately represented inservice.

Sl. No.	*Name of the Case*	*Year and citation*	*Facts*	*Questions of law/Articles*	*Decision/Activism*
3.	B.N.Tewari v. Union of India	AIR 1965 SC 1430	If sufficient number of reserved candidates were not available, the numbers of vacancies were to be carried forward. This 'carry forward' rule was challenged because the petitioner was denied of promotion from Grade IV Assistant to Section Officer.	Articie 16 (4) and the Rule regarding 'carry forward'	Carry forward Rule as modified in 1955 was held invalid. and unconstitutional.
4.	Triloki Nath Tiku v. State of J & K	AIR 1967 SC 1283	Reservation based on religion-between Hindus and Muslims- was challenged for the petitioner was denied promotion to a gazetted rank.	(I) Whether backward classes under 16(4) could only be based on the sole criterion of inadequate representation in state? (ii) What percentage of reservation for the backward classes was reasonable?	(I) Merely inadequate representation of a class in service of the state not criterion of backwardness. Whether the class of citizens were backward in social and educational terms should also be taken into consideration. (ii) Provision for reservation should be less that 50%.

Sl. No.	Name of the Case	Year and citation	Facts	Questions of law/Articles	Decision/Activism
5.	C.A.Rajendran v. Union of India & Others	AIR 1968 SC 507	Government Office memo of Railway Board secretariat Service, was challenged on the ground that it violated Article 16 (4)	Whether a constitutional duty was imposed on government by Article 16(4) to make reservation in favour of backward classes?	Article 16(4) did not confer any fundamental right on backward classes as regarding reservation of posts. Rather, it was a discretionary power on the state to make a reservation of appointments in favour of backward class of citizens which in its opinion was not adequately represented in the service of the States. The government was even empowered to give up the policy of reservation, if adopted earlier, by a subsequent order.
6.	Triloki Nath Tiku v. State of J & K	AIR 1969 SC 1	Promotion was denied because of the improper order of the government.	Relevant orders of the Government of J&K and Article 16 of the Constitution.	Government Orders were vague and contrary to the provisions in Article 16 (1) and (4)

Sl. No.	*Name of the Case*	*Year and citation*	*Facts*	*Questions of law/Articles*	*Decision/Activism*
7.	Hiralal v. State of Punjab	AIR 1971 SC1777	The respondent was denied promotion and a person belonging to Scheduled caste and junior to the respondent was promoted. Hence the Government rule of reservation was challenged.	Whether the reservation made under Article 16(4) offended Article 16(1) ?	Reservation of appointments under article 16(4) could not be struck down on hypothetical grounds or on imaginary possibilities, because reservations under article 16(4) were not violative of Article 16(1).
8.	Makhan Lal v. State of J & K	AIR 1971 SC 2206	Petitioner challenged the J&K Government Rules regarding reservation. (Refer Trilokinath case)	Whether reservation on communal ground was valid under Article 16(4) for the backward classes?	Court rejected the plea to make reservation on the communal lines as done by the State of Jammu & Kashmir because these reservations were contrary to the provisions of Article 16(4) of the Constitution.

Sl. No.	Name of the Case	Year and citation	Facts	Questions of law/Articles	Decision/Activism
9.	Janaki Prasad v. State of J & K	AIR 1973 SC 930	Equal treatment denied in regard to reversion owing toreservation made under the government orders in promotion as headmasters. The reservation order comes under the protection of Article 16 (4).	(I) What was the scope of expression backward class of citizens under Art.16(4)	SC set aside selection made by promotion committee. 1. Expression 'backward class of citizen" under article 16(4) was synonymous to the term 'socially and educationally backward classes under Art 15(4). Backwardness must be decided on the basis of both social and educational backwardness and net either of them.
10.	N.M.Thomas v. State of Kerala	AIR 1976 SC 490	Promotion in the service denied because of the reservation rules.	(a) Whether classification among the backward classes could be made for the reservations under Article 16(4) (b) Whether Article 16(4) was an exception to Article 16(1) ?	(a) Court held that a reasonable classification of employees could be made for the purpose of appointment and promotions for the reservations made under Article 16(4). (b) The Article 16(4) was not an exception to the Article 16(1) but an emphatic statement.

Sl. No.	*Name of the Case*	*Year and citation*	*Facts*	*Questions of law/Articles*	*Decision/Activism*
11.	Akhil Bhartiya Soshit Karamchari Sangh v. Union of India.	AIR 1981 SC 298	The validity of the ten circulars issued by the Railway Board favouring SC/ST candidates is to be declared	Whether reservation for backward classes could be made against a single post ? Art. 14,16,46,335	If there was only one post, the vacancy could not be filled on the basis of reservation. However, the reservation for backward classes could be carried forward to the next year. The circulars were held valid
12.	S.S.Sharma v. Union of India	AIR 1981 SC 588	Denied the opportunity for promotion because of departmental test limited to Scheduled castes and Scheduled Tribes candidates. Hence the relevant Rule was challenged.	Article 14, 15 and 16 and The Central Secretariat Service Rules (1962) R. 12 {2A	Sub-rule 12 (2A) does not contravene Article 14, 15 and 16. Different avenues for promotion to SC and ST candidates are justifiable.

Sl. No.	Name of the Case	Year and citation	Facts	Questions of law/Articles	Decision/Activism
13.	Bihar State Harijan Kalyan parishad v. Un ion of India	AIR 1985 SC 983	The decision of Steel Authority of India that resulted in the denial of opportunity to SC/ST candidates.	Official letters that practically denied promotion to SC/ST candidates Articles 309 and 335 and the relevant Presidential directive to Chief Executives.	The decision of the High Court reversed. SC/ST candidates should be given promotion.
14.	P&T Scheduled Caste /Tribe Employees Welfare Association (Regd.) v. Union of India	AIR 1989 SC 139	The concession that was given to the SC/ST candidates in regard to promotions was indirectly withdrawn by executive decisions. Hence this writ petition.	Articles 14, 15, 16, 29, 330, 332 and 335. The new policy of promotion in P&T does not provide the advantage that SC/ST candidates enjoyed	The extra advantage to SC/ST must be restored to them. They must be given those advantages as other departments provide to such candidates.
15.	Smt. Chetan Dilip Motghare v. Bhide Girls Education society,nagpur	AIR 1994 SC 1917	The petitioner claims that the single post of 'principal' is to be reserved. It should be considered promotional post and benefit of reservation is to given.	Articles 14 and 16 (4)	In the present case reserving single post would be unconstitutional as principle of reservation would not apply in the case of an isolated post

Sl. No.	Name of the Case	Year and citation	Facts	Questions of law/Articles	Decision/Activism
16.	Vishwas Anna Sawant v. Municipal corporation of Greater Bombay	AIR 1994 SC 2408	M was given promotion when he approached the High Court. He was an employee belonged to Backward class. Another employee who was similarly placed was denied promotion.	Articles 14 and 16.	The discrimination was held illegal
17.	R.K. Sabharwal and others v. State of Punjab	1995 SC 1371	Petitioners who belonged to general category challenged the validity of the Rules of Promotion in favour of SC/ST candidates in Punjab Service Engineers PWD Rules	Article 16 (4) and the Roster point fixed by the government. The Punjab Service of Engineers Class I.P.W.D. (I.B.) Rules	In the event of non-availability of a reserve candidate at the roster point it would be open to the State government to carry forward the point in a just and fair manner.
18.	National Federation of SBI v. Union of India	AIR 1995 SC 1457	Promotion by selection within Class I- Employees of SC/ST	Article 16 (4) and the relevant Official Memorandum.	With regard to promotions within Class I there cannot be any reservation. Only concession could be allowed.

Sl. No.	Name of the Case	Year and citation	Facts	Questions of law/Articles	Decision/Activism
19.	State of Karnataka v. Kumari Gowri narayana ambiga	AIR 1995 SC 1691	Special Rule providing for appointment only local candidates of SC/ST.	Article 16 (4) and 309 and Karnataka State Civil Services (Direct recruitment of SC/ST) to Class III posts.	High Court had held the rules void and the Supreme Court upheld the judgment of High Court.
20.	P.S. Ghalaut v. State of Haryana	AIR 1996 SC 351	In Haryana Medical Education Services, appellant whose seniority was ignored and a junior was promoted. This was challenged.	Article 16 (4). Haryana Medical Education Services Rules 1965.	When appointments are made to fill up the vacancies in the order of roster, the order of merit prepared by the Selection Committee gets changed. Hence appeal dismissed.

Sl. No.	*Name of the Case*	*Year and citation*	*Facts*	*Questions of law/Articles*	*Decision/Activism*
21.	Union of India v Virpal Singh Chauhan	AIR 1996 SC448	This appeal is against the judgment of the Tribunal regarding seniority vis-a -vis promotion.	question of claim of seniority in higher grade by the reserved candidates who obtained promotion by reservation	Even if SC / ST candidate is promoted earlier by virtue of rule of reservation/roster than his senior general candidate and the Senior general candidate regains his seniority over such earlier promoted SCs/STs candidate. The earlier promotion of the SC/ST candidate in such a situation does not confer upon him seniority over the general candidates even though the general candidates is promoted later to that category.
22.	S.Vinodkumar v. Union of India	1996 SOL case No. 237	The promotion of SC/ST candidates based on the relaxed evaluation norms questioned.	Whether reservation in eligibility conditions	No relaxation in the matter of qualifying standards where qualifying exam is held to determine the fitness of the candidates for promotion. A provision for lower qualifying marks or lesser level of evaluation is not permissible in the matter of promotions

Sl. No.	Name of the Case	Year and citation	Facts	Questions of law/Articles	Decision/Activism
23.	Ajith Singh Januaja v State of Punjab (Ajith Singh I)	**AIR** 1996 SC 1189	Appeal file against the judgment of Punjab and Haryana High Court. Government Rules regarding appointments and promotion between general category and reserved category are challenged.D51	whether a person belonging to scheduled caste or backward caste (SC or BC) can claim a seniority in promotion in general category in the higher grade when he reached the higher grade by virtue of reservation in the lower grade (roster system).	The members of the SC or BC class who have been appointed or promoted on the basis of reservation and system of roster cannot claim promotion against general category posts in the higher grade ,on the their seniority being achieved in the lower grade because of accelerated promotion .The equality principle requires exclusion of the factor of extra weightage of earlier promotion to a reserved category candidate because of reservation alone, when he competes for further promotion to a general category with a general category candidate ,senior to him in the panel. Art 16(4) reservation gives accelerated promotion but not accelerated consequential seniority.

Sl. No.	*Name of the Case*	*Year and citation*	*Facts*	*Questions of law/Articles*	*Decision/Activism*
24.	State Bank of India Scheduled Caste/ Tribe Employees Welfare Association v. State Bank of India	AIR 1996 SC 1838	The Association challenged the reservation policy framed by the State bank of India.	Article 16 (5). State Bank of India Act 1955 S. 43	The Court upheld the policy.
25.	Commissioner of Commercial Taxes, A.P Hyderabad v. G.Sethumadhave Rao	AIR 1996 SC 1915	The appeal arises from the Order of the Administrative Tribunal Andhra Pradesh. AP State and Subordinate Service Rules -not applicable in the case of Assist. Comm. Tax . Officer.	Article 16 (4) (4A), 309 and Relevant GOs of Andhra Pradesh Subordinate Service Rules	The stand taken by the Tribunal would apply only for direct recruitment and not for promotion. is illegal. Appeal allowed.

Sl. No.	Name of the Case	Year and citation	Facts	Questions of law/Articles	Decision/Activism
26.	Ashok Kumar Gupta v. State of U.P	1997 5 SCC 201	The pctitioners seek writ of mandamus to restrain the State (first respondent) from giving effect to the promotion of respondents 2 to 10	Whether right to promotion to Dalits and Tribes is constitutionally valid?	By virtue of Constitution amendment in Art. 16(4A), promotion is a fundamental right to the SCs and STs. Article 16 (4A) read with Articles 16 (1) and 14 guarantees a right to promotion to Dalits and Tribes as fundamental right where they not have adequate representation consistently with the efficiency in administration.
27.	Scheduled Castes and Scheduled Tribes Officers Welfare Council v. State of U.P."	AIR 1997 SUPREME COURT 1451	Challenging the Memo issued by the U.P. Government that introduced merit and ability as criteria for posts and promotions in the Health Department. Memo was alleged to be mala fide.	Article 16, 162 and The Memo issued by the U P Government.	The Court quashed the memo. and other incidental instructions.

Sl. No.	*Name of the Case*	*Year and citation*	*Facts*	*Questions of law/Articles*	*Decision/Activism*
28.	Union of India v. Brij lal Thakur	AIR 1997 SC 2101	Single post reservation was alleged to be 100% reservation and hence challenged successfully before the Central Adm. Tribunal. Hence the appeal by the Union Government.	Article 16, 14 and the relevant Rules.	The roster promotion even if in a single post is not unconstitutional. Tribunal's decision was incorrect. Hence the appeal allowed.
29.	Superintending Engineer, Public Health, U.T.Chandigarh v. Kuldeep Singh	AIR 1997 SC 2133	Post reserved for ST, but suitable candidate was not available. Hence Sc claims the post.	Articles 16 (1) (4) (4A)	The claim of the Sc candidate was to be considered. But promotion could not be given to a general candidate and eligible SC candidate was to be preferred.
30.	Chief General Manager, Telecom, Kerala Circle, Trivandrum v. G.Renuka	AIR 1997 SC 2138	Respondent challenged the power of the Government in promoting SC/ST candidates after reviewing selection.	Article 16 and the decision of the Central Adm: Tribunal.	Government has the power to review the selection.

Sl. No.	*Name of the Case*	*Year and citation*	*Facts*	*Questions of law/Articles*	*Decision/Activism*
31.	Jagdish lal v. Union of India	AIR 1997 SC 2366	Special leave arising from Division bench Judgment of P&H High Court. General candidate Challenging the promotion of the reserved candidates	Art. 16, 16 (4A) and 14	By virtue of Constitution amendment in Art. 16(4A), promotion is a fundamental right to the SCs and STs
32.	Suresh Chandra v. J.B.Agarwal	AIR 1997 SC 2487	Special leave arising from Bihar High Court judgment against single post reservation in connection with promotion.	Article 16 (4)	Leave granted Rule of roster held valid.
33.	Union of India v. Madhav Gajanan Chaubal	AIR 1997 SUPREME COURT 3074	Appeal from the judgment of the central Adm. Tribunal, Bombay. A single post promotion- hence no promotion. This decision of the Tribunal was challenged by the Union Government.	Article 16 (4)	Appeal allowed

Sl. No.	Name of the Case	Year and citation	Facts	Questions of law/Articles	Decision/Activism
34.	Ajith Singh v. State of Punjab (Ajith Singh II)	AIR 1999 SC 3471	Seniority vis-à-vis promotion of the reserved candidate challenged	Article 16 (1) 16 (4) 16 (4A) and 335	Article 16(4) and Article 16(4A) do not confer any fundamental right nor do they impose any constitutional duty on the State to promote the SCs and STs. It is only an enabling provision vesting direction in the State to consider providing reservation if the circumstances mentioned in those Articles so warranted and the court also linked up 'efficiency' factor as found in Article 335.
35.	Ram Prasad v. D.K.Vijay	AIR 1999 SC 3563	The Special Leave Petition arises from the judgment of Rajasthan High Court.	Article 16, 309. Rajasthan Police Service Rules (1954) R.. 8 and 33 as amended on 1-4-1997.	Amendment made valid. Guidelines regarding fixing seniority between general candidate and reserved candidates

Sl. No.	Name of the Case	Year and citation	Facts	Questions of law/Articles	Decision/Activism
36.	Dr. (Mrs.) Sandhya Jain v. Dr. Subhash Garg	AIR 2000 SC 29	The Dental college sanctioned five posts of readers The Recruitment Rules provide procedure for filling only four posts of readers in four disciplines. In such circumstances the past practice was to fill up the fifth post by appointing a lecturer from any one of the branches. It is left to the administrative decision of the government. This was challenged and the Court did not see any merit in the challenge.	Art. 16. The law involved was M.P. Medical Education (gazetted) Service Recruitment Rules (1987).	It is left to the administrative decision of the government.Dr. Garg's appointment held valid
37.	Haridas Parsedia v. Urmila Shakya	AIR 2000 SC 278	Relaxation of marks by 10% for reserved candidates for recruitment in the Transport Department. Of M.P.	Articles 16, 16 (4) and 309 Transport Department service Rules(1971) R. 11 A, 20	Relaxation held valid

Sl. No.	Name of the Case	Year and citation	Facts	Questions of law/Articles	Decision/Activism
38.	S.R.Murthy v. State of Karnataka	AIR 2000 SC 450	Single post cadre reservation- Head of section of Ceramics- was challenged.	Article 16 (4)	Reservation held invalid.
39.	M.G.Badappanavar v. State of Karnataka	AIR 2001 SUPREME COURT 260	The general candidates challenging the promotion of reserved candidates beyond certain level- to the level of Executive engineers.	Article 16 and Karnataka Government Servants (Seniority) Rules 1957 R.4	Seniority of the general candidates to be restored.

As certain constituencies in the elections to legislatures are reserved there are election cases in which caste becomes the central issue. In this case the returned candidate claimed that he belonged to Bhovri caste, which was listed in the President's Order. The rival candidate who challenged the election argued that the returned candidate belonged to Voddar caste, which was not a Scheduled one. The Election Tribunal[129] set aside the election of the returned candidate as it accepted the rival candidate's argument. In appeal the High Court came to the conclusion that though Bhovri caste was not mentioned in the Order, it was no other than Voddar. The rival candidate approached Supreme Court. Having gone through the caste names that changes from region to region but the caste status remained the same; the Court observed that Voddar was also Bhovri.[130]

More or less a similar issue was involved in *Parasaram v. Shivchand.*[131] This is also connected with election. In a reserved constituency in Punjab the election was challenged on the ground that the nomination papers of one Krishna Lal were rejected even though he was a Hindu and belonged to the Scheduled Caste namely *Chamar*. It was found that that Krishna Lal was a *Mochi* and not a *chamar*. Here the Court did not accept the contention that *Chamar* and *Mochi* were the same caste. The Court went by the President's Order and rejected the appeal. Another similar case that was also concerned with an election petition was over the 'Tribal name'.

In *Soosai v. Union of India,*[132] the issue was whether a person, who belonged to Scheduled Caste and converted himself to Christianity, was eligible to get the benefits of protective discrimination. The Court answered this question in the negative. The petitioner Soosai belonged to Adi-Dravida community, which was included in the list of Scheduled Castes. Later the petitioner embraced Christianity. He was cobbler by profession. Khadi and Village Industries Board allotted bunks free of cost to the Adhi-Dravida cobblers under Special Central Assistance Scheme of the Government of India for the welfare of the Scheduled Castes. The Government Order in this regard clearly pointed out that a person belonging to Scheduled Caste loses his position as a member of Scheduled Caste when he is converted to another religion. The petition was for the above reason dismissed.

The Punjab and Haryana High Court asserted that a family earning higher income could not enjoy the benefit of reservation to the backward classes under Articles 15(4) and 16(4).[133] In *Kumari Aruna v. State of Karnataka*[134], the Court again expressed its opinion that the benefits of reservation should not be given to those with a higher income.

The question whether caste alone could be the criterion for deciding backwardness, the Supreme Court answered in the negative. The Court ruled that caste-cum-means approach could be adopted to identify the backward classes. In the Court's opinion poverty should be given due weightage while deciding the backwardness of a class.

The Bihar High Court held that the provisions under article 16(4) were related to the promotional cases of selection and non-selection posts.[135] In *Janardhan Paswan v. State of Bihar*[136] the question was whether the sole post could be reserved for the candidate of the backward class under Article 16(4). The Court considered this a violation of the principle of equality.

A. Periya Karuppan v. State of Tamil Nadu[137] was indeed a landmark case in respect of the issue of reservation. The candidates challenged the unit-wise selection of Medical Colleges including the reservation for backward classes. Another significant question was the determination of backwardness on the sole basis of caste. Hegde J. observed that 'a caste has always been recognized as a class'. The learned Judge perhaps was not aware of the consequences of such observations. The pertinent question, here is, will it help abolish caste. The question whether 41 per cent reservation for Scheduled Castes, Scheduled Tribes and Other Backward classes could be valid. The apex Court declared that the unit-wise reservation for SCs, STs and OBCs was violative of Articles 14 and 15. But the classification of backward classes on the basis of caste was held to be within Article 15 (4). The Court also observed that 41 per cent reservation was not excessive. Commenting on this aspect of the judgment Anirudh Prasad (1991) writes: "*Rajendran, Balaram* and *Periyakaruppan* appear to present a 'retreat' from judicial efforts to search secular and rational criterion."[138]

In *Gopalakrishna v. State of Maharashtra,*[139] two questions cropped up. One, whether a carry forward formula could be adopted in reservation under Article 16(4) and what could be its extent. Two, whether neo-Buddhist or converted Buddhists from Scheduled castes could claim the benefit of reservation under article 16(4) even after renunciation of Hinduism? The Court observed that the carry forward formula was part of the reservations under Article 16(4) and the limit could not be more than 50 per cent . The ratio of the court was that the neo-Buddhists were still in the category of backward classes, as the conversion had not changed their social position. They were still subjected to social ostracism and continue to be under the social stigma of untouchability.

In *Rajesh Mullick v. state of M.P*[140]. The question was whether reservation for backward class could be made for the purposive reasons. In the present case the issue was that some post graduate admissions in the Medical Colleges were reserved for the medical practitioners in the rural areas. The Court held that such a reservation was permissible.

In *Deepak Sibal v. Punjab University*[141] the Supreme Court observed that there could not be cent percent reservation for one class of people. Fifty percent reservation for Scheduled castes, Scheduled Tribes and other backward classes could be justified. Rest of the seats was to be rationalized with a view to have scope for other categories of people as well.

In *State of Maharashtra v. Kumari Tanuja*[142] the question is whether the nomadic tribe of Bawas who claim to be a synonym of Gosavis. The benefits that were accorded to these communities were limited to those who were natives of Maharashtra region and those of these communities who migrated from Sindh were denied of this benefit. The case came before the Supreme by an appeal from the State of Maharashtra against the verdict of the High Court. The Supreme Court expressed its agreement with the finding of the High Court. The Supreme Court observed that

> These decisions have specifically held that if the Executive or the Legislature wants to render a judicial decisions ineffective, it can only do so by removing or altering or neutralising the legal basis of the judgment which is sought to be made ineffective and that neither the Legislature nor in the Executive has the power of simply declaring the earlier decisions of the Courts as invalid or not binding. In the instant case judgment in Vijay Daulatani's case (1985 (2) Bom Cr 488) was rendered after considering all the existing Government Resolutions and Circulars. It is by interpreting these Resolutions and Circulars, the Division Bench of the Bombay High Court came to the conclusion that the community 'Bawa' which migrated from the State of Sindh, was included in the list of Nomadic tribes. This finding was affirmed by this Court while dismissing the special leave petition filed by the State against the said judgment. A perusal of the Resolution dated 1-4-1987 shows that the said Resolution merely reiterates the various Resolutions passed earlier by the Government, which were considered and rejected in Vijay Daulatani's case. The State has not considered any fresh material nor has it received any fresh report from competent bodies other than the one that

was placed before the Division Bench in Vijay Daulatani's case to declare by way of clarification that the 'Bawa' community of Sindhi Samaj are not entitled to be included in the list of Vimukta Jati and Nomadic tribes. As stated by the Full Bench of the High Court, a perusal of the Resolution dated 1-4-1987 shows that, in effect, it was merely overruling the judgment of the High Court in Vijay Daulatani's case, which is not permissible in law. The State has not altered or neutralised the legal basis of the judgment of the High Court in Daulatani's case by producing relevant additional material or by applying its mind to the reasons given by the Bombay High Court in Daulatani's case. Therefore, we are of the opinion that the Full Bench of the Bombay High Court was right in coming to the conclusion that the Government Resolution dated 1-4-1987, read as a whole, shows that it came to be issued to set at naught or to get over the decision of the Bombay High Court in Vijay Daulatani's case (1985 (2) Bom CR 488).

In *K.C. Vasanth Kumar v. State of Karnataka*[143] the Court was requested to give guidelines, which may serve as a guideline to the Commission, which the Government of Karnataka proposes to appoint, for examining the question of affording better employment and educational opportunities to Scheduled Castes, Schedules Tribes and other Backward Classes. According to Seervai, this case 'is unique in the history of our Supreme Court, and it is to be hoped that it will have no successor.'

According to Justice Chandrachud:

The reservation in favour of Scheduled Castes and Scheduled Tribes must continue as at present, there is, without the application of a means test, for further period not exceeding fifteen years. The means test, that is to say, the test of economic backwardness ought to be made applicable even to the Scheduled Castes and Scheduled Tribes after 2000 AD. In so far as the Other Backward Classes are concerned, two tests should be conjunctively applied for identifying them for the purpose of reservations in employment and education: One, that they should be comparable to the Scheduled Castes and Scheduled Tribes in the matter of their backwardness; and two, that they should satisfy the means test such as a State Government may lay down in the context of prevailing economic conditions. The policy of reservations in employment, education and legislative institutions should be reviewed every five years or so. That will at once afford an opportunity (i) to the State to rectify distortions arising out of particular facets of the reservation policy and (ii) to the people, both backward and non-back ward, to ventilate their views in a public debate on the practical impact of the policy of reservations.

According to Justice Desai:

A time has come to review the criterion for identifying socially and educationally backward classes ignoring the caste label. The only criterion, which can be realistically devised, is the one of economic backwardness. To this may be added some relevant criteria such as the secular character of the group, its opportunity for earning livelihood etc., but by and large economic backwardness must be the load star. Chronic poverty is the bane of Indian Society. The bank balance, the property holding and the money power determine the social status of the individual and guarantee the opportunities to rise to the top echelon. How the wealth is acquired has lost significance. Purity of means disappeared with Mahatma Gandhi and we have reached a stage where ends determine the means. This is the present disturbing situation whether one likes it or not. Reservation in one or other form has been there for decades. If a survey is made with reference to families in various castes considered to be socially and educationally backward, about the benefits of preferred treatment, it would unmistakably show that the benefits of reservations are snatched away by the top creamy layer of the backward castes. This has to be avoided at any cost. If economic criterion for compensatory discrimination or affirmative action is accepted, it would strike at the root cause of social and educational backwardness, and simultaneously take a vital step in the direction of destruction of caste structure which in turn would advance the secular character of the Nation. This approach seeks to translate into reality the twin constitutional goals: one, to strike at the perpetuation of the caste stratification of the Indian Society so as to arrest progressive movement and to take a firm step towards establishing a casteless society; and two, to progressively eliminate poverty by giving an opportunity to the disadvantaged sections of the society to raise their position and be part of the mainstream of life which means eradication of poverty. This approach does not deal with reservation in favour of Scheduled Castes and Scheduled Tribes. Thousands of years of discrimination and exploitation cannot be wiped out in one generation. But even here economic criterion is worth applying by refusing preferred treatment to those amongst them who have already benefited by it and improved their position. And finally reservation must have a time span otherwise concessions tend to become vested interests.

Per Chinnappa Reddy, J. :-

One of the results of the superior, elitist approach is that the question of reservation is invariably viewed as the conflict between the meritarian principle and the compensatory principle. No, it is not so. The real conflict is between the class of people, who have never been in or who have already moved out of the desert of poverty, illiteracy and backwardness and are entrenched in the oasis of convenient living and those who are still in the desert and want to reach the oasis. Efficiency is very much on the lips of the privileged whenever reservation is mentioned. There is neither statistical basis nor expert evidence to support the assumptions that efficiency will necessarily the impaired if reservation exceeds 50 per cent, if reservations is carried forward or if reservation is extended to promotional posts. (Para 35, 36)

In view of Arts 15 (4) and 16 (4), so-called controversy between the meritarian and compensatory principles is not of any great significance, though, it is true that efficiency should not be sacrificed. The question really is, who are the scheduled castes, scheduled tribes and backward classes, who are entitled to special provision and reservation in regard to admission into educational institutions and representation in the services.

If poverty be the cause, caste is the primary index of social backwardness, so that social backwardness is often readily identifiable with reference to a person's caste. So sadly and oppressively deep-rooted is caste in our country that it has cut across even the barriers of religion. The caste system has penetrated other religious and dissentient Hindu sects to whom the practice of caste should be anathema and today we find that practitioner of other religious faiths and Hindu dissentients are some times as rigid adherents to the system of caste as the conservative Hindus.

Class poverty, not individual poverty, is the primary test. Other ancillary tests are the way of life, the standard of living, the place in the communal hierarchy, the habits and customs, etc., etc. Despite individual exceptions, it may be possible and easy to identify social backwardness with reference to caste, with reference to residence, with reference to occupation or some other dominant feature. Notwithstanding our antipathy to caste and sub-regionalism, these are facts of life, which cannot be wished away. If they reflect poverty, which is the primary source of social and educational backwardness, they must be recognised for what they are along with other less primary sources. There is and there can be nothing wrong in recognizing poverty wherever it is reflected as an identifiable group phenomena whether it is seen as a caste group, a sub-regional group, an occupational group or some other class. Once the relevant factors are taken into consideration, how and where to draw the line is a question for each State to consider since the economic and social conditions differ from area to area. Once the relevant conditions are taken into consideration and the backwardness of a class of people is determined, it will not be for the Court to interfere in the matter. But lest there be any misunderstanding, judicial review will not stand excluded.

In the words of Justice AP Sen:

Economic backwardness is only one of the tests to determine social and educational backwardness. If that test were to be the sole criterion of social and educational backwardness, the reservation for the advancement of such classes to special treatment under Art. 15 (4) would fail. The predominant and the only factor for making special provisions under Art. 15 (4) or for reservations of posts and appointments under Art. 16 (4) should be poverty, and caste or a sub-caste or a group should be used only for purposes of identification of persons comparable to Scheduled Castes or Scheduled Tribes, till such members of backward classes attain a state of enlightenment and there is eradication of poverty amongst them and they become equal partners in a new social order in our national life.

Since the problems pertaining reservation can never be resolved through litigation in the Courts, the Central Government should consider the feasibility of appointing a permanent National Commission for Backward Classes, which must constantly carry out sociological and economic study from State to State and from region to region within a State. The framers of the Constitution by enacting Article 340 clearly envisaged the setting up of such a high-powered National Commission for Backward Classes at the Centre.

> The doctrine of protective discrimination embodied in Arts. 15 (4) and 16 (4) and the mandate of Art. 29 (2) cannot be stretched beyond a particular limit. The State exists to serve its people. There are some services where expertise and skill are of the essence. In such services or posts under the Union or States there can be no room for reservation of posts; merit alone must be the sole and decisive consideration for appointments.

Venkataramiah, J observed:

> The questions have to be tackled with sympathy for persons who are really in need of the benign assistance at the hands of the State and with due regard to the interests of the general public.

It is now necessary to re-determine the question of backwardness of the various castes, tribes and communities for purposes of Art. 15 (4) and Art. 16 (4) in the light of the latest figures to be collected on the various relevant factors and to refix the extent of reservation for backward classes. The reservation of 15 per cent now made under Art. 15 (4) and Art. 16 (4) but which may be traced to Art. 14 and Art. 16 (1) to "special group" based on occupation-cum-income can in any event be availed of by members of all communities and castes. At this stage it should be made clear that if on a fresh determination some castes or communities have to go out of the list of backward classes prepared for Art. 15 (4) and Art. 16 (4), the Government may still pursue the policy of betterment of weaker sections of the population amongst them in accordance with the directive principle contained in Art. 46 of the Constitution. There are poor people in all castes and communities. If they are given adequate opportunity and training may be able to compete successfully with persons belonging to richer classes. The Government may provide for them liberal grants of scholarships, free studentships; free boarding and lodging facilities, free uniforms, free mid-day meals etc., to make the life of poor students comfortable. The Government may also provide extra tutorial facilities, stationery and books free of cost and library facilities. These and other steps should be taken in the lower classes so that by the time a student appears for the qualifying examination he may be able to attain a high degree of proficiency in his studies.

In Marri Chandra Rao v. Dean, Medical College[144] the question was whether a person belonging to a caste or a tribe and migrates to another could claim the benefits he/she would have enjoyed in the first State. This question has come up again and again before many High Courts. The different High Courts had arrived at different conclusions. Hence the Supreme Court in its Constitution Bench analyzed the issue and ruled that such a person could not claim the benefits, which the person could have enjoyed in his/her native state.

In spite of the above decision of the Supreme Court, the same issue was raised again in Action Committee v. Union of India. This was public interest litigation. The Action Committee on the Issue of Caste Certificate in the State of Maharashtra approached the court because the State Government had denied the benefits given to Scheduled castes and Scheduled tribes to those from outside the State. The names and status of different castes are different in different states. Thus in this issue it is the State Governments that has to decide whether the particular class of people belong to Scheduled Caste or Scheduled Tribe.

Many disputes have arisen with regard to certificates issued to prove whether a person belong to Scheduled caste or Scheduled Tribe. One aspect of this issue was discussed in Aparna Bhayae v. State of Maharashtra. [145] A student claiming that she belonged to the Scheduled Tribe called 'Mahadeo Koli'. In support she tendered certain caste certificate. According to the rules the application was sent to scrutiny Committee. The primary school records of her father showed that he belonged to 'son koli' caste, which was not included in the Scheduled Tribes. The Court therefore dismissed the appeal.

Whether a re-converted person can claim the status of the Scheduled Caste, was the issue in C.M.Arumugam v. S.Rajagopal.[146] This was a case related to election from a seat reserved for Scheduled caste candidates. In 1972 the nomination of Rajagopal was rejected on the ground that he did not belong to Adi Dravida Community because he had been converted to Christianity. But Rajagopal claimed that he had been reconverted to Hinduism since long and was accepted by the Adi Dravida Community. The Court held that if a person can be reconverted to Hinduism why he should not come back to his original caste. Hence Rajagopal was to be considered a Scheduled caste candidate. As his nomination had been wrongly rejected, the election of C.M.Arumugam was set aside.

In *Jagdish Negi v. State of U.P.*[147] the question before the Court was whether the residents of the Hill areas were entitled to the benefits of the backward classes.

Constitution of India, Art.16(4), Art.15(4) and the U.P. Public Services (Reservation for Scheduled Castes, Scheduled Tribes and Other Backward Classes) Act, 1994 give benefit enjoyed by the backward classes The Act granted to residents of hills and Uttarakhand areas of State of U. P. as they formed socially and educationally backward class of citizens. The Court observed that backwardness, however, cannot continue indefinitely - State is, therefore, entitled to take its own decision whether citizens cease to belong to reserve category and review its reservation policy.

In Action Committee v. Union of India,[148] Public Interest Litigation, the question is whether a person belonging to a Scheduled caste could claim the privilege in another State. There was an earlier case Marri Chandra Rao in which the Court had already held that such a person could not claim the privilege in a State other than his/her native State. This was because a particular caste was considered Scheduled Caste in one State but the very name of the caste in another State would be attributed to a non-Scheduled caste. This would definitely create confusion. Therefore it is the State and not the center is the authority to decide whether a particular class.

In *Union of India v. Dudh Nath Prasad*[149] the respondent was a candidate for IAS examination, He belonged to Nuniya caste, which was a Scheduled Caste in West Bengal. But In Bihar Nuniya Caste was not a Scheduled Caste. His parents were from West Bengal and where they were born and brought up and were ordinarily resident. They were residing in West Bengal for 30 years prior to examination. It was held that the candidate belonged to Nuniya caste of West Bengal. He was entitled to benefit reservation.

In *Ashok Kumar Gupta v. State of U.P.*[150] the petitioners sought writ of mandamus to restrain the first respondent from giving effect to the promotions already given to respondent 2 to 10. Quoting many previous judgments the petitioners argued that the Rules regarding promotions in the Utter Pradesh Service of Engineers (Public Works Department) (Higher) Rules 1990 effective from 15-10-1990. The Court was of the opinion that the right to promotion was not a fundamental right. The Court observed:

> It is already seen that the rule of reservation in promotions was in vogue in the State of Utter Pradesh right from 1973 and the promotions came to be made from 1981 onwards to Respondents 2 to 10 The U.P. Act saves the existing policy of reservation in promotions. The judgment in *Mandal* case saves the promotions already made. In *Sabharwal* case also a Constitution Bench has upheld the validity of the promotions given in excess of the roster; otherwise also those promoted on their own merit were held to be validly promoted. Even excess promotions remained undisturbed and the law became operative only from the date of the judgment. This Court upheld the previous promotions, though in excess of the roster system, as constitutional and valid. Therefore, we hold that the promotions of the respondents are legal and valid and they do not become void or unconstitutional as contended.

In *Bimlesh Tanwar v. State of Haryana*[151] the basic question was concerned with the determining inter se seniority among the officers of Haryana Judicial Service. The core question was whether on the basis of merit in terms of merit list or the date of joining seniority was to be fixed. The Court held that: "Seniority is not a fundamental right. It is merely a civil right. Inter se seniority of the candidates who are appointed on the same day would be dependent on the rules governing the same. Only in the absence of any statutory rules, the general principles may be held to be applicable." The Court also held that the merit list prepared by the State was not arbitrary.

Indra Sawhney v. Union of India[152] is a significant case. Based on the recommendations of the *Mandal Commission Report* (the Second Backward Class Commission) the government decided to provide reservation for backward classes and subsequently an OM was issued 'that 27 per cent of the vacancies in civil posts and services under the Government of India shall be reserved for Socially and Educationally Backward Classes.' Consequently there was a backlash, which formed the background for this case. The central issue in the case was the Government's Order dated August 13, 1990 reserving 27 per cent of the seats in the government services based on the recommendations of the Mandal Commission. This Order was to come to effect on August 7, 1990.

Much has been written on this case.[153] The Supreme Court pronounced certain important decisions: *First*, the identification of social and educational backwardness on the basis of caste was held constitutional.

Second, it was declared that reservation based on the economic criterion alone was not permissible under the Article 15(4). Under this Article the classification as backward and most backward was permissible. *Third*, the total reservations in the government jobs under backward classes should not cross the prescribed limit of 50 per cent . However when the reservations on the basis of caste were to be provided, it should be given subject to the exclusion of creamy layer, which was to be determined by a permanent Commission to be set by the Government for this purpose. *Four*, reservations in certain technical and super-specialty areas were not permitted under the provision of Article 15(4). *Five*, the Court gave a significant verdict that the reservations were only permissible in case of initial appointments and would not be permitted to promotions and finally the Court also put forward a new doctrine of creamy layer. This doctrine is aimed at finding out the creamy layer or the upper crust of the backward class and excluding the same from the domain of beneficiaries.[154]

Based on the direction of the Supreme Court, the Union Government constituted an expert committee under the Chairmanship of a retired Judge of Patna High Court Sri. Ramanandan Prasad. Based on this Committee's recommendations, the Union Government issued an Official Memo (OM). The States too have the authority to formulate their own criteria for detecting the 'creamy layer' in the respective states. Each State has to formulate norms to determine upper crest of the backward classes so that that upper crest could be disconnected from the rest of the backward classes. But often such formulation in the form of subordinate legislation is challenged.

Discrimination between similarly placed candidates-in this case within the Backward Classes- is violative of the principle of equality embodied in Article 14 and Article 16(1). This was held in *Vishwas Anna Sawant v. Municipal Corporation of Greater Bombay.*[155]

Reservation for Scheduled castes/Scheduled Tribes Indian Administrative Service men in the process of being allocated to various States was challenged. The Government made reservation for such candidates as far as possible in the home state. This rule was challenged in *Union of India v. Rajiv Yadav of* IAS[15] The Court was of the opinion that in this regard the government has the power to make such allocation.

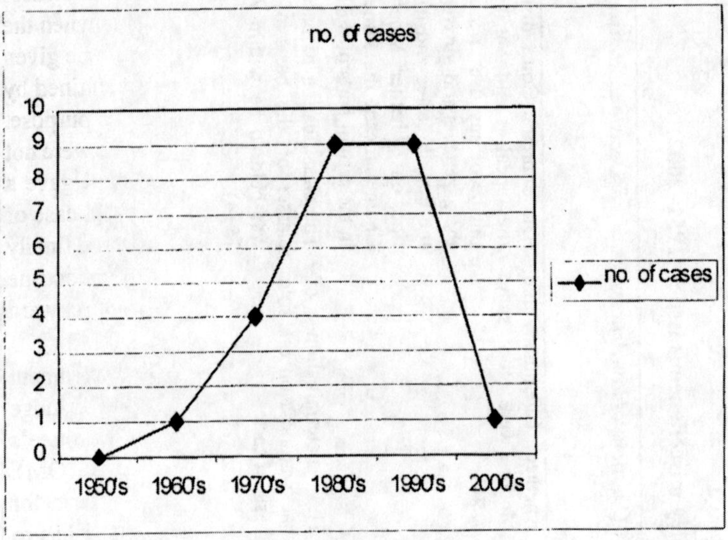

Figure 4.4.
Number of Supreme Court cases on reservation on miscellaneous issues

Table 4.4

Supreme Court Cases on Reservation Policy miscellaneous issues (1951–2002)

Sl. No.	*Name of the Case*	*Year and citation*	*Facts*	*Questions of law/Articles*	*Decision/Activism*
1	Parasaram v. Shivchand	AIR 1969 SC 597	an election case in which the caste name was in dispute	whether Chammar and Mochi were the same caste	The Supreme Court dismissed the appeal. it said that it would not be of any use to look into the gazetteers and glossaries on the Punjab castes and tribes to find out whether Mochi and Chamer meant the same caste in the certain parts of the state
2	A.Periakaruppan v. State of T.N	AIR 1971 SC 2303	The respondent was denied promotion and a person belonging to Scheduled caste and junior to the respondent was promoted. Hence the Government rule of reservation was challenged determination of backwardness on the sole basis of caste.	The determination of backwardness on the sole basis of caste	The classification of backward classes on the basis of caste was held to be within Article 15 (4).

Sl. No.	*Name of the Case*	*Year and citation*	*Facts*	*Questions of law/Articles*	*Decision/Activism*
3	N.E. Horo v. Smt. Jahan Ara	AIR 1972 SC 1840	By election to Khunti (ST) parliamentary constituency in Bihar, Jahan Ara filled nomination papers. She stated that she was the widow of a member of the Munda ST. another candidate objected to her claim, stating that she was a non tribal.	This case raised questions of corruption in a election petition, one important argument was regarding the status of a non tribal marrying a tribal.	The Supreme Court held that in this particular case, the customary marriage gave the status of a tribal to the non tribal wife.
4	C.M. Arumugam v. S. Rajagopal	AIR 1976 SC 939	political rivals fought over a SC reserved seat nomination of Rajagopal was rejected on the ground that he was not an Adi Dravida as claimed by him but a converted Christian	reconversion to Hinduism, whether a person be able to come back to his caste	ruled that a Hindu who converted to Christianity and was reconverted to Hinduism is a Hindu if his fellow caste men accepted him

Sl. No.	Name of the Case	Year and citation	Facts	Questions of law/Articles	Decision/Activism
5	Guntur Medical College v. Mohan Rao	AIR 1976 SC 1904	The parents of Mohan Rao originally professed Hindu religion and belonged to Madiga(SC) caste. They were both converted to Christinaty.The boy was born after that	question was the status of a reconverted Hindu	On conversion to Hinduism, a person can once again become a member of the caste in which he was born and to which he belonged before conversion to another religion of the members of the caste accepted him as a member.
6	Nishi Maghu v. State of J&K	AIR 1980 SC 1975	The selection of candidates to the Government college in Jammu was challenged in this petition by some who were not selected. the selection was challenged on several grounds.	18 per cent seats were reserved for rectifying regional imbalances and some seats for 'social castes	selection of candidates to the State medical college to "correct regional imbalances" without identifying the areas was illegal.but it upheld selection on the basis of 'social castes' with reference to their occupation
7	State of Maharasthra v Abhay	AIR 1985, SC 328	A candidate was selected on a strength of a provisional caste certificate issued by the concerned authority that he belong to 'hamba' claimed to be ST in Maharasthra.	Whether halba caste is ST,	issuing 'provisional 'certificates on caste states and after admission to the reserved seat ,the caste finding is reversed , it creates problem for the selected candidates as well as for others

Sl. No.	*Name of the Case*	*Year and citation*	*Facts*	*Questions of law/Articles*	*Decision/Activism*
8	K.C.Vasant Kumar v. State of Karnataka	AIR 1985 SC 1495	The Karnataka Government sought advice of the Supreme Court -some guidelines for its Backward Commission.	Whether caste alone could be the criterion for determining the backward classes?	Caste-cum-means approach could be adopted to identify the backward classes. Caste alone could not be the criterion for such delineation. Poverty should be given due weightage while deciding about the backward classes.
9	Soosai v. Union of India	AIR 1986 SC 733	Petitioner Soosai belonged to Adi-Dravida community, which was included in the list of Scheduled Castes. Later the petitioner embraced Christianity. He was cobbler by profession. Khadi and Village Industries Board allotted bunks free of cost to the Adhi-Dravida cobblers under Special Central Assistance Scheme of the Government of India for the welfare of the Scheduled Castes.	Whether a person who belonged to Scheduled Caste and converted himself to Christianity, was eligible to get the benefits of protective discrimination.	a person belonging to Scheduled Caste loses his position as a member of Scheduled Caste when he is converted to another religion. The petition was dismissed.

Sl. No.	*Name of the Case*	*Year and citation*	*Facts*	*Questions of law/Articles*	*Decision/Activism*
10	Bharat Sevashram Sangh v. State of Gujarat	AIR 1987 SC 494	The Gujarat Secondary Education Act 1973 was assailed on several grounds. One of the provisions challenged was Section 34(1).It provided that 15 per cent of vacancies of teaching staff of a registered private school shall be filled up by SC/ST candidates	Section 34(1).The Gujarat Secondary Education Act 1973	Supreme Court upheld the provision for reservation of teaching posts in Gujarat schools for SC/ST.
11	The Comptroller and Auditor General v. K.S Jagannathan,	AIR 1987, SC 537	The SC/ST employees working in the Indian Audit and Accounts Department ,Madras, sought relaxation in marks for their promotion from selection grade auditors to section officers	deals with relaxation of qualifying marks in respect of SC/ST for promotion	candidates can move the high court if they are not this benefit

Sl. No.	Name of the Case	Year and citation	Facts	Questions of law/Articles	Decision/Activism
12	Sarish Chandra v. State of Tripura	AIR 1987,SC1601	The petitioner, a resident of Tripura, claimed that he belonged to Laskar community which has been treated as ST with in the state. the government ,without any justification,delisted the community from ST category	What can be done when a ST community is excluded from the benefits given them under the Presidential Order	that if the community was not included in the presidential order, it would be open to the petitioner to take further steps available in law
13	State of AP v. Nagam Chandrasekhara	AIR 1988, SC 1309	Chandrasekhara was elected in the IAS against a vacancy reserved for SC. That was done on the basis of the social status certificate produced by him certifying that he belong to the Beda Jangam community	whether a particular communityBeda Jangam belonged to the Schedule Caste category in AP was the issue here	appeal dismissed

Sl. No.	*Name of the Case*	*Year and citation*	*Facts*	*Questions of law/Articles*	*Decision/Activism*
14	Deepak Sibal v. Punjab University	AIR 1989 SC 905	The exclusion of employees of Government / Semi-Government and other institutions to avail legal education .Changed rule restricting admission to employees of govt. / semi-govt. and similar institutions challenged	Art. 15(4).Changed rule restricting admission to employees of govt. / semi-govt. and similar institutions , whether valid	There could not be cent percent reservation for one class of people. Fifty percent reservation for Scheduled castes, Scheduled Tribes and other backward classes could be justified. rule restricting admission to employees of govt. / semi-govt. and similar institutions - Rule is discriminatory.
15	Marri Chandra Rao v. Dean, Medical College	AIR 1990(3) SCC 130	he sought admission to a medical college in the ST quota, which was denied.ST	Where a person belonging to a caste or tribe in one state migrates to another state, can he claim the benefits under their constitution in the new state	Rejected the contention that the new state should also recognize the SC/ST certificate and grant benefits according to it. he was denied admission to the medical college.

Sl. No.	*Name of the Case*	*Year and citation*	*Facts*	*Questions of law/Articles*	*Decision/Activism*
16	Comptroller & Auditor General v. M.L.Mehrotra	AIR 1991,SC 2288	Four senior officers challenged the circular issued in 1973 by the Comptroller And Auditor General of India providing for reservation for SC/ST officers in promotion posts	reservation in the audit department where there was no reservation for promotion	held that the government could direct reservation by executive orders.
17	Bimlesh Tanwar v. State of Haryana	AIR 1994 SCW 1508	determining inter se seniority among the officers of Haryana Judicial Service	Whether on the basis of merit in terms of merit list or the date of joining seniority was to be fixed.	Seniority is not a fundamental right. It is merely a civil right. Inter se seniority of the candidates who are appointed on the same day would be dependent on the rules governing the same. Only in the absence of any statutory rules, the general principles may be held to be applicable

Sl. No.	Name of the Case	Year and citation	Facts	Questions of law/Articles	Decision/Activism
18	Vishwas Anna Sawant v. Municipal corporation of Greater Bombay	AIR 1994 SC 2408	M was given promotion when he approached the High Court. He was an employee belonged to Backward class. Another employee who was similarly placed was denied promotion.	Articles 14 and 16.	The discrimination was held illegal
19	Action Committee v. union of India	AIR 1994 SC	public interest petition by the action Committee on the issue of denial of Caste Certificate to SC/ST in the state of Maharashtra	Articles 14,15(1),16(2) and 19 of the constitution.	Migrant SC/ST could not claim benefits in the new state.
20	Union of India v. Rajiv Yadav IAS	AIR 1995 SC 14	Reservation for SC/ST Indian Adm. Service men in the process of being allocated to various States is challenged; because the Govt. made a reservation for them as far as possible in their home states.	Article 16 (4) 307. Indian Administrative Service (Cadre) Rules 1954.R.5. Govt. Letter dated 31-5-1985	Appeal by the Government allowed.

Sl. No.	*Name of the Case*	*Year and citation*	*Facts*	*Questions of law/Articles*	*Decision/Activism*
21	Ashok Kumar Gupta v. State of U.P	1997 5 SCC 201	The petioners seek writ of mandamus to restrain the State (first respondent) from giving effect to the promotion of respondents 2 to 10	Whether right to promotion to Dalits and Tribes is constitutionally valid?	By virtue of Constitution amendment in Art. 16(4A), promotion is a fundamental right to the SCs and STs. Article 16 (4A) read with Articles 16 (1) and 14 guarantees a right to promotion to Dalits and Tribes as fundamental right where they not have adequate representation consistently with the efficiency in administration.
22	Jagdish Negi v. State of U.P	AIR 1997 SC 3505	This was originally a Public Interest litigation for benefit of reservation to the residents of Hill and Uttrakhand area	Articles 15 (4) and 16 (4) U.P. Public Service (Reservation for SC/ST and Other backward Classes) Act 1994	The petition was partly allowed.

Sl. No.	Name of the Case	Year and citation	Facts	Questions of law/Articles	Decision/Activism
23	State of Maharashtra v. Kumari Tanuja	AIR 1999 SC 791	Whether nomadic tribe from Sindh could be considered as Scheduled Tribe in Maharashtra	Article 16 (4) and the Resolution issued by the State of Maharashtra.	Appeal by the State of Maharashtra was dismissed. Judgment went in favour of Bawa community.
24	Union of India v. Dudh Nath Prasad	AIR 2000 SC 525	A person belonging to a scheduled caste in West Bengal stayed in Bihar for studies. He claims the status of reserved category for his parents still lived in West Bengal	All India Services Act 1951 and Article 16 (4) of the Constitution.	The person to be treated as scheduled caste. The decision of the Tribunal upheld.

The following chart would give a graphic idea of the cases that came before the Supreme Court.

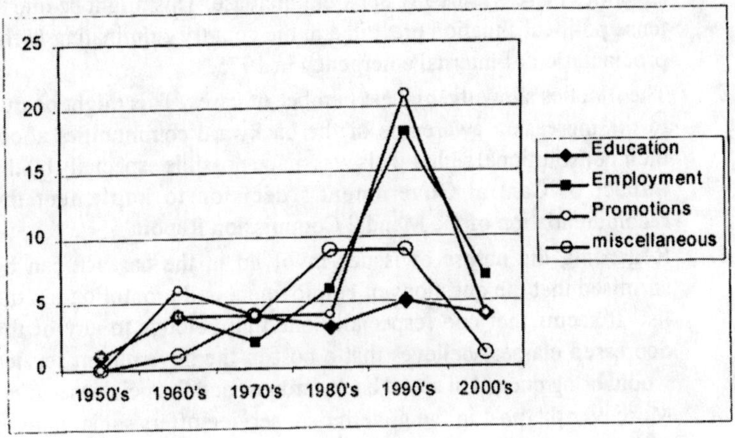

Figure 4.5

Number of Supreme Court cases on reservation in education, employment and promotion

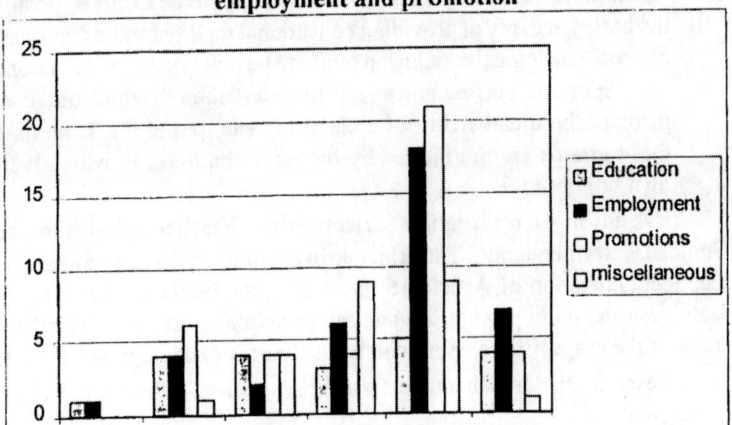

Figure 4.6

Number of Supreme Court cases on reservation in education, employment and promotion

The cases pertaining to protective discrimination or reservation that came up before the Supreme Court up to the year 2000 reveal following trends.

1. There is an increase in the number of reservational cases, but in the seventies there wasn't any apparent increase. This might be due to tense political situation prevailed in the country culminating in the proclamation of internal emergency in 1975.
2. The nineties show the highest number of cases. This might be due to the increasing awareness of the backward communities about their constitutional rights. This was made possible especially by the impact of Central Government's decision to implement the recommendation of the Mandal Commission Report.
3. Regarding the nature of issues involved in the cases it can be surmised that the questions of employment and promotion top the list. It seems that one (especially one that belongs to any of the depressed classes) believes that a post in the government service would bring one out of social backwardness and financial insecurity. Moreover the post in the government service offers social dignity and sense of sharing power.
4. Cases regarding 'education' also show that most of them are concerned with the admission to Medical Colleges or such other institutions. No case has come before the Supreme Court regarding the basic necessity of providing educational facility for the depressed classes. The logical conclusion ought to be that 'elite groups' among the depressed classes are trying to assert their 'rights' obtained through the membership of a class or caste, but at the same time these groups are not moved by the poor condition in which their own brethren live.

Evolution of reservation jurisprudence has been described as 'Judicial Gerrymandering' The principle of equality, caste-class confusion, reconceptualization of Article 16, increasing the quota of the reserved seats, reservation in promotions and the principle of 'carry forward' are some of the major issues upon which the Court is called upon to decide.

Reservation for Scheduled Castes, Scheduled Tribes is not at all questioned.

Summarizing the evolution of judicial observations, Nesiah says: "The courts have largely followed the lead of the legislature and the executive and when they did intervene occasionally it was mainly to regulate and modify, rather than to innovate or redirect policies. Except during a brief period...the role of the Supreme Court in advancing preferential policies had, up to the nineties been modest. But some recent judgments, notably *Indra Sawhney* (1993), may be heralding of enhanced judicial action in the years to come."[161] What enhanced judicial action is in store for the future cannot be predicted. But the issue of reservation has been highly politicized and consequently a judicial settlement of emerging issues will also be wrought with political paradigms.

References

1. A.I.R. 1951 SC 226.
2. AIR 1962 SC 36 This case can also be cited under 'promotions'.
3. AIR 1984 SC 1831.
4. AIR 1988 SC 925.
5. AIR 1968 SC 1012.
6. AIR 1980 SC 1975.
7. AIR 1989 SC 139.
8. AIR 1994 SC 1528.
9. AIR 1996 SC 351.
10. AIR 1997 SC 1095.
11. AIR 2000 SC 450 One of the issues in this case was that of promotion.
12. AIR 1999 SC 3471.
13. (1997) 6 SCC 129.
14. AIR 1997 S C 2101.
15. 1996 (9) JT (SC) 320,
16. (1974) 1 SCC 87, AIR 1974 SC 532.
17. (1996) 7 SCC 512, 1996 AIR SCW 2248.
18. (1996) 5 SCC 167.
19. (1995) Supp (1) SCC 432.
20. AIR 2000 SC 609.
21. By seventy-seventh Amendment (1995) Article 16 (4A) was introduced and Eighty-fifth Amendment (2000) added the phrase 'in matters of promotion, with consequential seniority'.
22. AIR 1997 SC 1451.
23. AIR 1997 SC 303.
24. AIR 1997 SC 2133.
25. AIR 1997 SC 3687.
26. AIR 1998 SC 1767.
27. AIR 2000 S C 1296.
28. AIR 1973 All 295.

29. AIR 1973 All 592.
30. AIR 1972 SC 1375.
31. AIR 1975 SC 1.
32. Backwardness in law perhaps is different from backwardness in economic development and educational attainments. Thus a political solution was found when a new State was carved out of U.P. namely Uttaranchal.
33. AIR 1972 SC 2381.
34. AIR 1988 SC 481.
35. AIR 1981 SC 2945.
36. AIR 2001 SC 3006.
37. AIR 1995 SC 1421.
38. AIR 1996 SC 1378.
39. AIR 1997 SC 1120 .
40. AIR 1998 SC 680.
41. AIR 1999 SC 2894.
42. AIR 2001 SC 717.
43. AIR 2001 SC 3006.
44. AIR 2001 SC 3262.
45. AIR 2000 SC 72 .
46. A.I.R. 1951 SC 226.
47. AIR 1962 SC 36 This case can also be cited under 'promotions'.
48. AIR 1984 SC 1831.
49. AIR 1988 SC 925.
50. AIR 1968 SC 1012.
51. AIR 1980 SC 1975.
52. AIR 1989 SC 139.
53. AIR 1994 SC 1528.
54. AIR 1996 SC 351.
55. AIR 1997 SC 1095.
56. AIR 2000 SC 450 One of the issues in this case was that of promotion.
57. AIR 1999 SC 3471.
58. (1997) 6 SCC 129.
59. AIR 1997 S C 2101.
60. 1996 (9) JT (SC) 320.
61. (1974) 1 SCC 87, AIR 1974 SC 532.
62. (1996) 7 SCC 512, 1996 AIR SCW 2248.
63. (1996) 5 SCC 167.
64. (1995) Supp (1) SCC 432.
65. AIR 2000 SC 609.

66. By seventy-seventh Amendment (1995) Article 16 (4A) was introduced and Eighty-fifth Amendment (2000) added the phrase 'in matters of promotion, with consequential seniority'.
67. AIR 1997 SC 1451.
68. AIR 1997 SC 303.
69. AIR 1997 SC 2133.
70. AIR 1997 SC 3687.
71. AIR 1998 SC 1767.
72. AIR 2000 S C 1296.
73. AIR 1999 SC 3471.
74. AIR 1964 SC 179.
75 AIR 1962 SC 36.
76. AIR 1965 SC 1430.
77. Devanesan Nesiah, *Discrimination- With Reason?* (OUP 1997) p.167
78. This was again confirmed in *V.V.Giri v .S.Sura Dora (1959)*
79. *Laila Chacko v. State of Kerala.* AIR 1967 Ker. 124.
80. AIR 1967, A.P.353.
81. AIR 1969 SC 1.
82. AIR 1971 SC 2206.
83. AIR 1969 Cal 576.
84. AIR 1968 SC. The observation regarding Article 16 (4) can be cited on 'employment' also.
85. AIR 1968 Ker. 42.
86. See Chapter V.
87. AIR 1969 SC 1.
88. Dayabhai v. State of Gujarat, IL.R.,(II).1970,Gujarat,386
89 AIR 1970 Ori 224.
90. (1971) 1 Mys. L. J. 226.
91 AIR 1973 SC 930.
92. A.I.R.1975.Kerala,131.
93. *Urmila Ginda v. Union of India.* AIR 1975 Del 115
94. AIR 1976 SC 490.
95. In accordance with the Court's observations, the Parliament brought amendments to Article 16 of the Constitution. These amendments protected the promotion and seniority concessions to the SC, ST and other backward classes of citizens. See. The Constitution (Seventy-seventh Amendment) Act 1995, sec. 2 (w.e.f. 17-6-1995), The Constitution (Eighty-first Amendment) Act 2000 (w.e.f. 9-6-2000) and The Constitution (Eighty-fifth Amendment) Act, 2001 (w.e.f. 17-6-1995).
96. AIR 1981 SC 588.

97. *Akhil Bharathiya Soshit Sangh v. Union of India* AIR 1981 298.
98. *Km Usha Rani v. M.D. University, Rohtak* AIR 1984 P & H 297.
99. AIR 1985 SC 983
100. AIR 1989 SC 139.
101. AIR 1994 SC 1917.
102. AIR 1995 SC 1371.
103. AIR 1995 SC 1457.
104. (1996) 6 SCC 580.
105. AIR 1995 SC 1691.
106. AIR 1981 SC 298. The Court also discusses the scope of Article 16 (4) regarding the initial appointment.
107. AIR 1989 SC 139.
108. AIR 1996 SC 1915.
109. AIR 1962 SC 36.
110. AIR 1996 SC 448.
111. *The Commissioner of Commercial Taxes A.P. and another v. G.Sethumadhava Rao and others.* 1998.
112. (1995) 2SCC 745.
113. AIR 1997 SC 2366.
114. (1997) 5 SCC 201.
115. AIR 1977 SC 2137.
116. AIR 1997 SC 2138.
117. AIR 1999 SC 3471.
118. AIR 1999 SC 3563.
119. AIR 2000 SC 278.
120. AIR 2000 SC 450.
121. AIR 1999 SC 3563.
122. AIR 2000 SC29.
123. AIR 2000 SC 3385.
124. AIR 2001 SC 3299.
125. 1995 AIR SCW 4309.
126. Devanesan Nesiah, *Discrimination with Reason.* (OUP 1997) p.74 .
127. (1968) 1 SCR 721.
128. Anirudh Prasad, *Reservation, Policy and Practice* (1991) p. 372.
129. *N.M.Thomas v. Sate of Kerala* AIR.1976 S.C.490 at 531.
130. Anirudh Prasad, *Reservation, Policy and Practice* (1991) pp 169-189.
131. *Viswanath v. Government of Mysore.* AIR 1964 Mys p.136.
132. K.Srinivasan & Sanjay Kumar, 'Economic and Caste Criteria in Definition of Backwardness',*EPW* October 16-23, 1999.

133. Until 1966 Election Tribunal had the jurisdiction to hear the election petitions, but in 1966 the Election tribunal was abolished. Now the jurisdiction is vested with the High Courts.
134. *B. Basavalingappa v. D. Munichinnappa,* AIR 1965 SC 1269.
135. AIR 1969 SC 597.
136. AIR 1986 SC 733.
137. *Rajesh Agarwal v .M.D, University and Anil v, Dean, Government Medical College* AIR 1985 P & H 206.
138. AIR 1985 Kant 196.
139. *Sheod Singh v. State of Bihar.* AIR 1986 Pat 124.
140. AIR 1988 Pat 75.
141. (1971) 1 SCC 38.
142. Anirudh Prasad, *Reservation-Policy and Practice in India.* (New Delhi 1991) p.156.
143. AIR 1987 Bom 123.
144. AIR 1987 MP 184.
145. AIR 1989 SC 905.
146. AIR 1999 SC 791.
147. AIR 1985 SC 1495. A critical study of the case is found in H.M. Seervai, *Constitutional Law of India.* (1992) pp. 623-625.
148. 1990 (3) SCC 130.
149. AIR 1990 SC 2250.
150. AIR 1976 SC 939.
151. AIR 1997 S C3505.
152. AIR 1994 SC 153.
153. AIR 2000 S C 525.
154. Ibid 251.
155. 2003 AIR SCW 1508.
156. 1992 Supp (3) SCC 215.
157. Arun Shourie, 'The Mandal Report: The stench of casteism', *The Indian Express.* 24-8-1990. Swapen das Gupta, 'Curse on Mandal: Grotesque Caricature of Hinduism'; Andrew Beteille, 'Caste and Politics: Subversions of Public Institutions' and Prof. M.N. Srinivas, 'The Mandal Formula-Backwardness: Castes v. Individuals' *Indian Bar Review* Vol.17&18 1991. Palkhivala, 'Mandal Perpetuates Casteism' *The Hindustan Times* 30-11-1992.
158. *The Economic and Political Weekly* (April 22-28, 2000) in its editorial commented "Open competitions being what they are, even the creamy layer cannot translate its advantages into tangible benefits without the aid of the sturdy reservation policy."
159. AIR 1994 SC 2408.
160. AIR 1995 SC 14.
161. Devanesan Nesiah, *op.cit at* p.74 .

5

Legal Mechanics of Reservation and Judicial Balancing of The Conflicting Interests

The word 'mechanics' denotes 'theoretical and practical knowledge of the design, construction, operation and care of machinery.'[1] Here the word is figuratively used to mean law, which engineers desirable changes in the political society. Thus phrase 'legal mechanics of reservation' is given the meaning of the existing legal provisions to protect the interests of the communities and groups of people whose interests need protection. These provisions could be classified into: (a) Constitutional, (b) Statutory and (c) those that are derived from Subordinate legislations like rules, regulations, orders, notifications and directions. The subordinate legislations are the creations of the executive.[2] By and large the subordinate legislations are based on the broader principles set out in the parent Act.

The Constitution of India under Article 141 gives the final authority to the Supreme Court to declare what is the law of the land. It means that the Court by its interpretation could ensure justice. Thus Court also plays a vital part in shaping the legal mechanics of reservation. The Court may give directions and occasionally even goes to the extent of making judicial legislation.[3]

Constitutional Provisions

The Preamble of the Constitution of India envisions 'equality' and 'justice' as the goals. 'Justice' is qualified by the words social. economic and political. Among these political justice has been achieved, seemingly at least, by the adoption of universal adult franchise. But economic justice and social justice have remained a mirage. The Forty Second Amendment to the Constitution added two terms, 'socialist' and 'secular' to the

Preamble. Socialism implies economic justice and secularism implies social justice. Often the policy of reservation has been viewed as a means to achieve social justice.

Though the Constitution envisages 'equality' as the basic principle, for obvious reasons it was considered desirable to have 'protective discrimination' as a policy to safeguard the interests of the marginalized sections of the polity. In other words it could be said that 'equality' as a right for all citizens is guaranteed by Article 14, 15 and 16 whereas 'equality' as a constructive policy has been incorporated in Articles 15(4) and 16 (4) (5).[4] This could be discerned from the wording of the provision. The sub clauses[5] empower the state to make laws in order to protect the interests of the communities who have been suppressed in the past. Hence once they achieve social equality and economic sufficiency the need for discrimination vanishes for the discrimination is only 'protective' In fact the policy reflected in Art. 15(4) were inserted by the First Amendment to the Constitution. It was a restatement of the policy of the Government and the restatement was necessitated by judgment in State *of Madras* v. *Champakam Dorairajan*[6] . The fact that the judgment went against the policy of the Government might have been the reason for such a restatement of policy through Constitutional Amendment. The political expediency behind the Amendment was reflected in the words of Nehru: "The House (Lower House of the Parliament) knows very well and there is no need for hush it up, that this particular matter in this particular shape arose because of certain happenings in Madras."[7]

But incorporating an apparently transient policy in the basic law of the land has its ramifications; because the Government may have to change the policies in accordance with the changing times and consequently the changing societal equations. But the basic law, that is, the Constitution is to be comparatively permanent. Thus the policy that ought to change in accordance with the changing times, when inserted in the basic law of the land has an adverse effect too. A few sections of people, at least, would like to remain as backward to get the benefits of preferential treatment and consequently this will lead to the perpetuation of social backwardness of castes.

Article 29 and 30 envisage 'protection' of minorities. These Articles give only cultural and educational rights to the minorities and hence do not have any direct nexus to the question of 'reservation'. A similar policy statement could be seen in Article 46 also, but this Article comes under Directive Principles of State Policy and hence not justiciable, although it could inspire the judges so inclined to receive some direction in interpreting law.

Part XVI of the Constitution contains special provisions for certain classes. Here the basic law provides for the reservation of seats in the legislature for certain classes of people. It is only commonplace to say that to be meaningful democracy must have a broader representation of the people concerned. As decision-makers of the country, the members of the legislatures enjoy much power and privilege. Obviously the reservation for seats in the legislature becomes essential for the weaker sections for their voice to be heard and to make their participation in law-making effective. Therefore it was only natural that the framers of the constitution wanted to incorporate the necessary provisions for the reservation of seats for Scheduled castes and Scheduled Tribes [8] and certain other weaker sections. Article 330 reserves seats in Parliament and Article 332 provides reservation of seats in the state legislatures. Originally such reservations were only for ten years; but as years went by Parliament through Constitutional Amendments extended the period[9]

Article 335 makes interesting reading. It says, "The claims of the members of the Scheduled Castes and Scheduled Tribes shall be taken into consideration, consistently with the maintenance of efficiency of administration, in the making of appointments to the services and posts in connection with the affairs of the Union or of a State." It is interesting because no mechanism was provided to gauge the impact of reservation upon the efficiency of administration.

Articles 341 and 342 of the Constitution empower the President to notify through a list the caste, race or tribe any State or Union Territory. Only the groups enlisted can claim the reservation benefits. At the same time Parliament has the power to include or exclude any caste or group of people in or from the list. Parliament shall do this by passing a law. Such Presidential Orders so far as the Court cannot make any change in the Order. The Court's enquiry is confined to interpreting what an entry in the Presidential Order is intended to mean.[10]

It is after a detailed enquiry that the Presidential Order is made. Any amendment to the presidential Order can be made only by legislation. In *Srish v. State of Tripura,* it was held that even if the Tribe (Laskars) was covered by the general description that by itself may not justify its inclusion in the Order as a Scheduled Tribe. Again the President has the power to declare that a caste or subcaste shall be deemed to be a Scheduled caste in a particular part of a state and not in any other part. It follows that a person who wants to be elected from a Scheduled caste constituency must show that he has been registered as a Scheduled caste in his electoral roll; the fact that his caste is recognized as a Scheduled caste in the constituency from which he seeks election is of no avail. That the Court has only a limited jurisdiction in this matter can be seen in the Supreme Court's observation in *Virendra v. Union of India.* Where a President's notification declares a caste to be Scheduled caste for the purposes of certain specified States, no Court will direct that caste to be declared Scheduled caste in relation to another State.

Sometimes one caste may have different names. In such cases people known in these areas as Scheduled castes or Scheduled Tribes are considered to be so.[11] According to the Circular issued by the Government of India on 6th August 1984 a person who is Scheduled Tribe in a State, as stated in the President's Order, continues to be a Scheduled Tribe person in another State to which he has migrated. [12] A similar observation was made in *Rajesh Arjunbhai Patel v. State Of Maharashtra.*[13] Bhils are recognized as Scheduled Tribes in Gujarat and Maharashtra. The petitioner's father had migrated to Bombay from Gujarat in 1961.There was reservation for Scheduled Tribes in Medical Colleges. But the petitioner's claim was rejected on the ground that the Government Instruction 17 (a) disallowed reservation for migrants from other States. The Court held that the relevant clause of the Instruction was violative of Articles 14, 15, 16, 19 and 342 of the Constitution.

There are certain contradictions in the determination of Scheduled castes. For instance, the Court was clear in stating that a person who is converted to another religion cannot claim his previous scheduled caste status.[14] In fact when Ambedkar, the legendary Dalit leader, along with his followers accepted Buddhism, they were denied the claims of being Scheduled Caste people. Only later the 'neo-Buddhists' were given those rights.[15] The problem of conversion to another religion in the context of 'reservational rights' is a legal question so far as the principle of 'equity' is to be adopted. It also has socio-political implications in the sense that such groups may also become powerful pressure groups and would try to tilt the balance in power equations by forming potent vote-banks. For instance in Kerala the Latin Catholic Christians and Christians whose forefathers had been low caste Hindus, enjoy the benefit of reservation for the backward.

A recent development is the Constitution (Amendment) Act 1993 that empowers the State legislatures to make law regarding the establishment of LSGIs. The Constitutional amendment has also made it mandatory the reservation of seats for scheduled Castes and Scheduled Tribes and their women.

State Legislations

It was a case from the erstwhile Madras State that caused the first amendment to the Constitution[16]. Again the present state of Tamil Nadu is the first sate to enact a statute in this regard. The Tamil Nadu Government enacted legislation namely *Tamil Nadu Backward Classes, Scheduled Castes and Scheduled Tribes (Reservation of seats in Educational Institutions and of appointments or posts in the Services under the State*) in 1993 and the President of India gave his assent on 19th July of the same year after consulting leaders of almost all political parties. Again in compliance with the request[17] from the Tamil Nadu Government, the said Act was brought within the purview of the Ninth Schedule of the Constitution and thereby the Court was deprived of its jurisdiction. The aim of the legislation is to continue 69 per cent reservation for the aforementioned communities. The immediate provocation for the Tamil Nadu Government to bring such legislation was a writ petition filed before the Madras High Court regarding the percentage of reserved seats in the admission to educational institutions.

In this regard *Madhya Pradesh Public Service Reservation for Scheduled Castes, Scheduled Tribes and Other Backward Classes (Amendment) Act 1995* is noteworthy. Kerala State has also had its share of legislation.

Subordinate Legislations

Constitutional provisions ought to be translated into administrative action to achieve the socio-economic equality. The subordinate legislation consisting of a heavy bulk of 'orders' 'notifications' and 'instructions' would be a suitable subject for a serious study in the realm of Administrative Law. It is common knowledge that the object of these legislations is to carry out the policy laid down by the relevant provisions in the Constitution. Between 1950 and 1991 for instance there were a dozen Constitution Orders. The Central Government issues separate orders for each state.[18] The main objective of these Orders is to identify the Scheduled castes and Scheduled Tribes and make necessary legal procedures thereof. This gives power to the concerned government to adopt such policy as to cater to the needs of communities, whose votes are a deciding factor in elections to Parliament and other various State Legislatures. The lists of Scheduled castes and Scheduled Tribes originally promulgated as part of the Constitution, have been modified, amended and supplemented from time to time. In most cases the driving force behind these changes in law is political expediency.

There are two opposing arguments regarding reservation policy. In 1956 the Union Government made it clear that Scheduled castes and Scheduled Tribes people who embraced Buddhism could not claim reservation. This was considered to be gross injustice to the concerned communities. But the fact remains that the people who convert themselves to Buddhism, Christianity or any other organized religion, do so because they no longer wanted to be subjected to caste-tyranny. Religions like Buddhism and Christianity do not recognize caste differentiation. Moreover, claiming reservation by Scheduled castes and Scheduled Tribes even after their conversion to religions that profess equality would only perpetuate the casteism. But unfortunately the reservation being related to vote banks and the vote banks playing significant role in a parliamentary majoritarian system, the issue of reservation for the benefit of Scheduled castes and Scheduled Tribes and other backward classes are to be viewed with this backdrop of political ramifications. For instance Ram Ganesh Kaspe while participating in the discussion on Constitution (Scheduled castes) Orders (Amendment) Bill, 1990 severely criticized the Congress party, the ruling party in 1956, for the order that the government issued at that time.[19] And the general trend of the discussion was that even if a person adopted a new religion, his position in society as a member of Scheduled castes would not change. If this argument were to be accepted would this not mean that it was giving a long lease to the caste structure in India? It is interesting to note that multicultural milieu is reflected once again in the policy of reservation.

But the subordinate legislations namely the Official Memos (MO) issued are said to be often not in favour of the aggrieved communities. For instance the Committee on the Welfare of Scheduled Castes and Scheduled Tribes observed:

> The Committee note with concern that the bureaucracy, i.e., Secretary, Joint Secretary, Director/Dy. Secretary of DOP&T ignored the relevant portion of the judgment, which is logical and reasonable to the Dalits and Tribes. Thus the Bureaucracy of the DOP&T adopted a policy of ignoring those parts of the judgment which appear to be beneficial and reasonable and just to SCs/STs but highlighting and implementing only those portions of judgments which are detrimental to the interests of SCs/STs. The Committee consider that the attitude and action of the bureaucracy is torturous and atrocious to the Government servants belonging to the weaker sections of society viz. Scheduled castes and Scheduled Tribe, which has

> caused immense harm to their service career. The Committee therefore recommends that steps should be taken to prosecute the officers concerned viz., Secretary, Joint Secretary, Director/ Dy. Secretary under Section 4 of Chapter II of the Scheduled Caste and Scheduled Tribe (Prevention of Atrocities) Act, 1989, apart from taking appropriate departmental penal action against them.[20]

Again the Committee goes on to delineate how the present bureaucratic set up is biased against the reservation policy. For instance it is pointed out that even Constitutional mandates are being violated. Article 338 provides that the Union and every State shall consult the National Commission for SCs and STs on all major policy matters affecting Scheduled castes and Scheduled Tribes. In accordance with the original Article 338 of the Constitution the Government of India appointed a Special Officer for Scheduled Castes and Scheduled Tribes. But instead of working as an effective monitoring agency, it remained a mere bureaucratic body.

But the Department of Personnel and Training (DOPT) did not do this because the DOPT felt that such consultation would serve no purpose.[21] In another place the Committee records:

> The Committee observed that the deliberations that took place in the Lok Sabha on 4-8-1998 throw light on the working of the DOP&T bureaucrats. Shri. Ram Vilas Paswan, who happens to be a former Minister for Railways in the Cabinet headed by PM Shri.DevaGowda and Shri Inder Kumar Gujral had mentioned in the Lok Sabha that he knew when he was in Government, how permanent bureaucracy dilutes the things and when Government become weak, bureaucracy become stronger and as a result any step proposed by the Government remains undecided. He further mentioned very specifically that the then Cabinet Secretary was against Scheduled castes and Scheduled Tribes...[22]

The Committee, then, expresses its apprehension about what might happen to the policy of reservation at the stage of implementation, which might be sabotaged by the partisan bureaucracy.

Article 338 provides for the appointment of a Commission for the purpose of investigating and monitoring of all matters relating to the safeguards provided for the Scheduled castes and Scheduled Tribes. Another duty of the Commission is to inquire into specific complaints with respect to their deprivation of rights and safeguards.

This Article originally provided for the appointment of a special officer for the Scheduled castes and Scheduled Tribes. Accordingly a special officer designated as the Commissioner was appointed in November 1950. After 15 years the Commissioner had 17 regional offices located in various States. Assistant Commissioners headed these regional offices and they were redesignated as Deputy Commissioners. In 1967 the restructuring was carried out and five zonal offices under the control of the newly created Directorate General of Backward Classes Welfare in the Department of Social Welfare.

The policy of the Government of India can be discerned from various resolutions adopted by the Ministry of Home Affairs and Department of Personnel and Administrative reform. The policy, generally, is to provide many concessions in favour of candidates belonging to Scheduled castes and Scheduled Tribes and Other Backward Classes (OBCs) Relaxation of upper age limit, of standards of suitability in direct recruitment, reservation of general pool Residential accommodation, Fee exemption for examination/selection, Traveling allowance to Scheduled castes and Scheduled Tribes called for interview/written tests, permission to write direct to Commissioner for Scheduled castes and Scheduled Tribes, Institutional training for Scheduled castes and Scheduled Tribes Employees are some of the privileges accorded to the aggrieved communities.

A significant MO demands that a person who claims that he /she belong to Scheduled Caste or Scheduled Tribe must produce a certificate to that effect from the competent authority[23] . It is often reported in the papers that false certificates have been obtained so that the high caste persons could get government employment.[24] Provisional appointment subject to verification can also be made,[25] but if it is proved that the person who got appointed in the reserved post, did make a false claim his services shall be terminated.[26] The caste status is verified not only at the time of initial appointment, but also at the time of promotion.[27] The privilege of reservation for Scheduled Castes and Scheduled tribes is given only for those belong to Hindu, Sikh or Buddhist sects. If a person belonging to Scheduled Caste or Scheduled Tribes converts himself to any other religion he/she loses the said privilege. The appointing authority should stipulate in the letter of appointment issued to the candidates of the Scheduled castes and Scheduled Tribes that they should inform such change of religion.[28]

The reservation scheme applies to all posts/grades belonging to Groups A, B, C and D under the Central Government. Similarly it is applicable to posts of Industrial workers in Industrial Establishments of the Government. An exception is made to appointments during emergencies like flood for flood relief work, etc. Regarding the daily-rated staff, it may not be practicable to apply Reservation Orders *in toto.* It is rather difficult to calculate beforehand the number of people to be employed in this category. It depends on the exigencies of work to be executed. Yet it should be ensured that persons belonging to Scheduled castes and Scheduled Tribes are employed in such a manner, as their overall representation does not go below the prescribed percentages for Scheduled castes and Scheduled Tribes respectively.[29] Appointing casual workers against regular posts is, in effect, direct recruitment. Hence all statutory requirements relating to such appointments should be followed while regularizing casual workers.[30]

Often the bureaucracy is accused of being biased against the backward classes of people. The Committees appointed by the Government themselves have come with such charges. Such accusations and counter charges would only aggravate the situation in which the civil society would be divided more or less permanently on lines of castes leading to a sort of Catch 22 predicament.

Exception to reservation is found in filling posts by transfer or deputation. Similarly if there is non-availability if suitable candidates from Scheduled castes and Scheduled Tribes in the case of services classified 'scientific or technical' or 'for conducting research' or 'organizing, guiding and directing research', candidates from other communities could be appointed with prior approval.[31]

How far the reservation policy is given effect at the implementation level, is an important question. In India the rate of law abidingness, in general, is at a low level. And observing legal provisions regarding reservation is also often criticized for non-implementation or violation. Thus the importance of subordinate legislation in implementing reservation policy in various departments therefore could be discerned in a number of cases that came before the Courts.

Judicial Intervention in Balancing the Conflicting Interests

The nineties of the last century registered the highest number of cases regarding the question of reservation. They were mainly concerned with services/posts in the Government. Finally the political development in the early nineties led to the landmark case that finally tried to settle the legal issues.

The Background

It all started with the *Mandal Commission Report* that had not been acted upon for a long time and the government headed by V.P.Singh decided to provide reservation for backward classes. The Second Backward Class Commission was constituted on December 20, 1978, B.P.Mandal, M.P. headed it. Apart from Mandal, there were five other members of whom S.S.Gill was the Member-Secretary. The terms of reference were: one, to determine the criteria for defining the socially and educationally backward classes, two, to recommend steps to be taken for the advancement of the classes of people so identified and three, to examine the desirability or otherwise of making provision for the reservation of appointments or posts in favour of such backward classes of citizens which are not adequately represented in public services both under the Union or any State and four, to present a report to the President regarding the above questions and make recommendations. The Commission may also examine the recommendations of the First Backward Commission and considerations that stood in the way of the acceptance of its recommendations by Government.[32]

The Commission presented the Report on December 31, 1980, but no action was taken on that.[33] In 1989 V.P. Singh became the Prime Minister of a non-Congress Government and subsequently an OM was issued that 27 per cent of the vacancies in civil posts and services under the Government of India shall be reserved for Socially and Educationally Backward Classes. Consequently there was a backlash, which formed the background for this case. The central issue in the case is not the Mandal Commission Report. What was called upon to decide, was the Government's Order dated August 13, 1990 reserving 27 per cent of the seats in the government services based on the recommendations of the Mandal Commission. This Order was to come to effect on August 7, 1990. This reservation is in addition to those already reserved for Scheduled Castes and Scheduled Tribes. Moreover the number of SBEC candidates recruited on merit in open competition was not to be counted in the 27 per cent. This reservation was to be implemented in all Central Government Departments and offices and public sector undertakings, including nationalized banks and financial institutions run by the Government. The decision of the Government created a social tension and political turmoil that caused serious questions of law and order. The agitation against the proposed reservation by the students forced the Government to clarify that it had no intention to implement the recommendation in the sphere of education.

Writ petitions were filed as PIL in the Supreme Court. At first the Court refused to interfere on the ground that the matter was a political one. In spite of the fact that the Court appealed to the nation that the matter was adjudicated upon and everybody's right would be worked out, the situation did not improve. Thereupon the Supreme Court Bar association moved a petition before a five-Judge-Bench. Subsequently the Court stayed the operation of the OM dated August 13, 1990 till final adjudication. In the meanwhile the process of identification of castes for locating the SEBCs was to continue.

> At first the Court was hesitant to intervene. The Court said:
> Three out of us[34] sitting as a bench on September 21, 1990, made an order after hearing the parties where we had indicated that the decision to implement three aspects of the implementation of the Mandal Commission was a political one and ordinarily the court would not interfere with such a decision.[35]

But the political fallout became so serious that Supreme Court Bar Association came forward with a petition to hear the case regarding the OM issued by the Government for reserving 27 per cent seats in the government services for the Socially and Educationally backward Classes (SEBCs). And the Supreme Court advanced the date of hearing the petition. Subsequently the five-judge Bench of the Supreme Court stayed the operation of the OM dated 13 August 1990. In the meanwhile there was a significant change in the political front. With the fall of V.P.Singh government at the center followed by the general election and the formation of a new government, the Court sought to know the clear stand of the new government on the issue. The Government submitted that it would modify the August 13, OM 'by (i) introducing the economic criterion in the grant of reservation by giving preference to the poorer sections of the SEBCs in the 27 per cent quota and (ii) and reserving another 10 per cent of the vacancies in the civil services for Other Economically Backward Sections ...' The constitutionality of this OM was also challenged. The Government failed in fixing economic criteria and hence the Court declined to vacate the stay for implementation of Memorandum. 'The constitution of the Special bench of nine judges became necessary to finally settle the legal position relating to reservation in view of the several earlier judgments of the Supreme Court not having spoken in the same voice. Similar questions also arose in respect of implementation of State Commission Reports, which were also directed to the Constitution Bench.'[36]

The Court tried to answer many complex questions. Its intervention and balancing the conflicting interests and finally introducing the concept of 'creamy layer' as a guideline for the executive to act upon, all converge in this landmark case. The indifference shown by the state governments in implementing the judgments led to *Indra Swahney* II and the Court was visibly active.

The case is considered to be a landmark case in the judicial history of reservational justice. Justice Sawant pointed out the political nature of the case in his observation:

> In a legal system where the Courts are vested with the power of judicial review on occasions issues with social, political and economic overtones come up for consideration. They are commonly known as political questions. Some of them are of transient importance while others have portentous consequences for generations to come. More often than not such issues are emotionally hyper charged and raise a storm of controversy in the society. Reason and rationalism become the first casualties, and sentiments run high. The Courts have, however, as a part of their obligatory duty, to decide them. While dealing with them the Courts have to raise the issues above the contemporary dust and din, and examine them dispassionately, keeping in view, the long-term interests of the society as a whole. Such problems cannot always be answered by the strict rules of logic. Social realities, which have their own logic, have also their role to play in resolving them. The present is an issue of the kind.[37]

The Petitions

As many as forty-six Writ Petitions were filed. The apex Court decided to hear all the petitions together. On the side of the Petitioners Sixty-one advocates and seven persons appeared. On the side of the respondents eighty-six advocates of whom sixty- nine represented the Union and various States and seventeen represented a private party.

Fourteen main issues were framed and the Honourable Judges went into these questions in detail and the nine-Judge bench took decisions and made observations on the constitutionality, validity and enforceability of the Order dated August 13, 1990. The majority of six judges made the final decision while three expressed their dissenting opinion.

The Issues

The issues framed by the Court encompassed a wider area of Reservation Policy and hence it needs to be quoted:[38]

1. (a) Whether the 'provision' contemplated by Article 16(4) must necessarily be made by the legislative wing of the State?

   (b) If the answer to clause (a) is in the negative, whether an executive order making such a provision is enforceable without incorporating it into a rule made under the proviso to Article 309?

2 (a) whether clause (4) of the article 16 is an expectation to clause (1) of Article 16.

   (b) Whether clause (4) of the article 16 is exhaustive of the special provisions that can be made in favour of 'backward class of citizens'? Whether it is exhaustive of the special provisions that can be made in favour of all sections, classes and groups?

3. (a) What does the expression 'backward class of citizens' in Article 16(4) mean? (b) Whether the backward classes can be identified on the basis and with reference to caste alone?

   (c) Whether the backwardness in Article 16(4) should be both social and educational?

   (d) Whether the 'means test' can be applied in the course of identification of backward classes? And if the answer is yes, whether providing such a test is obligatory?

   (e) Whether a class, to be designated as a backward class, should be situated similarly to the SC/STs?

   (f) Adequacy of representation in the services under the State.

4. (a) Whether backward classes can be identified only exclusively with reference to economic criteria?

   (b) Whether criteria like occupation-cum-income without reference to caste altogether, can be evolved for identifying the backward classes?

5. Whether backward classes can be further categorized into backward and more backward categories?

6. To what extent can reservation be made?

   (a) Whether the 50 per cent enunciated in *Balaji* [1963 Supp 1 SCR 439] is a binding rule of caution or rule of prudence?

   (b) Whether the 50 per cent rule, if any, is confined to reservation made under clause (4) of Article 16 or whether it takes in all types of reservations that can be provided under Article 16?

   (c) Further while applying 50 per cent rule, if any, whether a year should be taken as a unit or whether the total strength of the cadre should be looked to?

(d) Whether *Devadasan* [(1964) 4 SCR 680] was correctly decided?

7. Whether Article 16 permits reservations being provided in the matter of promotions?
8. Whether reservations are anti-meritarian? To what extent are Article 335, 38(2) and 46 of the Constitution relevant in the matter of construing Article 16?
9. Whether the extent of judicial review is restricted with regard to the identification of Backward Classes and the percentage of reservations made for such classes to a demonstrably perverse identification or a demonstrably unreasonable percentage?
10. Whether distinction made in the second memorandum between 'poor sections' of the backward classes and others permissible under Article 16?
11. Whether the reservation of 10 per cent of the posts in favour of 'other economically backward sections of the people who are not covered by any of the existing schemes of reservations' made by the Office Memorandum dated 25-9-1991 permissible under Article 16?
12. The concept of positive action and positive discrimination.
13. Desirability of a permanent statutory body to examine the complaints of over-inclusion/under-inclusion.
14. Should the matter go back to the Constitution Bench to go into the defects of the Mandal Commission Report?

The observations of the Judges to the questions formed from the submissions in the Writ Petitions could be summarized thus. Having analyzed the judgments made on cases pertaining to reservation in the past, Pandian J observed that even with executive order reservation could be made. Most Judges agreed with this and held accordingly. But it is submitted that the Honourable Justices have not given much attention to the question. The reservation being a very important policy matter it should not be left to the executive, which for all practical purpose means 'bureaucracy'. The apathy of executive in this regard has been pointed out by writers. Moreover it is the legislature which is the proper body to formulate policies. Debates in legislature would be helpful in making the backward class people aware of what is happening to their privileges. In a country where transparency in administration has not become a reality, entrusting the policy implementation with the bureaucracy is nothing but portentous.[39] According to Justices[40] as the expression 'other authorities' include all statutory authorities and other agencies and instrumentalities of the State Government/Central Government. Some of the local bodies and some of the statutory corporations may have their own legislative wings. In such a situation it would be unreasonable and inappropriate to insist that reservation in all these services should be provided by Parliament/legislature.' But there was a word of caution from Sawant J. who said, "Reservation by executive Order may not be invalid but since it was being made for the first time in services under the Union *propriety demanded that it should have been laid before parliament* not only to lay down healthy convention but also to consider the change in social, economic and political conditions of the country as nearly ten years had elapsed from the date of submissions of the Report, a period considered for evaluation if the reservation may be continued or not.'

Next issue is the enforceability of an executive order that makes a provision under Article 16 (4). Here too almost all judges agreed upon the efficacy of the executive order and that such a provision is effective the moment it is made. The question whether clause (4) of Article 16 is an exception to clause (1) is an intriguing one. Four Justices including Chief Justice Kania stated clearly that Clause (4) is not an exception to Clause (1) of Article 16. They further said "Yet it must be remembered that the equality of opportunity guaranteed by clause (1) is to each individual citizen of the country while clause (4) contemplates special provision being made in favour of socially disadvantaged classes. Both must be balanced against each other. Neither should be allowed to eclipse the other." But the justices did not go into the question of how long should the court go on balancing in this way. Again is it proper to consider that the clause (4) is only transient in nature and hence should have a time limit.

On the other hand Thommen J. describes 16 (4) as 'enabling provision conferring discretionary power on the State; an ameliorative harmonization of conflicting norms to stretch to the utmost extent the frontiers of equality; an emphatic assertion of equality between equals and inequality between unequals so as to achieve the maximum degree of qualitative and relative equality by means of affirmative action even to the point of reservation. It is in the nature of an exception or a proviso to the general rule of equality. The Supreme Court has generally treated clause (4) as an exception or a proviso to the general rule of equality enshrined in Article 16.' He also gives a warning, 'Clause (4) seen in whatever color, is a very potent weapon which causes lasting ill effects and damage unless justly and appropriately used.'

Kuldip Singh J. describes it as a special provision. Justice Sahai too clarifies Article 16(4) as enabling provision. 'Article 16 (1) is a fundamental right of a citizen whereas Article16 (4) is an obligation of the State. The former is enforceable in a court of law, whereas the latter is "not constitutional compulsion" but an enabling provision.'

To the question whether Article 16 (4) is exhaustive of the concept of reservations in favor of backward classes, Kania CJ and Venkitachaliah, Ahmadi and Jeevan Reddi, JJ replied affirmatively. '[Therefore] where the State finds it necessary-for the purpose of giving full effect to the provisions of reservation to provide certain exemptions, concessions or preferences to members of backward classes, it can extend the same under clause (4) itself. Sawant J, in a separate judgment voiced more or less the same opinion. But Thomman J. struck a different note when he said, 'Preferences without reservation may be adopted in favour of the chosen classes of citizens by prescribing for them a longer period for passing a test or by awarding additional marks or granting other advantages like relaxation of age or other minimum requirements. Such preferences can be extended to all disadvantaged classes of citizens, whether or not they are victims of prior discrimination.' (emphasis added). He included people like the handicapped. SahaiJ focuses on another aspect of Clause (4) with whom Kuldip Singh J agreed. In the words of Sahai J. 'Extension of reservation to new categories under Articles 15 (4) and 16 (4) beyond the 50 per cent rule laid down in Balaji and Devadasan, such as to government nominees, political sufferers, defense personnel, sportsmen, children of MISA and DISIR detenues, etc. under the cover of reasonable classification is a constitutional distortion and cannot be legitimately and legally accepted as valid.'

The question 3 (a), which seeks the meaning of 'backward class of citizens' in Article 16 (4), is a significant one. Kania CJ and Venkitachaliah, Ahmadi and Jeevan Reddi, JJ relying on previous judgments in this regard said, 'The opinions of the Supreme Court in *Venkitaramana, Rajendran, Periyakaruppan* and *Vasanth,* emphasise the integral connection between caste, occupation, poverty and social backwardness. They recognize that in the Indian context, lower castes are and to be treated as backward classes. *Rajendran* and *VasanthKumar* (opinions of Chennappa Reddy and Vekitaramaiah, JJ.) constitute important milestones on the road to recognition of relevance and significance of caste in the context of Article 16 (4) and Article 15 (4).' The caste-class rhetoric continues to haunt the judgments. As further clarification it was stated, '[Hence] from the use of the word "class" in article 16 (4), it cannot be concluded either that "class" is antithetical to "caste" or that a caste cannot be a class or that a caste as such can never be taken as a backward class of citizens. The word in Article 16 (4) is used in the sense of *social class*- and not the sense it is understood in Marxist jargon.'

A dissenting view was expressed by Sahai J. he posed the question, 'what is the meaning of the word, 'backward', 'class' and 'citizen' individually and taken together. How are they to be identified? By their caste, occupation, status, economic condition etc. Although the issue of reservation has been agitated before this court, time and again, the occasion never arose to lay down any principle or test for the determination of backward class.' Again he pointed out at the problematic aspect of backwardness. He added, 'Backwardness in such a vast country with divergent religions, culture, language, habits, social and economic conditions arising out of historical reasons, geographical locations, feudal system, rigidity of caste is bound to have regional flavour. Interactions of various forces have been responsible for backwardness in different parts of the country. *A caste backward in one State may be advanced in another.* (emphasis added) And he explicitly stated that 'Backward Class in Article 16 (4) cannot be read as backward caste.

Another difficult problem encountered by the honourable Court was the identification of backward class of citizens. While discussing this aspect of the issue, Kania CJ and Venkitachaliah, Ahmadi and Jeevan Reddy, JJ.stated that 'caste cannot be kept out of the process of identification for the purpose of Article 16 (4). Pandian J too stressed the role of caste in the determination of backwardness. According to him, 'A caste is also a class of citizens and that if that caste satisfies the requisite test of backwardness, then the classification of that caste as backward class is not opposed to Article 16 (4) notwithstanding that a few individuals of that caste are socially and educationally above the general average.' In identifying the backward class the dilemma that one might face can be discerned from the words of Sawant J. 'It is contended that the adoption of caste as a factor even for identifying backwardness would perpetuate casteism but it is not possible to redress the balance in their favour on any other basis. A different basis would perpetuate the *status quo* and therefore caste system instead of eliminating it. On the other hand, by giving discriminated caste groups the benefits in question, discrimination would in due course of time be eliminated and along with it casteism.' This argument, in a way, describes a sort of catch 22 situation. Kuldip Singh J. was of the opinion that constitution forbids classification on the ground of caste. He supported the observation in *Chitralekha* that caste can be totally excluded while 'identifying a backward class. In a similar vein Sahai J. also that the word 'class' cannot and was not used as caste as it was constitutionally considered to be destructive of secularism.' He also struck a warning note in his dissenting judgment saying, 'Accepting race, religion and caste as the remedy to undo the past evil would be against constitutional spirit, purpose and objectives. Disregard the Preamble and other provisions of the Constitution like Arts. 15 (1), 16 (2) and 29 (2) will plunge the nation into disaster.' In his opinion occupation should furnish the starting point of determination of backward class.

To the question whether the 'backwardness referred to in Article 16 (4) should be both social and educational, Kania CJ and Venkitachaliah, Ahmadi and Jeevan Reddi, JJ answered that backwardness in Article 15 (4) and in Article 16 (4) are different. They said. "Though Article 340 employs the expression 'socially and educationally backward classes' and yet the expression does not find a place in article 16 (4)". The reason is obvious: "backward class of citizens in Article 16 (4) takes in the Scheduled Tribes, Scheduled Castes and all other backward classes of citizens including the socially and educationally backward classes. Thus certain classes which may not qualify for Article 15 (4) may qualify for Article 16 (4) as backward class of citizens.' The Justices accepted the fact that "The accent in Article 16 (4) is on social backwardness. Of course, social, educational and economic backwardness are closely inter - twined in the Indian context." Thomman, J. in his dissenting judgment says that 'the backward class mentioned in Article 16 (4) is a synonym for the classes mentioned in Article 15 (4). But Kuldip Singh could not agree with this. He observes, "The expression 'backward 'in the context of Article 16 (4) is entirely different than the expression 'socially and educationally backward class' in Article 15 (4). When these two articles of Constitution in juxtaposition-enacted in consecutive years- use markedly different phraseology, well established canons of interpretation dictate that such meanings should be assigned to the words as are indicated by the difference in phraseology...Also what is to be identified under Article 16 (4) is not the 'backward class' but a 'class of citizens' which is inadequately represented in the State service...The judgments of this Court wherein it is assumed that the two expressions in Article 15 (4) and Article 16 (4) mean the same thing do not lay down correct law.'

The issue of 'means-test' is discussed as an answer to question 3 (d) According to Kania CJ and Venkitachaliah, Ahmadi and Jeevan Reddi, JJ, means test signifies imposition of an income limit. It is for the purpose of excluding persons (from the backward class) whose income is above the said limit and is often referred to as the 'creamy-layer' argument. The justices consider this to be a test for proper and more appropriate identification of a class. Sawant, Thomman, Kuldip Singh, and Sahai JJ. concur with this test. But the dissenting opinion comes from Pandian, J. His argument was that only after 42 years of the commencement of the Constitution the Government was taking steps to implement the scheme of reservation for OBCs under Article 16 (4). Another objection to creamy layer test is that the impugned OM does not speak about any creamy layer test. He says:

> It cannot be said by any stretch of imagination that the Government was not aware of some few individuals having come both socially and educationally above the general average and entered in the All India Services or any other civil services. Despite the above fact, the Government has accepted the listed groups of SEBCs as annexed to the Report and it has not thought prudent to eliminate those individuals. Therefore in such circumstances, it is doubtful whether the judicial supremacy can work in the broad area of social policy or in the great vortex of ideological and philosophical decisions directing the exclusion of any section of people from the accepted list of OBCs...Therefore when this Court is not called upon to lay a test or give any guideline as to who all are to be eliminated from the listed groups of the Report, there is no necessity to lay any test much less 'creamy layer' test.

To the question (e) whether a class, to be designated as a backward class, should be situated similarly to the SC/STs? Kania CJ and Venkitachaliah, Ahmadi and Jeevan Reddi, JJ answered in the negative. Only Thomman J. strikes a dissent. With regard to adequacy of representation Kania CJ and Venkitachaliah, Ahmadi and Jeevan Reddi, JJ are of the opinion that the State could assert from the facts or it may gather necessary material through a Commission/Committee, person or authority. In his dissenting judgment Kuldip Sing, J. says:

> The insertion of 'backward' at a later stage did not change the intention with which the original draft article 10 (3) was brought into existence. Dr. Ambedkar nowhere stated that reservations were meant for backward classes. In his speech (CAD, Vol. 7, pp 701-702) he was not referring to backward or non-backward communities, he was only referring to the communities, which were dominating the public services and

> those, which were not permitted to enter the said services... So the reservation under Article 16 (4) is not meant for backward classes but for backward sections of the classes, which are not adequately represented in the State services.

To the question whether backward classes can be identified only exclusively with reference to economic criteria, Kania CJ and Venkitachaliah, Ahmadi and Jeevan Reddi, JJ answer in the negative, but in the dissenting judgment Kuldip Singh J asserts that a backward class for the purpose of Article 16 (4) can be identified solely on the basis of economic criterion.

The fifth issue is whether a backward class can be further divided into backward and more backward. The majority opinion is that as there is no legal bar doing so, State may categorize. Sahai J. does not agree with this observation for according to him 'since the Constitution treats all citizens alike for purposes of employment except those who fall under Article 16 (4) any further classification or grouping for reservation would be constitutionally invalid.'

Majority view regarding the percentage of reservation is that Article 16 (1) and 16 (4) have to be harmonized for both aims at one thing namely 'equality'. Thus by 27 per cent reservation provided by the impugned Memorandums in favor of backward classes is well within the reasonable limits. Together with reservation in favour of Scheduled castes and Scheduled Tribes, it comes to a total of 49.5 per cent .

On the carry forward rule, which was struck down in *Devadasan,* the majority opines:

> The constitutionality of the carry forward rule was questioned in *Devadasan* on the ground that it resulted in violation of 50 per cent limit rule laid down in *Balaji.* The rule itself was struck down as on facts on 29 out of 45 seats appointments were made to SC/STs. But *on its own reasoning,* the decision *in so far as it strikes down the rule* is not sustainable. The most that could have been done in that case was to quash the appointments in excess of 50 per cent ...It is wrong to presume that always reservations would exceed 50 per cent as a necessary and the only consequence of the carry forward rule. When it does tend to in any subsequent year the authorities implementing the carry forward rule should ensure that it shall not result in reservation beyond 50 per cent in any given year.
>
> In his dissenting judgment Pandian, J "The percentage of

reservation at the maximum of 50 per cent is neither based on scientific data nor on any established and agreed formula. In fact Article 16 (4) itself does not limit the power of Government in making the reservation to any maximum percentage; but it depends upon the quantum of adequate representation required in the services."

On reservation in promotions Kania CJ and Venkitachaliah, and Jeevan Reddi, observe that the question as such does not arise because the impugned Memorandums do not provide for reservation in promotions. And Ahmadi J does not express any opinion at all. But Kania CJ and Venkitachaliah, and Jeevan Reddi opine that reference to the larger Bench was made with a view to "finally settle the legal position relating to reservations". And they are of the view that Article 16 (4) is confined to initial appointment and it cannot extend to promotions. Overruling *Rangachari* it is stated:

> It is true that *Rangachari* has been the law for more than 30 years and that attempts to reopen the issue were repelled in *Karmachari Sangh.* It may equally be true that on the basis of that decision, reservation may have been provided in the matter of promotion in some of the Central and State services but we are convinced that the majority opinion in *Rangachari* to the extent it holds that Article 16 (4) permits even in promotion, is not sustainable in principle and ought to depart from. However taking into consideration all the circumstances, we direct that our decision on this question shall operate only prospectively and shall not affect promotions already made; whether on temporary, officiating or regular/permanent basis.

In this regard the logical reasoning of Sahai, J is illuminating. According to him 'constitutional sanction is to reserve for backward class of persons. But promotion from a class or group of employees is not promoting a group or class but an individual. It is one against the other.'

Whether Reservation is Anti-Meritarian?

Another significant question is whether reservations are anti-meritarian. Kania CJ and Venkitachaliah, Ahmadi and Jeevan Reddi, held that 'the mandate of Article 335 is to take the claims of members of SC/ST into consideration, consistent with the maintenance of efficiency of administration.' Again 'lowering of minimum standard permissible under Article 15 would not be permissible under article 16 to which Article 335 applies' In his concurring judgment Sawant, J. struck a warning note when he said, 'For whomsoever,...reservation is made the efficiency of administration is not to be sacrificed, whatever the efficiency may mean. This is the mandate of the Constitution itself. To hold otherwise would not only be irrational but discriminatory between two classes of backward citizens.'

The justices also give a warning that [however] it would not be permissible to prescribe lower qualifying marks or a lesser level of evaluation for the members of reserved categories since that would compromise the efficiency of the administration.

Kania CJ and Venkitachaliah, Ahmadi and Jeevan Reddi answered the question of the scope of judicial review with regard to reservational law by saying that "The extent and scope of judicial scrutiny depends upon the nature of the subject-matter, the nature of rights affected, the character of the legal and Constitutional.

Reservation for Poorer Sections

The tenth question was whether there could be a classification of 'poorer sections' among backward classes under Article 16. The issue that emerges from the second Memorandum issued by the Government on 25th September 1991 is that whether distinction made in this Memorandum between the 'poorer' sections among the backward and others could be justified under Article 16. Such poorer sections are eligible to get 'preference' in reservation appointments. Kania CJ and Venkitachaliah, Ahmadi and Jeevan Reddi, JJ observed that the Government should notify which classes among the several designated other backward classes are more backward for the purpose of this clause and the apportionment of reserved vacancies/posts among the 'backward' and 'more backward'. On such notification, the clause will become operational. The Court by a majority held that though the criteria for finding out 'poorer' had not been evolved; it was obvious that the basis intended was economic. This according Court could not be sustained for it was not permissible under the Constitution. And the Court decided the eleventh issue of permissibility of the OM by observing that the OM was constitutionally invalid and accordingly being struck down.

The impugned OM contained provision for reservation of 10 per cent of the posts in favor of 'other economically backward sections' who are not covered by any existing schemes of the reservations. The issue here was whether it is permissible under Article 16. This classification according to Kania CJ and Venkitachaliah, Ahmadi and Jeevan Reddi, JJ did not come under either Article 16(1) or article 16(4). They observed, "Reservation of 10 per cent of the vacancies among open competition candidates on the basis of income/property holding means exclusion of those above the demarcating line from those 10 per cent seats. This is not constitutionally permissible. No bar can be created for a citizen from being considered for an appointment to an office under the State solely on the basis of his income or property holding." But Kuldip Singh, J was of the opinion that Government of India could make reservations solely based on economic criterion by a separate order.

Positive Actions and Positive Discrimination

Question twelve dealt with the jurisprudential questions of Positive Action and Positive discrimination. The majority judgment took note of the argument of Dr. Rajeev Dhavan and observed:

> Dr. Rajeev Dhavan describes Article 15 (4) as a provision envisaging programmes of positive action and Article 16 (4) as a provision warranting programmes of positive discrimination. We are afraid we may not be able to fit these provisions into this kind of compartmentalization in the context and scheme of our Constitutional provisions. By now it is well settled that reservation in educational institutions and other walks of life can be provided under Article 15 (4) just as reservations can be provided in services under Article 16 (4). If so, it would not be correct to confine Article 15 (4) to programmes of positive action alone. Article 15 (4) is wider than Article 16 (4) inasmuch as several kinds of positive action programmes can also be evolved and implemented there under (in addition to reservations) to improve the conditions of SEBCs, Scheduled Castes and Scheduled Tribes, whereas Article 16 (4) speaks only of one type of remedial measure, namely, reservation of appointments/posts.

Next issue is the desirability of a permanent statutory body to examine the complaints of over-inclusion/under-inclusion. In this regard the considered view of the Court was that there ought to be a permanent body in the nature of a Commission or Tribunal, to which complaints of wrong - inclusion or non-inclusion of groups, classes and sections in the lists of *Other Backward Classes* can be made. It should have the power to examine the complaints of the said nature and pass appropriate orders.

On Mandal Commission Report

The last question was weather the matter should go back to Constitution Bench to go into the defects of *the Mandal Commission Report.* In answering the above question the Court at the outset itself pointed out that each and every defect, if any, in the working and *Report* of the *Mandal Commission* does not automatically vitiate the impugned Office Memorandums. Then the Court observed that there were three factors to be kept in mind: (a) The *Mandal Commission Report* had not been accepted fully by the Government. The issue before the Court was not the validity of the *Mandal Commission Report* but the validity of the impugned OM. (b) The appointment of Commission to go into the question of Backward Classes was not necessary because even without a Commission the Government could have specified the OBCs on the basis of material as it might have had before. It could not be said that the criteria evolved by *the Mandal Commission* for identifying OBCs were irrelevant. In many States there have been reservations for OBCs, but only the Central Government had not implemented this kind of reservation. Finally the constitution of a permanent Commission to examine complaints would obviate the need for any such scrutiny by the Supreme Court. The Court also did not find it necessary to deal with *the Mandal Commission Report.* Partly concurring Pandian J. that all SEBCs brought in the list of *the Mandal Commission Report* should be given equal opportunity under the 27 per cent reservation in Central Government Services. He was also not in favour of 10 per cent reservation for poorer section of people for its unconstitutionality. Thomman and Kuldip Singh JJ dissented. Thomman J. could not find any proper application of mind in the impugned OM. He wanted the Government to reconsider the question of reservation under Article 16 (4). Kuldip Singh J in his dissenting judgment considered *the Mandal Commission Report's* identification of 3743 castes as beneficiary unconstitutional, invalid and could not be acted upon. According to him the identification violated Article 16 (4). The Commission did not determine the backward sections of the classes who are inadequately represented in the State services. The Commission did not go into the question of desirability or otherwise of making provision for the reservation of appointments or tests in public services. The honourable Justice came down severely on the *Mandal Commission Report* by commenting that 'out of the sources for preparation of the list of Backward Castes the socio-educational field survey was an eye-wash.' Again he remarked that 'Substitution Caste for Class in Article 16 (4) amounts to re-writing the Article. He further said that the application of caste criterion to non-Hindus is anti-secular and against the basic features of the Constitution. Moreover *the Mandal Commission* relied on the census 60 years old that is the census of 1931.Hence the basic calculation is illogical, absurd and against fair play. The Commission itself had admitted that the essential data before it was woefully inadequate and sketchy. In his dissenting judgment Sahai J. pointed out that the Commissions are only fact-finding bodies. The Constitutional responsibility of reserving posts rests with the Government. Unfortunately neither in 1990 nor in 1991 this duty was discharged constitutionally or even legally. It is the duty of the Government to go into the mistakes, if any, of the Commission. The Government should examine these things before issuing any order. "If the Government failed to discharge its duty then the exercise of power stands vitiated."

Law Declared by The Supreme Court

The main judgment gave 'Directions to the Government of India, State Governments and administrations of Union Territories. Herein lies the creativity of the Court in balancing the interests and ultimately upholding the spirit of the Constitution.

The Court had directed the Governments that they should within four months constitute a permanent body for entertaining, examining and recommending upon requests for inclusion and complaints of over-inclusion and under-inclusion in the lists of Other Backward classes of citizens. The advice tendered by such body should ordinarily be binding upon the Government. Secondly, the Court asked the Government of India specify the bases, applying relevant and requisite socio-economic criteria to exclude socially advanced persons/sections ('Creamy layer') from Other Backward Classes. The impugned OM should also be subject to exclusion of creamy layer. This direction is not fully applicable to the State Governments because some States had already implemented the reservation for Other Backward Classes.[41] But those states must also evolve the said criteria within six months. Thus they must also exclude the creamy layer. Any objection regarding the criteria evolved or equitable distribution of benefits of reservation should be agitated only before the Supreme Court.

The direction given by the apex Court was not complied with in time by the Government of Kerala. This led to *Indra Sawhney II.* A sizeable section of the Other Backward Classes in Kerala would come under the creamy layer. Perhaps it was the vote-bank politics and its compulsions made Kerala do nothing on the directions given in *Indra Sawhney I.*

Much has been written on this case.[42] The Supreme Court pronounced certain important decisions: *First*, the identification of social and educational backwardness on the basis of caste was held constitutional. *Second*, it was declared that reservation based on the economic criterion alone was not permissible under the Article 15(4). Under this Article the classification as backward and most backward was permissible. *Third,* the total reservations in the government jobs under backward classes should not cross the prescribed limit of 50 per cent . However when the reservations on the basis of caste were to be provided, it should be given subject to the exclusion of creamy layer, which was to be determined by a permanent Commission to be set by the Government for this purpose. *Four,* reservations in certain technical and super-specialty areas were not permitted under the provision of Article 15(4). *Five,* the Court gave a significant verdict that the reservations were only permissible in case of initial appointments and would not be permitted to promotions and finally the Court also put forward a new doctrine of creamy layer. This doctrine is aimed at finding out the creamy layer or the upper crust of the backward class and excluding the same from the domain of beneficiaries.[43]

Post–*Indra Sawhney* Scenario

Based on the direction of the Supreme Court, the Union Government constituted an expert committee under the Chairmanship of a retired Judge of Patna High Court Ramanandan Prasad. Based on this Committee's recommendations, the Union Government issued an Official Memo (OM). The States too have the authority to formulate their own criteria for detecting the 'creamy layer' in the respective states. Each State has to formulate norms to determine upper crest of the backward classes so that upper crest could be disconnected from the rest of the backward classes. But often such formulation in the form of subordinate legislation has been challenged.

The constitutionality of the criteria formulated by the Bihar and U.P. Governments for determining the 'creamy layer' was challenged in *Ashok Kumar Thakur v. State of Bihar and others*[44] through a writ petition. Two subordinate legislations, namely Bihar Reservation of Vacancies in Posts and Services (for Schedule castes, Scheduled Tribes and Other Backward Classes) (Amendment) Ordinance, 1995 and U.P. Public Services Reservation of Schedule castes, Scheduled Tribes and Other Backward Classes Act, 1994 were challenged.

Even though the Supreme Court gave the clear verdict that reservation in promotion is unconstitutional, the post-*Indra Sawhney* state of affairs does show that the subtle conflict between politically dominated executive and constitutionally committed judiciary has not ended. As a leading jurist puts:[45]

> Not against reservation, whilst arguing for the Ezhavas in the Mandal case (1992) I supported creating opportunities for the 'disadvantaged' and to enable them to share state power. But the reservation has become excessive. There is 80 per cent reservation for many posts and services. That is why I argued for a cap of 18-22 per cent on reservation for the SCs and the STs in the Sabharwal case (1995) and denying extra or accelerated seniority outside the reservation process in the Ajit Singh case (1999). Parliament amended the Constitution by 77th Amendment (1995), the 81st Amendment (2000) and 85th Amendment (2001) to strengthen the SC and the ST reservation in promotional posts at all levels. These matters are before the Supreme Court. *Even the Constitution has been forced to become a toy to yield to political pressure.*

If the Constitution itself has become a toy in the hands of the political executive what can Judiciary, which is supposed to be the guardian of the Constitution, do? This could be answered only by the unpredictable future political events.

References

1. Webster's New World Dictionary (1968).
2. These are also called delegated legislations for the power to make detailed rules etc, is delegated to the executive by the legislature. Though the legislature as well as the judiciary has control over this kind of law making, often the executive enjoys a free hand.
3. See *Unnikrishnan v. State of Andra Pradesh, AIR 1993 SC 2178.*
4. For a serious discussion of the two aspects of 'equality' especially in the Indian context, see also Andre' Beteille, *Society and Politics in India* (OUP 1992) pp 192-214.
5. See Article 15 (4) and 16 (4).
6. AIR 1951 SC226. A similar question of discrimination was discussed in *Jagwant Kaur* v. *Bombay* AIR 1952 Bom. 461.
7. Parliament Debates, Vol XII-XIII (Part II), col.9615. as quoted in Marc Galanter, *Competing Equalities.*p.165 n. 53.
8. But unfortunately the list of the Scheduled castes is not stable. The mobility of the groups and the existence of groups whose identity is confusing do make the lists unreliable. "{Thus} it cannot be said that the lists have been stable for the past thirty years but lot of changes have taken place either in the form of addition, deletion, restrictions of districts or generic names. Further it may be noted that even caste cannot be said to have been a foolproof basis for identifying the so called Scheduled castes to be included

in the Schedule for various reasons like fluidity of definition of specific castes from region to region and their social acceptability as also the pressures referred to by the Commissioner of Scheduled Castes" R.G.Misra and Gurvinder Kaur, *Reservation Policy and Personnel Selection* (New Delhi1990) p.33.

9. The Constitution (Seventy-ninth Amendment) Act, 1995.
10. B. *Basavalingappa* v. D.*Munichinnappa* AIR 1965 SC 1269.
    Bha iyalal v. Harikishan Singh, AIR 1965 SC 1557 (Scheduled Tribes).
    Dina V.Narayan Singh (1968) 38 ELR 212 (Scheduled Tribe).
    Parasram v. Shivchand AIR 1969 SC 567 (Scheduled caste).
    Bhaiya Ram Munda v. Anirudh Patar AIR 1971 SC 2533 (Scheduled Tribes).
    Sirish Kumar v. State Of Tripura AIR 1990 SC 991 (Scheduled Tribe).
    Virendra v. Union Of India. AIR 1992 All 147.
11. *R.O. v.Prafulla* AIR 1990 SC 727.
12. *State of Gujarat v. Patel,* AIR 1992 Guj 42.
13. AIR 1990 Bom 114, 117, 118.
14. *Soosai v.Union Of India.* AIR 1986 SC 733.
15. *ibid.*
16. *State of Madras v.Champakam Dorairajan* AIR 1951 SC 525
17. The Tamil Nadu Government's request contained following reasons for the inclusion: "The said Act attracts Article 31C of the Constitution, as falling within the purview of clauses (b) and (c) of Article 39 and Article 38 and 46 of the Constitution-vide section 2 of the Act. The Act has been passed relying on the Directive Principles of State Policy enshrined in Part IV of the Constitution....
18. *The Constitution (Jammu and Kashmir) Scheduled Castes Order, 1956.*
    The Constitution (Andaman and Nicobar Islands) Scheduled Tribes Order, 1959.
    As amended by the Scheduled Castes and Scheduled Tribes Orders (Amendment) Act 1976.
    The Constitution (Dadra and Nagar Haveli) Scheduled Castes Order, 1962.
    The Constitution (Dadra and Nagar Haveli) Scheduled Tribes Order, 1962.
    The Constitution (Pondicherry) Scheduled Castes Order, 1962.
    The Constitution (Uttar Pradesh) Scheduled Tribes Order, 1967 .
    The Constitution (Goa, daman and Diu) Scheduled Castes Order, 1968.
    The Constitution (Goa, Daman and Diu) Scheduled Tribes Order, 1970.
    The Constitution (Nagaland) Scheduled Tribes Order, 1970.
    The Constitution (Sikkim) Scheduled Castes Order, 1978.
    The Constitution (Sikkim) Scheduled Tribes Order, 1978.
    The Constitution (Jammu and Kashmir) Scheduled Tribes Order, 1989.

The Constitution (Scheduled Castes) Orders (Amendment) Act 1990.

19. Quoted in Jose Kananaikil(ed) *Scheduled Caste Converts in Search of Justice, (1993)* Part III. p. 6 "It is true that it (the introduction of the Bill) is a belated step, as it should have been done long back in 1956 itself. But it was deliberately shelved by the Congress leaders at that time and today we are trying to do it. It's better late than never, so I welcome the bill. I would like to tell the House what was done by Congress leaders in 1956. On 14th October, 1956. On 14th October 1956. i.e. on the *Vijayadasami* day, Dr. Baba Saheb Ambedkar along with his five lakhs Harijan followers adopted Buddhism at Nagpur. But some days prior to it on the 25th September 1956, orders to this effect were issued by the government that the benefits of reservation, etc would not be extended to Neo-Budh Harijans. Is it the kind of justice done to Neo-Budhs by the Congress regime? It is none but Congress Party alone which is responsible for it, for which they should beg pardon of this House."

20. See. *Sixteenth Report,* Committee On The Welfare of Scheduled Castes and Scheduled Tribes (2001-2002) submitted to Lok Sabha on 27th August 2001.

21. *ibid.*

22. *ibid.*

23. Orders 1and 53.

24. A movie *Ore oru Oorile,* in Tamil, which became the subject matter for a legal dispute, has a theme pertaining to this aspect. *Rangarajan v. Jagjeevan Ram* .

25. Order 53.

26. *ibid.*

27. Orders 33 and 42.

28. Order 9.

29. Orders 17 and 23.

30. Order 44.

31. Order 16.

32. 'Confused Report and Government Apathy' is the phrase that summarizes the fate of the First Backward Class Commisssion sometimes called Kaka Kalelkar Commission after its Chairman. See Anirudh Prasad, *Reservational Justice to Other Backward Classes* (New Delhi 1997) p. 32.

33. *ibid.* p. 52.

    "It[report] did not invite much criticism for a decade. The reason was obvious. The Congress Government at Centre adopted the well known administrative euphemism of 'acceptance in principle', which was the other name for a colourable non-implementation."

    Shash Ganshyam, 'Middle Class Politics-A case of Anti-Reservation Agitation in Gujarat' *Economic and Political Weekly,* Annual Number. 1987.

The report was placed before Parliament only in April 1982 as the backward class members of Parliament protested against the delay and held a 'dharna' in front of parliament Hose. Meanwhile there was anti-reservation agitation in Gujarat in 1985. The then Prime Minister Rajiv Gandhi promised to develop a national consensus on that issue, but this did not happen.

34. [Ed.: Ranganath Misra, CJ and K.N. Singh and M.H. Kania, JJ.]
35. 1992 Supp (3) SCC 211.
36. 1992 Supp (3) SCC at 219.
37. *Indra Sawhney v. Union of India.* 1992 S.C.C (Land S) P.205 (Para 395).
38. *Ibid.* pp. 220-221.
39. The right to information has been entrapped in the colonial law namely The Official Secrets Act,1923.
40. Kania CJ and Venkitachaliah, Ahmadi and Jeevan Reddi, JJ.
41. Kerala is one such state.
42. Arun Shourie, 'The Mandal Report: The stench of casteism', *The Indian Express.* 24-8-1990. Swapen das Gupta, 'Curse on Mandal: Grotesque Caricature of Hinduism'; Andrew Beteille, 'Caste and Politics: Subversions of Public Institutions' and Prof.M.N.Srinivas, 'The Mandal Formula-Backwardness: Castes v. Individuals' *Indian Bar Review* Vol.17&18 1991. Palkhivala, 'Mandal Perpetuates Casteism' *The Hindustan Times* 30-11-1992.
43. *The Economic and Political Weekly* (April 22-28, 2000) in its editorial commented "Open competitions being what they are, even the creamy layer cannot translate its advantages into tangible benefits without the aid of the sturdy reservation policy."
44. AIR 1996 SC 75.
45. Rajeev Dhavan, 'Reservation for All?' *The Hindu* 13 June, 2003.

6

CONCLUSION

One of the socio-political problems that have been plaguing the Indian polity is the question of bringing the traditionally backward sections of the people into the main stream of social life. Unfortunately communities in India exhibit a hierarchical structure cemented by a sort of religious belief that has held on to their social psyche and also by an economic structure of feudalism based on that hierarchy. This is popularly known as *caste*, peculiar to Indian society. This social structure has baffled the British rulers too. The issue of caste thus became a serious subject along with a broader issue of ending colonial rule. Since the beginning of nineteenth century the depressed classes began to organize themselves to demand social dignity and political power.

The British rulers gave some concession to these sections and put them into two categories namely, Scheduled Castes and Scheduled Tribes. When the Indian Union became a Republic with a democratic Constitution, this concession had to be continued and the Constitution itself guaranteed this. But the Constitution went further and empowered the State to make laws for giving such preferential treatment not only to the Scheduled Castes and Scheduled Tribes incorporated in the Government of India Act 1935, but also to Other Backward Classes that are socially and educationally backward. This preferential treatment is known as 'reservation', 'affirmative action' and 'protective discrimination'

During the British rule English language was introduced in education. It was the upper castes that made use of the opportunity and this was the starting point of the development of an oligarchic bureaucracy in India. Even after democracy ushered in, the bureaucracy exercised invisible but effective power mainly because it had inherited a power-complex from the civil service of the Colonial days. The members of the bureaucracy were mostly from the upper class. The depressed class had only little opportunity to be educated in English. These two factors were combined in such a way that it had been difficult to get their cooperation in implementing the policy of protective discrimination.

Nevertheless in the pre-Independence period itself a few princely States like Travancore and Mysore and Provinces like Madras were able to become aware of the need for special treatment to the depressed classes. In Madras, particularly, *Justice Party,* the first organized political party, came to power in 1920 and protective discrimination was given the legal form, namely, Communal G.O. that later came to effect the First Amendment to the Constitution.

In the post-Constitutional period this policy underwent many acid tests, due mainly to, the lack of cooperation from the Executive wing. Bureaucracy used to close their eyes to democratic values and indifferent about implementing the constitutional objectives with gusto would often overlook the fact that the Preamble of the Constitution has proclaimed the objectives of the Republic and the most important ones among them were *Equality* and *Justice.*

The Constitution empowers the State to make law to reserve seats in educational institutions, government services and legislatures. But with regard to legislatures there is a time limit for this reservation, although this limit has been extended through Constitutional Amendments from time to time. Regarding reservation in other two spheres it looks as if this were to go ad infinitum

There is an argument that 'efficiency' should be given priority in the appointments to the posts in Government services and in support Article 335 is cited. Efficiency depends upon education (in the formal sense) and training. Unfortunately the depressed classes have not had sufficient access to this. Mere reserving of seats in the educational institutions or giving scholarships are unlikely to make human resource efficient. What is needed is restructuring the educational system itself, both in its syllabus and infrastructure. Without providing proper education reserving posts in the Government service would be like putting the cart before the horse.

The policy of reservation as found in the Constitution of India could better be stated thus: Reservation has been made in favour of four classes of people namely:

1. Women and children belonging to all sections of society and all strata of society regardless of class, caste, race, religion etc. [Article 15(3)].

2. The socially and educationally backward classes [Article 15(4)]
3. The Scheduled Castes and Scheduled Tribes [Article 15(4), 16(4) and (4A), 332] and,
4. The 'weaker section,' which include Scheduled Castes and Scheduled Tribes also [Article 46]. But much controversy has arisen in the area of reservation of seats in educational institutions, which comes under Article 15(4) and reservation of posts in government services, which comes under Article 16(4). Hence this study focuses the preferential treatment envisaged in these Articles. From the analysis of cases attracting these Articles, it could be safely assumed that many disputes have arisen regarding reservation of posts and incidentally reservation in promotions in posts.

The political parties that dominate the Legislative Wing cf the Government are often motivated to hold the vote banks and satisfy their demands and the Executive wing, as has been already pointed out, show apathy towards the policy of protective discrimination. Consequently citizens are driven to seek justice from the Court. Thus befalls on Judiciary a greater responsibility of realizing the Constitutional objective of social justice and thus the judicial process, in reservation related disputes, becomes an important aspect of study. This naturally leads the discussion to Judicial Activism.

Judicial creativity in translating the policy into reality through a justice delivery system has been discussed from a jurisprudential angle. The cases relating to reservation have been examined to trace the general trend revealed by the Court in the past five decades. The epoch making case of *Indra Sawhney* stands as an excellent example for how Judiciary has saved the nation from a political turmoil and how has Judiciary balanced the conflicting interests in a judicious manner, casting away the initial apathy that had been generated mainly because the issue had been politically hyper charged.

Sharing power and resources is the crux of socio-political problems in any polity. The case analysis reveals the fact that much competition is discernible in sharing power through obtaining position in Government service. Thus, the hermeneutics of reservation, which ought to be viewed as an affirmative action, boils down to reserving seats in the positions of power. This may be due to many reasons like the one that the post in Government services has been attached to the idea of power since the days of the British. Besides Government job entails social status as well as provides economic security.

Having traced the evolution of reservational jurisprudence it could be safely surmised that Judiciary in the initial stages went by the rule book, giving due weight to the principle of equality [Article 14] and following a method of literal interpretation the Court went against reservation in the first couple of cases. This paved the way for the Parliament to amend the Constitution for the first time in this regard. But in late sixties, there was some kind of rethinking on the part of the Judiciary and backwardness due mainly to caste came to be recognized. Moreover in *Vasanth Kumar* Chinnappa Reddy, J went to the extent of saying that "...no one will think of describing Brahmins anywhere in the land as socially and educationally backward, however poor they might be." There is some truth in it because of the social stigma attached to 'the lower castes' the feeling of inferiority in them by itself might create social problems. Industrialisation and urbanisation might go a long way in mitigating this socio-psychic syndrome. Yet this is a problem to be reckoned with.

Mainly three trends could be seen in the judicial pronouncements:

(a) In *Balaji* and *Chitralekha* the Court adopted secular, scientific and rational criteria. The limit of reservation was fixed at fifty percent and caste played only an insignificant role in determining backwardness.

(b) But when the Court came to decide *Rajendran, Sagar* and *Periyakaruppan* caste was to be considered important and finally

(c) In *N.M. Thomas* and *Akhil Barathiya Soshit Karmachari Sangh* caste was restored to a significant place and promotion posts could also be reserved. This led one scholar to describe the phenomenon as 'judicial gerrymandering'. Another eminent lawyer rightly commented that "new ideas are added without old ideas being discarded" and "law does not evolve in the Supreme Court, it meanders." The reason for this meandering seems to be that there is a subtle conflict going on between the two wings of the State namely the Political Executive and the Judiciary. Whenever, the Judiciary comes out with a decision, which the Political executive might not relish, the latter resorts to amending the Constitution. This indeed is a limitation that Judiciary has to take note of. Therefore can one say that Judiciary has been displaying activism? If the term 'activism' in this context were to mean that the judiciary should interpret law in keeping with the spirit of the Constitution enshrined in the Preamble as "Justice social, economic and political", one might be tempted to say that by and large judiciary has tried to be active, of course, within the parameters set by the Constitution and the limitations imposed by Constitutional practices. This trend could be seen in the post-*Indra Sawhney* period also.

A study of *Indra Sawhney* is warranted because this could be described as a truly landmark case where the Supreme Court displayed activism especially in balancing various interests. In fact the court was hesitant at first to deal with an issue, which was politically sensitive. But once the political executive failed to resolve the issue and thereby leading the country into political turmoil and social tension, the court decided to go into the question. Obviously it did not confine itself to the impugned OM; instead it went beyond and wanted to resolve issues related to reservation for Other Backward Classes. 'What is backwardness? How to identify the backward class? These are some of the very important questions the Court tried to answer. Though the Court took a cautious step in the *Indra Sawhney* case, in the face of public opinion, which was expressed violently, compelled it to consider and introduce the 'creamy layer' standard to eliminate the elite group within the backward classes.

Thus it may be safely concluded that Judiciary did really become active when such an active role was expected of it. Here may be found the concern of the judiciary for the welfare of the nation at large. Whenever the executive fails or takes a wrong step, the judiciary is urged to intervene. And that is what happened in post-Mandal period.

The court refused to consider 'caste' as the sole criterion, for the goal of the Constitution is to establish a casteless society. This put an end to the existing ambiguity regarding whether caste could be taken as the sole criterion for measuring backwardness. But the Court conceded that 'caste' could be one of the factors in deciding backwardness. Palkhivala went to the extent of saying that the Court was trying to revive casteism, which the Constitution emphatically intended to end. Yet it could not be overlooked that the majority judgment leans more towards the economic criterion. And the minority judgment of Justices Thommen, Kuldip Singh and R.M. Sahai rule that casteism can never be the basis of reservation.

The court accepted the economic criterion as valid in determining backwardness. Incidentally it was the Nettur Commission appointed by the Kerala State that suggested the economic criteria for determining backwardness in 1968. And in 1992 in *Indra Sawhney* the Supreme Court introduced the doctrine of 'creamy layer' so that those individuals among the backward communities who no longer suffer from social and educational backwardness could be identified and set apart from the truly backward segments of society.

One of the focal points in this study is the issue of reservation in Kerala. The present study arrives at the inference that it is not a very sensitive issue in this State. Like the rest of India, Kerala too presents a caste-ridden society but in far less virulent form. Caste does not pose a threat as such to the polity. Urbanization and Westernization seem to have spread considerably throughout the territory. The erstwhile princely State of Travancore, which forms the bulk of modern Kerala State, did accept the reality of castes and recognised the necessity of reservation. Political movements in the former princely State of Travancore started as a confederation of neglected communities. The term 'neglected' is used here with a specific connotation as the administration was in the hands of upper castes namely Brahmins and Nayars. All other communities, hence, felt neglected. Thus was born the Joint Political Congress, a political movement spearheaded by these communities. The rulers also to an extent conceded to their demands and therefore, the idea of the necessity for reservation had already been internalized when the Republican Constitution of India came into existence.

This might be one of the reasons why the Supreme Court's directive in *Indra Sawhney* did not at first produce any sharp reaction in the state nor any reaction from the administration in Kerala. This trend could be perceived generally in south India because in North India riots broke out in the aftermath of Government's decision to implement Mandal Commission's recommendation. It goes to prove that there is a higher degree of political education among the people especially among the socially and educationally backward classes in the South and the upper classes in South Indian States have been able to internalize the need for reservation.

The cases analyzed in the study reveals a fact that the reservation policy is not administered in the proper manner. Any Report from the National Commission for Scheduled Castes and Scheduled Tribes would vouch for this. National Commission itself has not proved to be an effective mechanism, because of the lack of cooperation of the administration.

It is rather intriguing to note how the present legal mechanism of reservation is shoddily put to use. Often the policy of reservation is carried out through Official Memos and Official Letters. This could be easily inferred from the cases because in most of the cases the impugned law is an executive Order or Direction. As subordinate legislation or delegated legislation is also to be considered law the Court also accepts it as law. And in all cases pertaining to reservation, the Court considered Official Memos as law. But it is submitted that a serious policy matter like reservation should not be left to the bureaucracy to tinker with. For instance had V P Singh's Government put forward a *Bill* based on *Mandal Commission Report*, there would have been enough room for the members of Parliament to voice their opinion. The Press would have discussed it at length. A democratic debate would have mitigated the wrath of the upper class student community. Therefore resorting to the short cut route of executive orders, and avoiding Parliamentary debate is not in keeping with the best traditions of democracy.

Another significant issue is the process of identifying classes of people as Scheduled or Backward. Regarding Scheduled Castes and Scheduled Tribes it is the President who has the power to notify whether a group of people would come under the respective Schedules. In a vast country like India where multi-ethnicity is the hallmark one group of people may be depressed class in one region but the same class may not belong to depressed classes in another region. Therefore the power to determine the status of the classes should be left to the State Governments.

Reservation of opportunities for the Scheduled castes and Scheduled Tribes and Other Backward Classes, though made with the objective of creating an egalitarian society, has generated Social Political and Legal problems. How the concept of equality is to be translated into a political reality for the better functioning of democracy is a vexing question. And at the same time the social impact of reservation has caused many areas of conflict. Instead of acting as a catalyst in eradicating inequality by uplifting the hitherto socially backward, the policy of reservation coupled with the parliamentary system of democracy, has indirectly encouraged the social divisions of caste in transforming themselves into solid pressure groups bargaining for political favours, if not political power.

Formal political equality was easy to achieve for the Indian Constitution adopted 'universal adult franchise'. Even universal adult franchise gets its ideological content eroded when the electorate is illiterate and ill informed. Most of the people, who are included in the Scheduled castes and Scheduled Tribes and Other Backward Classes, have not had the advantage of education. Hence achieving political equality too becomes a dream for the populace and a pretension for politicians. And realizing the goals of economic and social justice, even after half a century of Constitutional practices, remains a mirage.

The philosophy of the individual changes in accordance with social changes and social changes are mainly the result of the transformations brought about by technology. For instance in the remote villages in India even today the discriminatory treatment of 'untouchability' is being practiced, but at the same time no one is troubled by the caste-based discrimination of untouchability in the crowded buses and trains of urban India. When in the former case untouchability is practiced in spite of Article 17 of the Constitution, the latter case shows that technology's impact has made Article 17 redundant. Thus the impact of technology is to be acknowledged as a significant initiator of social equality, if not a new kind of social mobility. The social environment undergoes a change in which it becomes impossible for practicing old ways of sustaining inequalities.

In India social inequalities have been inbuilt into life on traditional beliefs. The Western historians began to treat these beliefs as part of a religion, which later came to be called Hinduism, a word of Persian origin. However these beliefs have stronger roots in the ethos of the peoples of the sub-continent. This has produced psychological complexes of 'superiority' and 'inferiority' among the traditional groups. Offering them proper education could have removed this socio-psychological syndrome.

As Dworkin remarks there are two facets of equality namely equality as a right and equality as a policy. The latter one implies treatment with equal respect and concern. This demands a social behaviour, which could not be easily internalized in a society that has hitherto followed a behavioral pattern in keeping with hierarchic ethos and almost with a religious verve. By and large the social psychology of the people has not undergone any radical change. For instance the 'respect' attached to the so-called upper caste has created a situation in which many educated persons from the depressed classes, after gaining a better economic position try to have spouses from upper class and thus try to de-class themselves. How far would this social phenomenon, though helpful in a way to achieve an egalitarian society, help the community to which he belongs to rise up.

What exactly its impact on (a) the community concerned and (b) affirmative action envisaged by law. On the other hand when an upper class woman marries a man belonging to the depressed class the court does not give her the reservation benefits. The reasoning is that she does not suffer from social backwardness. But one has to disagree with this reasoning because in fact the woman suffers social stigma, which is more severe than the one a member of depressed may suffer. She may be an outcaste for the upper caste and the members of depressed class view her with askance.

Though the Constitution by one of its Directive Principles enjoins the State to offer compulsory education to all up to the age of fourteen, no serious step has been taken till today. Moreover in the name of 'administration' education has been treated as an industry to be regulated and this has led to the over-politicization of education. Instead of developing one's personality by providing means to improve one's talents, education has got commercialized. Obviously the depressed classes being economically poor find themselves victims of the changing scenario. For them education has become both unaffordable and uneconomic. And unfortunately the over-politicization divides people on party lines. The social psychology of division of people that has the basis on caste is now being reflected on the social psychology of political parties. There is no wonder that castes have come to organize political parties.

The economic equality, which goes a long way in ensuring social equality, has also more or less similar fate. When the Constitution was ushered in, it spoke about social and economic justice and in 1975 'socialism' was added to its Preamble. But the economic development has not been on the desirable lines. In the initial decades the Nehruvian socialism took precedence. The main features are the 'protected economy' and the 'mixed economy' in which public sector enjoyed prestige. In the public sector units 'reservation' has been adopted often without giving due weight to efficiency in governance. An important goal of governance ought to have been production of wealth. All other policies ought to be subservient to it. But unfortunately sharing the existing resources became the prime motive. This aggravated an unhealthy competition among the various groups in the society. This coupled with the electoral politics that aims at making majority in parliament and in various State Assemblies made the competition manipulative one, leading the groups to consolidate so that they would be strong enough to bargain for power. The policy of reservation is to be understood with this backdrop.

The identification of backward class too poses many a problem. There are mainly three aspects of backwardness: social, economic and educational. To quantify the backwardness certain parameters are to be formulated. Here comes the importance of the doctrine of creamy layer. Yet there are certain other factors that are also to be considered. Each State in Indian Union exhibits different rate of educational level, economic progress and social stratification. Perhaps that is why the states have been given the authority to decide the backwardness of the classes with regard to Other Backward Classes.

The proclaimed object of the policy of reservation is to achieve the meaningful equality among the people. The success of democracy too depends on realizing this desideratum. The road from *homo hierarchicus* to *homo equalis* is not smooth. But it is an obvious fact that the ideal of equality cannot be fully achieved. It is the feeling of 'being equal' and the recognition that one naturally gets in a society. This feeling, if it were inculcated would go a long way in removing social backwardness. But here too the State has not succeeded. There must be sufficient reasons for the failure and some of the reasons have been brought to light in the discussions in the study. The legislative wing and the executive wing of the government have to bear the bulk of the blame for the failure, whereas the judicial wing has tried to solve the complicated issue by making timely intervention and balancing of conflicting interests. Besides the legislative and executive wings do not emphasize the efficiency of the administration, whereas the judiciary at times wakes to the expediency of observing Constitutional stipulation regarding efficiency of the administration.

One of the important actors in the Constitutional practice is the political executive. In a Parliamentary democratic system it is the creation of the party or alliance of parties that could command majority in the legislature. This inevitably leads to a situation where the political parties vie with one another to woo the voters and in this process it is easy to surmise that they could not antagonize the bulk of the population, who hitherto enjoyed no power in the governance. The political executive being the projection of the majority in the legislature in the parliamentary system, the life span of the political executive depends upon the parties and their popularity. Since the late sixties of the last century the one party dominant system has been successfully challenged to produce in turn a multi-party system devoid of any ideological commitment. The avowed aim of these parties is to obtain majority in the legislatures. This makes them enact laws to satisfy the slogan mongering 'vote banks' rather than bring about a desirable impact of these statutes on society. At the same time the static mind set of the bureaucracy cast in the mold of British Colonial administration does not auger well with the sincere implementation of laws in general and laws regarding reservation in particular. It is only natural that in a given power structure or system some people get the chance to exercise power and the dominant group would never like change because change will upset their 'apple cart'. Thus they are wedded to status quo. Restructuring bureaucracy is the only solution to this problem. People with dedication and managerial skill should man it. Personal loyalty and self-centeredness should be replaced by an urge to realize the ideals set out in the Preamble of the Constitution. But unfortunately the Indian bureaucracy has been neither democratized nor modernized. The bureaucracy itself has become almost another pressure group that tries avowedly to preserve its privileges and prestige. This mind-set is, perhaps, the reason why the policy of reservation is not implemented in the proper way.

Moreover the Executive displays apathy towards, rather than obligation to follow, the directions given even by the apex Court. To evade contempt of Court the Executive adopts many methods too. This would create and undesirable mistrust between the two wings of Government and ultimately lowers the esteem of the Judiciary among the citizens.

The present study has tried to probe into how the legislature, executive and finally judiciary have viewed this issue and how judiciary tries to find out a solution by its active intervention. In this context it would be relevant to point out that the legislative and executive branches in India have the power and responsibility. The Constitution of India has empowered the Judiciary to declare finally what law is. Therefore judicial pronouncements become significant and the doctrine of 'creamy layer' is a concrete contribution in this direction.

The judiciary, thus, introduced 'economic' criterion, which is all the more important because economic welfare is the basis for advancement and lack of it causes all other kinds of 'backwardness'. Moreover the doctrine of 'creamy layer' tries to wean the so-called backward classes off the 'protective provisions' of the constitution, which only perpetuates the societal taxonomy of castes at the expense of a meaningful democracy. The doctrine of creamy layer tries to prescribe a pecuniary parameter to probe the degree of backwardness and thereby the more advanced among the formerly backward could be eliminated from the relief umbrella of 'protective discrimination'. This is in keeping with the spirit of the Preamble of the Constitution, which speaks about 'economic justice' and 'socialism'. It is to be noted at this point that Preamble is declared to be one of the Basic Structures of the Constitution. And judiciary may find it a useful tool for 'social engineering.'

But with regard to millions of Dalits (Scheduled Castes) and Adivasis (Scheduled Tribes) this parameter should not to be applied. The economic criteria in the long run will have an adverse effect of compartmentalizing these classes of people and prevent them from being brought into the mainstream of social life.

Recommendations

1. The Government should come forward to set up an Ombudsman like mechanism for hearing the complaints of depressed class people. Such an institution should have village level offices too. Moreover instead of making it more formal and legal, it would be better that such tribunals should be presided over by a team of persons not only from the legal field but also from other walks of life. It would be better if such legal mechanism be on the line of French Tribunals.
2. A comprehensive legislation to realize the above desideratum is the need of the hour.
3. Education should be structured in such a way that the depressed classes should get enough opportunity to develop their talents and personality. Primary education, in keeping with the spirit of the Directive Principles of State Policy, should be made available to the children of the depressed classes. It would be better if the educational curriculum were structured in such a way to develop traditional skills and knowledge.
4. The value and relevance of any policy will be judged only by the results it produces. Hence a monitoring Agency to assess the progress made each year in realizing the objectives of the policy of reservation should also be set up.
5. Many authors like Anirudh Prasad documented the absence of a database for assessing the impact of reservation policy. Even the Government appointed commissions have found it difficult to collect data. Hence it is submitted that a data bank in this regard is urgently needed to be established.

Areas for Further Research

1. The success of any policy is assessed by the result it produces. Have the provisions that envision affirmative action yielded desirable results or helped achieve the desideratum of building an egalitarian society by bringing the Depressed Classes to the main stream of civil society? Backward Classes other than Scheduled castes and Scheduled Tribes have registered some progress; but the position of the Scheduled castes and Scheduled Tribes has not made that much progress. A few studies in this area have appeared, but the fact that the upward mobility of the depressed classes varies from region to region. This in fact is an area where further research could be undertaken.
2. Whether criticizing the government, for their failures to achieve the goal of equality among the classes, is justified, or is there any other reason (or a reason) that has to be discerned from the politico-socio-economic life of the people of India? When competition is the hallmark of the globalizing process, is it wise to discard merit for realizing the elusive ideology of social justice and equality? What shall be the agenda for future when the very governance is inevitably intertwined with global agendas? Will it not be suicidal to discard merit? These are some of the pertinent questions for the scholars to probe further.
3. The Scheduled Castes, Scheduled Tribes and Other Backward Classes of people would think in terms of getting the privilege of reservation in the private sector also. This issue is being raised here and there even though no concrete program of agitation has begun. Reservation in the private sector has thus become an emerging problem with political and economic ramifications. How far will this reservation help the private sector in effectively participating in the economic development of the country is a significant question.
4. Commenting on a recent judgment of the US Supreme Court upholding affirmative action, a correspondent says that extending reservation in private sector is desirable. Once the reservation scheme became mandatory for the private sector how would it affect foreign investments and foreign collaborations in the economy of India? It should not be construed that the reservation policy *per se* affects efficiency adversely. In fact reservation policy does not attract real talents among the reserved category. In the highly politicized competition for seats within the percentage of seats allotted all

categories of candidates adopt their own ways and means to grab them. Here comes the notoriety of political nepotism and other corrupt practices. What are the solutions that can be suggested?

5. The impact of the British rule was seen in Westernization; but it happened only outwardly and it touched mainly the so-called upper castes. The British rule treated the communities on equal terms; but the encouragement that they gave to promote a sense of equality was fraught with motives to create division also. Perhaps the communities themselves might have become victims to this 'dividing syndrome' of the concept of equality when translated into political realities. The communities that hitherto enjoyed a higher status might invariably resent the 'equal status' came to be enjoyed by the former 'lower' communities. Similarly the communities that had hitherto been 'suppressed' might feel a certain amount of 'arrogance' from the newly obtained equality of status. Thus the very political doctrine of equality breeds a socio-psychological inequality. Unfortunately political leaders and legal luminaries do not take into account this phenomenon. This is an area that touches sociology, politics and social psychology. A genuine research in this area might be useful to the future policy makers.

Tables of Cases

1.	A.I.I.M.S Students Union v. A.I.I.M.S	AIR 2001 SC 3262
2.	A.K.Gopalan v. State of Madras.	AIR 1950 SC 27
3.	A.Periakaruppan v. State of T.N	AIR 1971 SC 2303
4.	Aarti Gupta v. State of Punjab	AIR 1988 SC 481
5.	Action Committee v. union of India	AIR 1994 SC 153
6.	Ajith Singh Januaja v. State of Punjab (Ajith Singh I)	AIR 1996 SC 1189
7.	Ajith Singh v. State of Punjab (Ajith Singh II)	AIR 1999 SC 3471
8.	Akhil Bhartiya Soshit Karamchari Sangh v. Union of India.	AIR 1981 SC 298
9.	Ameerkhan v. A. Gangadharan	AIR 2001 SC 3299
10.	Arati Roy Chaudhary v. Union of India	AIR 1974 SC 532
11.	Ashok Kumar Gupta v. State of U.P	1997 5 SCC 201
12.	Ashoka Kumar Thakur v.State of Bihar	AIR 1996 SC 75
13.	B. Basavalingappa v. D.Munichinnappa	AIR 1965 SC 1269
14.	B.N.Tewari v. Union of India	AIR 1965 SC 1430
15.	B.Venkataramana v. State of Madras and others	AIR 1951 SC 229
16.	Bhaiyalal v. Harikishan Singh,	AIR 1965 SC 1557
17.	Bhaiya Ram Munda v. Anirudh Patar	AIR 1971 SC 2533
18.	Bharat Sevashram Sangh v. State of Gujarat	AIR 1987 SC 494
19.	Bihar State Harijan Kalyan parishad v. Un ion of India	AIR 1985 SC 983
20.	Bimlesh Tanwar v. State of Haryana	AIR 1994 SCW 1508
21.	C.A.Rajendran v.Union of India & Others	AIR 1968 SC 507
22.	C.M. Arumugam v. S. Rajagopal	AIR 1976 SC 939

23. Champakam Dorairajan v. State of Madras AIR 1951 SC 226
24. Chatter Singh v. State of Rajasthan AIR 1997 SC 303
25. Chetan Dilip Motghare v. Bhide Girls Education society ,Nagpur AIR 1994 SC 1917
26. Chief General Manager,Telecom,Kerala Circle, Trivandrum Vs.G.Renuka AIR 1997 SC 2138
27. Commissioner of Commercial Taxes,A.P v.G.Sethumadhave Rao AIR 1996 SC 1915
28. Comptroller & Auditor General v. M.L.Mehrotra AIR 1991 SC 2288
29. Deepak Sibal v. Punjab University AIR 1989 SC 905
30. Dina V.Narayan Singh (1968) 38 ELR 212
31. Dr. (Mrs.) Sandhya Jain v. Dr. Subhash Garg AIR 2000 SC 29
32. Dr. Jagdish Saran v. Union of India AIR 1980 SC 820
33. Dr. Narayana Sharma v. Dr. Pankaj Kr. Lehkar AIR 2000 SC 72
34. Dr. Preeti Srivastava v. State of M.P AIR 1999 SC 2894
35. Dr.Chakradhar Paswan v. State of Bihar AIR 1988 SC 959
36. Dr.Sadhana Devi v. State of U.P AIR 1997 SC 1120
37. Fertiliser Corporation Kamgar Union v. Union of India. (1981) 1SCC 568
38. General manager Southern Railway v. Rangachari AIR 1962 SC 36
39. Guntur Medical College v. Mohan Rao AIR 1976 SC 1904
40. Hari Shamrao Nimje v. Union of India AIR 1977 SC 2137
41. Haridas Parsedia v. Urmila Shakya AIR 2000 SC 278
42. Hiralal v.State of Punjab AIR 1971 SC1777
43. Indra Sawhney v. Union of India AIR 2000 SC 498
44. Indra Swahney Vs. Union of India AIR 1992 SC 477
45. Jagdish lal v. Union of India AIR 1997 SC 2366
46. Jagdish Negi v. State of U.P AIR 1997 SC 3505
47. Janaki Prasad v. State of J & K AIR 1973 SC 930
48. Jatinder Pal Singh v. State of Punjab AIR 2000 SC 609
49. K.C.Vasant Kumar v.. State of Karnataka AIR 1985 SC 1495

50. K.Duraisamy v. State of T.N AIR 2001 SC 717
51. K.S.Jayasree v. State of Kerala AIR 1976 SC 2381
52. M. G. Badappanavar v. State of Karnataka AIR 2001 SC 260
53. M. P. v. Nivedita Jain AIR 1981 SC 2945
54. M.R.Balaji v. State of Mysore. AIR 1963 SC 649
55. Makhan Lal v. State of J & K AIR 1971 SC 2206
56. Maneka Gandhi v, Union of India AIR 1978 SC597
57. Marri Chandra Rao v. Dean, Medical College AIR 1990(3)SCC130
58. Minerva Mills Ltd. v. Union of India., AIR 1980 SC 1789
59. Minor P. Rajendran v. State of Madras" AIR 1968 SC 1012
60. N.E. Horo v. Smt. Jahan Ara AIR 1972 SC 1840
61. N.M.Thomas v. State of Kerala AIR 1976 SC 490
62. National Federation of SBI v. Union of India AIR 1995 SC 1457
63. Nishi Maghu v. State of J&K AIR 1980 SC 1975
64. P&T SC /ST Employees Welfare Association (Regd.) v.Union of India. AIR 1989 SC 139
65. P.G.Institute of Medical Education and Research Chandigarh,v. Faculty Association AIR 1998 SC 1767
66. P.S. Ghalaut v. State of Haryana AIR 1996 SC 351
67. P.Sagar v. State of AP AIR 1968 SC 1379
68. Parasram v. Shivchand AIR 1969 SC 597
69. Post Graduate Institute of Medical Education & Research etc.v. K.L.Narsimhan & and others AIR 1997 SC 3687
70. Pradip Tandon v. State of U.P. AIR 1975 SC 563
71. Prem Prakash v. Union of India AIR 1984 SC 1831
72. R.Chitralekha v. State of Mysore AIR 1964 SC 1823.
73. R.K. Sabharwal and others v. State of Punjab AIR 1995 SC 1371
74. Rajiv Mittal v. Maharshi Dayanand University AIR 1998 SC 680
75. Ram Prasad v. D.K.Vijay AIR 1999 SC 3563
76. Ritesh R. Sah v. Dr. Y.L. Yamul AIR 1996 SC1378
77. S.R.Murthy v. State of Karnataka AIR 2000 SC 450
78. S.S.Sharma v. Union of India AIR 1981 SC 588
79. S.Vinodkumar v. Union of India 1996SOLcaseNo.237
80. Sarish Chandra v. State of Tripura AIR 1987 SC1601

81. SBI SC/ ST Employees Welfare Association v. State Bank of India AIR 1996 SC 1838
82. SC/ST Officers Welfare Council v. State of U.P AIR 1997 SC 1451
83. Soosai v. Union of India AIR 1986 SC 733
84. Srish Kumar v. State Of Tripura AIR 1990 SC 991
85. State of A.P. v. USV. Balarama AIR 1972 SC 1375
86. State of AP v. Nagam Chandrasekhara AIR 1988 SC 1309
87. State of Bihar v. Bal Mukund Sah AIR 2000 SC 1296
88. State of Bihar v. Bageshwarki Prasad (1995) s(1) SCC 432
89. State of Karnataka v. Kumari Gowri Narayana Ambiga AIR 1995 SC 1691
90. State of Karnataka v. U.B.Urushabendra Kumar AIR 1994 SC 1528
91. State of Maharashtra v. Kumari Tanuja AIR 1999 SC 791
92. State of Maharasthra v. Abhay AIR 1985 SC 328
93. State of Punjab v. Dayanand Medical college and Hospital AIR 2001 SC 3006
94. State of Punjab v. G.S. Gill AIR 1997(4) SC 0605
95. State of Punjab v. Surjit Singh AIR 2000 SC 3385
96. State of U.P. v. Dr. Dina Nath Shukla AIR 1997 SC 1095
97. Subhash v .Union of India. AIR 1991 SC 631
98. Superintending Engineer,Public Health,U.T.Chandigarh v. Kuldeepsingh AIR 1997 SC 2133
99. Suresh Chandra v. J.B.Agarwal AIR 1997 SC 2487
100. T.Devadasan v. Union of India. AIR 1964 SC 179
101. The Comptroller and Auditor General v.K.S Jagannathan, AIR 1987 SC 537
102. Triloki Nath Tiku v. State of J & K AIR 1969 SC 1
103. Triloki Nath Tiku v. State of J & K AIR 1967 SC 1283
104. Union of India v. Dudh Nath Prasad AIR 2000 SC 525
105. Union of India v. Virpal Singh Chauhan AIR 1996 SC448
106. Union of India v. Brij lal Thakur AIR 1997 SC 2101
107. Union of India v. Madhav Gajanan Chaubal AIR 1997 SC 3074
108. Union of India v Rajiv Yadav IAS AIR 1995 SC 14
109. Valasamma Paul v. Cochin University AIR 1996 SC 1011
110. Venkateswarlu v. Govt. of A. P (1996) 5 SCC 167

111. Virendra v. Union o'f India. AIR 1992 All 147
112. Vishwas Anna Sawant v. Municipal corporation of Greater Bombay AIR 1994 SC 2408

High Court Cases

Andhra Pradesh

1. Ch. Rajaiah v. State of A.P; I.L.R.1973, A.P. 516
2. Desu Rayadu v A.P.P.S.C; AIR 1967, A.P.353
3. P.Sudarsan v State of A.P.; AIR 1958, A.P.569
4. V.Narayan Rao v. State of A.P.; AIR 1987, A.P.53
5. V.Raghuramulu v State of A.P ; AIR 1952, A.P. 129
6. Unnikrishnan v. State of Andhra Pradesh AIR 1993 SC 2178

Bihar

1. Abdul Latif v. State of Bihar A.I.R.1964, Patna, 393
2. Abhay Kumar v. Principal Darbhanga Medical College. A.I.R.1968, Patna, 504
3. Amalendu Kumar v. State of Bihar A.I.R.1980, Patna,1
4. Chaitram v. Sikander A.I.R.1968, Patna, 337
5. Dr. Anand Kumar Mishra v. State of Bihar A.I.R.1980, Patna 164
6. Hirdaya Narain v. Md.Sharif A.I.R.1968, Patna 296
7. Kakshan Parveen Shahabuddin v. State of Bihar A.I.R.1980, Patna 215
8. Nand Kishore Sharma v. State of Bihar A.I.R.,1965, Patna, 372
9. Padmaraj Samarendra v. State of Bihar A.I.R,1969, Patna,226.
10. Sheod Singh v. State of Bihar. AIR 1986 Pat 124
11. Umesh Chandra Sinha v. State of Bihar A.I.R.1968, Patna, 3

Gujarat

1. Dayabhai Chaturbhai v. State of Gujarat IL.R.,(II).1970, Gujarat, 386
2. State of Gujarat v. Patel, AIR 1992 Guj 42

Jammu & Kashmir

1. Lalitha Suri v. State of JK A.I.R.1965, J&K, 101
2. Sardool Singh v. Medical College. A.I.R., 1970, J&K, 45
3. State of J&K v. Jagannath A.I.R., 1958, J&K 14

Karnataka

1.	B.Sayeed Ahmed v. State of Mysore	L,J.(1), 1969, Mysore, 79
2.	G.N. Gudigar v. State of Mysore	L.J(2), 1972, Mysore, 202
3.	Keshava Iyengar v. State of Mysore	A.I.R.1956, Mysore 20
4.	Partha v. State of Mysore.	A.I.R.1951, Mysore 220
5.	Ramakrishna Singh v. State of Mysore	A.I.R.1960, Mysore 338
6.	Santhakumar v. State of Mysore	(1971) 1 Mys. L. J. 226
7.	Shetty v. State of Mysore	A.I.R.1969, Mysore, 48
8.	Subhashini v. State of Mysore.	A.I.R.1966 Mysore, 40
9.	Sudha v. S.C. of Medical College	A.I.R.1967, Mysore, 221
10.	Viswanath v. State of Mysore	A.I.R.1954, Mysore, 132

Kerala

1.	Hariharan Pillai v. State of Kerala	A.I.R.1968, Kerala.42
2.	Jacob Mathew v. State of Kerala	A.I.R.1964, Kerala, 39
3.	Kumari.T. Shameem v. Principal Medical College, TVM.	A.I.R.1975.Kerala, 131
4.	Laila Chacko v. State of Kerala	A.I.R.1967, kerala, 125
5.	State of Kerala v. Krishna Kumari	A.I.R.1976, Kerala, 54
6.	State of Kerala v. R.Jacob	A.I.R.1964, Kerala, 316

Madhya Pradesh

1.	Rajesh Mullick v. state of M.P	AIR 1987 MP 184

Maharashtra

1.	Gopalakrishna v. State of Maharashtra	AIR 1987 Bom 123
2.	Rajesh Arjunbhai Patel v. State Of Maharashtra	AIR 1990 Bom 114

Orissa

1.	Parvat Nalini Mallick v. State of Orissa	I L.R.,1972, Cuttack 1372

Punjab

1.	Gurinder Pal Singh v. State of Punjab	A.I.R.1974, Punjab,125
2.	Km Usha Rani v. M.D. University, Rohtak	AIR 1984 P & H 297
3.	Ramesh Chandra Garg v. State of Punjab	A.I.R.1966, Punjab 476

Tamil Nadu

1.	Champakam Dorairajan v. State of Madras	A.I.R.1951, Madras, 120

2. Natarajan v. The Director General Posts and Telegraphs A.I.R.1970, Madras, 459

Uttar Pradesh

1. Chhotey Lal v. State of U.P. A.I.R.1979, Allahabad, 135
2. Dilip Kumar v. State of U.P. A.I.R.1973, Allahabad, 592
3. Subhas Chandra v. State of U.P A.I.R.1973, Allahabad, 295

West Bengal

1. RN Pramanick v. Union of India. A.I.R.1969, Calcutta, 576

Amendments

1. **The Constitution (First Amendment) Act, 1951 art.15 (4)**

   Amendment of article 15.-**To article 15 of the Constitution, the following clause shall be added:-**

   "(4) Nothing in this article or in clause (2) of article 29 shall prevent the State from making any special provision for the advancement of any socially and educationally backward classes of citizens or for the Scheduled Castes and the Scheduled Tribes."

2. **The Constitution (Eighth Amendment) Act, 1956 art.330**

   Amendment of article 334.-In article 334 of the Constitution, for the words "ten years" the words "twenty years" shall be substituted.

3. **The Constitution (Sixty-Fifth Amendment) Act, 1990 art. 338**

   In Article 338 of the Constitution:-

   (a) for the marginal heading, the following marginal heading shall be substituted, namely:-

   "National Commission for Scheduled Castes and Scheduled Tribes".

   (b) for clauses (1) and (2), the following clauses shall be substituted, namely:-

"(1) There shall be a Commission for the Scheduled Castes and Scheduled Tribes to be known as the National Commission for the Scheduled Castes and Scheduled Tribes.

(2) Subject to the provisions of any law made in this behalf by Parliament, the Commission shall consist of a Chairperson, Vice-Chairperson and five other Members and the conditions of service and tenure of office of the Chairperson, Vice-Chairperson and other Members so appointed shall be such as the President may by rule determine.

(3) The Chairperson, Vice-Chairperson and other Members of the Commission shall be appointed by the President by warrant under his hand and seal.

(4) The Commission shall have the power to regulate its own procedure.

(5) It shall be the duty of the Commission:

(a) to investigate and monitor all matters relating to the safeguards provided for the Scheduled Castes and Scheduled Tribes under this Constitution or under any other law for the time being in force or under any order of the Government and to evaluate the working of such safeguards;

(b) to inquire into specific complaints with respect to the deprivation of rights and safeguards of the Scheduled Castes and Scheduled Tribes;

(c) to participate and advise on the planning process of socio-economic development of the Scheduled Castes and Scheduled Tribes and to evaluate the progress of their development under the Union and any State;

(d) to present to the President, annually and at such other time as the Commission may deem fit, reports upon the working of those safeguards;

(e) to make in such reports recommendations as to the measures that should be taken by the Union or any State for the effective implementation of those safeguards and other measures for the protection, welfare and socio-economic development of the Scheduled Castes and Scheduled Tribes; and

(f) to discharge such other functions in relation to the protection, welfare and development and advancement of the Scheduled Castes and Scheduled Tribes as the President may, subject to the provisions of any law made by Parliament, by rule specify.

(6) The President shall cause all such reports to be laid before each House of Parliament along with a memorandum explaining the action taken or proposed to be taken on the recommendations relating to the Union and the reasons for the non-acceptance, if any, of any of such recommendations.

(7) Where any such report, or any part thereof, relates to any matter with which any State Government is concerned, a copy of such report shall be forwarded to the Governor of the State who shall cause it to be laid before the Legislature of the State along with a memorandum explaining the action taken or proposed to be taken on the recommendations relating to the State and the reasons for the non-acceptance, if any, of any of such recommendations.

(8) The Commission shall, while investigating any matter referred to in sub-clause (a) or inquiring into any complaint referred to in sub-

clause (b) of clause (5), have all the powers of a civil court trying a suit and in particular in respect of the following matters, namely:

(a) summoning and enforcing the attendance of any person from any part of India and examining him on oath;

(b) requiring the discovery and production of any documents;

(c) receiving evidence on affidavits;

(d) requisitioning any public record or copy thereof from any court or office;

(e) issuing commissions for the examination of witnesses and documents;

(f) any other matter which the President may, by rule, determine.

(9) The Union and every State Government shall consult the Commission on all major policy matters affecting Scheduled Castes and Scheduled Tribes."

(c) existing clause (3) shall be renumbered as clause (10).

4. **The Constitution (Seventy-Seventh Amendment) Act, 1995 Art.16(4 a)**

Amendment of article 16.-In article 16 of the Constitution, after clause (4), the following clause shall be inserted, namely:-

"(4A) Nothing in this article shall prevent the State from making any provision for reservation in matters of promotion to any class or classes of posts in the services under the State in favour of the Scheduled Castes and the Scheduled Tribes which, in the opinion of the State, are not adequately represented in the services under the State.".

5. **The Constitution (Seventy-Ninth Amendment) Act, 1995 art. 334**

Amendment of article 334: In article 334 of the Constitution, for the words "fifty years", the words "sixty years" shall be substituted.

6. **The Constitution (Eighty-First Amendment) Act, 2000 art.16(4 b)**

Amendment of article 16: In article 16 of the Constitution, for clause (4A), the following clauses shall be inserted, namely: -

"(4B) Nothing in this article shall prevent the State from considering any unfilled vacancies of a year which are reserved for being filled up in that year in accordance with any provision for reservation made under clause (4) or clause (4A) as a separate class of vacancies to be filled up in any succeeding year or years and such class of vacancies shall not be considered together with the vacancies of the year in which they are being filled up for determining the ceiling of fifty per cent reservation on total number of vacancies of that year".

7. **The Constitution (Eighty-Second Amendment) Act, 2000 art.335**

Amendment of article 335: In Article 335 of the Constitution, the following proviso shall be inserted at the end,namely :—

"Provided that nothing in this article shall prevent in making of any provision in favour of the members of the Scheduled Castes and the Scheduled Tribes for relaxation in qualifying marks in any examination or lowering the standards of evaluation, for reservation in matters of promotion to any class or classes of services or posts in connection with the affairs of the Union or of a State".

8. **The Constitution (Eighty-Third Amendment) Act, 2000 art.243(d)**

Amendment of article 243M: In article 243M of the Constitution, after clause (3), the following clause shall be inserted namely:-

"(3A) Nothing in article 243D, relating to reservation of seats for the Scheduled Castes, shall apply to the State of Arunachal Pradesh

9. **The Constitution (Eighty-Fifth Amendment) Act, 2001 art 16**

Amendment of article 16.-In article 16 of the Constitution, in clause (4A), for the words "in matters of promotion to any class", the words "in matters of promotion, with consequential seniority, to any class" shall be substituted.

SC/ST Population and its trends based on 2001 census

Courtesy; Census of India report 2001

Trends in population size, proportion and decadal growth of Scheduled Castes and Scheduled Tribes population in India (1951–2001 Census)

Population in million

Census Year	*Total Population*	*Population*		*Proportion of Population*		*Decadal growth rate of population*		*Decadal growth rate of Non-SC/ST population*
		SC	*ST*	*SC*	*ST*	*SC*	*ST*	
1951	356.8	51.3	19.1	14.4	5.4	-	-	-
1961	439.2	64.4	30.1	14.7	6.9	25.5	57.6	20.4
1971	547.9	80.0	38.0	14.6	6.9	24.2	26.2	24.7
1981	665.3	104.8	51.6	15.7	7.8	30.9	35.8	18.4
1991	838.6	138.2	67.8	16.5	8.1	31.9	31.2	24.3
2001	1028.6	166.6	84.3	16.2	8.2	20.6	24.5	22.9

Population Size and Decadal Growth Rate of the Scheduled Caste Population in Top Five SC's Population States

State	*2001 Census SCs Population**	*1991 Census SCs Population*	*Decadal growth rate of SCs Population*	*Decadal growth rate of Non-SC/ST population*
Uttar Pradesh	35,148,377	28,044,139	25.3	26.0
West Bengal	18,452,555	16,080,611	14.8	18.9
Bihar	13,048,608	9,982,448	30.7	28.2
Andhra Pradesh	12,339,496	10,592,066	16.5	13.8
Tamil Nadu	11,857,504	10,712,266	10.7	12.0

*Recast figures.

The five states constitute 54.5 per cent of the total SCs population of the country.

INDIA
PERCENTAGE OF SCHEDULED CASTES TO TOTAL POPULATION 2001 (STATE/UT)

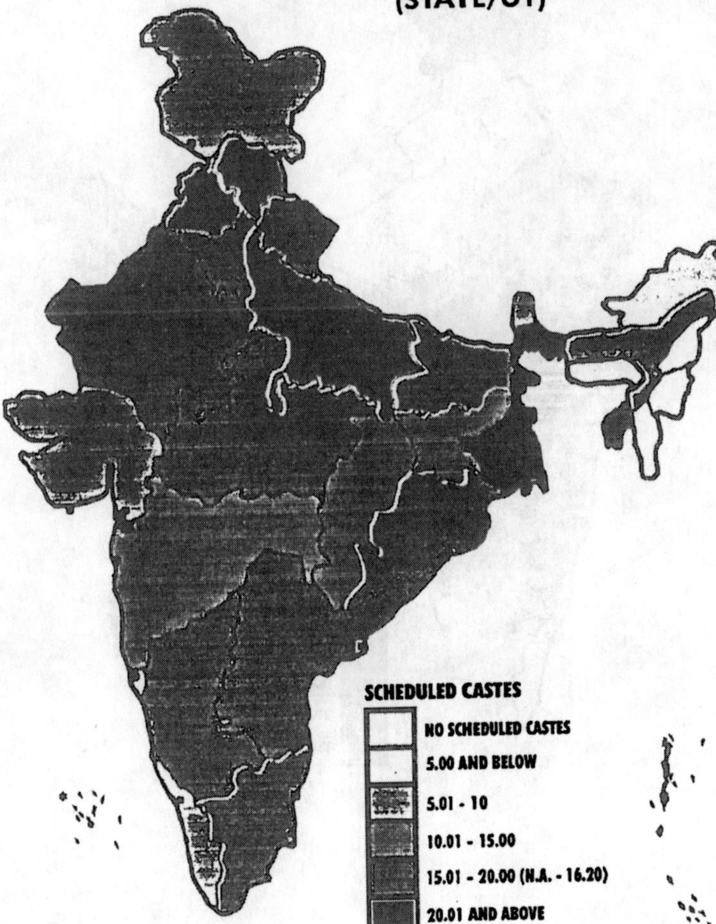

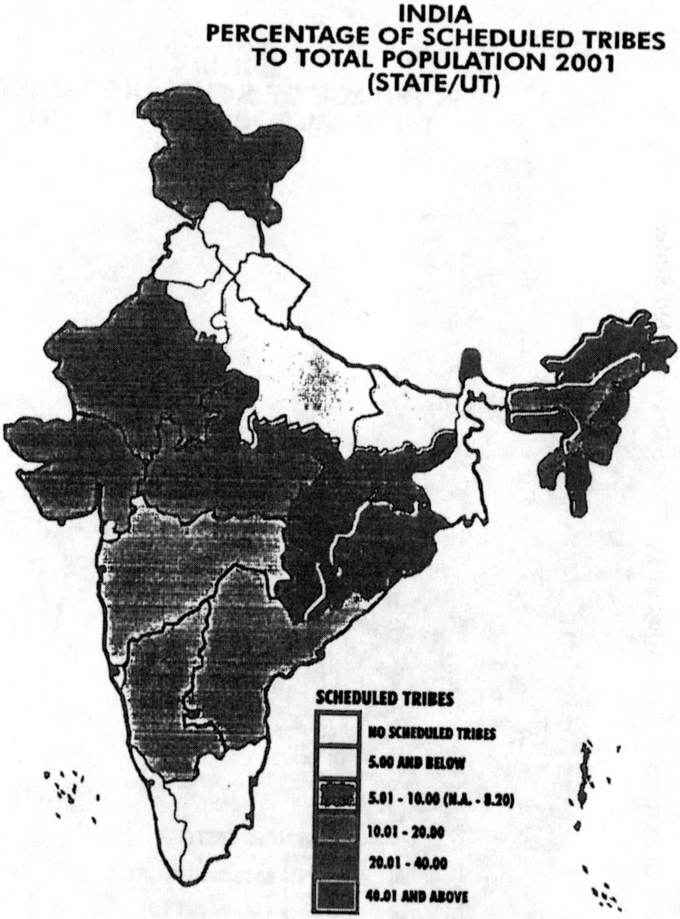
INDIA
PERCENTAGE OF SCHEDULED TRIBES
TO TOTAL POPULATION 2001
(STATE/UT)
SCHEDULED TRIBES
NO SCHEDULED TRIBES
5.00 AND BELOW
5.01 - 10.00 (N.A. - 8.20)
10.01 - 20.00
20.01 - 40.00
40.01 AND ABOVE

Decadal Growth of the STs Population in Top Five STs Populated States

State/Ut	*2001 Census STs Population*	*1991 Census STs Population*	*Decadal growth rate of STs Population*	*Decadal growth rate of Non-SC/ST population*
Madhya Pradesh	12,233,474	9,681,910	26.4	24.1
Maharashtra	8,577,276	7,318,281	17.2	24.8
Orissa	8,145,081	7,032,214	15.8	15.8
Gujarat	7,481,160	6,161,775	21.4	23.4
Rajasthan	7,097,706	5,474,881	29.6	28.4

Top 10 SC Populated Districts in India

State	*District*	*2001 Census SC Population*	*1991 Census SC population**
West Bengal	South Twenty Four Parganas	2,218,376	1,968,814
West Bengal	Barddhaman	1,860,754	1,660,493
West Bengal	North Twenty Four Parganas	1,840,397	1,564,689
West Bengal	Medinipur	1,576,337	1,361,828
West Bengal	Nadia	1,365,985	1,117,506
West Bengal	Jalpaiguri	1,248,577	1,035,971
West Bengal	Koch Bihar	1,242,374	1,123,719
West Bengal	Hugli	1,188,881	1,050,280
Uttar Pradesh	Sitapur	1,153,626	920,415
Uttar Pradesh	Hardoi	1,065,848	866,580

Top 10 ST Populated Districts in India

State	*District*	*2001 Census STs population*	*1991 Census STs population*
Gujarat	Surat	1,408,270	1,225,080
Rajasthan	Udaipur	1,260,432	957,559
Orissa	Mayurbhanj	1,258,459	1,090,626
Madhya Pradesh	Jhabua	1,211,116	968,372
Maharashtra	Thane	1,199,290	951,205
Maharashtra	Nashik	1,194,271	931,069
Gujarat	Dohad	1,182,509	911,833
Jharkhand	Ranchi	1,164,624	964,422
Jharkhand	Pashchimi Singhbhum	1,111,322	978,069
Rajasthan	Banswara	1,085,272	849,050

Top 10 Districts in India in Terms of Highest Percentage of SC Population

State	*District*	*Total population 2001 Census*	*SC population 2001 Census*	*Percentage of SC population*
West Bengal	Koch Bihar	2,479,155	1,242,374	50.1
Uttar Pradesh	Sonbhadra	1,463,519	613,497	41.9
Punjab	Nawanshahr	587,468	237,664	40.5
Punjab	Muktsar	777,493	293,539	37.8
Punjab	Jalandhar	1,962,700	739,762	37.7
West Bengal	Jalpaiguri	3,401,173	1,248,577	36.7
Punjab	Faridkot	550,892	199,257	36.2
Uttar Pradesh	Kaushambi	1,293,154	466,853	36.1
Punjab	Hoshiarpur	1,480,736	507,544	34.3
Rajasthan	Ganganagar	1,789,423	603,371	33.7

Top 10 Districts in India in Terms of Highest Percentage of ST Population

State	*District*	*Total Population 2001 Census*	*STs population 2001 Census*	*Percentage of STs population*
Mizoram	Serchhip	53,861	52,830	98.09
Meghalaya	West Khasi Hills	296,049	290,184	98.02
Mizoram	Champhai	108,392	104,924	96.80
Meghalaya	East Garo Hills	250,582	241,916	96.54
Ngaland	Phek	148,195	142,977	96.48
Mizoram	Saiha	61,056	58,742	96.21
Nagaland	Zunheboto	153,955	147,915	96.08
Nagaland	Tuensang	414,818	398,350	96.03
Meghalaya	Jaintia Hills	299,108	287,049	95.97
Meghalaya	South Garo Hills	100,980	96,616	95.68

Distribution of Districts by Percentage of SC ST Population (2001 Census)

Percentage of Population	*No. of Districts (SC)*	*No. of District (ST)*
Below 5	94	278
5-14	175	98
15-24	252	52
25-34	53	27
35-49	7	23
50+	1	75
Total	582	543

Distribution of Districts by SC & ST Population (2001 Census)

Population	*No. of Districts (SC)*	*No. of District (ST)*
Below 10,000	56	153
10,000-50,000	42	92
50,000-1 lakh	47	68
1 lakh-5 lakh	347	190
5 lakh-10 lakh	77	29
10 lakh and above	13	11

Five States/Uts in Terms of Highest & Lowest Sex-ratio (0-6 age group) of SCs Population (2001 Census)

State/Ut	*Sex-ratio (highest) of 0-6 population*	*Sex-ratio (0-6) Non SC/ST population*
Pondicherry	990	962
Jharkhand	984	955
Manipur	975	955
Andhra Pradesh	973	957
Chhattisgarh	968	962
	Sex-ratio (lowest) of 0-6 Population	Sex-ratio (0-6) Non SC/ST population
Jammu & Kashmir	899	939
Chandigarh	886	834
Gujarat	885	865
Haryana	865	807
Punjab	861	767

Five States/Uts in Terms of Highest & Lowest Sex-ratio (0-6 age group) of SCs Population (2001 Census)

State/Ut	*Sex-ratio (highest) of 0-6) Population*	*Sex-ratio (0-6) Non SC/ST population*
Dadra & Nagar Haveli	1009	911
Chhattisgarh	998	962
West Bengal	981	958
Tripura	981	956
Jammu & Kashmir	979	939
	Sex-ratio (lowest) of 0-06 Population	Sex-ratio (0-6) Non SC/ST population
Uttaranchal	955	876
Himachal Pradesh	955	897
Rajasthan	950	937
Tamil Nadu	945	937
A & N Islands	915	957

Five States/Uts in Terms of Highest and Lowest Sex-ratio Of SCs Population

State/Ut	*Sex-ratio (Highest) 2001 Census*	*Sex-ratio (Highest) 1991 Census*
Kerala	1048	1029
Pondicherry	1019	983
Manipur (Exce. 3-Subdivitions)	1006	976
Tamil Nadu	999	978
Chhattisgarh	994	988
	Sex-ratio (Lowest) 2001 Census	Sex-ratio (Lowest) 1991 Census
Uttar Pradesh	899	875
Punjab	892	873
Haryana	869	860
Delhi	852	834
Chandigarh	829	810

Five States/Uts in Terms of the Highest and Lowest Sex-ratio of ST Population

States/Ut	*Sex-ratio (Highest) 2001 Census*	*Sex-ratio (Highest) 1991 Census*
Dadra & Nagar Haveli	1028	1022
Kerala	1021	996
Chhattisgarh	1013	1009
Lakshadweep	1003	994
Arunachal Pradesh	1003	998
	Sex-ratio (Lowest) 2001 Census	Sex-ratio (Lowest) 1991 Census
Rajasthan	944	929
Nagaland	943	946
Uttar Pradesh	934	874
Bihar	929	923
Jammu & Kashmir	910	-

Total Literacy Rate and Female Literacy Rate in Top Five SC Populated States (2001 Census)

States	Total literacy rate
Uttar Pradesh	46.3
West Bengal	59.0
Bihar	28.5
Andhra Pradesh	53.5
Tamil Nadu	63.2
	Female literacy rate
Uttar Pradesh	30.5
West Bengal	46.9
Bihar	15.6
Andhra Pradesh	43.4
Tamil Nadu	53.0

Total Literacy Rate and Female Literacy Rate in Top Five ST Populated States (2001 Census)

States/Ut	Total literacy rate
Madhya Pradesh	41.2
Maharashtra	55.2
Orissa	37.4
Gujarat	47.7
Rajasthan	44.7
	Female literacy rate
Madhya Pradesh	28.4
Maharashtra	43.1
Orissa	23.4
Gujarat	36.0
Rajasthan	26.2

Five States/Uts in Terms of Lowest literacy Rate and Female Literacy Rate of SC Population (2001 Census)

States/Ut	*Literacy rate*
Karnataka	52.9
Rajasthan	52.2
Uttar Pradesh	46.3
Jharkhand	37.6
Bihar	28.5
	Female literacy rate
Orissa	40.3
Rajasthan	33.9
Uttar Pradesh	30.5
Jharkhand	22.6
Bihar	15.6

Five States/Uts in Terms of Lowest Literacy Rate and Female Literacy Rate of ST Population (2001 Census)

States	*Literacy rate*
Jammu & Kashmir	37.4
Orissa	37.3
Andhra Pradesh	37.1
Uttar Pradesh	35.1
Bihar	28.2
	Female literacy rate
Andhra Pradesh	26.1
Jammu & Kashmir	25.5
Orissa	23.3
Uttar Pradesh	20.7
Bihar	15.6

Five States/Uts in Terms of Lowest Literacy Rate and Female Literacy Rate of ST Population (2001 Census)

State/Ut	*Work participation rate*	*Work participation rate Non SC/ST*
Manipur	51.4	43.0
Andhra Pradesh	50.5	44.1
Himachal Pradesh	48.9	49.0
Tamil Nadu	48.1	43.7
Karnataka	46.3	43.7
	Female work participation Rate	Female work participation rate – Non SC/ST
Manipur	47.5	37.1
Andhra Pradesh	45.6	31.5
Himachal Pradesh	43.5	43.2
Tamil Nadu	40.3	29.2
Karnataka	38.4	29.8

Five States/Uts in Terms of Highest Work Participation Rate and Female Work Participation Rate of SCs Population (2001 Census)

State/Ut	*Work participation rate*	*Work participation rate Non SC/ST*
Tamil Nadu	54.9	43.7
Himachal Pradesh	54.6	49.0
Andhra Pradesh	53.9	44.1
Chhattisgarh	53.4	43.3
Mizoram	51.8	66.7
	Female work participation Rate	Female work participation Rate – Non SC/ST
Himachal Pradesh	52.7	43.2
Andhra Pradesh	52.0	31.5
Chhattisgarh	50.2	34.7
Tamil Nadu	49.5	29.2
Mizoram	48.1	29.7

Five States/Uts in Terms of Highest Work Participation Rate & Female Work Participation Rate in ST Population (2001 Census)

State/Ut	*Work participation rate*	*Work participation rate Non (SC/ST)*
Chandigarh	35.3	38.3
Uttar Pradesh	35.0	31.9
Assam	34.4	34.8
Tripura	32.6	33.6
Delhi	30.3	33.3
	Female work Participation rate	Female work participation rate (Non SC/ST)
Punjab	21.0	18.3
Assam	17.3	18.6
Chandigarh	15.1	13.9
Tripura	14.1	13.3
Delhi	10.0	9.2

Five States/Uts in Terms of Lowest Work Participation Rate and Female Work Participation Rate of SCs Population (2001 Census)

State/Ut	*Work participation rate*	*Work participation rate Non (SC/ST)*
Tripura	42.7	33.6
Nagaland	42.4	44.7
Uttaranchal	41.1	36.6
Uttar Pradesh	40.3	31.9
Lakshadweep	22.9	67.5
	Female work Participation rate	Female work participation rate (Non SC/ST)
Kerala	35.4	13.8
Andaman & Nicobar Islamds	35.0	14.8
Uttaranchal	31.9	26.8
Uttar Pradesh	30.1	15.3
Lakshadweep	7.1	12.5

Growth Trend of Urban Population of SCs & STs in India (1961 – 2001 Census)

Census Year	*Proportion of Urban population*		*Proportion of Non - SC/ST population*
	SC	*ST*	
1961	10.7	2.6	20.7
1971	11.9	3.4	22.9
1981	16.0	6.2	27.1
1991	18.7	7.4	29.2
2001	20.2	8.3	31.6

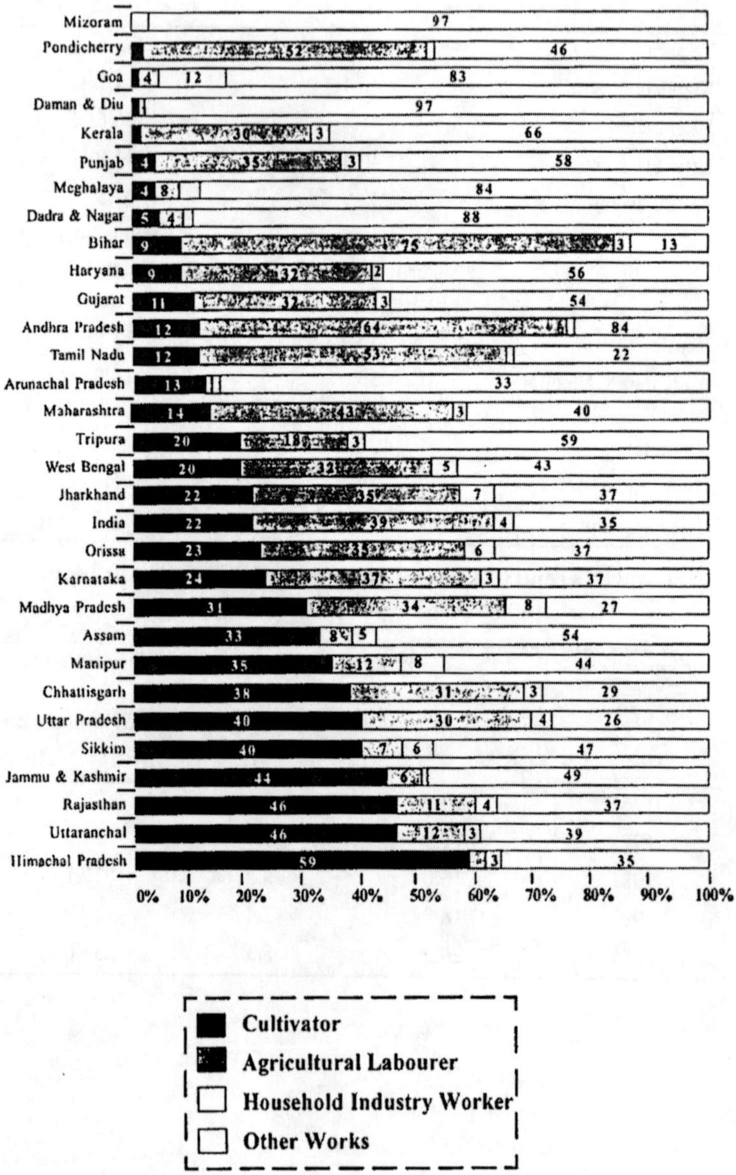

Mizoram 97
Pondicherry 52 46
Goa 4 12 83
Daman & Diu 97
Kerala 30 3 66
Punjab 4 35 3 58
Meghalaya 4 8 84
Dadra & Nagar 5 4 88
Bihar 9 75 3 13
Haryana 9 32 2 56
Gujarat 11 32 3 54
Andhra Pradesh 12 64 84
Tamil Nadu 12 53 22
Arunachal Pradesh 13 33
Maharashtra 14 43 3 40
Tripura 20 18 3 59
West Bengal 20 32 5 43
Jharkhand 22 35 7 37
India 22 39 4 35
Orissa 23 6 37
Karnataka 24 37 3 37
Madhya Pradesh 31 34 8 27
Assam 33 8 5 54
Manipur 35 12 8 44
Chhattisgarh 38 31 3 29
Uttar Pradesh 40 30 4 26
Sikkim 40 7 6 47
Jammu & Kashmir 44 6 49
Rajasthan 46 11 4 37
Uttaranchal 46 12 3 39
Himachal Pradesh 59 3 35
0% 10% 20% 30% 40% 50% 60% 70% 80% 90% 100%
Cultivator
Agricultural Labourer
Household Industry Worker
Other Works

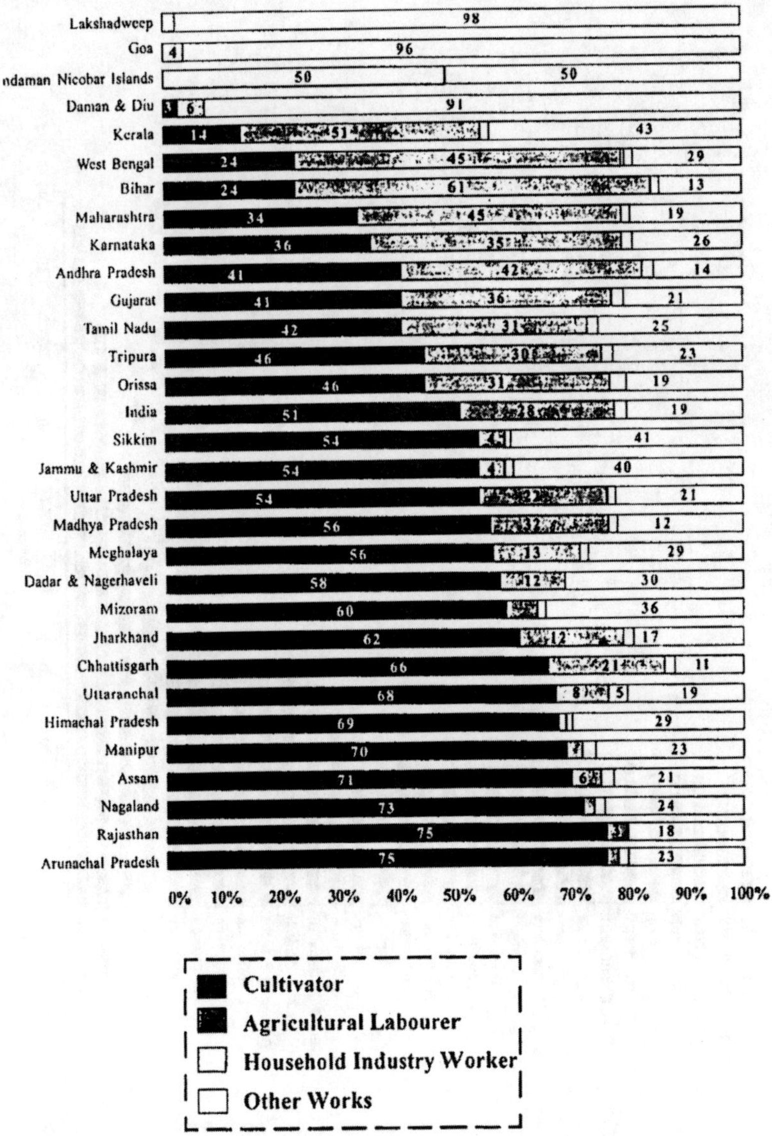
Lakshadweep
Goa
ndaman Nicobar Islands
Daman & Diu
Kerala
West Bengal
Bihar
Maharashtra
Karnataka
Andhra Pradesh
Gujarat
Tamil Nadu
Tripura
Orissa
India
Sikkim
Jammu & Kashmir
Uttar Pradesh
Madhya Pradesh
Meghalaya
Dadar & Nagerhaveli
Mizoram
Jharkhand
Chhattisgarh
Uttaranchal
Himachal Pradesh
Manipur
Assam
Nagaland
Rajasthan
Arunachal Pradesh
0% 10% 20% 30% 40% 50% 60% 70% 80% 90% 100%
Cultivator
Agricultural Labourer
Household Industry Worker
Other Works

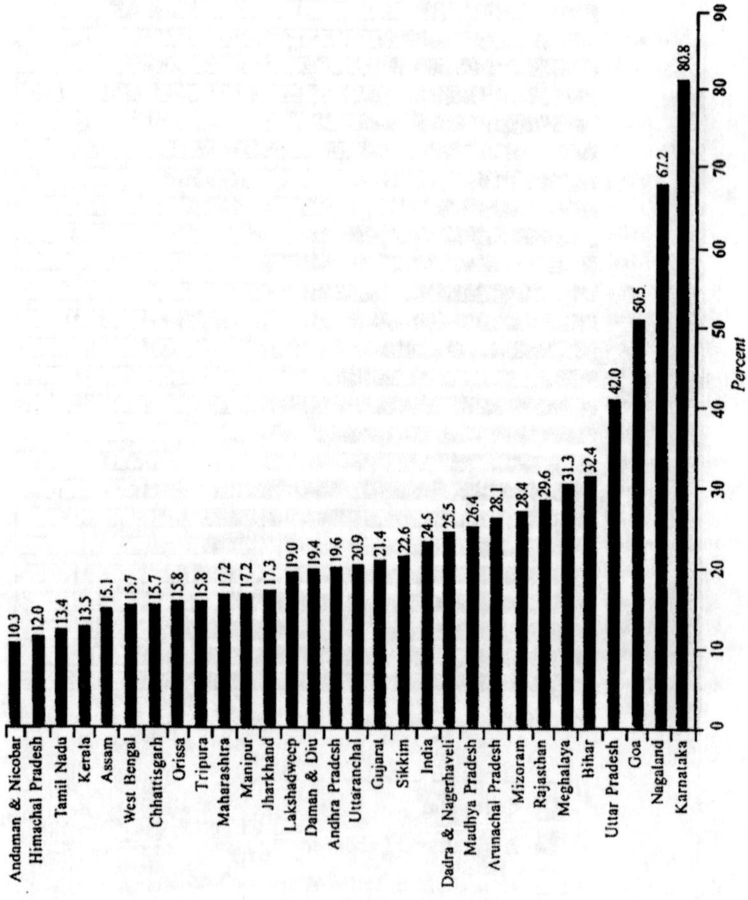
Andaman & Nicobar 10.3
Himachal Pradesh 12.0
Tamil Nadu 13.4
Kerala 13.5
Assam 15.1
West Bengal 15.7
Chhattisgarh 15.7
Orissa 15.8
Tripura 15.8
Maharashtra 17.2
Manipur 17.2
Jharkhand 17.3
Lakshadweep 19.0
Daman & Diu 19.4
Andhra Pradesh 19.6
Uttaranchal 20.9
Gujarat 21.4
Sikkim 22.6
India 24.5
Dadra & Nagerhaveli 25.5
Madhya Pradesh 26.4
Arunachal Pradesh 28.1
Mizoram 28.4
Rajasthan 29.6
Meghalaya 31.3
Bihar 32.4
Uttar Pradesh 42.0
Goa 50.5
Nagaland 67.2
Karnataka 80.8
0
10
20
30
40
50
60
70
80
90
Percent

DECADAL GROWTH OF THE SCHEDULED CASTES POPULATION (1991-2001)

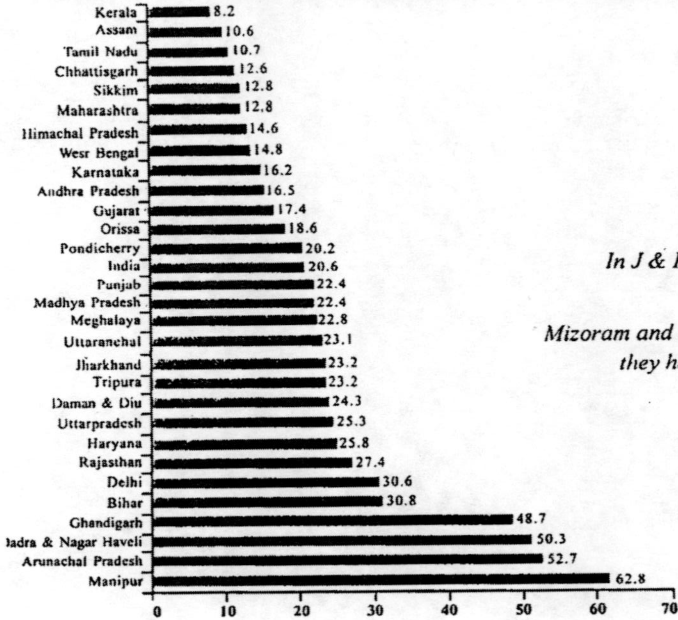

In J & K there was no Census in 1991.

◆

Mizoram and Goa are excluded from the Figure, as they have very small SC population.

Relevant Provisions of the Indian Constitution

Article 15. Prohibition of discrimination on grounds of religion, race, caste, sex or place of birth.

[(4) Nothing in this article or in clause (2) of article 29 shall prevent the State from making any special provision for the advancement of any socially and educationally backward classes of citizens or for the Scheduled Castes and the Scheduled Tribes.]

Article 16. Equality of opportunity in matters of public employment.

[(4A) Nothing in this article shall prevent the State from making any provision for reservation in matters of promotion to any class or classes of posts in the services under the State in favour of the Scheduled Castes and the Scheduled Tribes which, in the opinion of the State, are not adequately represented in the services under the State.]

[(4B) Nothing in this article shall prevent the State from considering any unfilled vacancies of a year which are reserved for being filled up in that year in accordance with any provision for reservation made under clause (4) or clause (4A) as a separate class of vacancies to be filled up in any succeeding year or years and such class of vacancies shall not be considered together with the vacancies of the year in which they are being filled up for determining the ceiling of fifty per cent. reservation on total number of vacancies of that year.]

Article 29. Protection of interests of minorities.

(2) No citizen shall be denied admission into any educational institution maintained by the State or receiving aid out of State funds on grounds only of religion, race, caste, language or any of them.

Article 46. Promotion of educational and economic interests of Scheduled Castes, Scheduled Tribes and other weaker sections.

The State shall promote with special care the educational and economic interests of the weaker sections of the people, and, in particular, of the Scheduled Castes and the Scheduled Tribes, and shall protect them from social injustice and all forms of exploitation.

Article164. Other provisions as to Ministers.

(1) The Chief Minister shall be appointed by the Governor and the other Ministers shall be appointed by the Governor on the advice of the Chief Minster, and the Ministers shall hold office during the pleasure of the Governor:

Provided that in the States of Bihar, Madhya Pradesh and Orissa, there shall be a Minister in charge of tribal welfare who may in addition be in charge of the welfare of the Scheduled Castes and backward classes or any other work.

243D. Reservation of seats.

(1) Seats shall be reserved for-

(a) the Scheduled Castes; and

(b) the Scheduled Tribes,

in every Panchayat and the number of seats so reserved shall bear, as nearly as may be, the same proportion to the total number of seats to be filled by direct election in that Panchayat as the population of the Scheduled Castes in that Panchayat area or of the Scheduled Tribes in that Panchayat area bears to the total population of that area and such seats may be allotted by rotation to different constituencies in a Panchayat.

(2) Not less than one-third of the total number of seats reserved under clause (1) shall be reserved for women belonging to the Scheduled Castes or, as the case may be, the Scheduled Tribes.

(3) Not less than one-third (including the number of seats reserved for women belonging to the Scheduled Castes and the Scheduled Tribes) of the total number of seats to be filled by direct election in every Panchayat shall be reserved for women and such seats may be allotted by rotation to different constituencies in a Panchayat.

(4) The offices of the Chairpersons in the Panchayats at the village or any other level shall be reserved for the Scheduled Castes, the Scheduled Tribes and women in such manner as the Legislature of a State may, by law, provide:

Provided that the number of offices of Chairpersons reserved for the Scheduled Castes and the Scheduled Tribes in the Panchayats at each level in any State shall bear, as nearly as may be, the same proportion to the total number of such offices in the Panchayats at each level as the population of the Scheduled Castes in the State or of the Scheduled Tribes in the State bears to the total population of the State:

Provided further that not less than one-third of the total number of offices of Chairpersons in the Panchayats at each level shall be reserved for women:

Provided also that the number of offices reserved under this clause shall be allotted by rotation to different Panchayats at each level.

(5) The reservation of seats under clauses (1) and (2) and the reservation of offices of Chairpersons (other than the reservation for women) under clause (4) shall cease to have effect on the expiration of the period specified in article 334.

(6) Nothing in this Part shall prevent the Legislature of a State from making any provision for reservation of seats in any Panchayat or offices of Chairpersons in the Panchayats at any level in favour of backward class of citizens.

Article 244. Administration of Scheduled Areas and Tribal Areas.

(1) The provisions of the Fifth Schedule shall apply to the administration and control of the Scheduled Areas and Scheduled Tribes in any State other than [the States of Assam [Meghalaya, Tripura and Mizoram]].

(2) The provisions of the Sixth Schedule shall apply to the administration of the tribal areas in [the States of Assam, [Meghalaya, Tripura and Mizoram]].

Article 275. Grants from the Union to certain States.

(1) Such sums as Parliament may by law provide shall be charged on the Consolidated Fund of India in each year as grants-in-aid of the revenues of such States as Parliament may determine to be in need of assistance, and different sums may be fixed for different States:

Provided that there shall be paid out of the Consolidated Fund of India as grants-in-aid of the revenues of a State such capital and recurring sums as may be necessary to enable that State to meet the costs of such schemes of development as may be undertaken by the

State with the approval of the Government of India for the purpose of promoting the welfare of the Scheduled Tribes in that State or raising the level of administration of the Scheduled Areas therein to that of the administration of the rest of the areas of that State.

Article 330. Reservation of seats for Scheduled Castes and Scheduled Tribes in the House of the People.

(1) Seats shall be reserved in the House of the People for-

(a) the Scheduled Castes;

b) the Scheduled Tribes except the Scheduled Tribes in the autonomous districts of Assam; and]

(c) the Scheduled Tribes in the autonomous districts of Assam.

(2) The number of seats reserved in any State [or Union territory] for the Scheduled Castes or the Scheduled Tribes under clause (1) shall bear, as nearly as may be, the same proportion to the total number of seats allotted to that State [or Union territory] in the House of the People as the population of the Scheduled Castes in the State [or Union territory] or of the Scheduled Tribes in the State [or Union territory] or part of the State [or Union territory], as the case may be, in respect of which seats are so reserved, bears to the total population of the State [or Union territory].

[(3) Notwithstanding anything contained in clause (2), the number of seats reserved in the House of the People for the Scheduled Tribes in the autonomous districts of Assam shall bear to the total number of seats allotted to that State a proportion not less than the population of the Scheduled Tribes in the said autonomous districts bears to the total population of the State.]

[Explanation.-In this article and in article 332, the expression "population" means the population as ascertained at the last preceding census of which the relevant figures have been published: Provided that the reference in this Explanation to the last preceding census of which the relevant figures have been published shall, until the relevant figures for the first census taken after the year [2026] have been published, be construed as a reference to the [1991] census.]

Article 332. Reservation of seats for Scheduled Castes and Scheduled Tribes in the Legislative Assemblies of the States.

(1) Seats shall be reserved for the Scheduled Castes and the Scheduled Tribes, [except the Scheduled Tribes in the autonomous districts of Assam], in the Legislative Assembly of every State

Article 335. Claims of Scheduled Castes and Scheduled Tribes to services and posts.

The claims of the members of the Scheduled Castes and Scheduled Tribes shall be taken into consideration, consistently with the maintenance of efficiency of administration, in the making of appointments to services and posts in connection with the affairs of the Union or of a State. Provided that nothing in this article shall prevent in making of any provision in favour of the members of the Scheduled Castes and the Scheduled Tribes for relaxation in qualifying marks in any examination or lowering the standards of evaluation, for reservation in matters of promotion to any class or classes of services or posts in connection with the affairs of the Union or of a State

Article 338. [National Commission for Scheduled Castes and Scheduled Tribes.]

(1) There shall be a Commission for the Scheduled Castes and Scheduled Tribes to be known as the National Commission for the Scheduled Castes and Scheduled Tribes.

(2) Subject to the provisions of any law made in this behalf by Parliament, the Commission shall consist of a Chairperson, Vice-Chairperson and five other Members and the conditions of service and tenure of office of the Chairperson, Vice-Chairperson and other Members so appointed shall be such as the President may by rule determine.

(3) The Chairperson, Vice-Chairperson and other Members of the Commission shall be appointed by the President by warrant under his hand and seal.

(4) The Commission shall have the power to regulate its own procedure.

(5) It shall be the duty of the Commission-

(a) to investigate and monitor all matters relating to the safeguards provided for the Scheduled Castes and Scheduled Tribes under this Constitution or under any other law for the time being in force or under any order of the Government and to evaluate the working of such safeguards;

(b) to inquire into specific complaints with respect to the deprivation of rights and safeguards of the Scheduled Castes and Scheduled Tribes;

(c) to participate and advise on the planning process of socio-economic development of the Scheduled Castes and Scheduled

Tribes and to evaluate the progress of their development under the Union and any State;

(d) to present to the President, annually and at such other times as the Commission may deem fit, reports upon the working of those safeguards;

(e) to make in such reports recommendations as to the measures that should be taken by the Union or any State for the effective implementation of those safeguards and other measures for the protection, welfare and socio-economic development of the Scheduled Castes and Scheduled Tribes; and

(f) to discharge such other functions in relation to the protection, welfare and development and advancement of the Scheduled Castes and Scheduled Tribes as the President may, subject to the provisions of any law made by Parliament, by rule specify.

(6) The President shall cause all such reports to be laid before each House of Parliament along with a memorandum explaining the action taken or proposed to be taken on the recommendations relating to the Union and the reasons for the non-acceptance, if any, of any of such recommendations.

(7) Where any such report, or any part thereof, relates to any matter with which any State Government is concerned, a copy of such report shall be forwarded to the Governor of the State who shall cause it to be laid before the Legislature of the State along with a memorandum explaining the action taken or proposed to be taken on the recommendations relating to the State and the reasons for the non-acceptance, if any, of any of such recommendations.

(8) The Commission shall, while investigating any matter referred to in sub-clause (a) or inquiring into any complaint referred to in sub-clause (b) of clause (5), have all the powers of a civil court trying a suit and in particular in respect of the following matters, namely:-

(a) summoning and enforcing the attendance of any person from any part of India and examining him on oath;

(b) requiring the discovery and production of any document;

(c) receiving evidence on affidavits;

(d) requisitioning any public record or copy thereof from any court or office;

(e) issuing commissions for the examination of witnesses and documents;

(f) any other matter which the President may, by rule, determine.

(9) The Union and every State Government shall consult the Commission on all major policy matters affecting Scheduled Castes and Scheduled Tribes.]

(10)] In this article, references to the Scheduled Castes and Scheduled Tribes shall be construed as including references to such other backward classes as the President may, on receipt of the report of a Commission appointed under clause (1) of article 340, by order specify and also to the Anglo-Indian community.

Article 340. Appointment of a Commission to investigate the conditions of backward classes.

(1) The President may by order appoint a Commission consisting of such persons as he thinks fit to investigate the conditions of socially and educationally backward classes within the territory of India and the difficulties under which they labour and to make recommendations as to the steps that should be taken by the Union or any State to remove such difficulties and to improve their condition and as to the grants that should be made for the purpose by the Union or any State and the conditions subject to which such grants should be made, and the order appointing such Commission shall define the procedure to be followed by the Commission.

(2) A Commission so appointed shall investigate the matters referred to them and present to the President a report setting out the facts as found by them and making such recommendations as they think proper.

(3) `The President shall cause a copy of the report so presented together with a memorandum explaining the action taken thereon to be laid before each House of Parliament.

Bibliography

Primary Sources

Reports, Memoranda, Monographs and Dissertations

1. *Constituent Assembly Debates* Vol. II pp. 1-36.
2. *Census of India* 1961.
3. Chitnis, S. 'A Long Way to Go ... Report on a Survey of SC High School and College Students in Fifteen States of India' [*ICSSR Report of Mammoth Survey*, 1977]. New Delhi: Allied 1981.
4. Cohn, B. *The Chamars of Senapur: a Study of the Changing Status of a Depressed Caste.* Unpubl. DPhil thesis, (Cornell University 1954).
5. Desai, I.P. Water facilities for the Untouchables in rural Gujarat. *Occasional.*
6. *Gazette of India Part* I July 7, 1934.
7. Heider, S. 'Lifting the Veil of Silence: Jamuna's Narrative of Pain' [Chamar], *Sociological Bulletin* 44, 1995: 241-54.
8. Houska, W. *Religious Belief and Practice in an Urban Scheduled Caste Community.* Unpublished PhD thesis, Syracuse University, N.Y. 1981.
9. Jans, J. *The Depressed Classes: a Chronological Documentation.* 12 parts, Ranchi/Kurseong: St Mary's College c. 1935/7.
10. Malik, S. *Social Integration of Scheduled Castes* [PhD Survey of 5 colonies in Ambala Town]. New Delhi: *Abhinav* 1979.
11. Mohanty, R.K. Factors affecting Social Mobility among Scheduled Castes: Survey of Literature Published from 1972-1984. Unpubl M.Phil dissertation, Institute of Advanced Studies, Meerut, 1985.
12. *Monographs* No. 8. New Delhi: ICSSR 1973.
13. Office Memorandum No. 36012/31/90-Estt (SCT), Government of India, New Delhi, 25th September 1991.

14. Office Memorandum No. 36012/31/90-Estt (SCT), Government of India, New Delhi, 13th August 1990.
15. Oommen, T.K. Scheduled castes and scheduled tribes. In S.C. Dube (ed.) *Indian Since Independence - Social Report on India - 1947-72*. New Delhi: Vikas 1977.
16. Prashad, V. Revolting Labour: The Making of the Balmiki Community. Unpubl. PhD dissertation.
17. Report of the (First) Backward Commission, 1955 (Kaka Kalelkar Commission).
18. Report of the (Second) Backward Commission, 1980 (Mandal Commission).
19. Report of The Backward Classes Commission, Government of Kerala 1970.
20. Report of the Backward Classes Reservation Commission (P.D. Nettur Commission) Government of Kerala.
21. Report of the Backward Commission (Justice K.K.Narendran Commission), Government of Kerala 2000.
22. Report of the Commissioner for Scheduled Castes and Scheduled Tribes.
23. Sharma, B.D. Scheduled Castes and Tribes: a status report, Lokayan Bulletin 8/6 1990.
24. Singh, D.R. *Rural Leadership among Scheduled Castes* [Standard PhD thesis: Mirzapur District, UP]. Allahabad: Chugh 1985.
25. Sixteenth Report of the Committee On The Welfare of Scheduled Castes and Scheduled Tribes (2001-2002) submitted to Lok Sabha on 27th August 2001.
26. Study of Customary Rights and Living and Working Conditions of Scavengers in Two Towns [Haryana and UP]. *Monograph Series* Vol. I, Part XI, D. 1966.
27. *T.M. Varghese and the Struggle For responsible Government* (Ph.D. Thesis, University of Kerala 1984).
28. Tuinmin, H. *The Political Economy of Untouchability*. (Unpublished Thesis, University of New South Wales, Sydney, 1984).

Secondary Sources

Books

1. Agarwal L.B. *The Harijans in Rebellion*. (Bombay: Taraporewala 1934).

2. Agarwal P.C. *Equality Through Privilege: A Study of Special Privileges Granted to Scheduled Castes in Haryana.* (New Delhi : ICSSR 1977).
3. Aggarwal P.C. *Halfway to Equality.* (New Delhi: Manohar 1983)
4. Alte I.D. *Rural Employment of Scheduled Castes.*(New Delhi: Deep & Deep.
5. Ambedkar, *Emancipation of Untouchables* (Bangalore 1992).
6. Ambedkar, B.R. *What Congress and Gandhi Have Done to the Untouchables.*(Bombay Thacker 1945).
7. Anant S.S. 'Changing Caste Hindu Attitudes Towards Harijans - a follow-up after four years.' In G.R. Gupta (ed) *Cohesion and Conflict in Modern India.* (New Delhi: Vikas 1978).
8. Augustine, P.A. *Social Equality in Indian Society.* (New Delhi: Concept 1991).
9. Bailey, F.G. *Caste and the Economic Frontier.* (Manchester: MUP 1957).
10. Bains Ravinder Singh (1994) in his book *Reservation Policy and Anti Reservationists,*(B.R.Publishing Corporation, Delhi).
11. Bajpai Anilkumar, *Judicial Response to the problems of Reservation* (Khama Publishers New Delhi).
12. Bakshi S.R. *Jagjivan Ram: the Harijan Leader.* (New Delhi: Anmol 1992).
13. Barker Earnest, *Principles of Social and Political Theory.* (London 1967).
14. Basu Durga Das, *Commentary On The Constitution Of India,* (S.C Sarkar & Sons Pvt. Ltd. 1964).
15. Baxi Upendra, *Courage, Craft and Contention* (Bombay 1985).
16. Baxi Upendra, *The Right To Be Human* (1987).
17. Bayly Susan, *Caste, Society And Politics In India* (OUP 2000).
18. Ben and Peters, *Social Principles and Democratic State* (London 1975).
19. Benjamin Joseph, *Scheduled Caste in Indian Politics and Society* (Ess Ess Publications, New Delhi, 1989).
20. Berreman G. *Hindus of the Himalayas: Ethnography and Change.* (Berkeley: University of California Press 1963).
21. Berreman G.D. *Caste and Other Inequities.* (Meerut: Folklore Institute 1979).
22. Beteille Andre, *The Idea of Natural Inequality and Other Essays* (1983).

23. Beteille Andre. *The Backward Classes in Contemporary India.* (Delhi: OUP 1992).
24. Beteille,Andre , *Society and Politics in India* (OUP 1991).
25. Bhai, N. *Harijan Women in Independent India.* (Delhi: BR Publishing 1986).
26. Bharadwaj, A.N. *Problems of Scheduled Castes and Scheduled Tribes in India* (New Delhi: Light & Life 1979).
27. Bhatia K.L. (1997), Judicial *Review and Judicial Activism* (Deep and Deep Publication, New Delhi).
28. Bhatia K.L., *Judicial Review and Judicial Activism* (1997).
29. Bhave, S. *Pan on Fire: Eight Dalit Women Tell Their Story.* (New Delhi 1988).
30. Bhowmik, K.L. (ed.) 'Development of Scheduled Communities' [1985 Conference papers on tribals]. *Current Anthropological and Archaeological Perspectives*, Vol. 6. (New Delhi Inter-India Publications 1988).
31. Bickel.A. The *Least Dangerous Branch.* The Supreme Court and the Idea of Progress (1970).
32. Borale, P.T. *Segregation and Desegregation in India. A Socio-legal Study* (Bombay: Manaktelas 1968).
33. Bose, N.K. *The Structure of Hindu Society* (New Delhi Orient Longman,1975).
34. Briggs, G. *The Doms And Their Near Relations.* (Mysore Wesley 1953.
35. Briggs, G.W. *The Chamars.* (Calcutta Association Press 1920).
36. Burman, B.K. Roy (ed.) Social Mobility among the Sweepers of India. Mimeo. (New Delhi Registrar General, Ministry of Home Affairs).
37. Burman, B.K. Roy Social *Mobility Movements among Scheduled Castes and Scheduled Tribes of India.* (Delhi Government of India Press 1970).
38. Burman, B.K. Roy The problem of Untouchables. In Romesh Thapar (ed.) *Tribe, Caste and Religion in India.* (Delhi Macmillan 1977.
39. Burman, B.K. Roy Beyond *Mandal and After: Backward Classes in Perspective.* (New Delhi Mittal 1992).
40. Centre for Social Studies, Surat (ed.) *Caste, Caste Conflict and Reservation.* (Delhi Ajanta 1985).
41. Chalam.K.S (1993), *The relevance of Ambedkarism in India* (Rawat Publications, New Delhi).

42. Chandel, M.P.S. *A Social Force in Politics: Study of Scheduled Castes of UP*. (New Delhi Mittal 1990).
43. Chandra Bipin, *India's Struggle For Independence.*(New Delhi 1999).
44. Chandra Bipin, *Modern India* (NCERT, New Delhi 1986).
45. Chandra Mouli.V (1994),B*R.Ambedkar: Man and his Vision* (Sterling Publications, New Delhi).
46. Chandra, V. *Handbook on Scheduled Castes and Scheduled Tribes.* (New Delhi Office of the Commissioner for SC&ST 1968).
47. Chatterjee, S.K. *The Scheduled Castes in India* (New Delhi: Gyan 1996).
48. Chaube S.K., Constituent *Assembly of India.* (Calcutta 1976).
49. Chaudhari Nirad.C., The *Continent of Circe.* (New Delhi 1965).
50. Chousalkar, A.S, *India; Idea of Political Resistance* (Ajanta Publishers New Delhi-1990).
51. Cohn, B.S. *An Anthropologist among the Historians and Other Essays.* (Delhi OUP 1990).
52. Cohn, B.S. The changing status of a depressed caste [Chamars, eastern UP] in McK. Marriott (ed.) *Village India.* (Chicago: UP 1955).
53. Danda, A.K. *Weaker Sections in Indian Villages.* (New Delhi: Inter-India 1993).
54. Das, A.C.R. *Handbook on Scheduled Castes and Scheduled Tribes of West Bengal.* (Calcutta Tribal Welfare Dept., Government of West Bengal 1966).
55. Das, Bhakta A *Glimpse of Scheduled Castes in Assam.* (New Delhi Omson 1968).
56. Das, D.P. *The Untouchable Story.* (New Delhi Allied 1985).
57. Desai, A.R. *Caste and Communal Violence in India.* (Bombay: Popular 1985).
58. Desai. I.P. *Untouchability in Rural Gujarat.* (Bombay Popular Prakashan 1976).
59. Deshpande, N. *Towards Social Integration: Problems of Adjustment of Scheduled Caste Elite in India.* (Delhi 1986).
60. Dhavan, Rajeev, *Supreme Court in India- Socio-legal critique of its jurisdiction Techniques* (Tripathi Bombay. 1977).
61. Dicey, *Law of the Constitution* (London 1924).
62. Diwan, Paras *Indian Constitution* (Allahabad law Agency-1984).

63. Dube M.P, *Role of Supreme Court in Indian Constitution* (Deep and Deep New Delhi 1987).
64. Dubois Abbe J.A., Hindu *Manners, Customs and Ceremonies.* (Oxford 1906).
65. Dushkin, L. 'Scheduled Caste politics.' in J.M. Mahar (ed.) *The Untouchables in Contemporary India.* (Tucson: University of Arizona Press 1972).
66. Dworkin Ronald, *Taking Rights Seriously, (*London 1977).
67. Elamkulam, *Studies in Kerala History.*
68. Eysenk Hans: *The Inequality of Men* (London 1970).
69. Freeman, J.M. 'The Consciousness of Freedom Amongst India's Untouchables.' in D.K. Basu & R. Sisson (eds) *Social and Economic Development in India.* (New Delhi Sage 1986).
70. Freeman, J.M. *Untouchable. An Indian Life History.* (London Allen & Unwin 1979).
71. Freeman, J.M. *Scarcity and Opportunity in an Indian Village.* (Menlo Park. Cal. Cummings 1977).
72. Fuchs, S. *At the Bottom of Indian Society. The Harijan and other Lower Castes* (New Delhi Munishiram Manoharlal 1981).
73. Fuchs, S. *The Children of Hari. (*Allahabad New Order 1949).
74. Galanter M, *Competing Equalities* (Oxford 1984).
75. Galanter, M, Competing *Equalities – Law and Backward classes in India.* (Oxford University Press, New Delhi, 1984).
76. Galanter, M. 'The Abolition of Disabilities - Untouchability and the Law'. in J.M. Mahar (ed.) *The Untouchables in Contemporary India.* (Tucson University of Arizona Press 1972).
77. Galanter, M. *Competing Equalities: Law and the Backward Classes in India.* (Berkeley University of California Press 1984).
78. Galanter, M. *Law and Society in Modern India.* (Delhi1989).
79. Galanter, M. Pursuing equality. 'An Assessment of India's Policy of Compensatory Discrimination for Disadvantaged Groups.' in D.K. Basu & R. Sisson (eds) *Social and Economic Development in India.* (New Delhi: Sage 1986).
80. Gandhi, M.K. *The Removal of Untouchability.* (Ahmedabad Navajivan 1954).
81. Gandhi, M.K. *All are Equal in the Eyes of God. Selections From Mahatma Gandhi.* (Delhi Ministry of Information and Broadcasting 1964).

82. Ganesan, L. *Relevance of Reservation.* (Madras Valentina 1991)
83. Ghosh, S.K. *Reservation in Service,* (Akshara Publication, NewDelhi 1996).
84. Ghosh, S.K. *Protection of Minorities and Scheduled Castes.* (New Delhi Ashish 1980).
85. Ghurye, G.S. *Caste and Race in India.* (Bombay Popular 1969).
86. Ghurye, G.S. *The Mahadev Kolis* (Bombay: Popular Book Depot 1957).
87. Gillespia Judith & Lazarus Stuart, *American Government Comparing Political Experiences* (Prentic Hall, Inc. Englewood cliff, New Fussy 1979).
88. Glazer.N, *Affirmative Action Ethnic Equality and Public Policy,* (Basic Books New York 1975).
89. Glen M. & Johnson, S.B. 'Social Mobility Among Untouchables'. in G.R. Gupta (ed.) *Cohesion and Conflict in Modern India.* (New Delhi Vikas 1978).
90. Gokhale J. *From Concessions to Confrontation: the Politics of an Indian Untouchable Community.* (Bombay Popular Prakashan 1993).
91. Gomango, G. *Constitutional Provisions for the Scheduled Castes and Scheduled Tribes.* (Bombay Himalaya 1992).
92. Gooptu, N. 'Caste and labour: Untouchable Social Movements in Urban Uttar Pradesh in the Early 20th Century.' in P. Robb (ed.) *Dalit Movements and the Meanings of Labour in India.* (Delhi Oxford University Press 1993).
93. Granville Austin *The Indian Constitution: Cornerstone of A Nation.*
94. Grenville Austin, *The Indian Constitution Corner Stone of a Nation* (Oxford University Press Bombay 1966.).
95. Gupta, Bharatbhusan, *The Welfare State in India a Critical Commentary.* (Central Book Depot-Alahabad 1969).
96. Gupta, K. 'Economic deprivation of socially deprived in Uttar Pradesh.' in Bhowmik K.L.(ed.) *Development of Scheduled Communities.* Current Anthropological and Archaeological Perspectives (New Delhi: Inter-India Publications 1988).
97. Gupta, M.R. *The Untouchable.* (Delhi Rajkamal 1948).
98. Gupta, P.K. *Commentaries on the Scheduled Castes and Scheduled Tribes (Prevention of Atrocities) Act, 1989.* (Lucknow Eastern 1992).
99. Gupta, S.K. *Scheduled Castes in Modern Indian Politics: Their*

Emergence as a Political Power. (New Delhi Munshiram Manoharlal 1985).

100. Gwyer and Appadorai, *Speeches and Documents on Indian Constitution* (London 1921).
101. Haines Charles Grove, *The American Doctrine of Judicial Supremacy* (New York 1959).
102. Hainrich, J.C. *The Psychology of Suppressed Classes* (London, Allen & Unwin 1937).
103. Hayek. F.A. *The Constitution of Liberty* (London. 1960).
104. Hazari Malik, M.A. *I Was an Outcaste*. (New Delhi Hindustan Times 1957).
105. Heimsath, C. *Indian Nationalism and Hindu Social Reform*. (Princeton- Princeton University Press 1964).
106. Henninger, F. *The Bhangis. Religious Life of India Series*. (Calcutta Association Press).
107. Hobhouse L.T., *Elements of Social Justice*.(London. 1922).
108. Hutton, J. H. *Caste In India*. (Oxford Oxford University Press, 1951).
109. Indian School of Social Sciences *Bonded Labour in India: a Shocking Tale of Slave Labour in Rural India*. (Calcutta ISSS 1975).
110. Isaacs, H.R. *India's Ex-Untouchables*. (New Delhi Asia 1965).
111. Ivan Reid *Social Class differences in Britain* (London 1989).
112. Iyer Krishna V.R., *Social Justice and Undone Vast* (New Delhi 1991).
113. Iyer Krishna, V.R *Some Half-hidden Aspects of Indian Social Justice* (Eastern book Co. Lucknow).
114. Iyer Krishna, V.R. (1991) *Social Justice and the Undone Vast*, B.R.Publishing Corporation, New Delhi.
115. Iyer Raghavan (ed.) *The Moral and Political Writings of Mahatma Gandhi*, Vol. I. (Oxford Clarendon Press 1986).
116. Jagadeesan P, *Marriage and Social Legislations in Tamil Nadu*.(Madras 1990).
117. Jain, M.P, *Indian Constitutional Law*, (N.M. Tripathi Pvt. Ltd. Bombay 1974).
118. Jain, P.C., Jain Shashi & Bhatnagar, Sudha *Scheduled Caste Women*. Jaipur Rawat 1997.
119. Jaswal S.S., *Reservation Policy and the Law*.(New Delhi 2000).
120. Jeffery,Robin, *The Decline Of Nayar Dominance* (London1976).
121. Jeffery, P. *et al*. 'Contaminating States: Midwifery, Childbearing

and the State in Rural North India.' in H. Afshar (ed.) *Women, State and Ideology*. (Basingstoke: Macmillan 1987).

122. Jeffrey, P., Jeffrey, R. & yon, A. *Labour Pains and Labour Power*. (London: 2ed 1988).
123. Jennings Ivor, *The Constitutional Problems in Pakistan* (London 1951).
124. Jones K. *Socio-Religious Reform Movements in British India*. (CUP 1989).
125. Joshi, B. *A Democracy in Search of Equality: Untouchables, Politics and Indian Social Change*. (New Delhi: Hindustan 1982).
126. Joshi, B.R. (ed.) *Untouchable! Voices of the Dalit Liberation Movement*. (London Zed and MRG 1986).
127. Juergensmayer, M. *Religion as Social Vision: the Movement against Untouchability in Twentieth Century Punjab*. (Berkeley: University of California Press 1982).
128. Juergensmayer, M. *Religious Rebels in the Punjab: the Social Vision of the Untouchables*. (India: Ajanta 1989.
129. Julius Stone, *Human Law and Human Justice* (Bombay 1965.
130. Kamble J.R, *Rise and Awakening of Depressed Class in India* (New Delhi 1979).
131. Kamble, J.R. *Rise and Awakening of the Depressed Classes in India*. (New Delhi National 1979).
132. Kamble, N.D. *Scheduled Castes*. (New Delhi Ashish 1982).
133. Kamble, N.D. *Atrocities on Scheduled Castes and Scheduled Tribes in Post-Independence India*. (Delhi Ashish 1982).
134. Kamble, N.D. *Poverty within Poverty*. (Bangalore ISEC 1979.
135. Kananaikil, J. *Christians of Scheduled Caste Origin*. (New Delhi Indian Social Institute1983).
136. Karlekar, M. 'A study of Balmiki women in Delhi' in L. Dube (ed.) *Visibility and Power: Essays on Women in Society and Development*. (Delhi OUP 1986).
137. Karlekar, M. *Poverty and Women's Work: a Study of Sweeper Women in Delhi*. (Delhi Vikas 1982).
138. Khare, R.S. *The Untouchable as Himself. Identity and Pragmatism among the Lucknow Chamars*. (Cambridge: CUP 1985).
139. Khosla, D. 'Untouchability - a case study in law and life.' in A. Podgovecki et al. (eds) *Legal Systems and Social Systems*. (London 1985).

140. Khosla, D. *Myth and Reality of the Protection of Civil Rights Law: a Case of Untouchability in Rural India.* (Delhi1987).

141. Knorringa, P. *Economics of Collaboration: Indian Shoe Makers in Between Market and Hierarchy.* (New Delhi Sage 1996).

142. Kodian *Atrocities on Harijans.* (New Delhi: Communist Party 1978).

143. Kolenda, P. 'Widowhood among 'Untouchable' Chuhras.' in A. Ostör *et al. Concepts of Person. Kinship, Caste and Marriage in India.* (Cambridge, Mass. Harvard UP 1982).

144. Kolenda, P. 'The Mother Goddess Complex among the North Indian Sweepers.' in G.R. Gupta (ed.) *Religion in Modern India.* (New Delhi Vikas 1983).

145. Kolenda, P. 'Untouchable Chuhras through their humor: 'equalizing' marital kin through teasing, pretence and farce.' in O. Lynch (ed.) *Divine Passions: the Social Construction of Emotion in India.* (Berkeley: University of California Press 1990).

146. Kshirsagar, R.K. *Untouchability in India: Implementation of Law and Abolition.* (New Delhi Deep & Deep 1986).

147. Lal Shyam 'Asprashyeekaran - Dalitisation' in S.M. Michael (ed.) *Dalits in Modern India. Vision and Values.* (New Delhi Vistaar 1999).

148. Lal Shyam *The Bhangi: a Sweeper Caste - its Socio-Economic Portraits. With Special Reference to Jodhpur Ciy.* (Bombay Popular Prakashan 1992).

149. Lal Shyam, *The Bhangis in Transition.* (New Delhi Inter-India 1983)

150. Lal Shyam, *Caste and Political Mobilization: the Bhangis.* (Jaipur: Panchsheel 1981).

151. Lal Shyam, *From Higher Caste to Lower Caste. The Process of Asprashyeekaran & the Myth of Sanskritization.* (Jaipur Rawat 1997).

152. Lal, A.K. 'The Educated Harijans as Elite.' in Sachchidananda & A.K. Lal (eds) *Elite and Development.* (New Delhi Concept 1980).

153. Lal, A.K. *Dalits in Action. An Evaluation of Bihar Dalit Vikas Samiti.* (New Delhi Concept 1997).

154. Lal, A.K. *The Politics of Poverty.* (New Chetana 1977).

155. Lal, K.S. *Growth of Scheduled Tribes and Castes in Medieval India.* (Delhi Aditya 1995).

156. Lal, S.K. & Nahar, U.R. *Extent of Untouchability and Pattern of Discrimination.* (New Delhi Mittal 1990).

157. Laski Harold. J; *A Grammar Of Politics* (London. 1951).
158. Laski, Harold; *Inequality and Justice* (1974).
159. Leach, E.R. Introduction, *Aspects of Caste*. (Cambridge UP 1962).
160. Lynch, O. 'Rural cities in India: continuities and discontinuities.' in P. Mason (ed.) *India and Ceylon: Unity and Diversity*. (London OUP 1967).
161. Lynch, O. *The Politics of Untouchability. Social Mobility and Social Change in a City of India*. (New York Columbia UP 1969).
162. Macpherson C.B. *Democratic Theory: Essays in Retrieval* (London 1975).
163. Massey, J. *Dalits in India: Religion as a Source of Bondage or Liberation*. (New Delhi Manohar 1995).
164. Mathew, J. *Protest and Reform*. (New Delhi Amerind 1987).
165. Maurya, R.L. 'Changing Status of the Scheduled Castes.' in Tripathi R.S. & Tiwari P.D. (eds) *Dimensions of Scheduled Caste Development in India*. (New Delhi Uppal 1991).
166. McKean Warwick, *Equality and Discrimination Under International Law*.(London 1983).
167. Mehta, Haroobhai & Patel Hasmukh's. The *Dynamics of Reservation Policy* (Patriot Publishers, NewDelhi 1985).
168. Mendelsohn O. & Vicziany, M. 'The Untouchables.' in O. Mendelsohn & U. Baxi (eds) *The Rights of Subordinated Peoples*. (Delhi OUP 1994).
169. Mendelsohn O. & Vicziany, M. *The Untouchables. Poverty, Pollution and the State in Modern India*. (Cambridge CUP 1998).
170. Mendelsohn, O. & Vicziany, M. 'The Untouchables Today.' in J. Manselos (ed.) *India, Creating a Modern Nation*. (Delhi Sterling 1990).
171. Menon V.P., *The Story of The Integration Of Indian States*.
172. Michael, S.M. (ed.) *Dalits in Modern India. Vision and Values*. (New Delhi Vistaar 1999).
173. Minority Rights Group *The Untouchables of India* (London: MRG 1982; Bangalore: Dalit Sahitya Akademy 1984).
174. Mishra Jitendra *Equality Versus Justice* (Deep and Deep Publication, New Delhi 1996).
175. Mishra R.G & Kaus Gurvinda- *Reservation Policy and Personal Selection*, (Delhi Uppal Publishers 1990).
176. Molund, S. *First We are People ...: The Koris of Kanpur between*

Caste and Class. (Stockholm: Department of Anthropology, University of Stockholm 1988).

177. Moon, Vasant, *Ambedkar Writing & Speeches* (Vol 1 to 15 Govt. of Maharashtra (1979-1991).
178. Moore, B. *Injustice: the Social Bases of Obedience and Revolt.* (New York Sharpe 1978).
179. Mukerjee, H.N. *Gandhi, Ambedkar and the Extirpation of Untouchability.* (New Delhi People's 1982).
180. Mukherjee, A.B. *The Chamars of U.P. A Study of Social Geography.* (New Delhi Inter-India 1980).
181. Mukherjee, D. *Caste and Outcaste.* (New York 1929).
182. Mukherjee, P. *Beyond the Four Varnas. The Untouchables in India.* (Shimla: Indian Institute of Advanced Study; Delhi: Motilal Banarsidas 1988).
183. Mungekar, B.L. 'State, market and the Dalits: analytics of the New Economic Policy'in S.M. Michael (ed.) *Dalits in Modern India. Vision and Values.* (New Delhi: Vistaar 1999).
184. Murugar, L. *Dalit Panther Movement in Maharashtra: a Sociological Appraisal.* (Bombay Popular Prakashan 1991).
185. Muthuswamy and Brinda's Reservation *and concessions,* (Swamy Publishers, New Delhi 1998).
186. Nair Ramakrishnan, *Constitutional Experiments in Kerala.* (Trivandrum 964).
187. Nandu Ram *Beyond Ambedkar: Essays on Dalits in India.* (New Delhi: Har- Anand 1995).
188. Nath, Ram *Dalit-Muslim Unity. Why? And How?* (Bangalore Dalit Sahitya Akademy 1995).
189. Nath, Trilok *Politics of the Depressed Classes.* (Delhi 1987).
190. Nehru.J, *The Discovery of India* (Asia Publishing House 1961).
191. *Nehru: The First Sixty Years* (ed.) Dorothy Norman. (Asia Publishing House, 1965).
192. Nesiah ,Devanesan in *Discrimination with reason?* (Oxford University Press, NewDelhi.1997).
193. Nesiah Devasenan, *Discrimination With Reason? Policy of Reservation in the United States, India and Malaysia* (Oxford University Press, Delhi 1997).
194. Ojha, G.P. *Politicisation of Scheduled Castes in Bihar.* (Patna: Jagjivan Ram Institute of Parliamentary Studies and Political Research 1990).

195. Omvedt, G. *Dalits and the Democratic Revolution: Dr Ambedkar and the Dalit Movement in Colonial India.* (New Delhi Sage 1994).
196. Opler, M. 'North Indian themes: caste and untouchability.' in J.M. Mahar (ed.) *The Untouchables in Contemporary India.* (Tucson: University of Arizona Press 1972).
197. Padhy ,K.S. and Jayashree Mahapatra *Reservation Policy in India* (Ashish Publishing House, New Delhi 1988).
198. Pai V.A.& Panandiker, ed., *The Politics of backwardness: Reservation Policy in India(1997).*
199. Pandey, R.S. 'Social profiles of Scheduled Casres in perspective of development programmes: a case study of Koraon Block [UP].' in R.S. Tripathi & P.D. Tiwari (eds) *Dimensions of Scheduled Caste Development.* (New Delhi Uppal 1991).
200. Parel Anthony J. (Ed.) *The Hind Swaraj* (Cambridge 1997).
201. Parikh, Sunita *The Politics of Preference. Democratic Institutions and Affirmative Action in the US and India.* (Ann Arbor: University of Michigan Press 1997).
202. Parmar, Y.A. *The Mahyavanshi: The Success Story of a Scheduled Caste.* (Delhi Mittal 1987).
203. Parry, J. *Death in Banaras.* (Cambridge CUP 1994).
204. Parry, J. *Caste and Kinship in Kangra.* (London Routledge 1979).
205. Parvathamma, C. *Scheduled Castes at the Crossroads.* (Ashish, New Delhi 1989).
206. Parvathamma, C. *Scheduled Castes and Tribes: Socio-Economic Survey.* (New Delhi Ashish 1984).
207. Pathak, B. *Road to Freedom. A Sociological Study on the Abolition of Scavenging in India.* (Delhi 1991).
208. Pawar, D. *Ma vie d'intouchable.* (Paris: La Découverte 1990).
209. Potty, Seetharaman S. *A handbook on reservation in public services and educational concessions in kerala for scheduled castes, scheduled tribes and other backward classes* (Thiruvananthapuram Kerala Services publications 2001).
210. Prabhakar, M.E. (ed.) *Towards a Dalit Theology.* (Delhi Indian Society for Promoting Christian Knowledge 1989).
211. Prabhash J, *Affirmative Action and Social Change-Social Mobility of Dalits.*(New Delhi 2000).
212. Prakash, D.R. *How to Erase Untouchability.* (New Delhi Bookwala 1979).

213. Prakash, G. (ed.) *The World of the Rural Labourer in Colonial India.* (Delhi OUP 1992).
214. Prakash, G. 'Becoming a Bhuinya: Oral Traditions and Contested Domination in Eastern India.' in D.Haynes & G. Prakash (eds) *Contesting Power. Resistance and Everyday Social Relations in South Asia.* (Delhi OUP 1991).
215. Prakash, G. *Bonded Histories: Genealogies of Labour Servitude in Colonial India.* (Cambridge CUP 1990).
216. Prasad ,Anirudh *Reservational Justice to Other Backward Classes (OBCs)* (Deeep and Deep Publication,New Delhi. 1997).
217. Prasad ,Anirudh *Reservation Policy and Practice in India, A means to an end,* (Deep and Deep Publication, New Delhi 1991).
218. Prasad ,Ishwari *Reservation Action for Social Equality* (Criterion Publications, New Delhi 1986).
219. Prasad Anirudh, *Reservation, Policy and Practice in India* (New Delhi 1991).
220. Prasad, R.R. & Rajani Kanth, G. *Development of Scheduled Caste Leather Workers.* (New Delhi: Discovery 1991).
221. Prasad, R.R. *Change and Continuity among SC Leather Workers.* (Rajendranagar, Hyderabad: National. Institute for Rural Development 1986).
222. Pritchett C.Herman, *The Federal system in Constitutional Law.* (1978).
223. Pundir, J.K. 'Social Development Through New Institutions And Scheduled Castes In The Rural Setting.' in R.S. Tripathi & P.D. Tiwari (eds) *Dimensions of Scheduled Caste Development.* (New Delhi Uppal 1991).
224. Pundir, J.K. 'Weaker Sections: Scheduled Castes And Beyond In Rural Settling.' in A.P. Sarasevat (ed.) *The Poor and the Poverty - Social, Economic and Political Dimensions.* (Meerut: Sawrup 1989).
225. Pundir, J.K. *Changing Patterns of Scheduled Castes.* (Jaipur: Rawat 1997).
226. Purohit, *B.D.* & Purohit, S.D. *Handbook of reservation for Scheduled Castes and Scheduled Tribe* (Jainsons Publication, New Delhi 1997).
227. Quigley, D. *The Interpretation of Caste.* (Oxford OUP 1993).
228. Radhakrishnan, S. & Kumari, R. *Impact of Education on Scheduled Caste Youth in India. A Study of Social Transformation in Bihar and Madhya Pradesh.* (New Delhi Radiant 1989).
229. Ram Jagjivan *Caste Challenge in India.* (New Delhi Vision 1980).

230. Ram Ratan 'The changing religion of the Bhangis of Delhi: a case of Sanskritization.' in *Aspects of Religion in India*, L.P. Vidyarthi (ed.). (Meerut Kedar Rathnam Rath 1960).

231. Rao K.V, *Parliamentary Democracy of India: A Critical Commentary*, (New Delhi *2nd* Ed.).

232. Rath ,Rajalaxmi (1995) *Reservation And Social Transformation Among Scheduled castes And Scheduled Tribes* (Inter India Publication, New Delhi).

233. Ravindran T.K., *Asan and Social Revolution in Kerala* (1972).

234. Rawls John, *A Theory of Justice.* (London 1972).

235. Redish Martin H.. *The Constitution As Political Structure.*(New York 1995).

236. Robb, P. (ed.) *Dalit Movements and Meanings of Labour in India.* (Delhi OUP 1993).

237. Rohner, R.P. & Chaki-Sircar, M. *Women and Children in a Bengali Village.* (Hanover, NH University Press of New England 1988).

238. Roy, A.K. *New Dalit Revolution.* (Patna 1980).

239. Roy, R. & Singh, V.B. *Between Two Worlds: A Study of Harijan Elites.* (Delhi Discovery 1987).

240. Rudolph, L.I. & Rudolph, S.H. 'Untouchability: A Test of Fellow Feeling'. in *The Modernity of Tradition. Political Development in India.* (Chicago University of Chicago Press 1967).

241. Russell Bertrand, *Roads to Freedom* (London 1919).

242. Saberwal, S. 'Status, mobility, and networks in a Punjabi industrial town.' in his *Beyond the Village: Sociological Explorations.* (Simla IIAS 1972).

243. Saberwal, S. *Mobile Men: Limits to Social Change in Urban Punjab.* (Delhi Vikas 1976).

244. Sachchidananda, T. *The Harijan Elite: a Study of their Status, Networks, Mobility and Role in Social Transformation.* (Haryana Thompson 1977).

245. Saksena H.S. (ed) *Safeguards for Scheduled castes and Tribes-Founding Fathers' Views* (1981).

246. Saksena, H.S. *Safeguards for Scheduled Caste and Tribes* (Uppal Publishing House, New Delhi1981).

247. Saksena, H.S. *Safeguards for Scheduled Castes and Scheduled Tribes: Founding Father's View.* (New Delhi Uppal 1981).

248. Sangwan, O.P. (ed.) *Dalit Society and the Challenge of Development.* (New Delhi Commonwealth 1995).

249. Sangwan, O.P. (ed.) *Social System and the Dalit Identity*. (New Delhi Commonwealth 1995).

250. Sanjana, J.E. *Caste and Outcaste*. (Bombay Thacker 1946).

251. Santhakumari, R. *Scheduled Castes and Welfare Measures*. (New Delhi Classical 1994).

252. Santoshi, H. *Daliton Mein Dalit*. (New Delhi Nav Sahitye Academy 1990).

253. Sanyal, S. & Roy Burman, B.K. *Social Mobility Movements among Scheduled Castes and Scheduled Tribes of India*. (New Delhi: Government of India 1970).

254. Sathe S.P., *Judicial Activism in India* (OUP 2002).

255. Saxena, P.K. *The Scheduled Caste Voter*. (New Delhi Radha 1990).

256. Searle-Chatterjee, M. 'The Polluted Identity of Work.' in S. Wallman (ed.) *The Social Anthropology of Work*. (London Academic Press 1979).

257. Searle-Chatterjee, M. *Reversible Sex-Roles: The Special Case of Benares Sweepers*. (Oxford: Pergamon 1981).

258. Searle-Chatterjee, M. Urban untouchables and Hindu nationalism, *Immigrants and Minorities* 13 (1994).

259. Seervai H. M., *Constitutional Law of India*. (Bombay 1994).

260. Shah, A.M . 'Untouchability, the Untouchables, and Social Change in Gujarat.' in P. Hockings, (ed.) *Dimensions of Social Life*. (Berlin Mouton 1987).

261. Shah, G. 'Anti-untouchability movements.' in Centre for Social Studies, Surat (ed.) *Caste, Caste Conflict and Reservation*. (Delhi Ajanta 1985).

262. Shah, G. *Politics of Scheduled Castes and Tribes*. (Bombay).

263. Shah, G. *Social Movements in India*. (New Delhi Sage 1990).

264. Shah, V.P. & Patel, T. *The Educational Problems of SC & ST College Students: a Statistical Profile*. (Delhi: Allied for CSSR).

265. Shah, V.P. & Patel, T. *Who Goes to College? SC/T Post-Matric Scholars in Gujarat*. (Ahmedabad: Rachana Prakashan 1977).

266. Sharma B.D, *Dalits Betrayed*, (Har Anand Publications, New Delhi, 1994).

267. Sharma Gopal & Singh Harilal in *Reservation Politics in India Mandalisation of the Society* (Deep and Deep Publications, New Delhi 1995.

268. Sharma O.P., *Reservation- A Gimmick* (New Delhi 1994).

269. Sharma S.P. *Reservations Bane or Boon,*(NewDelhi 1991).

270. Sharma U. 'Berreman Revisited: Caste And The Comparative Method.' M. Searle- Chatterjee & U. Sharma (eds) *Contextualising Caste: Post-Dumontian Approaches*. (Oxford Blackwell 1994).

271. Sharma, G.S. *Legislation and Cases on Untouchability and Scheduled Castes in India*. (Delhi Indian Council of Social Science Research / Bombay: Allied 1975).

272. Sharma, O.P. *Reservation: A Gimmick,* (Kar Kripa Publishers, New Delhi 1994).

273. Sharma, S.K. *The Chamar Artisans: Industrialisation, Skills and Social Mobility*. (New Delhi BR 1986).

274. Sharma, S.K. (ed.) *Reform, Protest and Social Transformation*. (New Delhi Ashish 1987).

275. Sharma, S.K. *Social Movements and Social Change*. (Delhi BR Publishing 1985).

276. Shasmal K.C. *The Bauris of West Bengal. A Socio-economic Study* (Calcutta: India Publications 1972).

277. Shrirama 'Untouchability and Stratification in Indian Civilisation,' in S.M. Michael (ed.) *Dalits in Modern India. Vision and Values*. (New Delhi Vistaar 1999).

278. Shukla, K.S. & Verma, B.M. *Development of Scheduled Castes and Administration*. (New Delhi Uppal 1993).

279. Shukla, V.N *Constitution of India* (Lucknow 1996).

280. Singh ,S.N. *Reservation Policy for Backward classes* (Jaipur Rawat Publication 1996).

281. Singh Ravindar Bains, *Reservation Policy and Anti-Reservationists* (New Delhi 1994).

282. Singh Vatsa, Rajendra, *The Depressed classes of India* (Geethanjali Prakashan Delhi 1977).

283. Singh, K.S. '*The Scheduled Castes*'- *People of India National Series, Vol. II Anthropological Survey of India* (OUP, Delhi, 1993).

284. Singh, P. *Equality, Reservation and Discrimination in India. A Constitutional Study of Scheduled Castes, Scheduled Tribes and Other Backward Classes*. (New Delhi Deep & Deep 1982).

285. Singh, S.N. *Reservation: Problems and Prospects*. (New Delhi Uppal 1987).

286. Singh, S.S. & Sundaram, S. *Emerging Harijan Elite: a Study of their Identity*. (New Delhi Uppal 1985).

287. Sivaramaya.B. 'Affirmative Action: Scheduled Castes and

Scheduled Tribes.' in *International Perspective on Affirmative Action.* (USA Rockeıeller Foundation 1984).

288. Srinivas, M.N: *Caste: its Twentieth Century* (New Delhi Viking 1996).
289. Srivastava, S.N. *Harijans in Indian Society.* (New Delhi Chand .1979).
290. Stevenson, S. *Without the Pale: Life Story of an Outcaste.* Religious Life of India Series. (Calcutta Association Press 1930).
291. Subramanian, K.S. 'Caste Violence Against the Scheduled Caste' *Social Science Probing,* 3, 4, 1986.
292. Tewary, S.N. 'Scheduled Caste women in rural Bihar - a study in sociology of poverty.' in Chaudhary, S.N. & Chaudhary, P. (eds) *National Development and Women.* (New Delhi Har-Anand & Vikas 1992).
293. Thomas Blom Hansen and Christophore Jaferelot (ed) *The BJP and the compulsions of Politics in India,* (Oxford University Press 2001).
294. Thomas Mathew, Caste *and Class Dynamics* (dTech, New Delhi 1992.
295. Thomas Mathew, *Caste And Class Dynamics-Radical Ambedkarite Praxis.*(New Delhi 1992).
296. Toynbee, Arnold.J. *A Study of History* (London 1962).
297. Tripathi, R.S. & Tiwari, P.D. (eds) *Dimensions of Scheduled Caste Development in India.* (New Delhi Uppal 1991).
298. Trivedi H.R. *Scheduled Castes' Quest for Land and Social Equality.* (New Delhi Concept 1995).
299. Upadhyay, H.C *Reservation for Scheduled Casts and Scheduled Tribes,* (Anmol Publication, NewDelhi 1991).
300. Vakil, A.K. *Reservation Policy and Scheduled Caste in India* (Ashish Publishing House, New Delhi 1985).
301. Varkey M.M. *Ormakaliloode* (Kottayam 1976).
302. Verma, G.P, *Caste Reservation in India-Law and the Constitution* (1980).
303. Vidrohi, M.R. *Dalit Dastavaij.* (New Delhi Dalit Sahitya Prakashan Sanstha 1989).
304. Vidyarthi, L.P. & Mishra, N. *Harijan Today. Sociological, Economics, Political, Religious and Cultural Analysis.* (New Delhi Classical 1977).
305. Vithal BPR, 'Evolving Trends in Bureaucracy' in *State and Nation*

in the Context of Social Change.(Ed. T.V. Sathyamurthy) (OUP 2000).

306. Vlastos. G, '*Justice and Equality*' *in Theories of Rights* (Jeremy Waldron (ed) London 1989).

307. Webster, J.C.B. 'Who is a Dalit?'in S.M. Michael (ed.) *Dalits in Modern India. Vision and Values.* (New Delhi: Vistaar 1999).

308. Wolpert Stanley, *A New History of India* (OUP 1982).

309. Zelliot, E. *From Untouchable to Dalit: Essays on Ambedkar Movement.* (New Delhi Manohar 1992).

Articles

1. Ahmadi A.M. J, 'Dimensions of Judicial Activism' *http://www.iosworld.org/ J ahmadi.htm . accessed on 08-07-*

2. Baboo, B. 'Cognition and Structure: Explaining the 'Exploitation' of An Untouchable Caste in Orissa', *Eastern Anthropologist* 39, 1986: 187-93.

3. Baxi ,Upendra , 'Legal Activism Judicial Tryst With Indian Destiny', *The Hindu* August 19,1997.

4. Beteille, A. & Srinivas, M.N. 'The Harijans of India' *Scientific American* 213, 1965: 13-18.

5. Das Bhagwan, 'Moments in a History of Reservations', *Economic and Political Weekly* October 28, 2000.

6. Bharti, I. 'Bihar's Most Wretched', *Economic & Political Weekly* Sept 22, 1990: 2124-25.

7. Bhatia, B. 'Massacre On the Banks of the Sone', *Economic & Political Weekly* XXXII, 51, 1997: 3242-45.

8. Bhatt, G.S. 'The Chamars of Lucknow', *Eastern Anthropologist* 3, 1945/54?: 24-41.

9. Bhowmik, K.L. The Bauris: 'A Dominant Scheduled Caste of West Bengal' *Bulletin of Cultural Research Institute*, 4, Nos. 1/2, 1966.

10. Bose, P.K. 'Social Mobility and Caste Violence: A Study of Gujarat Riots.'*Economic & Political Weekly* 16, No. 16, 1981.

11. Chalam, K.S. 'Caste and Economic Reform' *Seminar* 471, Nov. 1998: 33-37 (*Dalit* ...) [G].

12. Mowli Chandra, V. ''Jogin'. Girl-Child' *Labour Studies*. New Delhi: Sterling 1992.

13. Cohen, S.P. 'The Untouchable Soldier - Caste, Politics and the Indian Army' *Journal of Asian Studies* 28, 3, 1969.

14. Cohn, B.S. 'Chamar Family in a North Indian Village: a Structural Contingent' *Journal of Asian Studies* 19, 1960.
15. Corrie, B.D. 'A human development index for the Dalit child in India' *Social Indicators Research* 34, 1995.
16. Contursi, J. 'Militant Hindus and Buddhist Dalits: Hegemony And Resistance in an Indian Slum' *American Ethnologist* 16, 1989.
17. Desmond, E.W. Anti-Caste Revolution, *Time*, April 13, 1992.
18. Dhar, H. 'Escalating violence on Harijans' [UP], *Economic Political Weekly* 19 September 1992: 2023-4.
19. Dogra, B. 'First Stirrings and Repressio. A Report from Palamau '[Bihar]], *EconomicPoliticalWeekly* Vol XX No 1985:.
20. Venugopal. P (Justice), 'Implementation of Social Justice through Reservation' website (site) accessed on 29th March 2003.
21. Souza, V. 'An Operational Definition of Backward Groups in India' *Indian Journal of Agricultural Economics* 13, 1958.
22. Souza, V. 'Castes,Out-Castes and Sociology of Stratification, *International Journal of ?*
23. Souza, V. 'Changing status of Scheduled Castes', *Economic& Political Weekly of India* 16, 48, 1961.
24. Gill, S.S. 'The Reservation Muddle', January 24, 1997 *The Hindu.*
25. Gill, S.S. "The Empowered: A Grand Illusion', August 1, 1991, *The Indian Express.*
26. Gokhale, J.B. 'The Dalit Panthers and The Radicalization of the Untouchables' *Journal of Commonwealth & Comparative Studies* 17, 1991.
27. Gokhale, T.J. 'Bati or Vidroha: Continuity and change in DalitSahitya, Journal ofAsian & African Studies1980: 29-42.
28. Gumperz, J. Dialect differences and social stratification in a North Indian village, *American Anthropologist* 60, 1958: 668-82.
29. Gupta, T.D. Caste complications in agrarian conflict [Bihar], *Economic & Political Weekly* 2 May 1992.
30. Guru, G. Reservations and the sanskritization of Scheduled Castes-some theoretical aspects, *Sociological Bulletin* 33, 1984.
31. Guru, Gopal, 'The Shifting Sites of Reservation' *The Hindu.* 2 December-1997.
32. Hantal, B. 'BSP Gaining Strength', *Economic & Political Weekly* 31,21, 1996.
33. Deshpande J.V., 'Reservation Policy: Real Issues' in *Economic and Political Weekly* April 29. 2000.

34. Jain, R.K. 'Hierarchy, Hegemony and Dominance. Politics of Ethnicity in UP', 1995, *Economic & Political Weekly* 31, 4, 1996: 215-23.
35. James, P.A. & Sreenivas, 'R.G. Commissioner for Scheduled Castes and Scheduled Tribes', *Economic & Political Weekly* XIV (26) June 20, 1979.
36. Joshi, B. 'Scheduled Caste voters: New Data, New Questions', ? *Economic and Political Weekly* c1982: 1357-1361.
37. Katyal ,K.K. 'Need for Judicial Activism', *The Hindu,* 4 March, 1996,.
38. Khanna ,H.R. 'Judicial Activism', *The Hindu* 27 September,1995.
39. Khare, Harish , "*Judicial activism ... the good and the not so good*", 2nd *March 1997,T*he Hindu.
40. Khare ,Harish 'Some Perceptions' , *Frontline* 3rd May, 1996.
41. Khare ,Harish, 'For the Sake of a Civil Society', *The Hindu* 14th January-1996.
42. Kirpal, V. Higher Education for the Scheduled Castes and Scheduled Tribes, *EPW*, Jan. 28, 1978.
43. Kothari, R. Rise of the Dalits and the renewed debate on caste, *EPW* 29, 25 June 1994: 1589-94.
44. Krishnan, P.S. Untouchability and atrocities: the emerging Dalit identity, *Social Action* 43, 1993: 412-26.
45. Lal, A. K. "*protective discrimination and the scheduled caste*", October - December 2000, Journal of rural development.
46. Mahendra. P, Singh 'Are Article 15 (4) and 16(4) Fundamental Right?' (1994) 3 SCC (June) 33.
47. Malik, Bela Untouchability and Dalit women's oppression, *EPW* 34, 6, 1999: 323-324 [G].
47. Mendelsohn, O. A 'Harijan Élite? The Lives of Some Untouchable Politicians', *EPW* 21, 12; 22 March 1986: 501-9.
48. Mendelsohn, O. A 'Life and Struggles in the Stone Quarries of India', *Journal of Commonwealth and Comparative Politics* 29, 1, 1991: 44-71.
49. Mendelsohn, O.A The transformation of authority in rural India [Rajasthan], *Modern Asian Studies* 27, 1993: 805-42.
50. Cunningham Clark D & Menon Madhava N.R. *Michigan Law Review* Vol. 97, No. 5 March 1999.
51. Mohanty, R.K. Dynamics of atrocities on Scheduled Castes in rural

India [Bihar etc.], *Indian Journal of Social Work* 49, 1988: 51-66.

52. Mohanty, R.K. Scheduled Castes as minorities, *Mainstream* 23, No. 18, 1984.
53. Mohapatra, B.N. & Bhattacharyya, D. "Tribal-Dalit conflict. Electoral politics in Phulbani", *EPW* 31, 2/3.
54. Mohapatra, B.N. "Understanding indignities", *Seminar* 471, Nov. 1998: 43-46 (*Dalit* ...).
55. Nambissan, G.B. "Equity in education. Schooling Dalit children in India", *EPW* 31, 1996: 1011-24.
56. Nandu Ram *The Mobile Scheduled Castes: Rise of a New Middle Class*. Delhi: Hindustan 1988 [Reviews *Contributions to Indian Sociology* 23, 1989: 375-6 & *EPW* 25, 1990, 47: 2599-2600].
57. Narayana, G. "Rule making for Scheduled Castes: analysis of Lok Sabha debates 1962-71", *EPW* 15, 1980: 433-40.
58. Narayana, G. "Social background of SC Lok Sabha members 1962-71", *EPW* 13, 1978: 1603-08.
59. Narayana, G. "The political elite among the Scheduled Castes", *Journal of Constitutional and Parliamentary Studies* 8, 1974: 214-19.
60. Nauriya, A. "Dalit-Intermediate Caste alliance. Call to greatness" [UP], *EPW* 2 July 1994: 1640- 43 [G].
61. Nayak, V. & Prasad, S. "On levels of living of Scheduled Castes and Scheduled Tribes", *EPW* 19, 30, 1984: 1205-13.
62. Omvedt, Gail "*Dalits: miles to go", 15th August*-1997, India Today.
63. Pai, Sudha "Dalit assertion in UP: implications for politics", *EPW* 32, 37, 1997: 2313-4.
64. Pai, Sudha "The BSP in Uttar Pradesh", *Seminar* 471, Nov. 1998: 38-42.
65. Parmar, Y.A. "Occupational change among Mahyavanshisa - Scheduled Caste", *Indian Journal of Social Work* 39, October 1978.
66. Parry, J. Egalitarian values in a hierarchical society, *South Asian Review* 7, 1974: 95- 124.
67. Pinto,Ambrose , S.J 'Is reservation the answer for dalit empowerment?', *Journal of Rural Development* October - December 2000.
68. Prasad, P. Rise of kulak power and caste struggle in North India, *Economic & Political Weekly* 17 Aug. 1991: 1923-26.
69. Prashad, V. 'The Untouchable Question' *EPW* 31, 9, 1996: 551-59.

70. Sagar, M. & Pan, I. 'SCs and STs in Eastern India. Inequality and Poverty Estimates' *EPW* March 5, 1994: 576-74.

71. Sattanathan,A.N.'Reaction to Brahminism: DMK's Heritage' *The Indian Express (Madurai Edition)* 24 August 1967.

72. Shah, G. Caste, class and reservation, *EPW* XX, 1985: 132-36.

73. Shah, G. Social backwardness and the politics of reservation, *EPW* XXVI, 1991: 601- 10

74. Sharma, K.L. 'Caste and class: factors affecting social mobility among the Scheduled Castes', *Journal of Sociological Studies* 3, 1983: 43-71.

75. Sharma, K.L. 'Class Stratification and Atrocities' *Seminar* No. 243, 1979: ??

76. Shetty, K.P. Krishna, 'Judicial activism is essential in a democracy', *The Hindu*. 10 December,1996.

77. Singh, Jagpal 'Dalits in Haryana Politics', *EPW* 32, 43: 2787-8.

78. Srivastava, B.N, 'Working of the constitutional safeguards and protective measures for the scheduled castes and scheduled tribes', *Journal of rural development*. October - December 2000,

79. Swamy Praveen 'The Judiciary Supreme Concern, Judicial Activism in Action', *Front Line* 3 May,1996.

80. Swarup, Ram, 'Logic behind perversion of caste' *Indian Express*. 13 September, 1996.

83. Sowell Thomas, 'Judicial Activism Reconsidered' http://www.amatecon.com/etext/jar/jar.html accessed on 08-07-2003.

84. Thorat, Sukhadeo ' Programmes for Empowerment and Reducing Inequality: Long Way to Go for Untouchable', *Journal of Rural Development* October - December 2000.

85. Vicziany, M. 'The Demography of Untouchability, Bihar' 1872-1971. Unpublished Paper, *Asian Studies Association of Australia*, 5th National Conference, Adelaide 1984 (see Mendelsohn, O. & Vicziany, M.).

86. Tom Campbell, 'Judicial Activism- Justice or Treason?' Working Paper Number 2002/17 http://law.anu.edu.au/news/webdocuments/tomcampbell notes.pdf. accessed on 08-07-2003.

87. Benjamin, J. 'Social mobility among Scheduled Castes in Bihar': a case study of Barh Block, *Man in India* 71, 1991: 425-38.

88. Bhatt, G.S. 'Trends and Measures of Status Mobility Among the Chamars of Dehradun', *Eastern Anthropologist* 14, 1961: 229-42.

89. Bhattacharya, B. 'A Short Note on Clubs and Libraries of the Backward Communities', *Bulletin of the Cultural Research Institute* 4, 1965: 53-7.
90. Bhattacharya, B. 'A short note on the Scheduled Tribes and Scheduled Castes Population of West Bengal', *Bulletin of the Cultural Research Institute* 3, 2, 1964: 63-6.
91. Bhattacharya, B. 'The Cult of Bhutadamara', *Man in India* 11, 2, 1931: 83-115.
92. Chakravarti, N.K. & Subedi, S. 'Origin of Untouchability in Hinduism', *Man in India* 75, 1995.
93. Chandna, R.C. 'Distributional Pattern of Scheduled Caste Population in India', *Population Geography* 2, 1980).
94. Chitnis, S. Education for Equality: Case of Scheduled Castes in Higher Education, *EPW* 7 (31-33), August 1972.
95. Cohn, B.S. 'Changing Traditions of a Low Caste', *Journal of American Folklore* 71, 1958.
96. Cohn, B.S. Madhopur revisited, *Economic & Political Weekly* 11, 1959: 963-6.
97. Das, B. 'Untouchability, Scheduled Castes and Nation Building', *Social Action* 32, 1982: 269-82.
98. Desai, I.P. 'Anti-reservation Agitation and Structure in Gujarat Society, *EPW* 16, No. 18, 1981.
99. Souza, V. 'Does Urbanism Desegregate Scheduled Castes? Evidence from a District in Punjab', *Contributions to Indian Sociology* 11, 1977: 219-39.
100. Souza, V. 'Scheduled Castes and Urbanization in Punjab: An Explanation', *Sociological Bulletin* 24, 1975: 2-12.
101. Souza V. 'The Religious Factor and the Scheduled Castes', *Social Action* 32, 1982: 283- 91.
102. Dunn, D. 'Gender Inequality in Education and Employment in the Scheduled Castes and Tribes of India', *Population Research and Policy Review* 12, 1993: 53-70.
103. Gangrade, K.D. 'Social Mobility in India: a Study of Depressed Castes', *Man in India* 55, 3, 1955.
104. Gellner, D.G. 'Structure and consensus among 'untouchables' in South Asia', *Journal of Royal Anthropological. Institute.* 1, 1995: 395.
105. Gupta, M. 'Rehabilitation of Criminal Tribes', *Eastern Anthropologist* 17, 1, 1964).

106. Gupta, S.K. 'Violence Against the SCs: Parameters and Trends, *The Downtrodden India* 1, 2, 1994: 20-43.
107. *Indian Bar Review* Vol.17&18 1991.
108. Interview with justice V.R. Krishna Iyer 'Judiciary it is Affirmative Action' May,1996, Frontline.
109. Jha, M. 'Problems of Scavangers of a Tribal City: a Case Study of Ranchi, Chotanagpur', *Man in Asia* 7, 2, 1994.
110. Jha, V. Stages in The History of Untouchables, *Indian Historical Review* 2, (1975).
111. Joshi, B. 'Recent Developments in Inter-Regional Mobilization of Dalit Protest in India', *South Asia Bulletin* 7 (1987).
112. Kananaikil, J. 'Marginalisation of the Scheduled Castes: a Sociological interpretation', *Social Action* 32, 1982.
113. Khare, R.S. 'Indian Sociology and the Cultural Other,' *Contributions to Indian Sociology* (n.s.) 24, 1990: 177-99.
114. Khare, R.S. 'The Other's Double - the Anthropologist's Bracketed Self: Notes on Cultural Representation and Privileged Discourse', *New Literary History* 23, 1992: 1-23.
115. Kharwara, P.C. *et al.* 'Comparative Adoption of Improved Technology By Female and Male headed Scheduled Caste Families' [Himachal Pradesh], *Journal of Rural Development* 10. 1991: 343-51.
116. Kolenda, P.M. 'Religious Anxiety and Hindu Fate', *Journal of Asian Studies* 23 (Special Issue: *Aspects of Religion in South Asia*, 1964: 71-81.
117. Kolenda, P. 'Micro-ideology and Micro-Utopia in Khalapur. Changes in the Discourse on Caste Over Thirty Years', *EPW* August 12 1989: 1831-38.
118. Kumar, K. & Taragi, R.C.S. 'The Socially Deprived: a Case of Scheduled Caste Population in Uttar Pradesh', *Man in India* 71, 1991.
119. Lal, S. 'Acquiring a Dalit Identity' *Sociological Bulletin* 44, 1995: 86-8.
120. Lambert, R.D. Untouchability as a social problem: theory and research, *Sociological Bulletin* 7, 1956: 33-61.
121. Lapoint, E.C. & Lapoint, D.N. Socio-economic mobility among village Harijans, *Eastern Anthropologist* 38, 1985: 1-18 [G].
122. Lerche, J. Is bonded labour a bound category? - reconceptualising

agrarian conflict in India [UP], *Journal of Peasant Studies* 22, 1995: 484-515 [G].

123. *Lokayan Bulletin* The Golana Massacre [Gujarat], *Lokayan Bulletin* 4, 3/4, 1986: 74-8 [G].
124. Lorenzen, D. Traditions of non-caste Hinduism: the Kabir Panth, *Contributions to Indian Sociology* 21, 1987: 263-83.
125. M.N.Rao, *Judicial Activism.* appeared in *EbcIndia* from web.
126. Mathew, G. & Nayak, R.C. Panchayats at work: what it means for the oppressed? [*sic*: MP atrocities] *EPW* 31, 27: 1765-7.
127. Mohanty, P. K, "*Development of Scheduled Castes and Scheduled Tribes in independent India: Leads and Lags*", October - December 2000, Journal of rural development.
128. New Criteria For Backwardness' *The Indian Express.* 24-12-1983.
129. Oommen, T.K. Panchamas to Dalits. The context and content of identity, *Times of India*, 11.5.94.
130. Oommen, T.K. Sources of deprivation and styles of protest, *Contributions to Indian Sociology* 18, 1984.
131. Parry, J.P. The Koli dilemma, *Contributions to Indian Sociology* (NS) 4, 1970.
132. Parui, S.S. Untouchability in the early Indian society, *Journal of the Early Indian Society* 39, 1961.
133. Prasad Rao, C.R. & Radhakrishna Murty Dalit consciousness and Brahminism. A multiplex question. (*Eastern Anthropologist* 46, 1993).
134. Pundir, J.K. Social change among SCs in North India [UP mainly, includes reports of unpublished studies by Meerut students], *Social Change* 25, 4, 1995: 109-19 [G].
135. Radhakrishnan Menon, K.P. Justice constitution sets the limits-Judicial Activism, 8th February, 2000, *The Hindu.*
136. Randeria, S. Carrion and corpses: conflict in categorizing untouchability in Gujarat, *European Journal Of Sociology* 30, 1989.
137. Saberwal, S. Receding pollution: intercaste relations in urban Punjab, *Sociological Bulletin* 22, 1973: 234-59.
138. Sankaran, S R, "Welfare of Scheduled Castes and Scheduled Tribes in Independent India –'An overview of state policies and programmes' October - December 2000, *Journal of rural development.*
139. Schwartzenberg, J. The distribution of selected castes in the North Indian plain, *Geographical Review* 55, 1965: 477-95.
140. Shah Ganshyam, 'Social Backwardness and Politics of Reservations'

in *Economic and Political Weekly* Annual Number Vol. XXVI Nos. 11 and 12, March 1991.

141. Shyam Lal 'Acquiring a Dalit Identity' *Sociological Bulletin* 44, 1995.

142. Shyam Lal 'Sanskritization and social Change Among the Bhangis in Jodhpur City: A Case Study' *Indian Journal of Social Work* XXXIV, 1973: 37-41.

143. Shyamlal 'De-Sanskritisation And High Caste Converts into Bhangis' *Indian Journal of Social Work* 53, 1992: 273-

144. Singh, S. & Jammu, P.S.'Untouchability In Rural Punjab: An Analysis,' *Man in India* 76, 1996.

144. Singh, Shyam Nand, 'Impact of Reservation Policies for Tribals in India' *Journal of rural development* October - December 2000, 146.

145. Vasanthi Raman, Commentary 'Women's Reservation and Democratization-An Alternative Perspective' in *Economic & Political Weekly*. December 11-17, 1999.

146. Vidyarthi, L.P. & Agarwal, R. 'Economic Transition Among the Chamars in Bihar', *Journal of Social Research* 27, 2, 1984.

147. Vincentnathan, L. Nandanar, 'Untouchable Saint and Caste Hindu Anomaly', *Ethos* 21, 1993.

148. Vincentnathan, L. 'Untouchable Concepts of Person and Society', *Contributions to Indian Sociology*, 27, 1993.

149. Vincentnathan, S.G. & Vincentnathan, L. Equality and hierarchy in untouchable intergenerational relations and conflict resolution, *Journal of Cross-cultural Gerontology* 9, 1994: 1-20.

151. Virnius Xaxa, 'Protective Discrimination: Why Scheduled Tribes Lag Behind Scheduled Castes' in *Economic & Political Weekly*, July21, 2001.

152. Waldman, P. 'Reforms Bring Little Change for India's 'Untouchables' [Scavengers, Rajasthan], *Wall Street Journal*, 20/6/96: 1.

153. Wiebe, P.D. & Ramu, G.N. 'Christian and Hindu Harijans: A Study of the Effects of Christian Programmes in India, *Eastern Anthropologist* 28, 3, 1975.

154. Wiebe, P.D. 'Elections in Peddur: Democracy At Work in An Indian Town, *Human Organization* 28, 1969: 140-47.

155. Yagnik, A.& Bhatt, A. The anti-Dalit agitation in Gujarat, *South Asia Bulletin* 4, 1984.

Index

E

F

G

H

I

J

K

L

M

N

O

S